New Englanders on the Ohio Frontier

New Englanders on the Ohio Frontier

The Migration and Settlement of Worthington, Ohio

— ❖ —

Virginia E. McCormick

and

Robert W. McCormick

THE KENT STATE UNIVERSITY PRESS

Kent, Ohio, and London, England

© 1998 by The Kent State University Press, Kent, Ohio 44242

Library of Congress Catalog Card Number 97-36189

ISBN 0-87338-586-1

Manufactured in the United States of America

04 03 02 01 00 99 98   5 4 3 2 1

Library of Congress Cataloging-in-Publication Data

McCormick, Virginia E. (Virginia Evans), 1934–
    New Englanders on the Ohio frontier : migration and settlement of
  Worthington, Ohio / Virginia E. McCormick and Robert W. McCormick.
      p. cm.
    Includes bibliographical references (p.   ) and index.
    ISBN 0-87338-586-1 (cloth : alk. paper)
      1. Worthington (Ohio)—History.   2. Frontier and pioneer life—
  Ohio—Worthington.   3. Land settlement—Ohio—Worthington—
  History—19th century.   4. New Englanders—Ohio—Worthington—
  History—19th century.   5. New England—Population—History—19th
  century.   6. Migration, Internal—United States—History—19th
  century.   I. McCormick, Robert W. (Robert William), 1921–
  II. Title.
    F499.W92M384   1998
    977.1'56—dc21   97-36189
                                                                      CIP

British Library Cataloging-in-Publication data are available.

Contents

— ◈ —

List of Illustrations

— ◆ —

Acknowledgments

— ◈ —

MANY PEOPLE HAVE generously given advice and assistance during recent years as we have probed for information about the New Englanders who founded Worthington, Ohio. We are most grateful that the Scioto Company members were a literate group who kept company records and that descendants of key pioneers such as the Griswold, Kilbourn, and Buttles families deposited at least some of their personal records with historical societies for future generations.

Descendants of some of these pioneers have also shared with us unpublished family materials. We are grateful to Christopher Davenport of Vero Beach, Florida, for Andrews family material; to Nancy Kamlukin of Mequon, Wisconsin, for Buttles family material; to Lucile Bent of Oakland, California, for Job Case family material; to Ann Campbell of Gloucester, Massachusetts, for Griswold family material; to Winfield Darr of Perrysburg, Ohio, for Plumb family material; to Anne Lamb Miles of Reynoldsburg, Ohio, for Lamb/Sloper family material; and to Mary Anne Cummins of Delaware, Ohio, for Stanbery family material.

Many members of the Worthington Historical Society, too numerous to recognize individually, have encouraged our efforts and raised challenging questions. We are particularly indebted to Curator Jane Trucksis, Executive Director Kay Van Meter, and the late longtime librarian Lillian Skeele for their assistance in locating and making illustrations available.

While many people in the Worthington community have encouraged our research, we especially appreciate the generosity of David Faust in making available the Griswold manuscript materials, which he purchased at auction to preserve for the community, and the support of Susan Porter, former editor of the *Worthington News,* who first encouraged us to write a column probing Worthington's heritage.

During visits to New England we received valued assistance from Carol Laun, curator of the Salmon Brook Historical Society at Granby, Connecticut; Mary L. Nason, archivist of the Simsbury Historical Society; and Doris W. Hayden, Blandford, Massachusetts, historian.

We owe an enormous debt to the Ohio Historical Society, particularly to George Parkinson director of the archives and library division, whose manuscript collections and microfilms of early Ohio newspapers and government records made this research feasible. Many staff members of this division have assisted us over the years, but we would be remiss without a special thanks to Gary Arnold, Stephen Gutgesell, Marjorie Haberman, and Jeff Thomas.

We appreciate the editorial suggestions of Kathryn Grover, editor of *Old-Time New England,* regarding an excerpt from this manuscript that was published, in the journal of the Society for the Preservation of New England Antiquities, as "New England Culture on the Ohio Frontier"; and the suggestions of Robert L. Daugherty, editor of *Ohio History,* regarding an excerpt published in the journal of the Ohio Historical Society as "Episcopal Versus Methodist: Religious Competition in Frontier Worthington."

We are particularly grateful to the historians who read all or part of this manuscript and offered helpful criticisms and suggestions: George W. Knepper, Professor Emeritus of the University of Akron; Andrew R. L. Cayton of Miami University; and John L. Brooke of Tufts University.

Of course we appreciate the persons at The Kent State University Press who make this book possible, particularly Director John T. Hubbell for believing in the project, Julia J. Morton, Editor-in-Chief, and Linda K. Cuckovich and Joanna Hildebrand, Managing Editors, for following through on all the details which turn a manuscript into a book.

And we do, indeed, appreciate the patience of family and friends who doubtless wonder at times whether we are living in the twentieth or the nineteenth century.

We are most grateful for the many people who have challenged us, advised us, encouraged us, and rescued us from embarrassing errors. If there are errors that have crept through to the final product, we accept full responsibility.

Robert W. and Virginia E. McCormick

Introduction

— ❖ —

A STRANGER TO COLUMBUS traveling north from the Ohio State capitol building finds that High Street leads past high-rise offices and hotels to a steady flow of small stores, residences converted to commercial use, the main campus of Ohio State University, supermarkets, movie theaters, and fast-food restaurants. It is a typical urban landscape. But suddenly, about nine miles north, brick buildings—old brick buildings—line the very edges of the sidewalk. Before one can adequately comprehend the change, a traffic light forces a brief stop in the center of a picturesque New England village green, anchored by the attractive steeples of two churches. As the traveler drives on, there is no time to answer the question of why a New England village, apparently an old New England village, lies surrounded by this metropolitan area of over one million people.

Continuing a few miles north, the stranger might begin to wonder whether those quaint buildings had been an optical illusion. But citizens of Worthington, Ohio, know the New England appearance of their metropolitan suburb is an important manifestation of its heritage. Residents gather on warm summer evenings for concerts on that same village green, third graders studying local history make tombstone "rubbings" as they become acquainted with the trials of pioneers, and realtors emphasize the advantages of a community that has long taken pride in its educational system. Even though that school system now enrolls students from more than fifty nationalities, it is the heritage of the New England model of community life that provides unity. There is no doubt that the original proprietors of the village intended to transplant the New England culture with which they were acquainted. How much, though, was the new community influenced by the diversity of migrants who were attracted to the frontier?

We began this project with questions about community development: what are the factors that make a lasting difference, and are there answers to be found in migration and early settlement? Worthington is older than Columbus, founded in the same year that Ohio became the first state carved from the vast richness of the Northwest Territory. We soon began to realize that there were many answers in the records of this community's early settlers, who migrated west from Connecticut and Massachusetts. They were people who came with a purpose, and they left a wealth of primary data—letters to family members and friends, business records, justice-of-the-peace records, militia lists, school records, early newspapers, church records, and sometimes diaries, not to mention public materials such as estate inventories and tax and deed records. These documents constitute an unusually rich historical resource.

As we studied these fascinating materials and began to examine them in the context of the times, we naturally began to question how this experience of migration and settlement in Ohio compared with others on the westward-moving, nineteenth-century frontier.[1] Both historians and popular writers have noted the disproportionate influence of New Englanders in establishing western communities based on the New England town model.[2] It became the American ideal of small-town life.

Several historians have demonstrated the value of a microperspective analysis of a single community.[3] In Worthington we found, for instance, that the community's growth and character needed to be understood in relation to the charismatic and entrepreneurial leadership qualities of James Kilbourn.[4] Family kinship networks also demanded analysis to help explain who came west and who remained in the community.[5] The founders were a homogeneous group who organized themselves as the Scioto Company and founded what some have described as a "covenanted community."[6] Such communities were of a typical New England form, and they traced their origins all the way back to the Massachusetts Bay Company that established the English colony. Like many western migrants, the Worthington pioneers shared a common geographic heritage and religious faith. Although they continued to attract like-minded others, rapid growth led to diversity and sometimes to friction on issues such as religion and emerging nineteenth-century social issues such as slavery and temperance. Like most communities of the trans-Appalachian frontier, Worthington's development was influenced by its environment as well as by the heritage of its founders.[7]

The Scioto Company's dealings with land speculators—rather than the U.S. government—provides an illuminating perspective on early public land policy.[8] Although expanded land ownership was the common magnet for westward migration in this group as in most others, this settlement's diversity of occupational skills called for an analysis of manufacturing enterprises as well as of those commonly associated with agricultural production.[9] The timing of the development of local enterprises in relationship to national events such as war and economic depression emphasizes the limitations of self-sufficiency and local determination.[10]

The speed with which this community developed a cultural focus based on its subscription school and library, its Episcopal Church, and its Masonic Lodge announced its role as a competitor, not only as a destination for other westward migrants, but as a contender for the state capital, as a port on the canal linking Lake Erie with the Ohio River, and as the site of a college for higher education.[11] Citizens from this community played leadership roles in establishing a number of other towns in Ohio and farther west, such as the community of Worthington, Indiana.

An analysis of migration and settlement in Worthington, Ohio, lends itself to chronological divisions, from the formation of the company in New England to the incorporation of the town in Ohio thirty-three years later. Within these years we have chosen to focus on four stages: the process of preparing for and executing the migration, the struggles of a frontier community that compressed within a decade the process of conquering the wilderness and creating a material culture equal or superior to that which they had known in New England, the economic boom generated by a wartime economy and the ensuing depression that crushed infant western communities, and finally stabilization as a nineteenth-century market town with a town council and mayoral government.

 We do not present the establishment and early development of Worthington as either a unique or a typical experience, but simply as a case study of one community that provides a perspective from which historians might better understand the process of westward migration and frontier settlement.

Westward Migration,
1802–1804

— ❖ —

❖ CHAPTER I ❖

A Company to Make Settlement Northwest of the Ohio

— ❖ —

I T WAS SPRING, a time of new beginnings. The men who gathered at midday on May 5, 1802, at the home of Rev. Eber B. Clark in Granby, Connecticut, spent little time, however, noticing the New England spring bursting around them. They were meeting to consider a move that would change each of their lives forever.[1]

Most were present at the invitation of James Kilbourn, a Berlin, Connecticut, merchant who also served as an ordained deacon in the Episcopal Church. Kilbourn was an enthusiastic, self-made man who came from modest circumstances.[2] He was born at Farmington, on October 19, 1770, to parents who were unable to provide money for his formal education. Although he learned to read and do basic mathematics at home, he was a hesitant speller and innocent of proper grammar.

In James's sixteenth year, his father's circumstances became so reduced that James was forced to leave home and make his own way in the world. On October 1, 1786, he accepted a four-year apprenticeship working and boarding seven months of the year in a weaving mill at Granby. The mill site was adjacent to the prosperous farm of Elisha Griswold, and there Kilbourn found additional work during the harvest season. In exchange, he was tutored during the winter by his employer's son, Alexander Viets Griswold, an accomplished scholar four years older than Kilbourn.[3]

Young Griswold became his mentor, and Kilbourn converted from the Congregational Church of his birth to become an Episcopalian.

This was a significant decision in a state that was founded in Congregational philosophy and in a town that had not formally separated religious life from town government until 1739.[4] Although Episcopalians had been a tolerated minority, the fact that many of their ministers were educated in England placed them under suspicion of being agents of the Crown during the Revolutionary War. Rev. Viets, the namesake of Kilbourn's mentor, had, in fact, been imprisoned as a loyalist and had eventually migrated to Nova Scotia. As Kilbourn studied and accepted Episcopalian religious theology, it is quite likely that he absorbed some of the Episcopalian's prejudices about their perceived mistreatment and minority status in Connecticut.

Kilbourn's skills at the mill improved rapidly, and his apprenticeship was terminated at the end of the third year. In 1789, he married Lucy Fitch and became the mill manager. He prospered and was able to repurchase the twenty-five acre farm at Farmington that his father had been forced to sell and bought an adjoining seventy-five acres as well. By 1792, however, Kilbourn became seriously ill from inhaling the poisonous fumes of the dyes used in the textile mill and was forced to give up this work. He briefly attempted to farm with his father, but he was unable to withstand the rigors of agricultural life and in 1796 established a retail store in Granby.

This business prospered, and Kilbourn became prominent in community affairs, serving as town assessor and participating actively in the Masonic Lodge, the Episcopal Church, and the Granby subscription library. In 1800, he took deacon's orders and moved his business to Berlin so that he could conduct bimonthly Episcopal services both there and at Wethersfield. About the same time he became interested in moving west and traveled to New York State to explore settlement possibilities in the Genessee Valley.

In the decade following the Revolutionary War, many New England men became discouraged by poor land, differing religious opinions, taxes, and the harsh climate. Some eyed the west with longing just because they were curious "to see whether the grass on the other side of the mountain was greener."[5] The men of the Farmington River valley knew well the effort of holding a plow firmly in the thin soil of their fields and the backbreaking labor required each year to collect and haul off to the fence row the rocks loosened by winter's freezing and thawing. One who took his young son to the field to help plant

Fig. 1. James Kilbourn was a Connecticut businessman and Episcopal deacon who organized the Scioto Company that founded Worthington, Ohio, in 1803. (Courtesy of the Worthington Historical Society)

corn was startled to see tears in the boy's eyes and asked what was the matter. "I can't get enough dirt to cover the corn," the lad replied.[6]

The trans-Appalachian frontier beckoned seductively. No wonder these men listened eagerly to the stories western travelers told of land so fertile it sometimes took three or four men with arms outstretched to encircle the trunk of a single oak. New England neighbors who had settled near Fort Harmar, where the Muskingum River joins the Ohio, were amazed to find that their corn sometimes grew as much as nine inches in twenty-four hours.[7]

Like parents everywhere, the men meeting at Eber Clark's were anxious to provide a better future for their children, and New England was becoming crowded, even in the "back country" of western Connecticut and Massachusetts. The 1800 census revealed that 1,230 persons, nearly half of Granby's population of 2,735, were under sixteen years of age;[8] the numbers were similar in adjacent Simsbury and as far north as Blandford, Massachusetts. These three towns provided three-fourths of the men who gathered to consider moving west. Researchers like Greven have noted the extent to which early New England towns nourished extended patriarchal families, but by the middle of the eighteenth century New England life had evolved generational cycles of mobility in search of opportunity and the stability to enjoy its rewards.[9] By the end of the eighteenth century, opinions regarding the reasonable size of a farm needed to support a family had been revised downward, but opportunities to provide even a modest inheritance for children had become fewer and more expensive.[10]

Frederick Jackson Turner has emphasized the opportunity the American frontier offered for both native-born settlers and European immigrants to break the bondage of social rank and rise to the level of their own abilities.[11] Inexpensive land, Turner says, seemed to offer a vast opportunity, and each pioneer was anxious to secure a place for himself and his family before it vanished. Recent historians attribute this image of democratic egalitarianism to the time and place in which Turner himself came of age, rather than to the individualism he associated with frontier life, but Turner's work legitimized the hegemony of the nineteenth-century middle class.[12]

Thanks to his father-in-law, John Fitch, Kilbourn had by 1802 become excited about prospects for settlement north of the Ohio River, where land was cheaper and less inhabited than in New York. Fitch had a creative mind, which led to his development in 1786 of a craft that employed a series of oars linked to a crude steam engine. Successors of this first steamboat operated commercially on the Delaware River for a brief period, but Fitch felt that his invention's full potential would be best realized in the west. He had worked as a surveyor in what was then Virginia (now Kentucky) and had prepared an engraving of the Northwest Territory to raise funds for his steam-engine projects. He attempted unsuccessfully to obtain financial backing in Europe, and he died in Kentucky in 1798 without achieving his dream of steam navigation on the western rivers. His accounts of the richness of western lands had, however, influenced his son-in-law deeply.[13]

The men who convened at Eber Clark's in Granby were products of the democratic New England town meeting, and they certainly considered no other form of local government for their proposed settlement in the west. They may not have been aware that in seeking to transplant a New England village to the Ohio frontier they were modeling the same paternalistic colonizing role that proprietors had played in settling the Massachusetts Bay colony nearly two centuries earlier.[14] They began by immediately defining their purpose "of forming a company the object of which is to make a settlement in the Territory of the United States Northwest of the Ohio and between the Muskingum and the Great Miami Rivers."[15]

Organizing westward migration in terms of a "company" was by no means unique to the Granby group. Settlers from a number of the eastern states had used this procedure, and many of the best-known and most successful companies had been formed by New Englanders. The men meeting at Granby were undoubtedly well acquainted with the Ohio Company purchase, negotiated by Rufus Putnam and Manasseh Cutler, which led to the founding of Marietta in 1788.[16] Although this resulted in the first permanent settlement north of the Ohio River, it was a highly speculative arrangement involving the purchase of a tract of 1,781,760 acres for a down payment of five hundred thousand dollars and a like amount to be paid in government securities worth, perhaps, twelve cents on the dollar. After deducting the sections reserved for education and religion, many of the Ohio Company subscribers acquired substantial holdings at a cost of approximately thirty to forty cents per acre. Some of these holdings were now competing on the market, with or without improvements, with newly surveyed Congress lands priced at two dollars per acre.

Though the concept of using organized companies to settle the frontier involved a distinct minority of the westward migrants, their abilities in founding towns wielded an influence which far exceeded their numbers. The Scioto Company, founded by the men gathered at Granby, was certainly in the tradition of groups such as Ethan Allen's Onion River Land Company, in what is now Vermont, and Oliver Phelps's Connecticut Land Company, for which Moses Cleaveland had surveyed in the Western Reserve of Ohio—but there were also distinct differences.[17]

The Scioto Company was a classical example of a "covenanted community," as Page Smith defined such a group, bound in a special compact with God and with each other.[18] In fact, their articles of agreement began with just such wording: "We Do Each of us Individually and for Himself Covenant and agree with Each of the Others . . . ."[19] Smith was wrong, however, to indicate that election to this company required a unanimous ballot. The men who resolved in May 1802 to name their group the Scioto Company, made it clear from the beginning that theirs was to be a small group, limited to *settlers* rather than *speculators*, but that selection was by a democratic majority: "No person shall be admitted into this Company as a Subscriber and purchaser but upon the Vote of a Major part of the proprietors present at a meeting duly notified."[20]

The Scioto Company's decision to pinpoint the area between the Muskingum and the Great Miami Rivers may have indicated an incomplete knowledge of available land in the Northwest Territory. It would seem to demonstrate that they were aware that clear title had been gained in this region through the Greenville Treaty of 1795 and that initial surveys had been made. Perhaps they did not realize the different terms available for purchasing Congress Lands between the Muskingum and Scioto Rivers, land in the Virginia Military District between the Scioto and Little Miami Rivers, and land in the Symmes Purchase between the Little Miami and Great Miami Rivers.[21] But naming their group the Scioto Company and sending agents west to explore the fertile lands that Congress was aggressively marketing between the Muskingum and Scioto Rivers indicates this was their intended site. Within a few years, guides for emigrants and settlers would be published back east to analyze factors in the west such as climate, the availability of ground water and timber, topography, drainage, the quality of the soil, the legal security of one's claim, and the access to markets.[22] But most migrants in this early period relied heavily upon the information that had filtered back from explorers and earlier immigrants. Few had the resources to explore potential destinations and make a rational choice.[23] Compared to the squatters and adventurers who had begun streaming into the Northwest Territory more than a decade earlier, these New Englanders showed notable caution and organization.

Several of the Scioto Company members had served during the Revolutionary War, and all were proud of their rights as citizens of the new republic. None were anxious to move to a territory that offered them less than full citizenship. It was no coincidence that the recent session of Congress had passed legislation, which President Jefferson signed on April 30, 1802, enabling the creation of a new state north of the Ohio River.[24] Delegates to a constitutional convention were to be elected in October and, if they deemed statehood advisable, were to draft a constitution to be presented to the next congressional session. It appeared likely, then, that by the time Scioto Company members completed plans for westward migration they could count on the state of Ohio becoming a reality.

After defining their purpose, members of the Scioto Company proceeded to elect officers, choosing James Kilbourn as their president and Josiah Topping as secretary. Topping was an educated young man who had studied medicine with his physician father. He was born and reared in the Simsbury community, was two years older than Kilbourn, and like Kilbourn had a young family whom he anticipated moving west.[25]

The last major decision made at that first meeting was that "it be expedient to send two agents to explore sd Territory and report to the company." Reuben Humphrey of Simsbury and Kilbourn were chosen for that purpose. At a meeting two weeks later, Ezra Griswold of Simsbury and William Thompson of Blandford were selected as alternates for this trip. It would appear that the Blandford contingent had expressed a desire to be represented. Nathan Stewart of Blandford and Josiah Topping were designated to "open subscriptions & collect monies" to pay the exploration expenses of these agents.

Leadership was clearly evolving within the group, and it is equally clear that there was a conscious attempt to balance the influence of the Massachusetts and Connecticut contingents. After Humphrey, Griswold, and Thompson declined to make the western trip, "the proctors of this company in Blandford" in mid-June appointed Nathaniel W. Little to accompany Kilbourn west to explore potential sites.[26] Nathaniel Little was a merchant at Blandford, though born in Hartford County, Connecticut, and he was probably well known to both groups. Another advantage of Little's appointment was that as a trader he had previously traveled as far west as Pittsburgh and was therefore somewhat familiar with the territory.

At three meetings within the span of six weeks, a group that Josiah Topping referred to in his minutes as "Sundra persons" had formed a company to make a western settlement, had defined a geographic area for this settlement, had elected officers to conduct company business, and had selected two agents to journey west that summer and report back on potential sites. It was an auspicious beginning.

◆ CHAPTER 2 ◆

To Explore Said Territory
and Report to the Company

— ◆ —

I T WAS FRIDAY, JULY 30, before Nathaniel Little left Blandford to
begin "the journey to the Territory of the United States Northwest
of the River Ohio." He arrived at Kilbourn's home in Berlin the following day and attended church with him on Sunday. On Wednesday,
August 4, Little wrote in his journal that they "shipped . . . on board
the stage at Mr. Riley's" and arrived at New York the following day
after having "supped at Mott's in Norwalk [and] had the pleasure of
two hours sleep for the night."[1]

From New York, the agents continued by stage to Philadelphia,
where Kilbourn reported that they found yellow fever "raging with
great violence . . . people flying by thousands in every direction for
Safety . . . Coffins & Corpses . . . hurried along thro the Streets without any attendance or formalities." Concluding it was not safe to stay
in the city, they walked eight miles out the Lancaster road to await
the stage due the following day. Little was impressed with the stone
toll road which ran the sixty-two miles from Philadelphia to Lancaster. They continued across Pennsylvania through York to Shippensburg, and, as Kilbourn later wrote to his wife Lucy from Pittsburgh, there "the Stage Stoped & Came no further.—the next day as
we could not procure any Horses we Set out for this place on foot."

By Tuesday, August 10, they had "Made arrangements to send
on the portmanteau by the Pittsburgh wagon," and walked twenty-
four miles over the "Blue Mountains" to Fort Littleton. At this point
they were following the Forbes Road, a crude cut over the mountains

that had been built for military purposes during the French and Indian Wars.[2] By Thursday, Little had sore feet and a lame ankle, so they "hired a boy and horse and rode 14 miles." They continued in this manner, alternately walking and hiring horses, across the Allegheny Mountains to Pittsburgh. On Sunday, August 15, they attended church services in the city; on the following day Kilbourn wrote that he and Little "bought a large Cannoe & laid in our Stores for the passage & tomorough Morning we are to begin the practice of Navigation."

They proceeded downriver, stopping each night at huts on either the Virginia or the Northwest Territory side. One morning, reports Little, after going about two miles, "Mr. Kilbourn found out that he had left his watch. Put in shore and Mr. Kilbourn walked back while I got breakfast ready at a Dutch house on the Territory side." They arrived at Wheeling on Friday, August 20, where, since the water was too low for effective navigation, they "disposed of our canoe and hired horses on to Chillicothe." Following Zane's Trace, the only identifiable road in the Northwest Territory,[3] they rode through "sharp hills covered with white oak timber principally." Little commented on "numerous flocks of turkeys and gray and black squirrels in great numbers" as they approached the Muskingum River. They put up at Zane's Inn the night of August 22 and explored the area of present-day Zanesville. Little considered the soil good directly on the river, but "hard and thin" back away from it.

They arrived at "New Lancaster" the following day, where they found fine land crisscrossed by small streams and a "great prairie where they cut wild grass for hay." The following day they crossed the Pickaway Plains, broad prairies extending some twenty miles long and two to four miles in width. As they approached Chillicothe, they crossed the Scioto River, "a fine, clear stream, about 100 yards wide but very low." Little found Chillicothe, the seat of the Northwest Territorial legislature, "handsomely situated" with "about 390 dwelling houses . . . 8 goods stores," including "many handsome brick buildings." It had grown rapidly since its founding six years earlier, and Little judged it "bids fair to be a large and populous town."

On Wednesday the twenty-fifth, they went to the government land office and were somewhat disappointed to find that the choice lands along the Scioto River were largely taken up. They decided to investigate some sites north toward Franklinton on Walnut and Big

Belly Creeks.[4] For the next three days they explored this area, ending Saturday evening in a downpour that forced them to pick their way well after dark over logs and brush that nearly concealed the trail. Arriving finally at a "little cottage" near the Pickaway Plains, they took a "scanty supper and laid ourselves down on a miserable bed on the floor as wet as though we had been dipped in the river."

As they returned toward Chillicothe, they passed an Indian camp with a considerable number of bark huts and a large number of barking dogs which annoyed their horses. Little was fascinated by, and took time to explore, several of the ancient mound fortifications near the river, concluding, "These I think are a strong indication that many centuries ago this large extent of country was settled with a people more civilized than the present Indians." Kilbourn must have had much on his mind, for on the fourth day of exploring he again forgot his watch and had to ride back a couple of miles to retrieve it.

On Monday, August 30, they rode out from Chillicothe to Colonel Thomas Worthington's home and took tea with the government land agent and member of the territorial legislature. Worthington had spent much of the past year traveling throughout the territory to collect petitions in behalf of Ohio statehood, which he presented personally to the U.S. Congress. Although he was then living in a log cabin, Little found it "neatly furnished" and the location, about two miles from Chillicothe, "a very fine situation on a hill at least 300 feet above the level of the common ground." Although he was a couple of years younger than Kilbourn, Worthington had settled in the Virginia Military Tract four years earlier and had quickly established himself as a skilled political negotiator in the territorial legislature.[5] The three men must have talked at some length, for Little described Worthington in his diary as "one of the best informed men we have met in all the country."

Kilbourn and Little began their homeward journey by stopping at the salt licks southeast of Chillicothe, which Congress had reserved for public use. Although the saltwater springs extended for several miles, Little did not consider them well managed and noted that salt was selling for two dollars a bushel. They followed the Hocking River toward the Ohio River, Little noting with a somewhat superior tone that "This part of the country is settled with New England people, and have made very fine improvements. A great quantity of peaches are now on the trees and apple trees are improving fast. The people appear much in the New England style." This was part of the Ohio Company purchase west of Marietta, which had been settled for more than a decade. Here, Kilbourn and Little no doubt encountered a quality of buildings and farm improvements noticeably superior to the frontier lands they had been exploring farther north.

They ferried the Ohio River on September 4 to continue their journey on the more settled Virginia side. The following morning, after riding about five miles, "Mr. Kilbourn observed that he had left his portmanteau, which he went back after." They nevertheless reached Wheeling that evening. Not finding their baggage as expected, they returned again to Pittsburgh, where they stopped to visit the glassworks that manufactured window glass, tumblers, and bottles. They returned their hired horses and engaged "Mr. Johnson" to take them as far as Shippensburg, apparently in a farm wagon. They retraced the arduous journey across the mountains and arrived in Shippensburg on Sunday, September 12, where they "put up at Mr. Rippey's" to await the stage for Lancaster. Little noted, as though it were strangely inconsistent, that Rippey "keeps a good house, although he is a violent Democrat." The sharp political differences between New England Federalists and the Democratic-Republicans of the western states at the beginning of the nineteenth century are well known, but very little evidence speaks to the political sentiments of an individual who changed regions. Perhaps Nathaniel Little was about to experience the conversion of one who migrated from one region to another.

After crossing the Susquehanna and dining at Mr. Stump's tavern, "Some difficulty arose between Mr. Stump and the passengers on account of Mr. Stump's crowding a black in irons into the stage when it was full, with a man to attend to him." This is a curious observation, in which Little appears to make no objection to a black slave who was confined by shackles, but expresses consternation that this slave should be placed into a crowded compartment with paying passengers.

After again dodging the fever at Philadelphia, Kilbourn and Little this time sailed on a packet boat from New York to New Haven, where the two agents went their separate ways on Monday, September 20. Little arrived home in Blandford two days later, noting with satisfaction that he was in good health after traveling two thousand miles in the course of eight weeks.

Little's journal and Kilbourn's letter to his wife from Pittsburgh provide an illuminating glimpse of the widely differing travel conditions in the eastern and western parts of the country at the beginning of the nineteenth century. There was certainly great need for flexibility, and yet one senses a certain innocence, or a lack of preparation, on the part of these eastern men who hired horses somewhat randomly and briefly purchased a canoe for river navigation. New England roads permitted public transport, and New Englanders were accustomed to taking the stage for any extended journey between towns. Westerners who traveled to Washington or Philadelphia at that time rode horseback the entire way, knowing full well that most of the route offered neither public transportation nor livery stables with horses for hire. Kilbourn and Little were merchants, ill-prepared physically for the rigors of frontier life.

There is no hint of anything other than a congenial relationship between the two men, but Kilbourn was clearly the one who made the decisions and handled the funds. One cannot help noting that four times during this eight-week journey he began the morning by forgetting his watch, his purse, or his luggage. Clearly he had much on his mind, but it raises interesting questions about Kilbourn's attention to detail in business affairs, an issue which will arise again.

Little's account of this trip concluded on October 5, when he and Kilbourn reported to the company at Rev. Clark's in Granby. At this point the gaps in information become more fascinating than the resolutions recorded in the company minutes. There is no record of the very interesting discussion that must have taken place. It was agreed that the treasurer should immediately collect the subscriptions due from each member and pay over to the agents the sum due them for the expenses of their journey. It was also resolved that company membership would be limited to forty subscribers and that each new subscriber should pay $18.25 for company expenses, including the agents' trip to explore sites.

The key resolution of the meeting on October 5, however, was "That the purchase of the Congress Lands should be postponed till the terms of Doct. Stanbery and others shall be obtained." This is the first mention of Jonas Stanbery and the first suggestion that company members were considering an alternative site, even one none of them had seen. Stanbery, a New Jersey native, had become a physician in New York City, but was increasingly devoting himself to real estate investments in western land.[6] Although he was in financial partnership with Revolutionary War general Jonathan Dayton on this deal, it was Stanbery exclusively who dealt with Scioto Company members.

At the group's next meeting, three weeks later, the purchase decision was essentially settled. Kilbourn was "authorized to write to Col. Worthington Register of Land Office at Chillicothe to not hold in reserve for this company certain lands owned by the United States explored by our agents." He was also designated to go to New York City and confer with Dr. Stanbery, "to collect their terms of said payment & likewise to bargain conditionally for sd lands & to exhibit their terms to the company," and even to invite Dr. Stanbery to attend the next company meeting.[7]

The land parcels in question were twenty to thirty miles north of the Congress Lands that Kilbourn and Little had explored and tentatively reserved with Worthington. The Stanbery parcels were part of the two-million-acre U.S. Military District created by the Continental Congress in 1787 to satisfy claims from Revolutionary War soldiers who had been promised land in compensation for service. The land warrants ranged in decreasing amounts from eleven hundred acres for a major general to one hundred acres for noncommissioned officers and soldiers of the Continental line.[8]

It was 1797 before the U.S. Congress appropriated funds to survey this district into five-mile townships. The government intended to dispose of the entire district in quarter-township sections of four thousand acres each, which was, of course, much larger than any individual claim. Agents such as General Jonathan Dayton began grouping warrants, often purchasing them for a fraction of their value from veterans too old or uninterested to consider migrating west in person.[9] For the most part, this land, like the parcels the Scioto Company was considering, had now passed into private ownership and was being held for resale by land speculators.

What caused the Scioto Company to reject the Congress Lands that their agents had explored and within weeks to decide to contract with a speculator for land that no one in the group had seen? Obviously someone had talked to Kilbourn and Little about U.S. military lands north of the parcels they had explored. Was it during the afternoon tea at Thomas Worthington's home? Could the suggestion have come from a chance encounter with a surveyor at the land office? Perhaps it was encouragement from one of the many strangers they rode with during part of their journey or a suggestion from a fellow Episcopalian who knew that Dr. Stanbery had connections with General Jonathan Dayton.

There is no definite answer, but circumstantial evidence strongly points to Thomas Worthington and links him to the land in question. For example, James Scott, the surveyor who ran the section lines of this parcel in the U.S. Military District, had sent his report to Thomas Worthington, and Worthington had served as the agent for the original owner, John Dunlap, when in October 1802 Dunlap sold part of the land that Stanbery was assembling for the Scioto Company deal.[10] Since these military lands had already been conveyed to private ownership, they were, strictly speaking, no longer under the jurisdiction of the government land agent, but land agents were in position to benefit financially—and most did—from information that might today be categorized as "insider trading" or a conflict of interest.

It is important to realize, in the context of the time, that Thomas Worthington had inherited significant Virginia land from his father and that he had originally come to the Northwest Territory in 1795 to locate some Virginia military warrants he had purchased. He quickly became a business associate of Nathaniel Massie and Duncan McArthur, surveyors and speculators in the Virginia Military District, west of the Scioto River.[11] They were amassing large real estate holdings at the usual one-fifth commission for locating and surveying property. Massie felt that the federal land acts of 1796 actually helped speculators like himself. The government price of two dollars per acre made land in the Virginia Military District, which could profitably be sold for less, appear to be a bargain.[12]

After being appointed as the Chillicothe land office agent, Worthington continually struggled between his public and private roles in matters relating to land sales. Earlier in that summer of 1802, Elias Langham had filed a formal complaint against Worthington and the Chillicothe land office following an auction in which interested bidders were charged twenty-five cents to view the map of the sites being offered. Langham discussed a specific parcel and its potential price with Worthington and asked to be notified when it was offered for sale, since he had not seen the map and did not know the tract

number. It was a choice parcel that sold for $2.50 per acre, although
Langham had indicated to Worthington that he was prepared to offer
$8.00 per acre. Worthington reportedly received $1,600 on the deal,
and Langham's complaint protested, "How could I suspect that the
register would enter into a combination to prevent competition and
keep down the sale of public lands?"[13] Worthington was eventually
cleared of any charge of wrongdoing by Secretary of the Treasury
Albert Gallatin, himself a speculator in western lands.

For the Scioto Company, there were some clear advantages to the
U.S. Military District deal. The parcel which Stanbery and Dayton
were assembling for the company's purchase, although farther north
than the lands Kilbourn and Little had seen, offered river frontage on
the Whetstone River, a navigable tributary of the Scioto. The price
was $1.25 per acre compared with $2.00 per acre for Congress lands,
and Stanbery and Dayton were willing to accept both a four-year
mortgage and the New England real estate of company members as
down payment. The contract called for "Thirteen Thousand Dollars
to be paid in Obligations Well Secured payable within four years on
Everidge [average]" and "Seven thousand Dollars to be paid in Lands
& other Real Estate in New England."[14]

Much has been written, most with a justified negative bias, about
the roles of land speculators on the western frontier. Everyone agreed
that western lands would increase in value, but the rush to invest led
many to overextend their commitments. French aristocrat Charles-
Maurice de Talleyrand, on an American visit a decade earlier, perhaps
saw the problem more clearly than native investors. He warned that
many land speculators who were relying on a rapid resale to repay
their credit obligations would find that the increase in land values
failed to keep pace with their overextended ambitions. This was exactly what happened to the Ohio Company, Duer's Scioto group, the
Connecticut Land Company, and John Cleves Symmes on their land
commitments in the Northwest Territory during the 1790s. The mag-
nitude of their purchases made the inevitable costs, such as surveys
and taxes, an unbearable burden.[15]

Land speculation was sustained, however, by government regulations which required purchases in large parcels.[16] In 1800, to encourage sales, Congress dropped the minimum size of purchases in the
Congress lands to 320 acres and permitted a down payment of one-
fourth in cash and the remainder on credit for four years. This was

still beyond the means of many western migrants, and the credit option encouraged men unfamiliar with wilderness conditions to commit themselves for more land than they could clear and cultivate in time to pay their debt.

Stanbery and Dayton were fulfilling a role that has been described by some economic historians as "competitive middlemen."[17] They had three potential profit points: the resale of the New England lands they accepted as down payment, the accrued interest on the mortgages that they accepted, and the sale of the western land. The values of the first two are not known, but they made a handsome profit on the western lands in the Scioto Company transaction. Dayton already owned the two least desirable four-thousand-acre parcels, which he had acquired with military scrip. Stanbery put the deal together by purchasing the eight-thousand-acre site with the river frontage in two separate parcels, half at 50¢ and half at $1.00 per acre, just weeks before the partners sold the entire sixteen thousand acres for $1.25 per acre (see fig. 2).[18] The Scioto Company benefited by paying a lower price than they would have paid for government land and by being able to make the down payment—35 percent of the total—in New England real estate. The only loser in the deal was the United States government, which was attempting to sell western lands to obtain revenue to operate the federal government and to repay debts incurred during the Revolution.

Meanwhile, in the Northwest Territory, thirty-five elected delegates had been meeting in Chillicothe throughout November to draft a state constitution.[19] The Jeffersonian Democratic-Republicans, particularly those from Chillicothe, dominated this convention, with Worthington's brother-in-law, Edward Tiffin, serving as the presiding officer. The native New Englanders who had settled Marietta had tried to delay statehood by dividing the territory into two districts with their respective capitals at Cincinnati and Marietta. When the New Englanders were resoundingly defeated by the Virginians from Chillicothe and their allies, the Scioto Company leaders found themselves in the awkward position of favoring their new Virginia friends over their former New England neighbors.

Ohio constitutional convention delegates, many of whom had been frustrated for years by the autocratic power of the appointed territorial governor, Arthur St. Clair, crafted a document that limited the executive and placed most powers, including the appointment of

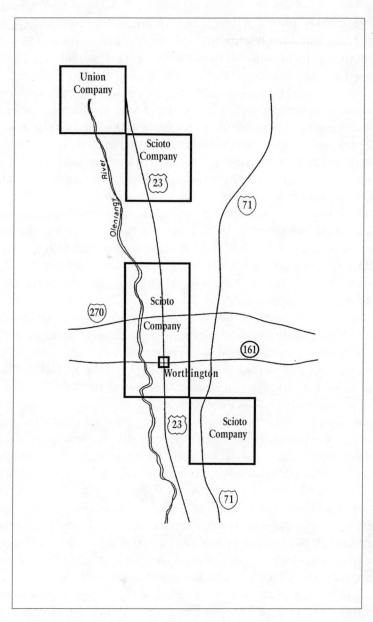

Fig. 2. Scioto and Union Company Purchases

supreme court judges, in the hands of an elected bicameral legislature. Although slavery within the Northwest Territory had been
forbidden by the Northwest Ordinance of 1787, the new Ohio constitution expressly forbade involuntary servitude and came within one
vote, a tie broken by chairman Tiffin, of enfranchising Negro males.
It contained a bill of rights that reaffirmed the freedom of speech, religion, and assembly guaranteed in the federal Constitution.

The constitution for the state of Ohio, which was completed by
November 29, was not submitted to the voters of the territory for approval, but was entrusted to Thomas Worthington to deliver personally to the United States Congress and press for quick acceptance
of Ohio as a state. By the time they completed their contract with
Dr. Stanbery in December 1802, it is probable that Scioto Company
members had some knowledge of the constitutional convention's
progress, but probably not of the details of the document itself.

Members drafted and signed their company's own "Constitution
and Articles of Agreement" on December 14. This legal document
spelled out the specific terms of the sale with Stanbery and Dayton,
such as the 6 percent interest to be charged on mortgages. It named
a committee of ten members who would represent the company on
the property transfer and hold title in common until the land was
divided. It specified that each new subscriber must "pay in cash at
the time of admittance Eighteen Dollars and twenty-five Cents," for
exploration costs.[20]

Most of the document, however, dealt with the procedure for
dividing the new property in Ohio. This was to remain undivided
"untill the major part of the subscribers shall Have arived upon the
spot provided they Shall Remove thither by the first Day of December
1803." Members determined that "there shall be laid out Two Roads
Leading north & south on each Side of the Whetstone River and
a Cross Road from East to West as near the middle of the tract as can
be with convenience." At the crossroad a "square Town Plat" was to
be laid out containing 164 lots. A central area was to be set aside as
a "Publick Square to remain for a green or parade." This was far
more pretentious than anything in the small New England towns that
these men were leaving. Until it was diminished by the creation of
Granby in 1786, Simsbury had stretched ten miles along either side of
the Farmington River, and the frame "meeting house" beside the road
served for both religious services and town meetings.[21]

The grid pattern of surveying land, which was introduced with the Land Ordinance of 1785, influenced both the location of towns, which frequently appeared at the intersection of township corners, and the layout of towns themselves.[22] The town plat for Worthington followed this grid pattern—an ancient form dating to Greek and Roman times, but associated in America with the city of Philadelphia, then the nation's largest and most elegant city. Such a plan ignored natural features and was inappropriate for hilly terrain, but it simplified surveying problems, minimized legal disputes over lot boundaries, and gave an illusion of orderliness and prosperity which was associated with eastern cities rather than country villages.[23] It was the pattern used to survey earlier Ohio communities such as Marietta, Cincinnati, and Cleveland. As Richard Wade has pointed out in his discussion of the urban frontier, western speculation involved towns as well as land. Town founders competed to attract new settlers, new businesses, and cultural institutions. The Scioto Company members were thinking ahead to the image their town would present, and their grid plan provided the means for orderly expansion.

They also committed themselves to a cultural presence by deciding to reserve a town lot and a farm lot "for the use and benefit of a Publick school" and the same again for the "use and benefit of a protestant Episcopal society." Although the latter was not illegal for a privately organized company, it appears somewhat inconsistent with a federal and state constitution guaranteeing freedom of religion. Scioto Company members were in essence declaring that this town, or at least its leadership, was to be Episcopalian. Like many religious converts, James Kilbourn, became more ardent than many who are born to their faith. He undoubtedly resented the fact that Episcopalians had been forced to pay taxes to support the Congregational Church until well after the Revolutionary War, when Connecticut ratified the federal constitution and joined the union. He was, in essence, reverting to an earlier time when church and state were linked and was attempting to reverse the tables and place himself and his followers in the majority.

The company's articles of agreement went on to establish a bidding system among proprietors that would determine the order of selection for town and farm lots. The proceeds from these bids were to go to the company to defray surveying expenses.

To enforce the company's goal of actual settlement rather than land speculation, it was agreed that each subscriber or his son would make settlement by January 1, 1805, or forfeit to the company twenty dollars for each one hundred acres subscribed. It is doubtful that this was ever enforced, for exceptions were immediately written for Russell Atwater and Ashel Deming, who were already seeking alternate settlers.

Although forty-two persons signed this contract, several were not officially accepted as members until January or February 1803, probably because that was when they were able to pay the exploration fee in cash. Dr. Stanbery was included as a member for a token one-hundred-acre subscription, but everyone understood that he was not planning to settle in the community.

In less than eight months, forty-one men had determined to commit themselves and their families to a new life on land they had never seen.[24] They had designed the outlines of the ideal community they planned to build. This almost certainly reflected Kilbourn's vision primarily, but he sold the concept and convinced an interesting group of men with diversified skills that a better life awaited them in the west.

❖ CHAPTER 3 ❖

A Place Most Favorable
for Our First Improvement

— ❖ —

Aᴌᴛʜᴏᴜɢʜ ɴᴏᴛ ᴀʟʟ ᴏꜰ ᴛʜᴇ subscribers had paid their exploration
fee and officially joined the company when the land purchase
was negotiated with Dr. Stanbery, everyone seemed confident that
they would attract the necessary number of subscribers before the
deed was officially recorded. At that same meeting of December 14,
1802, members began their detailed planning, resolving "That nine
men be sent forward as Labourors Including an agent & Carpenter for
the purpose of Building a Saw mill & make other necessary improvements."[1] A committee of three was appointed to conduct the hiring.

There was never any question that James Kilbourn would be the
agent in charge. By the next meeting, on January 13, seven young men
in their early twenties, all sons of members and four of them members
in their own right, were employed as laborers. They were to be paid
twelve dollars per month from the time of their arrival in the west
until the first of December. On February 22, members voted that Kilbourn should be paid four shillings and sixpence per day plus expenses
while "Acting in the Capacity of an over Seer for this company" and
that his older brother Lemuel should receive "Eight Shilling per Day
while working as a Carpenter" in building a sawmill. It is an interesting and unanswered question why the Kilbourn brothers were to
be paid in English currency rather than in U.S. dollars, but perhaps
they considered it more secure or negotiable. Deed records of the era
clearly show that both currencies were in use simultaneously.[2]

Kilbourn was anxious to head west as soon as spring weather
was sufficiently advanced. He departed early enough in the year, on

April 6, to encounter snow and other disagreeable weather before reaching Pittsburgh on April 21. He remained there several days obtaining mill irons, blacksmith's tools, iron, and other small supplies, which he shipped in care of William Russell, a tavern owner at Alexandria (now Portsmouth, Ohio), who was to send them up the Scioto River to Chillicothe. Kilbourn himself set out across country on horseback through Zanesville to Franklinton, arriving on Friday, May 6—"very wet, cold and much fatigued" from a snowstorm the previous day and swimming his horse through two rivers.[3]

But he was eager to see the company purchase and set off the next morning for three days, "in the woods viewing our lands, and choosing out a place most favorable for our first improvement" (see fig. 2). It was a week before he found time to write Lucy, but he was still exuberant about what he had seen. "I have been Carefully over the land & find it full as good as I expected, & I am fully persuaded that the half township lying on the River is worth all the Money we have given for the whole."[4] Kilbourn's enthusiasm invariably inspired and sustained his colleagues. He typified the aggressive Yankees whom Merle Curti has described as having glorious dreams of a new community, better both for themselves and for everyone else than anything they had known in the east.[5]

The half-township of eight thousand acres lying along the river, where Kilbourn determined to locate his town, had been perimeter surveyed by Israel Ludlow in 1797. Ludlow was a government surveyor who had worked primarily in the Symmes Purchase in southwestern Ohio. In the U.S. Military Tract he was paid three dollars per day and was expected to hire his own axmen and chainmen, the former to clear the brush and blaze the trees used as survey points, the latter to carry the chain which measured the distance. Such work was seriously hindered by trees in full leaf, heavy snow, or mud, so the preferred work period for professional surveyors was late fall and early winter. It was difficult work and a far cry from the glamorous legends commonly associated with western hunters, traders, and trappers. Surveyors, however, gained firsthand knowledge of the land and often benefited handsomely from knowing the location of the best quality land and streams that offered potential mill sites.

One can clearly envision Ludlow and his axmen and chainmen chopping their way through the wilderness near the Whetstone River in November of 1797. Although surveyors sometimes utilized a fifty-link chain for hilly terrain, Ludlow's crew evidently primarily relied in this area on the standard one-hundred-link chain, whose brass or iron links totaled sixty-six feet, or eighty chains to the mile.[6]

Ludlow must have been as impressed with the region as Kilbourn, for his survey notes described excellent farming land well timbered with oak, white and black ash, walnut, beech, and sugar trees. He measured the Whetstone River at "3 chains, 50 links wide," or approximately 231 feet; he particularly noted the "high bank" on the east side composed of "slate rock interspersed with sulphurous mineral bodies."[7] His team did their work well, placing posts every two and one-half miles to mark both the township corners and the midpoints that defined the quarter-township sections. When the perimeter was resurveyed in 1835, George H. Griswold was able to find sufficient posts, though some were broken at ground level, to mark the bearing and distance from Ludlow's "witness trees."[8] These blazed trees were usually hickory, ash, or oak, chosen for their longevity.

Kilbourn's choice for the town site was on the east side of the river, south of Ludlow's "high bank," which is now preserved as a Columbus metropolitan park. Kilbourn's town site was also on high ground, which promised a healthy situation free from flooding and marshes that produced ague fevers and yet an easy walk to the navigable river that provided access all the way to the port of New Orleans. This port at the mouth of the Mississippi had, until recently, been owned by the French and administered by the Spanish, who had intermittently blocked navigation.

The lower Mississippi ports of Natchez and New Orleans were already becoming important markets for the western farmers of both Kentucky and Ohio, but more importantly, an open port at New Orleans provided an alternative route to eastern markets, avoiding a struggle over the mountains. In 1802, Nathaniel Massie entrusted "ninety three barrels of Pork and four of hog lard" to a flatboat operator, instructing him to sell at Natchez if he could get ten dollars a barrel or twelve dollars at New Orleans. "I had rather take these prices than to risk a sale at any of the [Caribbean] Islands."[9] The flatboat, which was broken up for lumber on arrival, cost ten shillings per foot, and two hands were paid sixty dollars each plus provisions. Such trade flourished in succeeding months as President Jefferson's Louisiana Purchase was ratified and the threat of Spanish confiscation was eliminated. For the Scioto Company, however, that was in the future. For now, the Whetstone River was a natural highway in the wilderness that provided an immediate means for transporting supplies from Franklinton and Chillicothe.

When Kilbourn returned to Franklinton, the bustling settlement established by Lucas Sullivant nine miles south on the west side of the Scioto and Whetstone junction, he found the first of his work crew had arrived, the brothers Alexander and William Morrison of Blandford, Massachusetts. He immediately sent them downriver to Chillicothe to procure the supplies sent from Pittsburgh. He himself went by horseback and arrived ahead of the boat to purchase axes, chains, a smith's bellows, bar iron, and a variety of provisions, including thirty bushels of wheat and a barrel of whiskey.[10]

The availability of such diverse provisions for immigrants on the Ohio frontier was in marked contrast to the situation their ancestors had faced in coming to New England during the Great Migration of the 1630s. Those early migrants had been warned by Rev. Higginson, "when you are once parted with England you shall meete neither with taverns nore alehouse, nor butchers, nor grosers, nor apothecaries shops . . . in the midst of the great ocean, nor when you are come to land here are yet neither markets nor fayres to buy what you want."[11] It places a different perspective on the hardships of the pioneers who crossed the trans-Appalachian frontier the year Ohio became a state.

By the time Kilbourn returned to Franklinton, he found that the Connecticut workers—Israel P. Case, Abner P. and Levi Pinney, Adna Bristol, and Ebenezer Brown—had arrived within the hour. "When they had refreshed they went up the river with me, and went immediately to work."[12] Kilbourn was pushing himself and everyone else in the work party because the time was short to clear some land and plant seeds that would provide a crop for harvest before frost and before the first group of families arrived in the fall.

Kilbourn was also able to purchase a variety of provisions from settlers in the Franklinton community, which had in April been named the "seat of justice" for a new county named Franklin. This gave Franklinton an immediate advantage in terms of growth. Since county seats were usually twenty to thirty miles apart to permit travelers with a wagon or carriage to travel to county court and return the same day, Kilbourn's settlement only nine miles to the north was never going to enjoy the stimulus of becoming a county-seat town. Established only six years earlier, Franklinton was already able to offer a variety of products for sale. Kilbourn's provisions included thirty bushels of corn, fifteen of oats, and ten of potatoes; fifty pounds of bacon and eighty of pickled pork; a ball of soap; two cows with calves; two yoke of oxen at fifty dollars each; and a plow made to order. This is consistent with Utter's contention that the tide of immigrants furnished a sizable market for agricultural goods during their first year of residence, but that by the second year they became producers who added to the western surplus, which had no transportation to eastern markets.[13]

In addition to the Franklinton settlement, the central Ohio wilderness had acquired several other inhabitants who were helpful. Kilbourn found a couple of squatters on the Scioto Company site and negotiated their removal, paying them for their cabin, which the advance party quickly moved into. The work party added to the squatter's initial clearing for a cornfield, "as we could sooner get a larger piece here to plant, than where we first began."[14] Kilbourn's report to the company made no mention of Indians living in the area, although Ludlow's survey notes marked an Indian trail running north and south near the river, which was apparently used by itinerant hunting parties. The Wyandot tribes that had occupied the general area prior to the Greenville Treaty apparently had no significant villages within the boundaries of the Scioto Company purchase.

Heading north to view the upper part of this purchase, Kilbourn took along corn to be ground at the "Yankee settlement" about five miles north, where the extended families of Nathan Carpenter and Thomas and Avery Powers had settled two years earlier. Kilbourn was pleased to have New England neighbors and, when he wrote Lucy, took pains to assure her that "There are several families settled very near us who appear to be very Clever people have got well agoing & More Settlement forming fast."[15] He was also pleased to find that the northern four thousand acres of the purchase were "better than I had expected." He judged that it would "afford a plenty of good pasture and mowing ground."[16]

Kilbourn's letter to his wife appears to take special care to assure her that the situation of the new town was healthy and that there were already neighbors settled in the area. He was apparently a devoted family man who missed his wife and children during his frequent absences. Only a week after his arrival, he wrote her that "I must say that if My affairs were well Settled & I had My Lucy in My

Arms & the Children around us I Could very well dispense with ever
going to Connecticut again." He certainly expected his letter to be
sent and hers to be received, although this would have to be done
at Chillicothe for Franklinton as yet had no post office. He admon-
ished her, "Do not fail to write me often. I think it quite enough that
I must be at this distance from you & not that I should be deprived of
hearing from you also — Tedious at best will be my summer."[17]

By the first of June the work party was burning brush and plowing
for corn. Kilbourn did not report the acreage that was cleared, but
most experts credit one man with the ability to clear and plant about
two to three acres the first year.[18] Without taking time to remove the
stumps, but simply plowing the ground and planting crops between
them, it is not unrealistic to estimate that the work party was able
to clear and plant an area that today might encompass about two
modern city blocks, or approximately thirteen acres.

On a trip to Franklinton for more supplies, Kilbourn "heard of
my brother in Licking wilderness, went out to meet him and on
Thursday the 9th, at evening conducted him safe to our cabin." With
Lemuel Kilbourn on hand to supervise the construction of a sawmill,
the advance work party was now complete. The following Wednesday James reported that they had "finished planting our corn, potatoes, etc."[19]

There was little time for random exploring, but the eight-thousand-acre New England–style town site contained an interesting prehistoric earthworks such as the one that had fascinated Nathaniel
Little near Chillicothe the previous year. This earthworks, on the
west side of the river, was well-covered by forest growth when the
pioneers arrived. It would eventually be measured as a rectangle,
630 feet east to west, 550 feet north to south, with entrances at the
northeast and southwest corners and the southern wall broken by a
truncated mound that measured 20 feet in height and 192 feet in diameter at the base. Two smaller circles outside the main works to
the southwest and northwest respectively measured 120 and 140 feet
in diameter, one broken by a single entrance and the other by three
entrances.[20] Speculations about the earthwork's use as a fortification
or burial grounds would intrigue the New England settlers for years.

For the Scioto Company work party, the summer of 1803 was a
time for what one observer of pioneers moving into the wilderness
described as proceeding to "prostrate the forest and deposit the seed

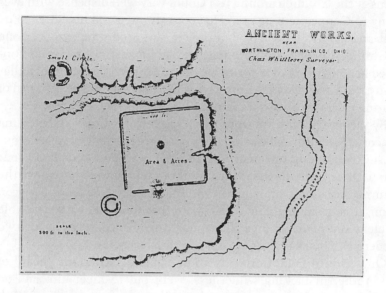

Fig. 3. A map of the Adena-Hopewell earthworks on Worthington farm lot no. 10 revealed these rectangular and circular mounds when it was surveyed in 1840. (Taken from *Ancient Monuments of the Mississippi Valley*)

of art and refinement."[21] With crops in the ground by mid-June, the laborers moved to their next priority—temporary log homes for the families who would be coming west that autumn. Typical frontier cabins were about sixteen by twenty feet, usually requiring twenty logs per side, or eighty in all.[22] Since the survey of town and farm lots would not be completed until after the arrival of the main party, these cabins had no pretense of permanence, but were simply "of rough, unhewed logs without windows, with puncheon floors, no chimney, only an opening in the roof for smoke to escape."[23] They would provide temporary protection for the settlers during their first winter in Ohio.

With the work laid out and provisions stocked, Kilbourn returned east to prepare his own family and the others who were making the westward migration that fall. It is a measure of Kilbourn's leadership to note that no formal meetings of the company were recorded during his absence. Other members had, however, been selling property and putting their affairs in order.

From January through March there had been a flurry of activity as the company formally accepted members who were paying their exploration fee and a few new subscribers to replace those who, for one reason or another, had dropped out. When the deed was recorded in Chillicothe, it contained the forty-two members from December, with subscriptions ranging in size from one hundred to twelve hundred acres each[24] (see appendix A). It was never intended that all members should have an equal four hundred acres. Actually, twelve subscribers held more than that and twenty-seven had less, but all had well over the forty acres that a typical frontiersman could cultivate alone with one horse.[25]

In the Scioto Company, young bachelors like Abner P. Pinney and Israel P. Case subscribed jointly for two hundred acres. Dr. Stanbery took a token share of one hundred acres. The largest subscribers were Blandford merchant Russell Atwater and James Kilbourn at twelve hundred acres each. But Atwater was also considering a move to New York State and, with the company's approval, was seeking replacement settlers. Kilbourn subscribed for an additional three hundred acres in the names of his nephews Asahel Hart and William Kilbourn, who were not yet twenty-one years of age.

Family networks were one of the keys to the company's formation and persistence. Not only had Kilbourn persuaded his brother Lemuel and his two nephews, who were too young to become members in their own right, to make the migration, but he was about to seek significant financial investment from his uncle by marriage, Jedediah Norton.[26] The Kilbourns were not the only family network in this migration. Sixty-eight percent, or twenty-six of the thirty-eight original proprietors who eventually shared in the land division, had fathers or fathers-in-law, sons or sons-in-law, brothers or brothers-in-law in the group (see appendix B). Far from being unique, this pattern of family networks appears to have been the norm for frontier migration and far more common than the rugged individualism routinely portrayed in historic narratives of the western movement.[27]

Besides Abner Pinney himself, the Pinney clan included his son Azariah and son-in-law William Vining. Abner's other sons, Abner P. and Levi, and son-in-law Ebenezer Brown were among the advance work party. The three Topping brothers, Josiah, Zophar, and John, were company members, as were Zophar's brother-in-law, Ezra Griswold, and Josiah's brother-in-law, Levi Hayes. Israel Case and Alexander Morrison both had sons who joined the company, and Israel was a brother-in-law of company member Job Case, while Morrison was a brother-in-law of company member William Thompson. Members Ambrose Case and Lemuel Humphrey were brothers-in-law, as were Thomas Phelps and Levi Buttles. The company was, for the most part, a closely knit group of New Englanders, linked in some cases by several generations of intermarriages.

But there were also geographic clusters within the group, primarily around the towns of Blandford, Massachusetts, and Granby and Simsbury, Connecticut (these two towns had been united until Granby was set off as a new town in 1786). The absence of any kinship connection between the Connecticut and Massachusetts factions suggests that their union in this company was based on business and Episcopal Church connections.

When it came time to put up the money, some members changed their minds and some deferred their move to the next year, but others put their affairs in order and sold property in preparation for the move. It was the opportunity to acquire significant land holdings that drew these families westward, even though most also had skills other than farming, like James Kilbourn's storekeeping or his brother Lemuel's carpentry, which provided a significant part of their income. Most of these company members considered themselves "farmers" in the Jeffersonian sense of a nation of yeomen. Land gave status and value far beyond its purchase price. It symbolized independence and the opportunity to build a family's future. As Clark has pointed out, when people spoke of themselves as independent they did not mean self-sufficiency, for they relied upon a complicated exchange of goods and services. Rather, they meant the freedom to conduct their own affairs, and this type of independence was deeply rooted in the possession of freehold property.[28] The persistent New England values regarding land, family, and religion in the founding of Worthington are remarkably similar to those Susan Gray reports in studying the Michigan frontier of thirty years later.[29]

Historians have recognized that migrations occur for positive reasons associated with the destination, negative reasons associated with the area of origin, or some combination of the two.[30] Nearly all of the Scioto Company were positively recruited, responding to factors associated with the destination, but some were also moving west because opportunities in the east had failed them. Ezra Griswold, son of Kilbourn's former employer and brother of his mentor, was involved in a series of lawsuits from February through August 1802. He attempted to convey everything he owned—some 142 acres of land with two dwelling houses, a barn, a dye house, a fulling mill, two gristmills, and a cooper's shop—to his brother Alexander V. Griswold for 5,600 pounds.[31] Subsequent judgments and land sales suggest this was a "paper" transaction that was only partially successful in sheltering his assets from creditors. Although Ezra was a key member in supporting the westward migration, his business troubles explain why he held no leadership position or financial responsibility in the group. Creasy has emphasized the importance of adding such psychological and opportunity costs when evaluating the decision whether to emigrate.[32]

Some members were able to liquidate their property assets by selling to friends and neighbors. In January, Roswell Wilcox sold two and one-half acres, a dwelling house, and his one-third share in a gristmill at Simsbury for $950.00.[33] At almost the same time William Thompson sold 172 acres on the road from Blandford to Granville, Massachusetts, for $3,000.00, or approximately $17.44 per acre.[34] This was toward the lower end of what good New England farms were selling for, and Thompson's farm probably had few improvements; but it was sufficient to allow Thompson to subscribe for one thousand acres of Scioto Company land and still have sufficient cash for moving expenses and constructing buildings on his new purchase.[35] There was ample motivation for migration when a family might establish itself amid land abundant enough to establish each child comfortably.

Although Wilcox's and Thompson's sales were private agreements, others sold to Jonas Stanbery as provided in the company contract. On February 28, Stanbery purchased ten acres with buildings and blacksmith's shop from Nathan Stewart of Blandford for $631.00 and ninety-one acres from Glass Cochran for $1,398.00, or $15.36 per acre.[36]

By the time the company met on August 10 and 11, for their final meeting in the east, the families who were moving that fall were busy concluding their preparations, and all other members were giving power of attorney to someone who was going west. Perhaps the most significant resolution of this meeting was that "the Town purchased & layed out by us . . . shall be hereafter called Worthington."[37]

This was a politically astute move, for Thomas Worthington had been elected in April by the Ohio legislature to represent the new state in the United States Senate. He was already being characterized by some as the "father of Ohio statehood." His name was known throughout Ohio and in the U.S. Congress, guaranteeing that a town named in his honor would have instant recognition.[38] His brother-in-law, Edward Tiffin, had been elected Ohio's first governor. Kilbourn was well aware that the friendship of men in such powerful positions would benefit his planned community.

Another interesting decision at this meeting was that "two Dollars be Appropriated out of the fund to Each Subscriber for a Library." While a two dollar subscription seems relatively insignificant by modern standards, it must be compared with the wages of twelve dollars per month paid the young men in the advance work party. Two dollars was a substantial commitment, equivalent to at least four days wages for these laborers. James Kilbourn and Levi Buttles were appointed as a committee to purchase books, and on September 2 the treasurer turned over $59.86 to the library committee. In an era when many books often sold for twenty or thirty cents and most for less than a dollar, it would appear that the community began its library with a significant number of volumes.

This commitment for a library was probably an outgrowth of Kilbourn's previous membership in the Granby subscription library. It is completely consistent with Doyle's analysis of Illinois communities, in which the New England community model was transported westward intact.[39] It was unusual to establish such a cultural institution before the community was actually settled, but it was eminently practical when preparing to move from an environment where books were available to one where they were not.

Frederick Jackson Turner, more than any other historian, has consistently defined American development in terms of a continual return to primitive conditions on an advancing frontier line.[40] The preparations of the Scioto Company, however, support more recent historical research, illustrating a realistic acceptance of the frontier environment but also a clear expectation that this would be a brief interval of hardship before building a community that equaled and surpassed those these families had known in the east. Every facet of the Scioto group's preparations reflected confident optimism.

◆ CHAPTER 4 ◆

If You Calculate for Smooth Roads
Free from Hills You Will
Be Disappointed

— ◆ —

B y September 1803, about half of the Scioto Company families
were preparing to join the work party that was already on site
in Ohio. Others had decided to postpone their departure until the
following year or were reconsidering their decision completely. The
oldest of the members going west were in their fifties and had served,
usually brief militia duty, during the Revolutionary War. They did not
share the social class of the officers who organized the Society of Cincinnati, but philosophically they typified the Roman citizen-soldier,
Cincinnatus, who left his wife and plough when duty demanded that
he take up the sword on behalf of his country.[1]

From Blandford this group included company treasurer William
Thompson, his wife Annah, and their seven children, who were from
five to twenty years of age. Alexander Morrison's two oldest sons
had gone out with the work party, and his oldest daughter had married and was remaining in the east, but he prepared to leave with his
wife Mehitable and their four youngest children. The Morrisons left
behind the grave of a young daughter who died in August 1802 (evidently that had been a very sickly time in Blandford, for Nathan and
Anna Stewart also left behind two daughters who died in the same
epidemic). Although Anna Morton Stewart's father was a Presbyterian minister educated in Scotland, Nathan, like the others from
Blandford, was one of the founders of the local Episcopal Society.[2]

In the same fifty-year age bracket were David Bristol and Samuel
Beach from Barkamsted, Connecticut. Bristol's oldest unmarried son,

Adna, was in the work party, and two married daughters had recently moved to New York State; but the two youngest children came west with David and their stepmother. Samuel and Desiah Beach were moving with their three children, who were from nine to nineteen years of age. During the Revolution Samuel had served as a fifer during the Bennington and Saratoga campaigns.[3]

The leaders of the Scioto Company were, for the most part, younger men in their thirties with young families. While the older generation felt they had fought for and won liberty, the younger generation inherited a concept of equality of opportunity. Thomas Jefferson's inauguration as president just two years earlier was a dramatic turning point that shifted power from a strong central government to the collective leadership of individual states.[4] Both the leadership of Ohio and the leadership of Worthington represented this new generation of leaders.

James Kilbourn celebrated his thirty-third birthday during the trip west. Accompanied by his nephew, Asahel Hart, he and his wife were traveling with their four children, and Lucy was, in the biblical sense, "great with child." Ezra Griswold was two years older, and he and his wife Ruth were accompanied by six children, the youngest born the previous January. They were joined by her sister Lois, married to thirty-year-old Zophar Topping, and their two children. The youngest Topping brother, John, was still single. The oldest, thirty-five-year-old Dr. Josiah Topping, had a family of four children, the youngest a babe whom his wife Mehitable carried in her arms as she made the journey on horseback.[5]

From the Massachusetts contingent, Glass and Mehitable Cochran of Blandford also had a young family of six children, and he was distinguished from other members of the group for withdrawing from the Episcopal Society to become one of the founders of the Blandford Baptist congregation. Nathaniel Little was unmarried, but was accompanied by his brother William. Twenty-one-year-old Noah Andrews came west to take up the subscription of his father, Revolutionary War veteran Moses Andrews, who had recently moved from New Britain, Connecticut, to Montague, Massachusetts.[6]

Levi Buttles, Job Case, and Thomas Phelps, neighbors from "the Notch" area of North Granby, where the Massachusetts-Connecticut border had been in dispute, joined the company late and decided to come out alone that fall and make preparations, but to go back and bring their families the following year. They also intended to explore potential sites for a group of neighbors from Granville, Massachusetts, who had recently formed a company to consider western settlement and had chosen Buttles as their president.[7] Buttles and Case were to investigate possible sites near Worthington and make a recommendation when they returned the following spring.

The majority of the Scioto Company members were heads of household who had established their families in New England, and they were, on average, a little older than the English emigrants to New England during the Great Migration of the 1630s.[8] Such migrations by family groups were common both from the Old World to the New and from east to west across the new continent. Even in a rural area with no significant town, Faragher describes a community of "families in association."[9] A social support network and the practice of reciprocal work exchange, based upon family ties, were deeply embedded in the cultural fabric of rural and small-town society.[10]

Like the advance work party, various family groups headed west at slightly different times. Kilbourn and Little had doubtless warned the others that accommodations for western travelers were small, crude cabins, completely unsuitable for large groups. Ezra Griswold's party left their home in Simsbury on September 15, and his plodding ox-drawn wagon was the first to reach the site of the new settlement on October 29, 1803.[11] It was a feat his descendants recounted with pride, chiding the families of those who had chosen teams of horses. This information was also quickly conveyed to those who were planning trips the following year.

None of the one hundred men, women, and children who traveled west to Worthington in the autumn of 1803 took time to record their feelings on leaving their old homes or to note their daily experiences on the road. One is left to ponder the mysteries of how the women felt while bidding farewell to family members they might never see again. One particularly wonders about Lucy Fitch Kilbourn, who was forced to stop at Catfish Camp (now Washington, Pennsylvania) to give birth to a baby daughter on October 15. Did the rigors of the journey advance the birth that they had hoped would occur in their new home, or did she willingly set off into the unknown, trusting that help would be at hand when her time came? Perhaps she had been separated from her husband too often during the previous two years of exploration to bear the thought of waiting in the east another year.

Fig. 4. "Scioto Settler," a terra cotta relief with an ox team and buckeye branches symbolizing the Ohio pioneers, was executed for the Worthington Post Office by WPA artist Vernon Carlock. (Courtesy of the National Archives)

Perhaps Kilbourn felt it was necessary to set an example to the company by having his family be among the first settlers to spend a winter in the new community. In any event, they named the infant Orrel after a sister who had been born and had died in Granby before her first birthday.[12] James Kilbourn exulted in the fact that Orrel's birth rounded out the company at an even "One Hundred souls" who would spend the first winter in Worthington.[13]

For most of these travelers, it was a difficult journey lasting from six to eight weeks. Although some westward migrants traveled in the spring to clear land and plant crops, members of this company delegated that responsibility to a work party, and both they and their neighbors who founded Granville followed the common wisdom of westward migration, leaving in the autumn after the dangers of the summer fever season abated.[14] Dr. Daniel Drake, Cincinnati's best-known pioneer physician, strongly urged emigrants from regions north of Ohio to plan to arrive in late autumn and make their home for the first season on an upland farm to avoid the fevers and chills associated with river bottoms and decaying vegetation.[15]

Those in the Worthington migration who started late encountered snow before they reached their destination. Every family had a horse or ox wagon, sometimes a cart, and perhaps one or two horses for riding. The wagons were too small and too heavily loaded to provide enough room for anyone other than very young or ill passengers. All but the youngest children walked, sometimes driving a prized sow and her piglets along with them. Lura Buttles's granddaughter, whose mother was eleven when the family came west, recalled her saying that "many were the tears she shed and as they dropt on her dress would freeze, as [they] traveled through the snow over the mountains her stockings would freeze to her shoes. . . ."[16]

There were extensive and sometimes costly preparations to be made for the westward trip, such as new wagon wheels and "iron to tire them." One account book recorded paying eight dollars "for making one pair of hind wheels to the Horse-wagon" and twenty-one dollars "for the Ox-wagon, axeltrees and wheels and [k]nees."[17] Teams and wagons were invariably the most expensive possessions these pioneers owned. In contrast with the large prairie schooners that later traveled the National Road and crossed the plains to California, these were flat-bottomed farm wagons with high sideboards. They were, however, topped with wooden staves that supported a sailcloth or heavy linen covering.[18]

From Carlisle to Pittsburgh the Pennsylvania State Road paralleled an old Indian path, a distinctive example of the utilitarian practicality of these native American routes.[19] By the time they reached western Pennsylvania, the travelers had reached poorer roads, and deep ruts mired wagon wheels to their hubs when it rained. On the steepest roads over the mountains, teams were doubled and wagons were brought forward in relays. At times during the descent, ropes had to be attached to the wagon bed, and men scrambled through the brush beside the trail, pulling the ropes tight to prevent the wagon from tumbling over.

Once the travelers were ferried across the Ohio River, the roads became little more than trails. From Zanesville across country to the Worthington settlement, even those who came a year or two later resorted to using axes to cut their way through forest growth.

After company member Levi Hayes brought his family west, a letter from his wife Ruhamah described the last part of the journey on the newly cut road: "We had to cut and tug three days in the wilderness & see no human being nor scarce any water. I thot it a poor time to be sick [which she had been] but the third day just at evening we came in sight of a small settlement. It gave me much joy to see the face of a woman."

Ruhamah offered pointed advice to her friend, Elizabeth Case, who was preparing to come west. "Bringing our clock was a wrong calculation. If I had brot the top part of my case of drawers it would have been better." She admitted that "If I was to take the journey again I would not use one article of crockery on the road for we broke the most of ours. Tin would do for almost any use & you can borrow the cups at most places where you put up." She minced no words in warning her neighbor, "If you calculate for smooth roads free from hills you will be disappointed. if you expect to dress to keep your clothes clean you will miss your aim."[20]

Two of the company members, Abner Pinney and Levi Buttles, both of whom came west in the autumn of 1804, died within months of their arrival in Worthington. The settlement of these men's estates provided a complete inventory and appraisal of their belongings that shows precisely what two of these pioneer families considered essential for the trip and for equipping their new home.[21] Both men left widows and large families. Five of Pinney's children were married, but four still shared the family home. Buttles's seven children ranged from four to seventeen years of age. Pinney's estate was valued at $454.51 and Buttles's at $547.26.[22]

Both Pinney and Buttles were slightly above average landholders among the thirty-eight company members.[23] In the eight-thousand-acre half of the purchase that was surveyed as the "town" of Worthington, the median holding for the twenty-four "heads of household" who actually came west was two town lots and 193 acres of farmland. Pinney ranked fifth in the company with three town lots and 237 acres, while Buttles was eighth with three town lots and 212 acres.[24] These rankings, on the lower edge of the upper third of the Scioto Company settlers, suggest that their estate inventories provide a representative view of the possessions these New England migrants brought west.

In each estate, the most valuable possession was their wagon and team. Pinney had an "ox waggon" worth sixty-five dollars and a "sett wagon harness with yolk &c." and a pair of oxen, "1 red the other brindle," valued at fifty-five dollars. He also had one cow and a white mare "having but one eye." Buttles had a "light waggon" worth forty-five dollars, an extra set of wagon "fore wheels," and a cart. His team of oxen was only valued at forty dollars, but he had a black mare worth fifty-five dollars, a horse, three cows and calves, and six sows with piglets and several shoats. The baby pigs, of course, would have been born in Ohio; the sows, each with six to nine piglets, apparently weathered their long walk very well.

Buttles had a "rifle gun" appraised at fifteen dollars, while Pinney had a six-dollar "musket with bayonet." It is worth noting that guns with a rifled barrel that produced greater accuracy were appraised at more than twice the value of a common musket. Buttles owned a "man's saddle" and a "sett carriage harness." One suspects that the former proved more useful on the frontier, for it was two decades before local roads improved enough for carriage travel.

Both estates contained a plow, a bell, and a variety of hand tools. Pinney's included two axes, three hoes, fifteen pounds of chain, a grass scythe, a drawing knife, a broad knife, six pounds of iron wedges, a steel trap, a pair of small steelyards, a log chain, and ten gimlets.[25] Buttles's tools included a brush scythe, two old sickles, five axes, one spade, an "english shovel," two "draught chains" and one log chain, ten pounds of steel, twenty one-half-pound bars of iron, a shaving knife, a hammer, a rasp, a handsaw, a gauge, two chisels, an iron hook and trammel, and a pair of small steelyards. The similarity between these lists suggests that axes for felling trees and chopping firewood, hoes for cultivating crops, scythes and sickles for cutting grass and grain, chains for dragging logs, small steelyards for weighing items, and iron for making tools and repairs were common equipment for every western emigrant.

Buttles's wardrobe was quite basic—one "sertoot coat," one great coat, one "Black strait Bodied coat," two waistcoats, two shirts, one pair of nankeen breeches, three pair of pantaloons, a pair of cotton stockings, a white neck handkerchief, and a "man's hat."[26] This inventory makes no mention of underclothes, which reflects either what the appraisers chose to include or what the pioneer wore. Pinney's wardrobe appears to have been more varied: he owned four "strait bodied" coats, three vests (one striped and one of silk nankeen), two pairs of small clothes (one of plain nankeen and the other of "damaged velvet"), eight pairs of worsted stockings (some "footed"), a bandanna handkerchief and cotton pocket handkerchief, one "knaped" hat and one "castor" hat, and a pair of boots.[27] The fact that Pinney's appraisers itemized three pairs of trousers, from "striped linen" to "brown tow," and four shirts, from "Irish linen" to "check linen" to "coarse muslin," clearly shows that he had garments appropriate for both work and social occasions. A pair of "silver shoe buckles" and one of "plated knee buckles" reflects the tastes of a man accustomed to attending parties, although the expectation of such in the frontier settlement seems somewhat optimistic.

Buttles's estate included two yards of blue broadcloth that was valued at nine dollars and was evidently purchased ready-made. Fine woolen broadcloth derived its name from the wider commercial looms used to produce it. Nine yards of "home made woolen cloth" was appraised at $10.12, a clear indication of the lower valuation of the homemade product. Pinney's estate included 4 "weavers reeds" in varying sizes, a "great spinning wheel" valued at two dollars, and 118 "hackle teeth."[28] It would appear that both families engaged in the home production of yarn and cloth, but that they also had access to machine-woven cloth. This would place them above the average American household of 1800, of which, Larkin contends, the majority were clothed in fabrics produced by the household.[29] Farmington merchants, however, who enjoyed a brisk trade with Europe, China, and the West Indies, were importing silk, tea, and porcelain goods by the 1790s. At the same time, domestic manufacturing, such as Stephen Brownson's mill, was producing woolen, cotton, and linen cloth.[30]

Cooking and eating utensils of iron, tin, and pewter were basic in both estates. The Buttles household had a frying pan, a dutch oven, a pot, an iron tea kettle, two brass kettles (one large and one small), eight tin pans, a wire sifter, three flat irons, a pair of andirons, a fire shovel, and tongs. The Pinneys had the same basic frying pan, dutch oven, tea kettle, and fifteen tin pans in varying sizes and shapes. They also had a roaster, a funnel, a candle base, a pail, and several cups of tin. Except for a seventy-five-cent teapot, their pewter was appraised by the pound according to its condition—eight pounds of new pewter at $4.00, eight and one-half pounds of "fourth worn" pewter at $3.27, and five pounds of old pewter at $1.25. Such groupings demonstrate that pewter utensils were considered rather common. The Pinneys also had three "japanned tumblers," the popular lacquer pieces decorated in the Japanese style, which were valued at fifty-one cents for the group.[31]

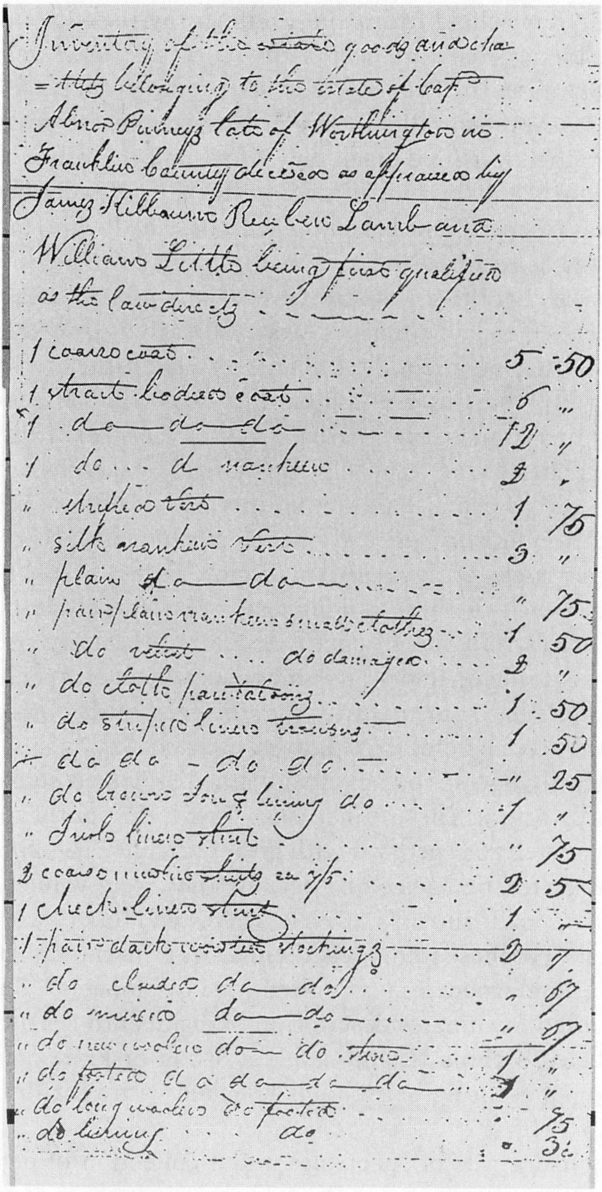

Fig. 5. Abner Pinney's death in November 1804 was the first in the community, and his estate inventory reveals the types of possessions the New England emigrants brought west. (Microfilm, Pinney estate)

The only household furnishings brought by these pioneers were beds. The Pinneys had four beds with "pillows & ticks" valued from $8.50 to $16.12 each. They also had sixteen linen sheets, eight flannel sheets, seventeen pillow cases, a "lock cumpass" coverlet, and two other coverlets (one black and white and the other black and yellow), four blankets, four pieced quilts, three "under bed ticks," and several "diaper" towels and tablecloths. The Buttles family also had four "beds and bedding," valued from $9.50 to $17.00 each. It would appear that these were featherbeds, but it is not clear whether the "under bed ticks" describes straw-filled ticks or a smaller size designed for use on a trundle bed. A "set Blue furniture" valued at $2.80 in the Pinney estate was enumerated with the bedding and may refer to a chamber pot, perhaps with a wash basin and pitcher. Two small chests were probably traveling chests as the largest was appraised at fifty cents. This was an impressive array of bedding for the western country, where early travelers frequently recorded sleeping on straw ticks without anything more than a blanket. One assumes that each of these homes also had some crude handmade benches, stools, and tables constructed after the family arrived that appraisers considered temporary and of no value worth including.

Each family had some luxuries that they obviously considered too precious to leave behind. Levi Buttles owned a $13.00 silver watch, and the family had a wooden clock valued at $18.00 and a looking glass worth $1.50. These must have made the journey over the mountains safely, but perhaps with great difficulty. The Pinneys also had seven plates, perhaps china because they were valued at $1.00, a 25¢ punch bowl, and a "sett New knives and forks" worth $1.25. The appraisal of these items sets them apart from the tin and pewter dinnerware and wooden spoons often used by pioneers.[32] Such items bring to mind Bushman's description of eighteenth-century estates that included a china teacup, a silver spoon or knife, and a book or two as representing households "flecked with gentility without being colored by it."[33]

Pinney had a pair of spectacles and a collection of eight books valued at $4.30 that included the Bible, a dictionary, and selections such as "travels of Cyrus, Winchesters Decalogues, Websters selections, Robinson Crusoe, Benjamins work, and Shakespeares Edward the Black prince." Such private ownership of books is particularly enlightening in view of the Scioto Company's early commitment to establish a subscription library.

Estate inventories from a company of landowners do not reflect the contents of the most humble households in a community, but, as noted earlier, these two men who died within months of their arrival can be considered representative of this particular group of New England settlers.[34] Their personal property contained essential wearing apparel, household furnishings and equipment, livestock, tools, and farm equipment. Fifty-two percent of Pinney's estate was devoted to personal apparel and household furnishings, compared to 32 percent of Buttles's estate. At the same time, 68 percent of Buttles's estate was reflected in the value of his livestock and tools, compared to 48 percent of Pinney's. These differences apparently reflect the different stages in life of the two men. Pinney was a man old enough to count on sons and sons-in-law to do the major farm work, while Buttles had a number of young children and expected to set up a farming operation in the new country.[35]

These families represented the New England "back country" of the late eighteenth century, and both had been "farmers" there. In Ohio, Pinney's sons and sons-in-law were farmers, coopers, blacksmiths, and tinsmiths; among Buttles's sons and sons-in-law were a merchant, a banker, a hornsmith, a brick mason, and several farmers.

These estates suggest families who were well dressed and had comfortable homes by the standards of the day. They appear to represent the middle class that Bushman describes as having acquired "vernacular gentility."[36] As household goods became less costly and more widely available, common people began to acquire the essentials for genteel living, such as feather beds.[37] Although both families brought several feather beds and bedding such as linen sheets and coverlets, bedsteads were not included. There was a clear expectation that bulky items such as tables, chairs, beds, and looms would be constructed after their arrival.

One suspects that each of these families, like Ruhamah Hayes, found "our loads were made a little too heavy or at least too bulky."[38] Decisions about what to take and what to leave behind must have been at least as difficult as the packing decisions of a modern traveler preparing for a trip around the world. How these western migrants must have hated to pare down a man's tools and a woman's housekeeping possessions to the size of a farm wagon that could be manhandled over steep mountain roads and hacked through dense forest.

❖ CHAPTER 5 ❖

In Perfect Health and Much
Pleased with Our Situation

— ❖ —

WINTER ARRIVED AT THE clearing in the forest that the new settlers called Worthington ahead of the Kilbourn family with their
infant daughter. According to their minutes, the Scioto Company
met for the first time "AT WORTHINGTON" on December 1, 1803,
at Mr. Bristol's cabin on the north side of the public square. It appears
that Kilbourn had just arrived and that there was unfinished business
relating to the cabins, the sawmill, and the harvest, as well as a need
to begin surveying as quickly as possible. A resolution authorized
"the Agent [to] Procure hands to finnish the Cabbins & to Secure the
Sawmill & Likewise to Procure two Chainmen to Carry the Chain
while Running out the forty farm Lots & Likewise to Secure the Corn
& Stoke & oxen & Horses."[1] The meeting adjourned until December 5, but was postponed to the seventh, the eleventh, and finally the
twelfth. Everyone was clearly too busy making the cabins, crops, and
livestock ready for winter to take time for a meeting.

More than thirty years later, Joel Buttles remembered his family's
arrival at the wilderness site as a "sorry time." He recalled that they
"had a cabin of one room for our numerous family and effects, and
this cabin was in the woods about twenty rods north of the public
square on Main Street. . . . Our cattle and horses had to be fed, though
not much."[2] When the first settlers arrived, the planned "public
square" was actually a maze of felled trees, only parts of which had
been reduced to logs for cabins.

The immediate priorities must have been "chinking" the spaces between cabin logs with clay to keep out the winter wind, constructing three-sided "lean-tos" to shelter livestock, and harvesting and storing corn and potato crops for human rather than wildlife consumption. The fact that the company met December 1 in David Bristol's cabin suggests that the "schoolhouse" was not yet ready for occupancy.

By December 12, company members got down to business, meeting in the "schoolhouse," a large double cabin on the east side of the public square. A committee of Buttles, Griswold, Stewart, and Thompson was appointed "to Settle Mr. Lemuel Kilbourn's Account," and it was resolved that "in Case of any Disagreement in Sentiment" a fifth member would be appointed. This is the first suggestion that there might be a problem with Lemuel Kilbourn's work on the sawmill and the amount he expected to be paid.

The relative importance of this issue can be judged by comparing this four-person committee with the appointment of a single individual, Nathan Stewart, as "a School Committee for this Society." It was also resolved that Ezra Griswold should be granted the right to "Keep a publick house for the Entertainment of Travelers if any there Should be. . . ." A school and tavern were clearly high priorities for the group, but there was also the problem of providing enough cabins for those who had already arrived. Several of the eleven families on site must have been crowded together, for the company resolved to "Call on Gentlemen . . . for Bilding Cabbins for themselves or other persons."[3]

The following day, company members agreed that "the Grindstone belonging to the Company Should remain as Publick property & for that use only" and that the company's "pair of Large Stillyards Should . . . be Kept at Mr. Ezra Griswolds."[4] The schoolhouse might be the official community center, but since Ezra Griswold's tavern was the place to sharpen tools and make official weights, it assumed a prominent place in the community's informal social structure.

On December 13, company members also resolved to petition the county court at Franklinton for a road from Franklinton to Worthington. This was presented to officials of the common pleas court on January 7, 1804, and the request was granted. Three "viewers" were appointed to determine the location of this road, and a surveyor was charged to "make a correct survey of the same and return it to this Court."[5] It is significant that no Worthington men were included among the three viewers, for Franklinton was on the west side of the river and Worthington on the east. A crossing point would have to be negotiated.

Earlier in this same January 7 session, county judges had approved a plan recommended earlier in the fall to open a road from Franklinton to Newark, requiring the road builders to make "said road thirty-three feet wide, and prepare and make it passable for loaded wagons or carriages." A petition from the Worthington settlers to intersect this road with a road to their community was granted, on condition that "the said petitioners defray all of the expense of viewing, surveying and opening the road." Thompson, Griswold, and Beach were appointed viewers, and James Kilbourn was designated the surveyor, to report at the court's next meeting.

The distinction between the two proposed Worthington roads is enlightening. A road north from Franklinton to Worthington was clearly in the interest of both communities and was therefore to be financed from county funds. Likewise, Franklinton was already committed to a road east to Newark; however, if Worthington residents wished to intersect it so that travelers and new settlers from the east could come directly to Worthington, the county officials decreed that the expense would have to be borne by the Worthington settlers themselves. On March 15, both groups reported again to the court. The township supervisor was ordered to open the road from Franklinton to Worthington and to "make it passable for loaded wagons." The report of the Worthington committee and Kilbourn's survey of a road from Worthington to intersect the Newark road was received and "ordered to be recorded."[6]

At the January 7 session of the Franklin County Court, which considered Worthington's request for roads, judges also granted "a license to keep a tavern" to Ezra Griswold, "he being recommended to the satisfaction of this Court; and he also paying into the Clerk's hands the tax required by law." At the same time, Nathan Carpenter, in the settlement about five miles north, was granted a license "to keep a house of public entertainment." The wording was evidently more significant than appears at first glance. Griswold's "tavern" served the alcoholic beverages typically associated with this term, while

Carpenter's "house of public entertainment," according to local tradition, was strictly a temperate establishment.

Although roads and taverns were certainly a high priority, it is interesting that most of the resolutions from the Scioto Company's meeting on December 14 dealt with the community's prospective library. Thompson, Griswold, Beach, Stewart, and Josiah Topping were appointed as the library committee. Zophar Topping was chosen to "Keep & take Care of the Library Belonging to this Company." James Kilbourn and Ezra Griswold were designated to purchase books, and Nathaniel Little to be the "Auditor of Accounts for sd Library." A meeting was set for four o'clock on Monday, December 19, for the "Making of by Laws & Drawing Books."

These bylaws were signed by subscribers or their "attorneys" on December 23, 1803. It was agreed that there would be four library meetings each year on the first Wednesday of March, June, September, and December, with officers elected by majority vote at the September meeting. The library was to be kept in Worthington, and at the quarterly meetings each subscriber was entitled "to draw two volumes whenever there are books enough" or only one if there were not enough books for all who wished them. Books to be taken were "put up to the highest bidder," with no book being loaned without "paying at least two cents for the benefit of the Library." A system of fines was established for books that were not returned after the second library meeting (a six-month loan); if a book was lost, the borrower "shall pay twice the value of the book lost." This was a subscription library. It was clearly stated that any "proprietor who shall lend a book belonging to the Library to any person who is not a proprietor, shall pay a fine of 12 ½ cents and all damages which shall be done to any book."[7]

While a library that was limited to subscribers and books that were loaned to the highest bidder may sound undemocratic in the modern era of tax-supported public libraries, subscription libraries were the norm in frontier communities *if* a community was to have any type of library at all.[8] Most did not. These December bylaws contained three or four signatures representing local settlers, such as Nathan Carpenter, which proves that the Scioto Company had opened library subscriptions to nonmembers for a fee. Such quick establishment of the library that the company had initiated in August is a dramatic testimony to the reading abilities and desires of these pioneers. Perhaps during that first winter, when inhabitants clustered around the open fires of their crude cabins for both light and warmth, evenings were made more bearable by sharing books, probably often read aloud to several listeners.

Kilbourn reported to Thomas Worthington that "We have laid a foundation (as I trust) for a flourishing Library. Dr. Stanbery of N. York has made a handsome present to it."[9] This gift appears to have been in much the same spirit as a modern realtor who presents a housewarming gift to the client who has recently purchased a new home. Kilbourn gave no indication whether these were volumes from Stanbery's own library or whether this was a financial gift to purchase titles recommended by the purchasing committee. In any event, books were acquired between mid-August and mid-September, and Kilbourn was reimbursed by the company for transporting them west. The gift was substantial enough for company members to name their institution the "Stanbery Library" in the donor's honor, a custom perpetuated today by college campuses and other institutions throughout the country who christen buildings for their financial benefactors. How one wishes that a complete list of the volumes in this original collection had been preserved.

At their meeting on December 14, Scioto Company members also made plans to survey town and farm lots. Job Case and Abner P. Pinney were each to be paid sixty-seven cents per day as chainmen. Thomas T. Phelps was to be paid forty-two cents per day as flagman, and Israel Case the same as axman. No mention was made of Kilbourn's role, but his name appeared as the surveyor on the farm plat filed with the county recorder.[10] Joel Allen, a company member described by his granddaughter as a "civil engineer," may have been involved at some point, but the minutes mention no payment. He drew the earliest map of the area surrounding the settlement (see fig. 6) and appears to have been running an account at the company store as early as December 1803.

Two key decisions had to be made about the sawmill. Who was to complete its construction and operate it, and what were the charges to be for sawing boards? When the committee made its recommendation, a distinction was made between hard timber and "soft timber such as blue ash, black walnut and other soft timber." Hard timber

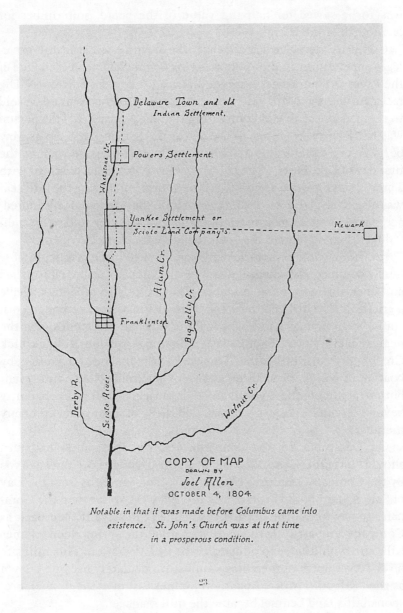

COPY OF MAP
DRAWN BY
Joel Allen
OCTOBER 4, 1804.

*Notable in that it was made before Columbus came into
existence. St. John's Church was at that time
in a prosperous condition.*

23

Fig. 6. Map drawn by Joel Allen, October 4, 1804

was to be sawed for half the value of the board, soft timber for one-fourth of the board's value.

Company members decided that "the Sawmill & all the mill privileges appertaining to the Spot including So much land on each Side of the River as Shall be necessary to Raise a Dam, erect buttresses, Dig races &c also for a Mill yard, not exceeding two acres" should be sold to the person capable of completing it and operating it. This person was to "Positively engage to Compleat the Sawmill as Soon as May be, & erect a Compleat grist Mill on sd Dam with a good boalt by the first day of Dec. Next." The company clearly wanted a gristmill with a proper sieve as soon as possible. The person purchasing the mill seat was also to be given the option to purchase the adjacent one-hundred-acre farm lot at a fair valuation. If the mill was not sold to an individual, it would remain the "publick property of the Company."[11]

It is not clear whether the dam was finished by December or how nearly complete the sawmill was, but the company wanted it finished and operating as soon as possible. They were also anxious to have a gristmill that utilized the same dam within a year. Although corn could be ground by hand, wheat flour required millstones, and the nearest facility was Thomas Worthington's mill on Kinnickikick Creek, north of Chillicothe. This was a trip of about forty miles by boat or, in winter, by sleds on snow-covered trails.[12] A commitment both to complete the sawmill and to build a gristmill was apparently beyond Lemuel Kilbourn's means and those of most other company members.

On December 19, the company resolved that James Kilbourn should "have the Sawmill & Saw Rag Wheel, gorgins & Crank at $500 By the Company Requiring the Dam to Stand 6 months from the Day of Sale & if it Should Sustain any injury by the water then the Company to pay for all the Repairs resonable & Receive it then Back as Company Property." If the dam withstood the spring floods, James Kilbourn would agree to undertake the mill operation. This mill site on the river north of the village almost immediately became known as the "Kilbourn Mill." Apparently James assumed the financial responsibility, and Lemuel became the mill manager.

At the same meeting, the company voted to "make a present to Mr. King of one fourth part of the apple and Peach trees that are now growing [in] the nursery" provided he remove them within a year. King was one of the squatters Kilbourn had displaced from the site the previous spring, even though he had apparently started saplings for an orchard. It is impossible to determine whether King was paid a fair price for his "improvements" in June, making this a benevolent gesture, or whether the company had simply confiscated the squatter's improvements. It clearly illustrates, however, that squatters who did not hold title to the land often made improvements, hoping that these might ultimately gain them possession.[13]

During this first month on the site, company members were faced with decisions large and small. Nathaniel Little was given permission to purchase "a Sertain Black Walnut Tree which is now Cut for the purpose of a Canoe." This must have been a particularly large and straight tree that could be burnt out in Indian style for a "dugout" canoe. Little was operating a store in the new settlement as he had in Blandford, and this required frequent trips downriver to transport merchandise.

As the surveying proceeded, a committee of trust was appointed "to take Care of the School Lot & funds." As soon as part of the one-hundred-acre lot reserved for the school could be cleared, the committee intended to rent the land and apply the proceeds to the support of the school. There were already men in the settlement who were not company members and who might become renters rather than landowners. Some had come into the area before the Scioto Company settlers arrived, others may have traveled west as hired hands, as Joel Buttles's diary described the persons in his father's party in 1804.[14]

Although renting might seem a strange choice in a region of abundant and relatively cheap land, it had been a common practice among land speculators for several years. Not everyone had cash for a down payment to buy land, but renting offered the opportunity to get started in farming and perhaps eventually earn enough to purchase land of one's own. As early as 1797, Nathaniel Massie reported to a client in Virginia that "I have leased the land for six years to have improved with two good hewed log houses and a stone chimney in each, intending to make two small farms. I am offered for this land ten pounds per hundred acres annually . . . and to make considerable improvements with orchards &c. . . ."[15] He subsequently reported opportunities to lease other tracts at the same rate.

Their first winter in Worthington, company agents apparently purchased items in Chillicothe or Franklinton as they were needed by settlers, keeping the accounts in the company ledger.[16] Many of these items were similar to those that the pioneers brought west: a large iron kettle, a bake oven, and a plough chain for Lemuel Kilbourn; a spider, a tea kettle, a tin poringer, and three iron teaspoons for Joel Allen; an ax, a tin pail, and a blanket for David Bristol. Lemuel Kilbourn and Adna Bristol each purchased a cow. Ezra Griswold and Nathan Stewart bought whisky barrels; Zophar Topping and Glass Cochran bought flour barrels; and Samuel Beach and Nathan Stewart each purchased a beehive. Nathan Stewart, curiously, purchased fifty dollars worth of blacksmithing tools, prompting one to recall that he had sold his blacksmith's shop in Blandford and to wonder whether he had brought some tools with him and was now expanding his business or had sold his tools in the east and had now changed his mind.

The Worthington store was also proving to be a convenience for neighbors such as Daniel Brown and Avery Powers who were already settled in outlying areas. Some names on the company ledger, however, are a mystery. Stephan Warren, who purchased a number of small tools and three oxen worth $65.20, is mentioned in no other company materials or early county records. The frontier demanded that neighbors help neighbors.

December 25, 1803, fell on the Sabbath, and Christmas was obviously commemorated with religious respect. On Monday, however, Kilbourn wrote to Senator Worthington that "an entertainment was prepared for the whole at the school house on the Companies expense."[17] He thanked Worthington for the donation he had made to the company the previous summer that supported this celebration.

A highlight of the feasting was a series of toasts that displayed the sentiments of the community with astonishing frankness.

1- To the Scioto Company, May prosperity attend our labours & grant to the spirit of perseverance which brought us hither, and prudence unite us in a friendly & Victorious Society 2- The Town of Worthington, While it perpetuates the memory of our worthy friend to whom it is named, May it become Conspicuous for Science, Enterprise and the Useful Arts 3- The State of Ohio, Young in the order of time, but old in the wisdom which formed her Constitution. May Wisdom & Prudence still preside in her Councils, While Commerce and Manufactor shall so emerse us as to equal the demands of the Agricultural Interest. 4- The

Literary Institutions of the Scioto Company, May the same spirit which
excited us to make the public appropriations still animate our endeav-
ours, till the wilderness so given, becomes a fruitful field yielding a rich
revenue & may youth become Patrons of knowledge and virtue. 5- Governor Tiffin, So wise and just. . . . 6- Hon. Thomas Worthington,
Benefactor and friend. . . . 7- Doct. Jonas Stanbery, the Liberal Patron of
our Library. . . . 8- The Fair Dames of Worthington, May they not be
disposed to return to the Old Hive, but rather to labor with a smile the
Heart of Labors do While Industry & Harmony are seen in their Domestic Circle.[18]

The first four toasts display typical New England optimism for a
town that aspired to become far more than a farming village. Like
the New Englanders who had settled Marietta a decade earlier, this
group envisioned moving well beyond the economic base of agriculture. They were focusing on the quick development of commerce
and manufacturing. It is particularly noteworthy that in a group
that included no record of a member with anything beyond a basic,
grammar school education, much emphasis was placed on "literary
institutions." This group's interpretation of providing the opportunities of a better life for their children was broad indeed.

In some ways, however, the final toast is the most poignantly
revealing. Kilbourn was, as usual, buoyantly optimistic, reporting to
Thomas Worthington, "We are all in perfect health, and much pleased
with our situation." The toast to the "fair dames of Worthington,"
however, strongly suggests that some among the women sorely
missed the comforts of their homes and the relatives left behind. It is
possible that some might even have been counseling friends and relatives to reconsider their decision about westward migration.

Kilbourn admitted that for the older residents the Christmas celebration closed after the toasts, when "those of us who had families
retired & left the young people to close the scene with a ball." There
must have been several occasions during those first weeks for young
people to pursue their attraction to the opposite sex, for on February 8
the entire community again gathered at the schoolhouse, this time to
celebrate a double wedding. The ceremony, performed by the justice
of the peace from Franklinton, united Abner P. Pinney to Polly Morrison and his younger brother Levi Pinney to Charlotte Beach.[19]

Both of these young men had been members of the advance work party and had probably seen few eligible females from May to October. It is not clear whether these young people knew each other in New England, but this seems unlikely with Abner and Polly, who were the first intermarriage between the Blandford and Simsbury contingents of the company. Regardless of the length of the courtships, the marriage of twenty-three-year-old Abner and seventeen-year-old Polly produced eight children and lasted until her death sixty-one years later, while the union of twenty-year-old Levi and sixteen-year-old Charlotte likewise reared eight children and lasted until her death fifty-seven years later.[20] Worthington did prove to be the healthful site its founder predicted, but it undoubtedly helped that some of these pioneers came from hardy stock.

The establishment of new families was only one of many new beginnings in the frontier community. Residents moved quickly to establish cultural institutions in addition to the library. That first winter, Thomas Phelps gave up assisting with the survey to teach school in the double cabin on the east side of the public square. Although no subscription list survives, there appears to have been at least twenty-three children, from five to fourteen years of age, in the settlement that winter. As soon as spring arrived, even boys of eight or ten probably left school and began helping to clear the land for crops. It is likely there were fewer and younger scholars when William Thompson's daughter, Clarissa, taught during the spring and summer terms. She was paid twenty-eight dollars for what were probably two ten-week terms.[21]

Very soon after the first families arrived, they must have begun meeting for religious services, probably with Ezra Griswold as the reading clerk. Church services were formalized at the schoolhouse after the arrival of Deacon Kilbourn, who was able to report to Thomas Worthington on February 7, "We have formed a regular Society for religious purposes & have Divine Service performed every Sunday in public."[22] Actually, the articles of agreement had been executed just the previous day.[23] Those who signed signified that they agreed "in Sentiment with the Faith, Worship, and principal Doctrines, of the Protestant Episcopal Church" and united to form a religious society known as "ST. JOHN'S CHURCH IN WORTHINGTON AND PARTS ADJACENT." This wording was specifically designed to accommodate persons within five miles of the town center, and elaborate regulations were drafted regarding those who might join from more distant settlements and the number of Sundays they would be entitled to receive services "according to their numbers and contributions." This was definitely the document of a church that was designed for expansion.

It was agreed that annual meetings of the voting congregation "shall be holden on the Monday, Next after Easter-Sunday" and that the officers to be elected would include a moderator, a reading clerk, three trustees to hold title to and manage all church property, a treasurer, two wardens, one or more tithing men, and "a sufficient number of Choiresters." In 1804, Easter Monday fell on April 2. On April 3 at the schoolhouse in Worthington, the following officers were elected: moderator, James Kilbourn; reading clerk, Ezra Griswold; first trustee, James Kilbourn; second trustee, Nathan Stewart; third trustee, William Thompson; treasurer, Nathaniel Little; wardens, Samuel Beach and Nathan Stewart; tithing man, William Little; choristers, Samuel Beach, Jr., Abner P. Pinney, and Noah Andrews. The selections reflect how firmly this church was under the leadership of James Kilbourn and Ezra Griswold. It is worth noting that several of the families already in the community—such as the Topping brothers, Alexander Morrison, David Bristol, Lemuel Kilbourn, and Glass Cochran—were not represented. There is no record of whether they attended services without being eligible for sacraments or whether they remained unserved by a formal religious organization. Wives were, of course, members of the congregation from the beginning, but could not be considered for an official position.

In addition to the school, the church, and the library, there was one other organization to be established in the frontier community as soon as possible. Kilbourn reported to fellow mason Thomas Worthington that before leaving Connecticut the group had obtained a charter from the Connecticut Lodge, "authorizing us to hold a Masonic Lodge in this town. Tho it will be Necessary that Some Brother should be authorized to Instal us . . . we have taken the liberty to send forward your name to the Grand Master."[24] Thirteen of the Scioto Company members had been masons in New England, and it was quite logical that they should wish to continue this brotherhood in Ohio as soon as practical.[25]

During the winter of 1803–4, the homogeneous membership of the Scioto Company had established a school, a library, a church, and a masonic lodge. The latter three, at least, were institutions unknown in six-year-old Franklinton and in many of the new communities like it throughout southern and eastern Ohio. The Worthington settlers were rapidly going about the business of developing on the western frontier what Robert Hine has described as the model New England town. He considered these self-contained, close-knit communities the ideal small town coveted by people throughout America.[26]

It is a description that would have delighted James Kilbourn. Within weeks of his arrival, he bragged to Senator Worthington, "I trust it will not be thought boasting if I say to a confidential friend, that we are doing something clever in our new settlement tho embraced in the bosom of the Forest."[27]

Wilderness Settlement,
1804–1812

— ❖ —

❖ CHAPTER 6 ❖

A Just and Legal Land Division

— ❖ —

O N PAPER, IT WAS an elegant town plat—this new settlement of Worthington. The public square of nearly five acres, which company members had planned back east, was bisected north and south by "Main Street" and east and west by "State Street," already sounding like the city its founders hoped to create.[1] The rectangular plat was bounded somewhat picturesquely on the east by "Morning Street" and on the west by "Evening Street," and many of the interior streets commemorated New England towns such as Hartford, Windsor, Blandford, Granby, and Berlin (see fig. 7).

As Wade has pointed out in studying the urban frontier, many settlers migrated west seeking promising towns as well as good land.[2] Infant cities offered important economic attractions for those who arrived early, and there was city speculation as well as land speculation. Men with capital often laid out towns in key locations and waited for the tide of settlement to increase their value. Unfortunately, a significant number of these "towns" never materialized beyond the stage of having their plats recorded at the county courthouse.

The Worthington proprietors, however, were committed to more than a paper plan. Their immediate creation of a cultural focus—which included an Episcopal church, a school, a library, and a masonic lodge—demonstrated this beyond words. One and a half acres on the east side of the public square was reserved for the school and the same for the Episcopal church. Significantly, both have been retained for this usage to the present day.

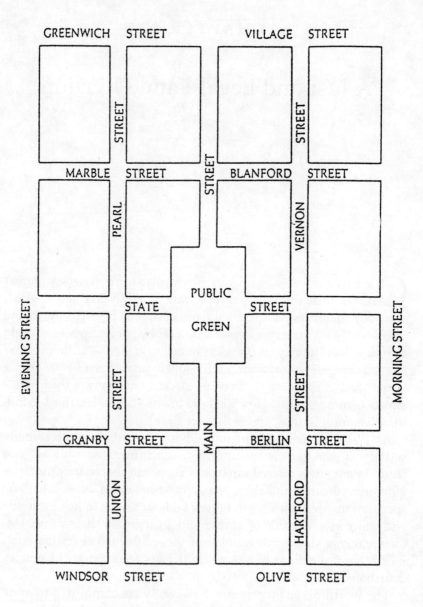

Fig. 7. Map of Pioneer Worthington streets

The school and church lots were double the three-quarter-acre size of the remaining 160 "town lots" that were established for residential and commercial use. This size was carefully chosen to provide for essentials such as a family residence, a stable for a cow and horse, a privy, a vegetable garden, and perhaps a few fruit trees. To maximize the number of buildings facing the principal streets, lots were twice as deep as their frontage.[3]

As they had agreed before migrating, company members bid to determine the order in which town and farm lots would be selected. In December 1803, thirty-seven persons bid from a high of fifty-three dollars to a low of twenty-five cents to select a lot, others who bid nothing were apparently given their choice at the end. This produced a total of $505.37 for company expenses such as surveying, but it is unlikely that the total was ever collected, because eight of the persons who bid were not included when the property was legally divided and the deed signed in August 1804 (see appendix A).[4] Membership among the original proprietors changed until the actual land division. This is reflected in the fact that Jedediah Norton, Kilbourn's uncle by marriage, was brought in as a major investor between December 1803 and August 1804.[5]

The most expensive town lots selected were the two on the north side of the public square, taken by Moses Byxbe and Ezra Griswold, and the two on the west side of the square, taken by William Thompson and Nathaniel Little. In fact, the map reveals exactly what one would expect. All of the first choice lots had frontage on either Main or State Streets (see fig. 8). Although James Kilbourn's bid of $12.10 gave him the thirteenth choice, one suspects that others deferred in allowing him to receive the select lot on the southwest corner of the public square.

Many proprietors probably intended to combine their home with some type of business, as Ezra Griswold did with his double-cabin home and tavern on the northeast corner of the public square. But at that time, the "square" was barely identifiable. As Joel Buttles recalled the scene in the fall of 1804, "trees on the square had been cut down only, falling across each other and every way, as they were naturally inclined. It was, of course, difficult getting about among these fallen trees, and going from house to house."[6]

The company had tried to deal with that problem at their meeting on April 23, 1804, with a resolution "That Liberty be given to any

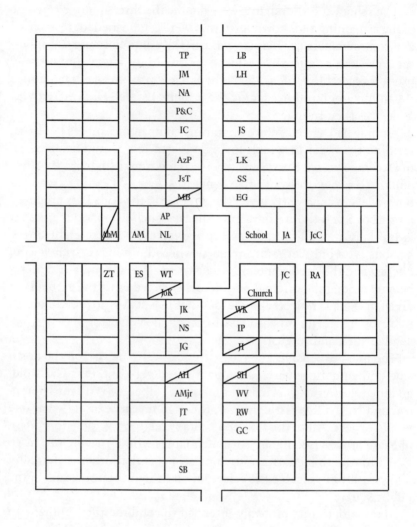

Fig. 8. Worthington Town Lots bid in December 1803

person or Persons to fence the Publick Square or Green on the four Sentral Corners by obtaining Permision of those who Live upon the Square By Leaving a Rode 4 Rods wide on Main & State Streets if they will Seed the Same to Grass & may improve the same till June 1805."[7]

One marvels at the unrealistic optimism of expecting any individual to voluntarily make such improvements on public property in a frontier community where everyone was overwhelmed by the work required to provide the necessities of life. There is ample evidence that the public square was not cleared for some time. Descendants of Mila Thompson Griswold, who arrived as a child in 1803, told the story of being sent from her father's cabin on the west side of the square for water at the community well on the church lot and becoming so thoroughly lost in the maze of fallen trees that her cries for help brought rescue from a neighbor.[8]

The town lots, plus the public square and streets, required approximately 130 acres. On the choice river bottom just west of the village, eighty acres of farmland was set aside for the support of the school and the same for the Episcopal church. A twenty-acre woodlot for each was reserved in an area that the settlers considered too rough for cultivation. This left approximately 7,670 acres of farmland in Worthington to be divided among company members.

The lay of the land made a significant difference in the size and configuration of farm lots, which had been referred to in neat multiples of one hundred acres when the company was organized in the east. The river was a major barrier, which decreed that farm lots must be on one side or the other. Kilbourn's survey crew established three tiers of lots running north and south, one on the west and two east of the river. To create lots of approximately equal acreage, those on the west were shorter and wider than the longer narrow ones on the east (see fig. 9). They ranged in size from 20 to 130 acres, with the average being approximately 93 acres.

The same bidding arrangement was used to determine the order of selection for farm lots. In general, the most desirable of these were in the middle tier, which extended west to the river and fronted the "county road" to Franklinton, which was an extension of Main Street south of town. Some proprietors sought specific features such as proximity to the village, a spring site for a distillery, or a clay bank with the potential for firing bricks.

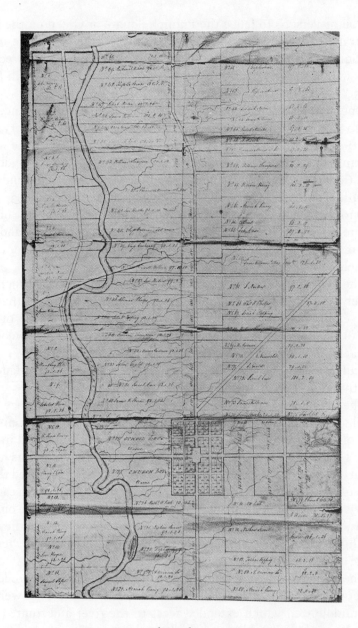

Fig. 9. Survey of Worthington Farm Lots

It is clear from company minutes in April 1804 that farm lots within the eight-thousand-acre "town" of Worthington had been assigned by that time. Reference was made to a lot south of town between Zophar Topping's land and Alexander Morrison, Jr.,'s land and to "pluss" lands adjoining Mr. Cochran, Major Thompson, and Mr. Curtis. Members had agreed in Connecticut that any unsubscribed, or "overplus," land would be held in common by the company until it was sold.[9]

All hands spent the spring of 1804 in hard physical labor. Some trees were girdled and left to die, to be removed later. Others were felled, and the brush and any unneeded logs were burned to prepare for planting the first crops. This process, which strikes modern citizens as a scandalous waste of timber resources and a regrettable rape of the natural environment, left a rich mineral ash on top of virgin soil that virtually guaranteed the productivity of early crops of corn and potatoes.

Meanwhile, the company was directing much attention to the location of roads. In addition to the Franklinton road, a committee was appointed to lay out a road from the "North End of Main Street in the best Direction to New Connecticut and those persons who own Land Where the Rode Shall Cross Shall Give their Lands for that purpose."[10] This strongly suggests that the Worthington settlers were expecting frequent interaction with the New Englanders who were settling in the Connecticut Western Reserve. A similar committee was appointed in May to lay out a road on the west side of the river, "in the most Eligable Situation," to travel from one end to the other of the western tier of farm lots.

Kilbourn's work in surveying the town lots and farm lots of Worthington took precedence over the survey of the outlots in the eight thousand acres of the purchase to the north and south of the town. It appears, however, that some members were anxious to complete the legal division of the land and gain title to the acreage they had committed to buy. On April 23, Nathan Stewart was appointed "to treat with Mr. Smith" and hire him to survey the two "out sections of land."

By August 11, 1804, the plat maps were complete, payments or notes promising payment had been collected, and deeds were prepared to "make and duly execute a just and legal division" of all sixteen thousand acres of the company purchase. Seventeen proprietors

Fig. 10. The survey chain, sextant, and pole used by James Kilbourn's crew in surveying the Scioto Company purchase is now part of the Worthington Historical Society Museum. (Photograph by the authors)

were present for the signing, and eleven others had given power of attorney to someone in Worthington. Separate deeds for Worthington and the outlying sections were legally executed before Justice of the Peace Ezekiel Brown, a resident already settled north of the Scioto Company purchase when the members arrived.[11]

These deeds present a straightforward description of land boundaries and the lot numbers assigned to each individual. However, it is difficult to believe, human nature being what it is, that thirty-eight men could make such significant decisions about their future with complete amiability. Several notes in company minutes suggest survey adjustments of an acre or two, probably to correct an error or adjust to the terrain. The only clue to a significant problem is the appointment of a committee of three members "to Adjust a Seartain Difficulty" in regard to Thomas Phelps's lot. They reported on August 8 that Phelps should be entitled to $18.33 in damages.[12] This was a significant amount considering Phelps's bid of $1.30 to determine his order in the selection of lots. It may be coincidence, but Thomas Phelps very shortly left Worthington and sold his three town lots and 258 acres of farmland to James Kilbourn and William Little.[13] His was the first departure among those who had actually come west.

A more pressing problem was the fact that the committee still held title to nearly four hundred unsubscribed acres in the outlying parcels, and the two largest shareholders, Jedediah Norton of Farmington with seventeen town lots and 1,548 acres of farm land, and Russell Atwater of Blandford with twelve town lots and 1,187 acres, had no intention of moving west. The company's commitment to have only settlers as members had been jeopardized by the necessity of raising funds for the down payment.

In view of Kilbourn's clear role as the company leader, it is something of a surprise to note that fifteen company members had larger holdings than his four town lots and 347 acres of land. His actual holding was far short of the 1,200 acres for which he had subscribed two years earlier, and his failure to meet this commitment suggests the reason for bringing in Norton. Subsequent land sales suggest that there was a somewhat nebulous line between Kilbourn's personal holdings, unsubscribed lands in which he represented the company as agent, and sales for eastern investors such as Norton for whom he held power of attorney. Kilbourn clearly controlled much more land than he owned.

It is noteworthy that, although both the leadership and the majority of the Scioto Company membership came from Connecticut, the eight company members from Blandford, Massachusetts, acquired sixty of the 160 town lots and nearly 6,000 acres of the total 16,000 acres of land. Based upon land ownership, they were a very influential minority (see appendix A).

The community also contained a majority with considerably less influence. These were the adult males who did not own property in Worthington. A list of township electors, recorded approximately six months after the partition of the company lands, contained forty-two names, only twenty of whom were Scioto Company members or their sons.[14] Surprisingly, only six of the remaining twenty-two names appeared on either the 1805 or 1806 militia lists. Some of these electors were too old for militia duty, and a few were settlers in the area north of Worthington that became part of a new county in 1808; but it is clear that there were a significant number of adult males in Worthington as early as the first winter who owned no property and who soon disappeared from the community.

This seems to be consistent with Lee Soltow's analysis of land ownership in the first decade of statehood, when the Ohio population increased by 400 percent. He estimated from tax records and census data that only 45 to 50 percent of the males over twenty-six years of age owned land in 1810.[15] Some of these laborers and renters remained in the community, but in Worthington many of them evidently moved on and left very little evidence of their presence.

The arrival of the first residents on the site did not mean the settlement was complete. The task of promoting Worthington had just begun, and Kilbourn was certainly the foremost advocate. A prime example is the case of Moses Byxbe, a wealthy hotel owner and storekeeper from Lenox, Massachusetts.[16] Byxbe had acquired a number of military warrants and had used them to purchase considerable land about ten or twelve miles north of the Worthington settlement. It would appear that someone in the Scioto Company attempted to convince him to settle at Worthington and open a store. In December 1803, although his name never appeared as a company member, he was recorded as the highest bidder and assigned lot 60—a choice lot on the north side of the public square. David Bristol received this lot in the partition, and there is no record that Byxbe ever owned it, but he did arrive in Worthington in August 1804 and, according to the Delaware County history, "stayed three months and built a two-story frame house" before moving about twelve miles north to settle on his own land at "Berkshire Corners."

Byxbe brought west an extensive inventory of store goods that he sold to Nathaniel Little "before opening the packages." Years later Joel Buttles, whose family arrived the first week in December 1804, recalled that the only buildings at that time were log cabins, "except a frame store house, built by Nathaniel Little on the north side of the public square."[17] Two things seem clear: the Scioto Company was actively recruiting new settlers and Moses Byxbe was accustomed to being the leader of his community. Within four years he abandoned Berkshire to found Delaware as the county seat of the newly erected county just north of Worthington.[18] It offered formidable competition as a destination for a continuing flow of migrants from the east.

Additional competition arose in the spring of 1804, when Scioto Company members Levi Buttles, Job Case, and Levi Hayes became actively involved in helping to form the Licking Company. That company's initial list of seventy-eight names included thirty-four from Granby, four from Hartland, Connecticut, five from Blandford, and twenty-eight from Granville, Massachusetts.[19] These were neighbors from back east who were also interested in moving west but had found the Scioto Company did not have room for them all.

Buttles and Case scouted prospective sites that spring and recommended an area about twenty miles east of Worthington, which led to the purchase of 26,000 acres by the Licking Company. Before bringing his family west to Worthington that fall, Buttles was elected president of that company, which was preparing to settle the community of Granville, Ohio, the following year. Buttles, Case, and Hayes had to make a choice between towns—as would a continuing flow of their relatives and neighbors and others.

But Kilbourn had his own excellent means of promoting continued settlement. On July 3, 1804, he was informed by the secretary of the treasury of his appointment as "district surveyor" for all of the U.S. Military Tract within the boundaries of the Chillicothe District.[20] Senator Thomas Worthington had almost certainly recommended him for this position, placing him directly in the flow of those seeking to buy or sell land in the rapidly developing U.S. military lands north and east of the Worthington settlement.

Kilbourn was particularly anxious to attract additional New Englanders who shared a similar vision for the Worthington community. When he returned east in 1805, he sought emigrants with specific

skills, and he offered land as an inducement. He successfully negotiated with James Parker of Perth Amboy, New Jersey, to purchase
four thousand acres on the Whetstone River about five miles north
of Worthington. This was sold to the Union Company, a group with
twenty-seven members, who were organized to purchase lands in
common with articles of agreement similar to the Scioto Company.[21]
Most of these men were relatives or neighbors of Scioto Company
members. The Union Company even included Scioto Company member Lemuel Humphrey, who decided to settle near some of his Case
relatives in the Union purchase, and Elias Vining, who settled there a
little north of his Scioto Company brother, William.

These men chose to concentrate on farming. There was no town
planned for the Union Company purchase, and some members, like
Ezra Griswold's brother Roger, were simply investing in Ohio land.
A number of the Union Company members who actually migrated
west settled in the town of Worthington, where they employed skills
that this rapidly growing community needed. This number included
the Goodrich brothers, skilled carpenters who had been members
of Kilbourn's Episcopal congregation in Berlin, and William Robe,
who soon became the teacher at the Worthington Academy. The formation of the Union Company appears to be an interesting attempt—
probably directed by James Kilbourn—to foster growth in the covenanted community of Worthington without diluting its New England
heritage.

After the Scioto Company land was divided and matters relating
to the church, school, and library were in the hands of each institution's trustees, there was no real need for the company to continue
its existence. On January 28, 1805, members resolved "That this
Company be Desolved." The minutes make no record of the preceding discussion, but at the same meeting Benjamin Chapman was
accepted as a settler, replacing Russell Atwater, who was Chapman's
relative by marriage. It was also agreed that anyone taking the
"Great Stillyards" from Mr. Griswold's for more than twenty-four
hours would pay twelve and a half cents per day "for the Company's
Benefit." This is evidence of business as usual right up to the very
end of the company's existence.

It appears that the resolution to dissolve the company was initiated by Kilbourn's resignation as agent. The following day he addressed the "Gentlemen of the Scioto Company." "Having, according

to my best understanding pursued to effect the various objects for which I was appointed your agent," he proposed to settle accounts and issue certificates "to all those who have ballances to receive from the Treasurey." The fact that the company owed money to some members suggests that Kilbourn's resignation may not have been completely voluntary. Perhaps some members were anxious to bring their group business to a close and settle all accounts. Kilbourn concluded, "believing that there now remains no further material service that I can render in this public capacity—I beg leave to <u>Resign</u> the Agency back to the Company whence I received it." He thanked members for their confidence in him and extended his best wishes for the "future prosperity, honour and happiness of this Company. . . ."[22]

Kilbourn's words certainly imply that the company would continue as an entity, and minutes do reveal two company meetings in May 1806—at the school house with Israel Case as chairman—but no business was conducted. The single resolution approved was that "this meeting be adjourned till the Committee See Cause to Call them to a meeting again." It would appear that the Scioto Company was Kilbourn's creation and that the group was finished when he resigned. But the company's stated purpose of making settlement in the territory northwest of the Ohio had been accomplished.

Kilbourn's charismatic leadership had been essential to that end. He exhibited all of the characteristics that Weber has attributed to such leaders: confidence, dominance, a sense of purpose, and the ability to articulate the goals that followers are prepared to accept. Such leadership frequently arises in times of crisis, and these characteristics are often associated with religious, political, or military leaders. Westward migration was certainly a crisis in the life of every family who undertook it, and Kilbourn's missionary fervor was clearly apparent in helping his associates negotiate this trial. Those who have researched charismatic leaders note that such leaders are often "more concerned with doing the right thing than with doing things right."[23] One senses this in Kilbourn's careless attention to detail even while his enthusiasm for the goal never faltered.

As late as April 1807, "the Scioto Company Committee," composed of James Kilbourn, Nathan Stewart, William Thompson, Josiah Topping, Alexander Morrison, and Zophar Topping, sold several parcels of land still in the company possession.[24] While the legality of such actions may be questionable, it appears that the company gradually faded away as all land was conveyed to private ownership and as its usefulness declined.

Although thirty-eight company members initially owned all eight thousand acres of the Worthington town and farm lots, they no sooner obtained title than they began to sell. Two weeks after the partition, Ambrose Case, Lemuel G. Humphrey, and Joel Mills all conveyed their joint "shares in the Scioto Company" to Ambrose's brother Isaac Case, who made settlement that fall.[25]

Within a couple of years, real estate prices reflected major land improvements. In December 1806, Nathan and Anna Stewart sold their ninety-three-acre farm lot south of the village to a new settler from Massachusetts for $1,000. It was a choice lot on the river and was bisected by the road to Franklinton, but a nearly tenfold increase in value within two years suggests that a significant amount of land had been cleared and buildings had been erected.[26]

About the same time, Kilbourn wrote to James Allen, who had returned east, and reported that "There is now an opportunity presents that your lot laying east of the Town, May be sold at Four Dollars per acre, by putting with it the two first city lots." One-fourth would be paid down and the remainder in three annual installments with interest. Kilbourn recommended this as a "good sale" and thought there were prospects for selling the rest of Allen's land at two dollars per acre, "and the purchaser will take the right in the Library and pay the value of it."[27] This is interesting evidence that the library membership was considered an asset that could be bought or sold along with the property.

In 1810, the eight-thousand-acre Worthington purchase had fifty-three parcels on the tax list. Two of these were owned by the Worthington Academy and St. John's Episcopal Church, and thirty-one of the remainder were owned by Scioto Company members or their heirs.[28] Within five years, twenty-one parcels had been acquired by persons who were not part of the original company. It is vivid evidence of the rapid mobility associated with the western frontier.

Until Worthington acquired a newspaper in 1811, it is difficult to determine precisely the nature of the improvements that had been made when land changed hands. In July 1811, however, Alexander Morrison advertised two farm lots for sale that probably typified development. A ninety-acre farm north of the village, bisected by the road to Sandusky, was described as having "30 acres of which has been deadened three years and is now in fine order for immediate improvement, and on about five acres the timber has been chopped down the same length of time, and ready for burning over." A second parcel of ninety-five acres adjoined the village lots on the east and was bisected by the "main east and west post road from Wheeling to Greenville." It had about twenty acres "under improvement" and "a one story BRICK HOUSE of two rooms."[29]

Morrison advertised that "These two tracts, for elegance of situation, quality of soil and convenience of living springs and running water, are inferior to none, and will be sold very low for CASH, but for cash in hand only." Therein lay the problem. Throughout the region cash was in short supply. Congress was still offering virgin land in Ohio for two dollars per acre with four years credit. Unimproved land in settled areas was worth more; but, as Ezra Griswold noted in a letter to his brother Roger, "land here was worth $3 per Acre but . . . it would not be easy to sell it for cash."[30]

It was not only the quality of the soil and the access to springs and streams that affected land value, but its location. Morrison's mention of roads was aimed directly at new settlers seeking convenient access to markets. The "post road from Wheeling to Greenville" was a particularly effective drawing card—and a bone of contention to the residents of Franklinton, who were vocal about the stupidity of routing the western mail over the Granville-Worthington "bridle-path" when it was obvious to them that the better route from Zanesville to Urbana lay through Franklinton.[31]

In less than a decade Worthington had become a challenge to the county seat as an attractive destination for new settlers.

❖ CHAPTER 7 ❖

An Elderly Gentleman Passed
Through with All His Posterity

— ❖ —

PERHAPS JAMES KILBOURN missed his own family, or maybe he was trying to reassure his wife about the number of families moving west. In any event, he took time during his exploratory trip with Nathaniel Little in 1802 to write from Pittsburgh about the steady stream of families passing through there to the Northwest Territory. He particularly noted that "one Elderly Gentleman passed last week with all his posterity. Which, including his Sones families Made the number of 45 persons."[1]

No one in the Scioto Company matched that, but the family of Abner and Ruth Pinney came closest. They migrated with their son Azariah with his wife and two infant sons; their daughter Ruth Brown with her husband Ebenezer and infant son and daughter; their daughter Hulda Vining, who with her husband William was expecting their first child; and two sons and two daughters, aged eight to sixteen. Their other sons, Abner P. and Levi, had come west with the advance work party and married during the first winter in the new town. This family included twenty members in the western settlement when the land was divided in 1804, and they experienced typical deaths and births in ensuing years. By the time Worthington was incorporated in 1835, the Pinneys' children, spouses, and grandchildren who lived in the local area numbered seventy-eight persons.[2]

Other family networks were similar, if somewhat smaller, and many encouraged the continuing migration of relatives and friends from New England over the first ten or fifteen years of Worthington's existence. An analysis of pioneer Worthington supports historians who have written of the importance of kinship networks in establishing a community on the western frontier; and contrary to the myth of frontier individualism, Worthington exhibited considerable social continuity among families.[3] As Boorstin succinctly points out, it was the explorers, hunters, and surveyors who were the loners. Settlers themselves traveled in groups, and this was a significant factor in shaping American institutions.[4]

Ties between Worthington and New England families remained strong throughout the frontier period. Men frequently returned east on business, and they not only encouraged new emigrants, but often brought back single female relatives who might find improved matrimonial prospects in the west. Cynthia Andrews, daughter of Scioto Company member Moses Andrews and sister of Worthington residents Noah Andrews and Beulah Hills, was one of these. On April 15, 1813, in Worthington, she married Eliphalet Barker, who that fall accompanied his pregnant wife to her parents' home in Montague, Massachusetts, to spend the winter awaiting the birth of their first child.[5] Such an arduous trip seems remarkable, but it may have resulted from Indian alarms in the Worthington area due to the war. Her husband and brother had been called out with the militia the previous fall and again in the spring. Cynthia's brother Jesse and sister Betsey Andrews left Montague for Worthington in November, and her friend Julia Buttles had returned east to visit relatives in Granby at the same time. Females wishing to travel west had little problem in finding an appropriate male escort.

No one encouraged continuing migration to the western settlement more ardently among his extended family than James Kilbourn. His descendants expressed pride in their family heritage, tracing its origins to Yorkshire, England, where the name Kilbourn meant "cold brook or stream."[6] James was one of ten siblings, only five of whom lived to adulthood, married, and reared families.[7] He successfully persuaded his brother Lemuel to join the Scioto Company and bring his family west when Lemuel became the supervising carpenter for the original sawmill. The Kilbourn brothers ran this venture jointly, with James financing it and Lemuel managing operations until 1806, when Lemuel sold his land and moved his family to the Chillicothe area.

No record survives to explain whether Lemuel accepted a better opportunity or whether he became dissatisfied playing a subservient role to his younger brother.

Scioto Company records do show that James unsuccessfully attempted to interest his older brother William in moving west, but several of William's children were eventually persuaded by their uncle James. His nephew John Kilbourn played an important role with the Worthington Academy; nephew Arius was active with the Worthington Manufacturing Company; and Homer Tuller, husband of his niece Eliza Ann, became a prominent Worthington storekeeper. Two of William's other sons settled in other parts of central Ohio. Kilbourn also persuaded his nephew Asahel Hart, son of his sister Anna, to come west with him even though Asahel was too young to legally share in the Scioto Company purchase. Hart married in Worthington and had three children, whom Kilbourn raised after their father's untimely death.

But the extended family network went even further, particularly as it related to business. Kilbourn's uncle by marriage, Jedediah Norton, became a key financial backer of the Scioto Company project, and although he had no children of his own, several of his Norton, Upson, Wright, and Wilcox nephews were influenced to move to the Worthington area.[8] James Kilbourn's sister-in-law, Sarah Sage, was a link to Joseph and Oliver Sage, who joined the Union Company purchase and settled just north of Worthington. It was a pattern historians have noted in the settlement of many pioneer communities, and it encouraged what Mary Ryan aptly describes as "the corporate family economy."[9]

Consciously or unconsciously, James Kilbourn played the role David Russo describes as the "patriarch-entrepreneur" of colonial Puritan society, always pooling family resources and creating family alliances in search of security.[10] As his oldest son Hector reached his teens, he learned the surveying business with his father, and he later surveyed the Lake Erie port city of Sandusky and attended to the Kilbourn family interests and investments there. Kilbourn's second marriage to Cynthia Goodale Barnes established a link to Cynthia's brother, successful Columbus businessman Lincoln Goodale. Further family-business alliances were established as his daughters married: Lucy to Matthew Mathews, Kilbourn's supervising manager at the Worthington Manufacturing Company; Laura to Rensselear Cowles, manager of that company's retail store in Worthington; Harriet to Worthington brick mason and builder Arora Buttles; and his step-daughter Lauretta Barnes to newspaper editor and Columbus businessman Joel Buttles. It was the latter who, with some humor and considerable accuracy, described his father-in-law as "the sachem of the tribe."[11]

Other family groups had similar linkages, particularly as they influenced continuing migration of related families. David Bristol's sons-in-law, Jordan and Abraham Ingham, averaged fifty miles a day walking from New York State to inspect the land south of town near their father-in-law, where they settled and had twenty-three children between them.[12] William Vining's brother, Elias, became a member of the Union Company and settled on its land in Delaware County. Lemuel Humphrey's brother-in-law, Isaac Case, bought his brother Ambrose's Scioto Company share and settled near their cousins Israel and Joanna Case. Even Scioto Company member Russell Atwater, who moved to New York and founded the town of Russell, was represented in Worthington by one of his wife's relatives, Benjamin Chapman, whose son operated a store in the village for a number of years. Recompense Stanbery, who became a leading Worthington citizen and a justice of the peace, was the nephew of land speculator Jonas Stanbery, who purchased a token membership in the Scioto Company after selling its members this western property.

It would be impossible to overemphasize the importance of family networks in both the initial settlement and in subsequent emigration. The pattern in Worthington described here is consistent with that reported in other studies of kinship as a factor in migration.[13] It seems likely, however, that such studies even seriously underestimate these networks because the names of married female relatives are not usually recognized and computed into the equation. Wives probably influenced some of those in the Scioto Company who changed their minds and decided not to migrate west. Joab Norton, however, was a later emigrant who might not have made the move without his wife's encouragement. His father-in-law, John Goodrich, was a warden in James Kilbourn's Episcopal congregation at Berlin, Connecticut; and on Kilbourn's trip east on business in 1805, Goodrich became convinced of the prospects in Worthington and decided to emigrate. "Mrs. Norton, seeing her father's family about to go, at once urged her husband to accompany them."[14]

Fig. 11. Orrel Whiting, Laura Cowles, and Harriet Buttles, daughters of James Kilbourn, married local businessmen and created a family business network that caused one son-in-law to describe Kilbourn as "the sachem of the tribe." (Taken from *Old Northwest Genealogical Quarterly*)

One cannot overestimate the emotional support that family members provided for each other in the frontier living conditions. The death of Levi Buttles in June 1805 left his widow with seven children, from three to eighteen years of age, and sent shock waves through the newly established community. James Kilbourn had already gone east on business, and Lucy wrote of the death, "which was sudden and surprising to us all . . . [from] a sudden cold which caused a plurisy in his head."[15] Lucy must have been one of many wives who, seeing a forty-two-year-old man stricken so quickly, realized it might easily have been her own husband. In her letter, she twice assured her husband that Mrs. Buttles wanted her friends in the east to know the cause of death "and not lay it to the country." Kilbourn responded with shock and encouraged Lucy, "I am sure your feeling heart will lead you to visit her frequently & do all in your power to cheer her spirits & encourage her resolution to support with fortitude so severe a disappointment and . . . the rest of her friends the same."[16]

The community undoubtedly did its best to rally to the family's support, but Sarah Buttles must have been a strong woman. Although she and the children certainly had days of despair, there is no evidence that she considered returning to her former home in New

England. Granddaughter Lura quoted her mother's remembering that fourteen-year-old Arora mourned his father so deeply, "he would go to the edge of the woods and seat himself on a log and bury his face in his hands, and moan for hours. he thought he was out of sight and hearing of any one, but they all heard him and it almost broke their hearts."[17]

That same fall, Joel Allen became so disconsolate over the death of his son, Augustus, that he experienced what modern psychiatrists would consider a nervous breakdown. He had been twice widowed and had apparently left his oldest son to conduct business in Southington, Connecticut, while he investigated prospects in Worthington, accompanied by sixteen-year-old Augustus. Perhaps he held himself accountable for the conditions that led to his son's death, for he left Worthington in despair, planning "to keep a school if my deranged state of mind & weakness of body would permit. . . ." He was unable, however, to face such a prospect and returned to Southington, where he described himself nearly a year later as being "in that low disagreeable state I have been ever since Augustus died."[18]

It is an oversimplification, of course, but some survived and some were defeated by the hardships of frontier life. The nineteenth-century western frontier did not place quite as many burdens on families as John Demos describes in the immigrant colonies of the seventeenth century, where the family served as the business, school, vocational institute, church, house of correction, welfare institution, hospital, orphanage, old people's home, and poor house.[19] School and church were strong in frontier Worthington, but families were a critical factor for survival. Marriages in the new community quickly formed new extended family networks.

The Scioto Company family network (see appendixes B and C) dramatically illustrates the relationship that family connections played, both in migration and in the community's persistence. Of the thirty-eight original proprietors who (by birth or marriage) had parents, children, or siblings in the company, only one failed to come to Worthington, and he sold his property to a brother who made settlement. Of the original proprietors who settled in Worthington, seventeen still had family members in the village by 1835. *All* of these had either parents, married children, or siblings in the community. One cannot presume that being the descendant of a proprietor held any particular attraction for prospective marriage partners—simple geographic proximity seems the important consideration in determining prospective spouses.[20] Whatever the selection criteria, however, the establishment of family connections through marriage appears to have been one of the significant factors related to a family's persistence in the community.[21]

It is interesting to speculate why some families who had migrated without family connections and made none in the pioneer community soon moved on. Nathan Stewart played leadership roles in the Scioto Company and in establishing the first school, library, and Episcopal congregation. He apparently had two sons, Josephus and Henry, who were old enough to appear on early militia lists, but the family sold all of its Worthington property in 1806 and left no trace of their destination. Glass Cochran, who was also from Blandford and one of the largest landowners in the new community, served as the township's justice of the peace and had four sons in their twenties by the time the family moved to Indiana in 1817.[22] One suspects it was the lure of better prospects that enticed these families. Yet the question remains: would their decision have been different if they had come with or had established kinship ties in the new community?

European travelers frequently remarked on the freedom of young people on the American frontier to interact with each other and select their own marriage partners. Class distinctions and economic factors, which played a significant role in the marriage decisions of the Europeans who could afford to travel in America, played little role on the frontier. Good health and the courage to work were sufficient recommendations for a pioneer son-in-law.[23]

Worthington rapidly grew beyond the covenanted community of its founders. By the end of the frontier period, growth was reflected in land ownership and church and militia membership, as well as in the selection of marriage partners. Of the forty-two marriages recorded in the community during the first decade, nine (21 percent) were between children of two original proprietors, fourteen (33 percent) were between a Scioto descendant and a later arrival, and nineteen (45 percent) were between two residents whose families had arrived after the original company.[24]

Contrary to the commonly held belief that the overwhelming percentage of frontier marriages occurred in March–April and November–December, before planting and after harvest, Worthington marriages during the first decade occurred in every month except August, and the peaks were in February and July.[25] Perhaps Worthington was less attuned to agricultural rhythms than the typical frontier community.

Although population growth in the pioneer community reflected a birthrate that exceeded the mortality rate, there was no remarkable difference between the generation that bore children in New England and migrated west and the first generation to raise their family in Worthington. The New England generation averaged 7.5 children during a marriage averaging 32 years in length, with the husband being 24.5 years of age and the wife 22.1 years at first marriage. The first Worthington generation averaged 5.49 children during a 25.6 year marriage, with the husbands being 25.3 years of age and the wives 21.9 years at first marriage.[26] Worthington did not experience the dramatic drop in the age of marriage or the rise in the number of children that some historians have associated with the availability of cheap land and abundant opportunity. This may be attributed to the brevity of Worthington's frontier period and the speed with which its settlers acquired a lifestyle similar to that which they had known in New England. It is consistent, however, with Margaret Walsh's findings that the number of children among frontier families was not markedly different from those elsewhere in that time period.[27]

Although there is no information for the total population of Worthington, available data regarding descendants of the original proprietors reflect a high degree of morality. This may be influenced by the fact that landowners were presumably the upper class of the community or by the church orientation of these proprietors. The descendants of the Scioto Company may or may not have been typical of the entire community. Of the forty-four marriages among these descendants for which the exact dates of marriage and the birth of the first child are known, only three were born within seven or eight months, and this may reflect either premarital sex or premature births. Thirty of the firstborn children, however, arrived within twelve months, and the average span between marriage and first birth was 13.3 months.[28] These pioneers may have been moral, but they were not sexually inhibited. Perhaps they reflected the New England Puritans for whom it was a duty of conjugal union to be fruitful and multiply.[29]

Divorce was as uncommon in this community as in most others during the nineteenth century. As numerous historians and sociologists have pointed out, for most women divorce was an economic impossibility. The only divorce prior to 1835 among the descendants of the Worthington proprietors was that of Harriet Thompson Platt from William Platt in 1822. Both were widowed when they had married in 1817 in Delaware, where Harriet had lived with her first husband Nathaniel Little. William Platt had established the first "Silversmith & Jewelry Shop" in Columbus in 1815.[30] Perhaps they never did agree on where to live, for she was in Delaware and he was in Columbus when the divorce was granted, on grounds of "extreme cruelty and adultery," and she was granted custody of their two children.[31] Harriet's father was one of the largest landowners in Worthington, her first husband had had the largest store in Delaware, and her second husband was a successful silversmith in the capital city. The court records gave no information regarding financial arrangements, but Harriet was in comfortable circumstances. She was married again two years later, to a Delaware, Ohio, physician; and her two children by William Platt shared in his estate in 1825. If the divorce created local gossip, it would appear that it was soon forgotten.

A particularly interesting view of female financial security occurred in this same family when William Thompson died in 1830. When his estate was settled by his surviving son, Charles, and his son-in-law Moses Wilkinson, payment was made to Clarissa, the oldest spinster daughter, for "five years labor" computed at three-quarter time, or thirty-nine weeks, per year. She was paid seventy-five cents per week for a total of $146.25. This settlement, sworn to before the local justice of the peace, was apparently agreed upon among the Thompson heirs as fair compensation for Clarissa's care of her parents.[32] Clarissa had taught school in early Worthington and Berkshire, but after the last of her six siblings married she cared for their elderly parents. Such household labor by a spinster relative was common, but financial compensation for these services was highly unusual. At least one historian has speculated that the low value attached to the work of spinster relatives carried over into later relationships with domestic help.[33] Magnanimous as Clarissa's compensation was by the standards of the early nineteenth century, payment at seventy-five cents per week for household labor when men were being credited one dollar per day for labor on the roads working off their taxes, reveals the true disparity assigned to the value of male and female work.

It is impossible to know how many single people were living and working in Worthington during the frontier period, but it is certain

Fig. 12. Clarissa Thompson Burr taught a subscription school in a log building on the public square during 1804–5, when she was twenty-one years old. For many years she was secretary of the Women's Tract Society of the Episcopal Church. (Taken from *Old Northwest Genealogical Quarterly*)

to say that nearly all lived "in family" with employers or relatives of some connection. It was common for brothers and sisters, nieces and nephews, cousins and orphans to find homes temporarily or permanently with other family members. Boys and girls in their teens, or even younger, lived with families where they were learning a trade or helping with the household labor. The family unit was the basic building block for community life on the frontier.

CHAPTER 8

A Tolerably Comfortable Cabin

— ❖ —

E VERYONE WHO CROSSED the mountains into Ohio country in
the first decade of the nineteenth century experienced the all-
encompassing forest. This wilderness was the dominating factor
of both farm and village life in frontier communities. In diaries and
letters travelers and settlers expressed their awe of the majestic trees,
the depression they felt in the darkness of the leafy canopy that
obscured the sun, and the terror of the unknown that lay hidden in
the forest depths. A clearing that admitted daylight and companions
within the call of a rifle shot alleviated the worst fears of those in the
new settlement, but nothing prevented the nervous tremors created
by a wolf pack howling in the night.

Wolves and panthers were so common in central Ohio when
the Scioto Company settlers arrived that Franklin County officials
awarded a bounty from the county treasury of one dollar "for the
head or scalp with two ears on . . . of each wolf or panther . . . under
six months old" and two dollars for the same over six months old.
This measure was not only for human security, but even more for
the protection of domestic livestock from attack. In 1805, seven of
the Scioto Company pioneers or their sons received these bounties,
and Jeremiah Curtis, who settled northeast of Worthington on Alum
Creek, killed seventeen wolves in three years.[1] Men with guns
quickly became the dominant animal of the frontier.

Turkeys, deer, and small game were plentiful, and although there
were no Indian villages within miles, hunting parties were frequently

seen in the area, generally camping near a stream "where water and wood were convenient." Joel Buttles recalled that "It was thought that the whites would soon kill or drive off the deer entirely; but this did not appear to be the case for several years. The whites were probably not as good hunters as the Indians, and being so much more engaged in other things, it was found that the deer increased more in the neighborhood of white settlements than at a distance where the Indians were more numerous."[2] Indians frequently brought furs such as raccoon and muskrat skins into the village to trade for goods.

When the Buttles family arrived in December 1804, a one-room cabin with a dirt floor was available for Levi and Sarah, their seven children, and three or four hired laborers who had come west with them. Levi immediately hauled logs to the sawmill north of the village and had them converted to "two-inch planks, thirteen feet long, which being set up on end, edge to edge, and spiked to suitable timbers, soon formed a house, such as it was." Both the roof and the floor were of rough boards, but within two weeks they had a house that, "though not warmer, was more roomy," with "two rooms below, and what answered to two above." Their son recalled that members of the household survived a severe winter, but all persons were "more or less ill, though not laid up. Every one had a diarrhea pretty much all the time, which, I have no doubt, saved us from worse diseases."

This dwelling bears little resemblance to the log cabins that were the typical pioneer home, but it speaks to the determination of a pioneer who wished to establish as quickly as possible some of the comforts his family had known in the east. The living conditions of the Buttles family were similar to the families who had arrived the year before. The summer had been unusually wet, with the river in flood stage making its water unsuitable for drinking. The pioneers dug shallow wells and used the water that filtered in, but by the time the Byxbe family arrived near the end of August, the settlement was in "woeful condition" with most of the community "shaking with the ague."[3] Such malarial illnesses were so common on the Ohio valley frontier, where decaying vegetation attracted insects, that most people soon accepted it as an inevitable fact of life over which they had no control.[4]

About the same time, Joel Allen wrote to his son, a merchant at Southington, Connecticut, "Do send on fifty sieve bottoms. . . . There is but one . . . and that is going around from cabin to cabin constantly in the neighboring settlement. They burn holes in skins to sift their flour and meal."[5]

But the weather was better, and the settlers were more comfortable when the Hayes family arrived a year later. They stayed temporarily with the Buttles family, and Ruhamah Hayes wrote to Elizabeth Case, who was preparing to come to Granville that fall, "If you wish to know how I am suited with this living here I can tell you that the Ladies in general apear to be well pleased but as for myself I do not make up my mind at once. . . ." She elaborated on the pros and cons in some detail: "Pork is easy made but no cellars to put it in, the best of beef but no cider. We have a barrel of whisky stands in one cornear of one of our front rooms. We have the best of wheat flour & I think the indian meal preferable to that in new england but we have no place to store it only in bags & we are over run with mice but I believe there is not a rat in Ohio." Such candid appraisal of frontier homes from a woman's viewpoint is rare. One can almost feel her disappointment being tempered by a Puritan resolve to be absolutely fair and balance each negative comment with a positive one.[6]

In terms of self-sufficiency, this frontier community was quite different from those initially established by English immigrants in the New England colonies. Although Mrs. Hayes found many settlers were "making cloth woolen & linnen," commercial goods were available in Worthington from the very beginning. In fact, some items were less costly in the west than in the east. She advised, "I should not bring any more beds than is wanted for the families use, feathers are cheaper a little distance from here than there." She suggested, however, that tin pans, "bonet paper," ginger and tea, as well as men's and women's shoes "will sell well here."[7]

The Griswold family's account with Stewart and Little's store the first year after their arrival included the purchase of a vest pattern, three-quarters of a yard of flannel, a dozen buttons, three yards of ribbon, nails, cloves and allspice, and a set of knives and forks.[8] Although the nearby river offered fish for the catching, it was not long before local storekeepers were also offering "salt fish just received from the Lake" for sale by the barrel.[9] In terms of home comforts, glass windowpanes to admit light were a high priority. Kilbourn wrote from Pittsburgh to Ezra Griswold in 1806, "I have attended to your business in geting the Glass, & a boat is to start for Chillicothe tomorough which will take it."[10]

To promote the new settlement and attend to both personal and community business interests, James Kilbourn returned east every year, leaving Lucy to cope with family responsibilities. This was consistent with Ralph Waldo Emerson's philosophy, accepted throughout the nineteenth century, that man's sphere was the world of business and government and woman's role was to create order and beauty in the home and family. Even those who defined and supported the domestic role of women approved such separation of sexual spheres.[11]

It must have been a difficult role for Lucy, alone in this frontier setting, but her letters reported family news in a matter-of-fact tone: "I am unwell and low spirited . . . the children are all well . . . our mare was taken sick last friday and her hide was taken off the next morning [after her death one assumes] we had a grate deal done for her but to no effect." Lucy had obviously done what she could and felt no guilt, but she did not hesitate to speak her mind about her husband's absence: "I hope you may do your business according to your mind with prosperity but Dear Sir do not agree to go to New England again before you get home which I hope you will return in some less time than you did last year."[12]

The loss of a horse was significant. Many persons did not own any horses, and, for those who did, horses were often their most valuable possessions. In frontier Worthington horses were typically appraised at forty to forty-five dollars, and they represented about 10 percent of the assets of the estates settled.[13]

During the first years of settlement, the pioneers had few possessions beyond those they brought west with them. John Topping's death in 1809, shortly after his marriage, revealed a young man with a bookcase and several volumes of sermons and evangelical history.[14] A churn, a cream tub, and ten pounds of cheese attested to his wife's dairy. Alexander Morrison's estate in 1811 revealed a prospering farmer whose livestock included a pair of oxen, five steers, three milk cows, two mares, and "a gang of about 35 hogs in woods which could not be rounded up for inventory."[15] Worthington residents, like most pioneers, fattened their swine by allowing them to forage for the abundant beechnut and acorn mast.

By 1811, the better homes were acquiring a few of the first pieces of handcrafted furniture. Morrison's inventory included one "elbow chair" and seven kitchen chairs. Three "bedsteads and cords," as well as four "beds and furniture," indicated that at least some family members now slept on feather mattresses on cord beds rather than on the straw ticks and feather mattresses that families initially spread on the floor or on wooden benches built into their log homes. Azariah Pinney's estate the same year included six "chair frames," suggesting that someone locally was making frames for rush seats.[16] It also included a "rag rug" valued at $1.50, the first mention of any floor covering of any type. Windows still had no curtains, few fireplaces had andirons, and no one yet had the brass candlesticks so beloved by modern antique dealers. Most homes had a single fireplace for heating and cooking, but even this required fifteen to twenty cords of wood annually.[17] Wood was plentiful, but chopping it was a laborious process.

Although there were several small frame or brick homes in Worthington before the war with England, log cabins still housed many families, particularly on outlying farm lots. Many prospective young farmers got their start by renting. Ezra Griswold advertised one such property as twenty to forty acres "in excellent order for any crop" and stated that "a tolerably comfortable cabin will be afforded for the convenience of a family if wanted."[18] In modern real estate parlance, one suspects this would undoubtedly qualify as a "handyman's special."

The Kilbourn home, begun late in 1804 on the southwest side of the public square, was the first brick structure in the community and the first residence that resembled those the settlers had left in New England. It faced Main Street and was but a single room in depth, but it set a standard with its two-story construction. When Griswold replaced his log home and tavern with a Georgian-style brick building in 1811, it continued as a community gathering place, reflecting the prosperity both this family and the community as a whole was achieving. That same year Arora Buttles advertised for sale a "large Brick Dwelling House," which he was building on the portion of his father's farm lot that he had inherited just north of the village.[19] This home, with three rooms on the first floor and three on the second, was much smaller than Griswold's, but spacious for the time. It is now preserved as a museum by the Worthington Historical Society with a cooking fireplace that portrays an affluent family's lifestyle in the frontier village.[20] Such improvements were gradual, and not everyone shared equally.

The Jedediah Lewis estate in 1807 included five deerskins, valued from forty to eighty cents each, and (to account for the skins no doubt)

Fig. 13. The cooking fireplace in the house Arora Buttles built and advertised for sale just before his militia unit was activated for service in the War of 1812 and is now part of a Worthington Historical Society museum. (Photograph by the authors)

a "rifle gun" worth sixteen dollars.[21] A particularly interesting item in this inventory, in view of Lewis's son and grandson's long leadership role in the Methodist Church, was a violin appraised at seven dollars. There were good times in the frontier community when spirits were high and a fiddle was welcome.

The large cabin, which served the first four years as both church and town hall, became a ballroom whenever the young people organized a dance. Joel Buttles, who turned eighteen shortly after his family arrived, recalled that dances occurred "probably once in ten days on an average."[22] There were more young men than women in the frontier community, and early arrival Ruhamah Hayes advised the daughter of a friend, "I would not that you should enlist for life until you have seen some of the smart lads here." Single women in the east were encouraged to come west specifically to find husbands, and Worthington wives were not shy about playing a matchmaking role. Hayes wrote Elizabeth Case regarding her niece: "I think she had better come here, there is a likely widower that wants a companion. I see nothing why she cant make herself happy & him likewise. . . ."[23]

Frontier life delineated men's and women's work and made both essential. It was assumed that nearly everyone would marry and that those who were widowed would soon remarry. On one occasion the newspaper saluted the village belles in a gallant poetic offering that resembles the flowery sentiments later popularized in high school yearbooks:

> As cupid through Worthington pass'd upon duty,
>   He sent up their names to the Goddess of beauty,
> As flowers whose attraction his notice had claim'd,
>   Which God in the form of a nosegay had fram'd . . . .
>   Miss C.A . . . we will to a lilly compare, No garden
>   e'er boasted a lilly more fair.
>   Miss A.M . . ., a rose of all hearts the desire, May
>   her charms long remain such delight to inspire.
>   Miss W . . .'s a touch-me-not, for if you do, Her wit
>   is wound up for the stroke to give two.[24]

At least half of the fun must have been in figuring out who was the object of each reference.

It seems likely that those who were accustomed to frontier life may have viewed their community differently than the travelers, both British and eastern, who most frequently wrote descriptions of the western region. Because of the time and cost involved, travelers tended to be from the upper classes of society who were accustomed to domestic comforts unavailable in frontier communities. Although men, as one would expect, traveled—on business and to explore the country—a surprising number of women also traveled, in both directions to visit relatives. When Charity Rotch attempted to reach Worthington in the spring of 1811 to visit the family of Dr. James Hills, she was at first prevented "by the height of the rivers." The following day, "determined to surmount every obstacle," their party procured good saddle horses and went three miles out of their way to take a ferry rather than to attempt fording the river. Although they were warmly welcomed by the Hills, she found "their house which tho equal to many in this country is not what we wish them to have & we are gratified to find they are going to another place more eligibly situated. . . ."[25]

Like Mrs. Rotch, local residents were frustrated by the road conditions, particularly during spring rains. They had little choice but to make the best of it. At one point the town's newspaper was forced to explain the lack of news; the mail that was due Wednesday had not arrived until Thursday evening. The editor noted that, due to poor roads, "It has not arrived at the proper time for six or eight weeks past."[26] Perhaps the postal service has changed less than one would have hoped in nearly two centuries.

It is not surprising that these immigrants, who began a subscription school within weeks of their arrival, would place a high priority on education during the frontier period. When new school committeemen were selected in December 1804, it was agreed that they would conduct a two-month school that winter, with each subscriber being required to deliver and stack one-half cord of wood for each scholar subscribed or pay seventy-one cents per cord to Levi Buttles who would hire it done.[27] A week later, James Kilbourn, Levi Buttles, and Ezra Griswold were elected trustees, and Alexander Morrison, Jr., was selected as the clerk of the "Worthington Academy." In the second winter of its existence, the community was already attempting to upgrade its image and offer more advanced studies. It was the following November before William Robe was "employed for one month on trial and then longer if all parties are agreed."[28] He was to teach a four-month subscription school at ten dollars per month. This was two dollars per month less than the laborers of the advance party had been paid the previous year—clear evidence of the comparative value of physical and mental labor, even in a frontier community that valued education.

During this time several local citizens purchased timber that had been cut from the school's farm lot, and Solomon Jones was given a contract to clear, fence, and plant seven acres in 1805 and again in 1806. As rent, he was to deliver "twelve bushells good Merchantable Shell Corn for each acre in the old clearing and ten for each acre to be cleared this spring. . . ."[29] More importantly, the Scioto Company, "in legal meeting" on May 17, 1805, voted to "unite with the Citizens of the Town of Worthington" to apply to the state legislature to incorporate "for the better management of the funds & directing the other important concerns of the Worthington Academy."[30] Although the Scioto Company had never been legally incorporated, the community of settlers already included other persons and was rapidly attracting more. To construct a substantial building for the "academy," there had to be a legal entity for property ownership.

A subscription list was circulated to construct a two-story brick building, which would be fifty-three feet long by twenty-seven wide with thirteen windows and a door both front and rear. There was to be a "cupolo in the center of the roof & a chimney at each end. . . ."[31] Over the next year or so, fifty men subscribed cash, materials, labor, or some combination of the three.

The plans to incorporate the academy, however, did not meet with the approval of everyone in the community. William Thompson, "in behalf of himself & others," requested the assistance of Mr. Baldwin, a Chillicothe resident and former Speaker of the Ohio House of Representatives, "to rid us of the diabolical plans that James Kilbourn & his associates have contrived in order to tax us without our consent or agreement." The problem Thompson outlined was that many who subscribed were unable to pay, and to keep the project alive Kilbourn proposed a property tax on all land within the eight-thousand-acre boundaries of "Worthington." Since a great number of the subscribers owned little or no property, Thompson, and probably several other large landowners, felt such a tax was unfair. Thompson pointed out that the company had set aside farmland that was now providing nearly one hundred dollars yearly in rental income to support the school. He gave no indication of it, but perhaps he was also aggrieved that his daughter Clarissa had been replaced as the teacher as the academy sought to offer a higher level of instruction.[32]

Although William Robe was a dwarf in terms of physical stature, he quickly earned respect in the community as a teacher, and the same year was appointed the village postmaster. In November 1806, his contract to teach a subscription school was extended to six months, "if twenty schollars or upward be subscribed." For this, he was to be paid eighty dollars and his board; if more than twenty scholars were subscribed, the cost would be averaged among those attending. Subscribers thus committed themselves to pay four dollars per student for a six-month term, with a possible reduction if more than twenty were subscribed. Ezra Griswold subscribed for three scholars, probably his two sons and a daughter between eight and fourteen years of age. James Kilbourn also subscribed for three scholars, probably his three daughters, from nine to thirteen years old.[33] This clearly shows that the academy at this time was co-educational. It also implies that Griswold and Kilbourn both considered their five-year-old children too young for academy schooling.

The community survived its first recorded rift about taxation, and the brick building was placed under construction as planned in the summer of 1807. On February 20, 1808, the Ohio legislature incorporated the Worthington Academy as a *subscription* school. Any person who paid five dollars was entitled to a membership certificate, which granted voting privileges in the corporation. Seven trustees were to be elected annually, and they had the power to "acquire, hold and possess any property . . . given, granted, sold, bequeathed or devised for the benefit of said Academy" so long as the income did not exceed ten thousand dollars annually. They were also given the power to make rules and regulations for the governance of the institution. The first trustees were James Kilbourn, Isaac Case, Moses Maynard, Ezra Griswold, Alexander Morrison, Jr., Thomas Palmer, and Noah Andrews.[34] They were a mix of original Scioto Company members and recent arrivals, which probably reflected the leadership transitions occurring in the growing village.

It would be two decades before Ohio seriously considered a property tax to support public schools. In the meantime, progressive towns like Worthington offered subscription schools, which in this case was subsidized by the rental income from the school's farmland.

The other founding institution, the Episcopal Church, was also feeling the effects of population that was diversifying as the community grew. When St. John's Episcopal Church was incorporated by an act of the Ohio legislature on January 27, 1807, three years after its organization, thirty men were listed as members; nineteen of them were Scioto Company members or their sons.[35] Most of the original bylaws being retained, the incorporation was simply a legal mechanism required by the state for holding property as a group. The election of officers on the Monday after Easter was retained, and the trustees at the time of incorporation were James Kilbourn, Ezra Griswold, and Thomas Palmer. Samuel Beach was chosen as treasurer and Ezra Griswold as clerk. Services were held in the log school until that was replaced by the brick academy building, into which the church also moved.

James Kilbourn and Ezra Griswold had served as trustees continuously from the congregation's organization; by contrast, William Thompson, who was also one of the original trustees and who also still lived in the community, was conspicuous by his absence. Given

Thompson's disinvolvement, Alexander Morrison and his sons were the only representatives of the Blandford contingent who were still members of the Episcopal congregation. Nathaniel and William Little and Nathan Stewart, who had originally been officers, were all preparing to leave the Worthington community. Glass Cochran was never recorded as part of the Episcopal Church.

Thompson had been an Episcopalian leader of the Blandford community, and his defection appears to have been a personal matter, perhaps connected to the school dispute. There were others in the community, however, who desired a church connection other than with the Episcopalians. The minutes of the Ohio Presbytery show that as early as 1805 two recently licensed "probationers for the gospel ministry" were assigned to preach at Worthington, Mr. Cyrus Riggs on the fourth Sunday in November and Mr. Reed Bracken on the second Sunday in December.[36] If they actually did so, they most certainly met a group gathered in someone's home, probably in the Carpenter-Powers settlement north of the village. It was common for Presbyterians to send young ministers on such missionary assignments on the western frontier to seek persons of that faith who might become the nucleus of a congregation.[37] It would be another decade, however, before that event occurred in Worthington.

Even more than the Presbyterians, Methodist "circuit riders" began to serve the religious desires of families on the frontier. Worthington's Methodists trace their roots to this "classic Methodist way"—a circuit rider by the name of Martin would occasionally preach to a group of settlers, who met first in 1808 at Samuel Beach's home south of the village and later in barns or in groves of trees.[38] In the words of one local historian, "things began to heat up" in the summer of 1811, when itinerant preachers Rev. Mitchell and Mr. Sabin held a revival meeting on the east bank of the Whetstone River south of town. Over the course of several days, a sufficient number of persons were converted to warrant the formation of a class meeting, with local resident Joab Hoyt as leader.

It is worth noting that Samuel Beach, who was the treasurer when the Episcopal Church was incorporated, was the same person who hosted the first Methodist circuit rider in his home. Several other families, such as the Pinneys, Bristols, Vinings, and Slopers, who were initially active in the Episcopal congregation became the nucleus of the Methodist class. Perhaps more than anything else, this threatened the cohesiveness of the covenanted community Kilbourn had envisioned.

Methodism was well suited to the frontier. In direct opposition to Calvinistic predestination, Methodist revivals freely offered salvation to everyone who sought atonement. God was not an unreachable abstraction, but a real presence even to the lowliest of persons.[39] In a time and place when life was drab, harsh, and fraught with uncertainties, the Methodist assurance that everyone was equally worthy of salvation was incredibly appealing. In Worthington, as in other frontier towns, the self-governing Methodists prospered. Wigger suggests that Methodists took advantage of the "free space" created by the abolition of state-sponsored religion after the American Revolution, increasing their membership from 1 in 800 persons in 1775 to 1 in 36 by 1812.[40] That year Worthington Methodists announced their regular quarterly meeting to be held a half mile west of town on Friday evening "at early candle lighting."[41]

The prosperity of school and church in Worthington reflected the rapid growth of the frontier community and the continuing optimism of its leadership. Some writers consider the triangulation of education, religion, and opportunity as the key element that supported small-town America for more than a century.[42]

When the federal census was taken in 1810, Ohio had sufficient population to increase its representation in Congress from one to four members. Although Cincinnati, which was the largest city in the state with 2,540 persons, had only 5 percent of the population of Philadelphia, the nation's largest city, it already surpassed the federal capital of Washington.[43] Chillicothe, the state capital, had 1,369 residents, compared with 685 in the Worthington area, but Cleveland, which had been surveyed seven years earlier than Worthington, only recorded 57 residents.[44]

When discussion arose about moving the state capital to a more central location, the citizens of Worthington eagerly proposed their town. As early as 1808, key citizens met to draft a proposition emphasizing its location, "near the center of the State and situated along a stream of water where there was ample opportunities for water power."[45] The academy was offered as a temporary facility until state buildings could be erected, and a subscription was circulated to secure pledges to construct accommodations for the legislature and state officials. By 1810, 136 subscribers had pledged $25,334. James Kilbourn and his financial backer, Jedediah Norton, accounted for $6,000, and four others pledged $1,000 or more; more broadly, fifty-seven pledges of less than $100 revealed widespread support across all economic levels of the community. A few names from as far north as Delaware and east to present-day Westerville indicated widespread geographic support.[46]

Seven sites were seriously considered for the new capital, but the ultimate choice was between three: a site offered by the Sells brothers on the west side of the Scioto River north of Franklinton that is the present city of Dublin; a site proposed by four investors who owned land on the high eastern bank of the Scioto east of Franklinton; and the Worthington proposal. In lobbying for the Worthington proposal in February 1812, Kilbourn attempted to meet the competition by offering to extend the town plat and to provide the state with 340 inlots of three-quarters of an acre each, 66 outlots of two-and-a-half acres each, 5,000 acres of nearby land, and $6,000 in cash, labor, and materials. He proposed to erect a state house to be 125 by 50 feet for legislative, executive, and judicial functions and a penitentiary building to be 150 by 30 feet.[47] Kilbourn was evidently counting heavily on being able to acquire the unoccupied land east of Worthington that was then owned by speculators.

But it was not to be. The legislature accepted the proposal for the site on the east side of the river opposite Franklinton, and it was here that a new city called Columbus was built. The investors who owned this property offered a ten-acre square for public buildings and the same for a penitentiary, with a state house, offices, and penitentiary valued at $50,000 to be completed by December 1817.[48] Worthington's offer had been a serious contender, but the New Englanders were outbid by a site on a larger river, a prime factor for commercial transportation and industrial power. It was also a more substantial financial package from investors who perhaps had better political connections. The loss was a serious disappointment; no one in Worthington at the time realized that this decision preserved their public square to be a twentieth-century "Village Green," rather than the site of a commercial skyscraper or asphalt parking lot.

The scope of Worthington's financial pledge must be considered in relation to the resources of this cash-starved community, where barter was commonly accepted. The subscription list for the Worthington

Academy had included contributions in bricks, lumber, shingles, labor, but all too seldom in cash. The newspaper accepted "wheat, flour, corn, pork, beef, tallow, honey, bees wax, butter, cheese, flax, linen, fowls, &c." as payment for its subscriptions.[49] Stores and artisans did likewise.

The community had no bank, and a complicated system of personal notes arose to meet the needs of borrowers and lenders. These notes were commonly exchanged and accepted as cash. This is illustrated by Ezra Griswold's arrangements in 1811, when his new tavern was being built. "In payment for brick which I am making for him," Amos Maxfield accepted a note from Griswold for $9.00, another for $12.00 that Griswold held against Israel Case, a $6.15 note against Azariah Pinney, the cancellation of Maxfield's own $5.00 note to Griswold, and Griswold's payment of Maxfield's $5.00 note to Erastus Parmenter. All together, this totaled $41.02 with interest.[50]

Like his original tavern, the new Griswold establishment continued to be the heart of community life. His account books are a litany of whiskey sales—by the glass, by the quart, or by the gallon. Several distillers were soon operating in the area, and Griswold bought by the cask, one fifteen-dollar receipt from Samuel Henderson being somewhat casual about the amount in a cask, "containing perhaps about 60 gallons."[51] But some persons were beginning to question the effects of such widespread use of alcohol. Under the headline, "The experienced man's advice to his son," the newspaper warned, "For he that places his supreme delight in a tavern, and is uneasy till he has drank away his senses, renders himself soon unfit for every thing else. Frolic at night is followed with pain and sickness in the morning."[52] For the moment, however, this was a minority view.

The intellectual and social life of the community was apparently thriving, although the available bits and pieces are more tantalizing than informative. In 1811, members of the "Conjunto Society" were notified that an election of officers would be held August 6, at E. Griswold's. Was this perhaps a musical group? No further information is known. About the same time the "Philological Society" announced its meeting at the academy. This, of course, was a literary society. Intellectual activity beyond the academy classroom was clearly being encouraged.[53]

By 1811, the newspaper office was also serving the community as a bookstore, providing the expected items such as Webster's dictionary, hymnals, and a variety of textbooks in arithmetic, surveying, Latin, English grammar, geography, and astronomy; but it also offered volumes of poetry, Ovid's *Art of Love,* the *Life of William Tell,* Steuben's *Military Exercise,* and more.[54]

News of the outside world, however, arrived slowly. The great earthquake, which became known to later generations as the "New Madrid Quake," was felt in Worthington on December 16, 1811, but it was January 1 before it was discussed in the newspaper. The editors noted that it was apparently more severe to the southwest and had damaged chimneys in Cincinnati and Chillicothe. There was no clue, however, that any word had yet reached Worthington of the devastation that changed the course of the Mississippi River and destroyed as many as forty or fifty boats and their crews.[55] The editor noted, "It is probable that some further information will be received, and it would be gratifying to us, to learn the cause of this popular convulsion of nature." Three weeks later it was reported that the previous day "an earthquake was very seriously felt in this place," being "most severe along river banks."[56] Without really understanding the scientific phenomena, local people became accustomed to the aftershocks, which continued, in varying degrees of severity, for nearly a year.

Problems that caused the community far greater difficulties were the pioneers' relatively futile attempts to fend off accidents and disease, which posed an ever-present threat of death. Some tombstones survive to mark frontier deaths, but we can only guess at the causes of death and at the anguish experienced by frontier families and their friends. Community prestige offered no protection from untimely death. Thirty-seven-year-old Lucy Kilbourn died in March 1807, like so many of her peers, in the unsuccessful birth of her eighth child. Death in childbirth was so common that women talked openly of their fears, having little recourse but to place themselves at the mercy of God's will.

There were undoubtedly infants who succumbed to diseases such as measles and diphtheria, which their immature immune systems could not fight. Nothing is known of the suffering their parents endured, not even when ten-year-old Charles Cochran drowned in the Whetstone River in June 1811.

The lack of such knowledge makes a letter from Joel Allen to his son James terribly poignant. Joel described the death of his son, Augustus, buried on what would have been his eighteenth birthday "in a black walnut Coffin—carried and attended by his young Mates and friends with no other relation than his father to lament the loss of a Son who was just ripening into manhood." Augustus, who was apparently working at Lemuel Kilbourn's mill, was taken sick on October 3 and died on October 23 despite the constant attention of his father and Dr. Lamb, who bled him and put "ten large blisters on his Arms and legs. . . ." Joel signed the letter "your afflicted and at present disconsolate father."[57]

The cause in this case was apparently an infectious illness, but accidents were also life threatening. Even a minor cut from an ax could lead to a fatal infection. Individual and family health reports were part of nearly every letter. When typhus struck in the autumn of 1810, it was devastating. It began with an infected visitor from Vermont who stayed with a family east of town. Several family members became sick and a daughter died and the disease spread from them throughout the community. From October to the following August, the epidemic caused nine deaths within eight miles of Worthington, and doubtless struck fear in many a heart. The newspaper's care in reporting the facts and in arguing that the origin of the disease was "foreign to this place" shows how disastrous the epidemic was to the community's reputation as a healthful site for new settlers.[58]

Sickness was far more feared than crime in this frontier community. The violence commonly portrayed in movie versions of the western frontier was not present in Worthington, perhaps because everyone was known and very likely related in some way to almost everyone else. That is not to say that petty theft or vandalism did not occur. Calvin Case offered a ten-dollar reward for the "almost new" saddle, "mounted before and behind with silver plate," that was stolen from Ezra Griswold's stable. This must have been the work of a stranger passing through, for such a distinctive saddle would have been instantly recognized anywhere near the village. In the same issue of the paper, James Kilbourn offered a five-dollar reward for information regarding the persons who "threw down fencing between Mrs. Lewis's farm pasture and the lower saw mill."[59] Whether this was a neighborly grudge or teenage vandalism, the need to restack the rails of a "worm" fence could certainly not be classified as serious destruction.

Worthington emerged from its frontier period with a much more diverse population than the company of original proprietors. It had lost some of its settlers because of personal disagreements or attractive options elsewhere, but it had become a closely knit community that shared tools and labor on community projects or that sat up with each other in times of sickness and death. Farm and village life was difficult but tolerable, and sometimes even enjoyable.

❖ CHAPTER 9 ❖

Squires with Muskets and Rifles

— ❖ —

W HEN THE WORTHINGTON pioneers arrived in the west, there
was no active Indian threat that required military preparedness.
The only pressing need for law and order involved civil affairs. Ohio
had adopted a county and township form of government, rather than
the self-governing towns these settlers had known in New England.
The first line of judicial authority, according to the Ohio constitution, was the township justice of the peace. This position traced its
roots to the fourteenth-century British legal system that granted
local statutory powers to appointed "conservators of the peace."[1]
When the New Englanders arrived, they found their projected town
was part of a large area identified as Liberty Township, with residents
Ezekial Brown and Zachariah Stephen as justices of the peace.

The authority of justices of the peace superseded any powers
granted to leaders of the Scioto Company by that group's constitution.
This was vividly illustrated by the double wedding of Abner Pinney
and Polly Morrison and Levi Pinney and Charlotte Beach on February 8, 1804. The presiding official was Justice of the Peace Zachariah
Stephen, not Episcopal Deacon James Kilbourn.[2] Only justices of the
peace and licensed ministers were authorized to perform marriages
under Ohio law.

James Kilbourn was elected a township justice of the peace the
following year, and for the remainder of the century there was at least
one and often two Worthington men serving in that capacity.[3] During

his three-year term, Kilbourn performed six marriages, and his own marriage in 1808 to Cynthia Barnes was performed by fellow Worthingtonian and justice of the peace Alexander Morrison.[4] It was somewhat ironic, considering the Episcopal commitment of the founding leadership of this community, that the first local marriage to be performed by a licensed minister was that of Samuel Sloper and Lydia Maynard, married in 1812 by Methodist minister Isaac Fisher.[5]

While marriages may have been one of the most pleasant duties of the justices of the peace, the greatest portion of their time was devoted to advertising and appraising stray animals, resolving conflicts regarding debts, writing deeds to transfer property, and administering oaths of office to local officials or militia officers. This was, of course, a part-time position and payment was based upon fees for services.

It was common for animals of all types to forage throughout the frontier community, but stray horses were valuable enough to be advertised either by the owner who lost them or by the justice of the peace who received them from the finder. A typical advertisement, placed by Joel Buttles, was for two runaway mares; he described one as "a very light grey, has a small piece clipt off her right ear, appears cross to strangers" and the other as "black with one hind foot white but not recollected which. . . ."[6] Judging from the number of horses that were advertised and appraised, there must have been many stray animals who were recognized by someone in the community and returned to their rightful owner without appearing in official records. During the many years Ezra Griswold served as justice of the peace, a small pasture near his tavern accommodated horses "taken up" by someone locally. Two local men were hired to appraise each animal, and the appraisal was published in the local newspaper and transmitted to the clerk of the county court. A typical appraisal by Arora Buttles and Hector Kilbourn involved a mare colt, "about fourteen hands high, the near hind foot white, with a white spot on the near side, two years old last spring," which they valued at $23.50.[7]

There was no trained lawyer in the Worthington community, but printed forms simplified the process of writing deeds or executing a debt. The Worthington men who served as justices of the peace were evidently respected for their common sense and fairness. Several were reelected for successive terms, and others advanced to become associate judges of the county's court of common pleas. Justices of the peace had a remarkable range of legal powers, particularly in the resolution of debts—the aspect of the job requiring by far the greatest amount of time and attention.

When a debt was referred to the justice for collection, a complaint was officially sworn, as by Orin Case in 1811: "I do solemnly sware that I am in danger of losing my debt against Joseph Pelton as he has left this State if I dont have an attachment against his property."[8]

After an official complaint, the township constable was ordered to summon the defendant, if he could be found; for example, "You are hereby commanded to summon Glass Cochran to appear before me at my dwelling house in said Sharon [township] on the 3rd day of December next at 11 oclock A.M. to answer William Robe in a debt of twenty-two dollars."[9] It is clear that Griswold held hearings in his home, and probably other justices in this time period did the same.

Sometimes the defendant admitted the debt but had no means to pay, as in the judgment of Thomas Palmer against James Russell. In September 1810, James Russell "confessed Judgment against himself in favour of Thomas Palmer" on a note for $28.88. In January the constable was notified of the judgment and commanded to "levy said debt & costs & interest from the date of Judgement on the goods & chattels of said Russel by distress & sale thereof returning the surplus if any to said Russel. . . ." If there was insufficient property to satisfy the judgment, the constable was ordered to "convey him to the Jail of the county there to be detained untill said debts & costs shall be paid or be otherwise legally discharged. . . ."[10]

Sometimes such a sale was carried out, as in the instance reported by Constable Joel Buttles in a judgment against Benjamin Chapman. Buttles reported he had "made service of this execution by the sale of property & collected ten dollars & sixty-two Cents & paid over to the plaintiff nine dollars & 66 Cents . . . received my fee, 103 Cents."[11] Sometimes the Franklin County jail served as a debtor's prison. One receipt from the jailor to the township constable testified that on a commitment by Griswold he received "the body of James Ashby into the Jail of Franklin County."[12] It is not clear how such matters were resolved, since no evidence exists of prisoners working off their debts or raising the money by other means.

If there was a dispute between a plaintiff and defendant, the justice of the peace had full power to subpoena witnesses. In 1811, Griswold ordered the constable to summon James Adams and Bela Tuller "to appear before me . . . to testify what they know concerning a suit in which the State of Ohio is Plaintiff & Alexander Basset Defendent."[13]

A contested judgment, however, could become quite expensive, as illustrated by the case of Zophar Topping versus Isaac Bartlet. The debt was $3.25, a summons to the defendant cost 12½¢, constable fee was 15¢, three subpoenas were 30¢ and the cost of serving one was 10¢, the judgment charge was 25¢, three witnesses were paid $1.50, the charge for swearing in six witnesses was 24¢, bail bond was 25¢, a transcript was 25¢, the execution cost 25¢, 10¢ interest was charged, and the discharge of the case was 10¢. The total cost of adjudicating this case was $6.86½—more than double the original debt. This illustrates that even a hearing before the local justice of the peace could be a complicated and expensive legal process. Perhaps this small debt involved a serious principle. However, even more surprising than the cost in this case is the fact that while Justice of the Peace Griswold and plaintiff Topping were married to sisters, Griswold apparently saw no need to disqualify himself from hearing the case.[14]

Although the actions before a justice of the peace were on the scale of a modern small-claims court, the fact that men with no legal training were given broad powers to subpoena witnesses, execute judgments, and commit defendants to jail jars our modern sensibilities. The system, however, evidently worked to the community's satisfaction, for no one from Worthington appealed a case to the county court during this frontier period. Data in this community contradict Clark's contention that lawsuits were rarely brought by one townsman against another and that most debt actions were between strangers who lived at some distance from one another.[15] Justice-of-the-peace records in Worthington suggest that legal actions between local residents were quite common, but that such cases were rarely extended to the county court.

While the justice of the peace was available to ensure the protection of individual rights, it was the militia that was designed to protect the community, and village leaders usually served in both capacities. The Uniform Militia Act, passed by Congress in 1792, remained the basic militia law throughout the nineteenth century. It enshrined the concept of universal military service and required the enrollment of all able-bodied white males between eighteen and forty-five years of age. Certain exemptions were permitted for physical disabilities or religious beliefs, such as the Quakers' opposition to bearing arms. Officers up to the rank of captain were elected by the troops, while field-grade officers were elected by the company officers they commanded.[16] Such elections were an excellent gauge of a man's leadership role as perceived by others in the frontier community, and frequently they became the route to political office.

In Worthington, the first election of militia officers for which the record survives was held on August 12, 1805, when the Sharon Township Light Infantry Company of the 2nd Division of the 4th Ohio Brigade elected Abner P. Pinney as captain, William Little as lieutenant, and Levi Pinney as ensign.[17] The thirty-three men in this company appear to have been young men under thirty, many the sons of Scioto Company members, including the twenty-six-year-old Captain Pinney. It seems likely that Captain James Kilbourn's militia company, which was identified as the Franklin County 1st Company on a muster roster taken April 24, 1806, had elected officers even earlier. In Kilbourn's company Aaron Strong served as lieutenant, Ezra Griswold as ensign, and there were four sergeants, four corporals, and three drummers.[18]

The fact that these two lists contain the names of seventy-seven different men who were available for community defense indicates dramatically just how rapidly the frontier community was growing. Only twenty-nine of these men were Scioto Company members or sons who had shared in the land division in August 1804.

Militia men were required to train at least twice a year, but military historians are united in portraying these "muster days" more as social affairs than as occasions for military drills. It would appear to have been so in Worthington, for Kilbourn's account with Griswold on April 28, 1806, included "5 quarts of whiskey to pay for what Lt. Strong & I had of him training day."[19] And only twenty-nine of the forty-six men in the company were present for that muster day! It is highly likely that the officers were more qualified for the social aspects of the job than they were skilled in military tactics.

The federal militia act specified that within six months of enrollment each recruit was to equip himself with a musket or a rifle, a bayonet, a belt, two spare flints, a knapsack, a bullet pouch, and at least twenty-four cartridges suited to the bore of his musket or a powder horn, a quarter pound of powder, and twenty balls suited to the bore of his rifle.[20]

The Worthington men who were present for drill in April 1806 were not badly equipped. Captain Kilbourn and Lieutenant Strong had swords, Ensign Griswold and 1st Sergeant Case had espontoons, and all the men except the drummers had flints and either a musket or a rifle, the latter about equally divided.[21] There were three drummers, but only one drum. No one had bayonets or cartridges, but six men each had a quarter pound of powder and twelve rifle balls. No one had a "Nap-Sack," but that probably posed no problem as long as the exercises were confined to the public square.[22] As time went on and there was no call for militia action, discipline may have actually declined. Two years later the same company contained fifty-five men under Captain Ezra Griswold, but only thirty-five reported for spring muster, nine without any weapon, and few had any of the other required equipment.[23] In the absence of a crisis, militia training was apparently not taken very seriously.

Governor Tiffin addressed the legislature about militia problems in 1806, and one letter writer responded that there were "few persons who view Militia duty in any other light than a burthen." The problem of obtaining enough qualified officers was even worse because "few of the inhabitants have leisure to attend to all the duties required by law, few have the means of equipment and a still less number choose to encounter the displeasure of their friends and neighbours for the empty name of an unproductive office in the Militia." This writer suggested that, as an inducement, officers should hold their commission for a specified time, such as four or five years, and then be exempted from all further militia duty.[24]

This did not happen, but ironically the rising talk of war with England sharpened militia discipline. The Ohio General Assembly passed an act that followed the federal guidelines, but sharpened discipline and imposed fines for noncompliance.[25] The 1792 militia act prescribed that the president might call militiamen into national service for not more than three months in any one year. In March 1809, James Kilbourn, by then a major commanding a battalion in the Ohio militia, ordered Captain Griswold's company to assemble at the public square, "with arms complete in every respect . . . for the purpose of detaching from your Company three men & officers by voluntary enlistment or draft."[26] This was to meet Worthington's share of the 2,384 men required from Ohio to meet the quota of 100,000 militiamen for United States service, as demanded by an act of Congress.

Fig. 14. An artistic interpretation depicts muster day on the public square, a major event in the pioneer village. (Courtesy of Andrea J. Myers)

As friction increased between the United States and Great Britain, sentiments about a declaration of war were divided. In general, the New England region that depended on maritime trade was opposed to war, while the western regions that feared British-inspired Indian attacks tended to favor war. Senator Worthington, however, felt that Ohio was vulnerable and militarily unprepared, and he voted against the declaration of war. The command of Ohio's militia had already been turned over to General William Hull, an elderly and somewhat corpulent Revolutionary War veteran who proved a most unfortunate choice.[27]

Militia units in the Worthington area had for several months been equipping themselves and training with more fervor. Captain Joab Norton's company, recruited from the area of the Union Company purchase about five miles northwest of Worthington, went so far as to specify an elaborate uniform. Members were fined fifty cents if they were not attired with a "black hat or cap, and a bearskin on the same, and a cockade, and a white feather with a red top on the left side of the same, said feather or plume to be of seven inches in length, also a black rifle frock or hunting shirt, trimmed with white fringe, and a white belt round the same, and a white vest and pantaloons and white hankerchief or cravat, with a pair of black gaiters or half-boots and black knee-bands."[28] Such dandified dress was unusual for the militia, and white pantaloons and vest were certainly more suitable for impressing the ladies at muster than for actually fighting the British or Indians, but the Ohio law had specified that each company "shall wear, while on parade, such uniforms as may be agreed upon by a majority of the company."[29]

In June 1812, this company was called out by Governor Meigs to defend the northern boundary of the frontier settlements.[30] As they departed Captain Norton addressed his men with stirring words about the barbarity of the enemy, reminding them that "you my brave fellows, are freedom's children. . . . Let Britons, let savages, or any others of equal numbers, encounter with us, and we will maintain our rights."[31] The service of this gaudily attired company that summer was primarily confined to the construction of defensive blockhouses on the northern border.

A number of Worthington men, however, marched north with Hull's army, and, even after a "fateaguing march of 25 days," Arora Buttles was cocky when he wrote to his brother Joel that they were camped on the banks of the Detroit River, "opposite Sandbridge, a small British town on the other side of the River, but I expect it will be smaller before another day is at an end for we calcilate to give them a hundred or two cannon balls for their breakfast in the morning. . . ." This attitude prevailed despite the fact that he had put on the poorest clothes he had to "go throu the brush and swamps," putting all his clothes and money on a ship that had been brought up to carry provisions. When that fell into the hands of the British, he was left "in a poor situation without either money or clothes even to exchange to wash."[32]

Military tactics and the organization for supporting the troops were obviously in shambles well before Hull's surrender to the British. Nearly thirty years later, Buttles traveled to Detroit on business by steamboat, and used the occasion to reminisce to his wife of the campaign years earlier, when "There were scarce 20 persons in an open crazy boat tilting over the waves expecting that probably every one would be the last that our leaky boat could ride out." He lamented for the "poor set of boys . . . wading through wilderness, swamps and rivers to Detroit only to be surrendered to the enemy by a coward. . . ."[33] Time did not heal the bitterness Ohio soldiers felt about Hull's surrender of the army on August 16, 1812.

In 1812, however, it was a bitterness mixed with rumors and panic. False alarms about Indian attacks caused the settlers north of Worthington to flee south or build blockhouses. For several weeks the hysteria bordered on that later occasioned by Orson Welles's 1938 radio program, "War of the Worlds." One person was detained for several days at Delaware, on suspicion of being a British spy, and the newspaper constantly reported on ominous movements by groups of Indians. Settlements like Worthington felt extremely vulnerable. As the newspaper pointed out, "The militia are almost all called into the field from the frontier settlements in this quarter, which leaves us in a very disagreeable situation, especially as a party of Indians might by avoiding the army stationed to the north of us, fall upon the inhabitants and massacre them without opposition. . . ."[34] These westerners expressed no fear of the British, but only of their Indian allies whom they considered capable of savage treachery.

The terms of Hull's surrender provided that Ohio militiamen who had not joined the federal army would be permitted to return to their homes, on condition that they "will not serve during the war." Soon these discharged prisoners were moving south, and on September 13 Thomas Russell paid Ezra Griswold $1.50 for "six suppers and one loaf & a half of bread . . . for six soldiers in Col. Mearthure's Regiment on the return home from the surender of Detroit."[35]

Actually, Worthington businessmen had found the war profitable from the beginning. Troops passing northwest to Urbana sought supplies; and after General William Henry Harrison assumed command of the army, he was in Worthington and Delaware making arrangements for wagoners to supply the troops. His orders of October 28, 1812, were issued from "Northwest Army Headquarters, Worthington, Ohio."[36] Wherever the general stopped became the army's temporary headquarters. Gradually, confidence in his command restored calm to Ohio.

The siege of Fort Meigs the following spring was a critical test of western defenses. Governor Meigs wrote Captain Barker and Captain

Case to request militiamen for the force he was assembling to march to Sandusky, requesting that they "rendezvous at this place [Delaware] to morrow evening with all the mounted men you can muster." He assured them he would "ask no man to perform or undertake what I will not do myself."[37] Worthington men were not involved in the bloody rescue of the fort's garrison, but its successful stand prevented the need for further activation of militia units.

No Worthington man earned glory or martyrdom in this war, although four militia companies served varying periods of duty. Captain Levi Pinney's company was with Hull's army at Detroit. Captain Chauncey Barker's company and Captain Israel P. Case's company went into service on August 24, guarding the settlements for several weeks after Hull's surrender and again in May 1813. Captain Aaron Strong's company did the same from October through December 1812.[38] Other Scioto Company descendants served with Delaware County militia units, making the total number of men who served from the Worthington area well over one hundred, but difficult to compute accurately because some returned from service with one company and went out with another.

Most militiamen served briefly and saw little actual combat, like their fathers before them in the Revolutionary War. Few men from Worthington served in U.S. Infantry regiments. Arora Buttles served early in the war as the drum major on Colonel Duncan McArthur's staff of the 1st Ohio Militia Regiment, and later he and Abner P. Pinney served as lieutenants with the 27th U.S. Infantry Regiment. A recruitment authorization from General Lewis Cass makes it clear that Buttles's rank was obtained by recruiting fifteen soldiers for federal service, but these names have not survived.[39] Zophar Topping died on September 7, 1814, while serving as a scout with friendly Indians, but his death was apparently from natural causes, and efforts to secure a pension for his widow were unsuccessful.[40]

Although Worthington residents experienced a year of fright from their proximity to the fighting in the west, their newspaper gave little indication that they were discussing the issues behind the conflict. The war's major effect on the Worthington community turned out to be a favorable stimulus for the economy. Local farmers were delighted when the quartermaster at Franklinton sought contracts for 2,000 bushels of oats.[41]

CHAPTER 10

Apprentice Wanted—Of Steady
Deportment and Industrious Habits

— ◈ —

IN TERMS OF WORK, the frontier village was dramatically different from a modern town in several important ways. Pioneers would have been completely mystified by the concept of unemployment. In their world, there was endless work to be done, and every man, woman, and child did what they could according to their abilities. Children began their preparation for the world of work at home: girls learned household skills from their mothers and boys learned farming or craftsmanship skills from their fathers or uncles. In their teens they might be apprenticed to learn a trade or sent to clerk in a store. Craftsmen who produced handmade products had no blueprints, but over time they developed three-dimensional memories that were highly accurate, just as the housewife learned to gauge the correct temperature of the oven for baking or the blacksmith to judge the heat required in his forge to produce a quality tool. Work was task-oriented rather than time-oriented, with farmers mobilizing all hands and working long hours during planting and harvest and sawmill operators doing the same when rainfall raised streams and water power was abundant.[1]

Most people were generalists rather than specialists, and family income was usually derived from several sources. This was true even when the head of the household was a recognized artisan, such as a blacksmith, or a professional, such as a physician. Social historians have long researched and discussed the "transition to capitalism," and Worthington exhibited all four patterns of household production described by Clark.[2] Household labor was evident in women's weaving and in seasonal activities by farmers such as broommaking and carving wooden handles for tools; itinerant workers were available for common labor and skills such as shoemaking and dressmaking; work was exchanged for needs such as carpentry or the use of a cider press; craftsmen working in their homes produced items as diverse as chairs and hats. No one typified the diverse sources of income more clearly than Ezra Griswold. He obtained a tavern license his first winter in Worthington and continued to renew it at the cost of four dollars per year.[3] Everyone in the pioneer village would certainly have identified Griswold as the tavern keeper, but that was not the only source of either his income or his influence. His daybooks show that many families kept a running account, and the volume of whiskey sales—for consumption both on and off the premises—made this a profitable business even at 6¢ per gill, 12½¢ per pint, and 37½¢ for a double bowl of sling or toddy. Family celebrations, as on November 3, 1806, "the evening he [Kilbourn] came home from New England," called for a twenty-five-cent quart of whiskey.[4]

When Griswold's new brick tavern was built in 1811, with a party room on the upper floor, nineteen young bachelors celebrated its completion with a ball that cost them $1.46 each. Griswold itemized the $27.75 charge to include $1.00 for the use of the room with candles and wood for the fire, $12.00 for six quarts of wine, $4.00 for two quarts of French brandy, $8.75 for thirty-five suppers at twenty-five cents each, and $2.00 for sugar. When ladies were present for supper, wine was more appropriate than whiskey, even though it carried a luxury price. A couple of months earlier, twenty-four men, who had apparently worked on the new tavern's construction, celebrated its completion with a meal of "hot stew" at thirty-one cents each and several bowls of sling. Most of Griswold's tavern business came from the local community. Even his occasional boarders were likely to be workmen who were newly arrived in the community and had no other lodgings. In September 1806, Kilbourn paid three dollars per week each for room and board for Amos Maxfield, who was developing a brickyard, and Jedediah Lewis, who was building a second sawmill in the community.[5]

Because of his recognized record-keeping abilities, Griswold soon became the clerk for many community organizations. He served the Episcopal congregation in this manner without pay; but when local elections were held at the tavern, it was natural that Griswold would be paid $4.50 "for carrying the election Poll book of Liberty Township to Chillicothe."[6] When he began the first of several terms as justice of the peace in 1808, he collected standard fees for services, usually twenty-five cents each for swearing militia officers, executing a debt, or filing a deed to transfer property.

Although Griswold acquired 209 acres of farmland in Worthington when the Scioto Company property was divided, he had no intention of farming this himself. He engaged tenants to begin clearing this land and farming it for a share of the produce, similar to the rental arrangements for the town's church and school property. In time these contracts became quite profitable.

With the tavern, public office, and rental farmland, it is somewhat surprising to discover that Griswold regularly received income from the day-to-day services that comprised a significant portion of the economic activity of the pioneer community. His stable was a place to rent a team of oxen for heavy-duty work at fifty cents per day or a horse for riding to Lancaster or Chillicothe. On occasion he would take his ox team and haul "sleepers" for a construction project or a load of iron from Franklinton. Many such items in Griswold's day-books were settled by an exchange of services with no cash changing hands. Other men were doing the same; Alexander Morrison charged the trustees one dollar per day for the use of his wagon during the construction of the academy.[7]

Perhaps Griswold's most unusual enterprise was his one-dollar purchase of "the exclusive privilege of Making and using John Sweets pattent Bee Hive." Griswold essentially bought the Worthington "franchise" for this improved hive, which consisted of several 16-x-14-x-6-inch boxes. Its advantage was the orifices near the center and one near the top so that the boxes could be stacked one on top of another, allowing the bees to move freely between them, but making it possible to remove any individual box to retrieve honey.[8]

Most men in the community engaged in similarly diverse activities, although many were also sought out when specific skills were needed. Nathaniel Little and Nathan Stewart were partners in the first store in Worthington, which Little evidently managed. Stewart apparently built, and perhaps hired others to work in, both a blacksmith shop and a distillery. Such combinations of production and sales in the new community were common. Although Stewart left in

1806, and Little moved to Delaware in 1808, others were already meeting these needs. Alexander Morrison, Jr., and James Kilbourn soon had stores. While company member Icabod Plumb was both a blacksmith and a carpenter, he moved to nearby Berkshire and specialized in making wagons. Levi Pinney became one of several blacksmiths who worked in the early village and pledged "$2 in smith work" as part of his subscription for the academy building.[9] His brother, Azariah, was a cooper who made the barrels and kegs so essential to the community. Distilleries were quickly established both north and south of the village. By 1812, Dan Case was offering his for rent, advertising that "Whiskey will be received in payment. . . ."[10]

James Kilbourn's trip east in 1805 was the first of several to seek new settlers for Worthington who could contribute specific skills to support the community's commercial growth. Quality residential and commercial structures were a high priority, and carpenter-house joiners such as Timothy and Ebenezer Goodrich and Eliphalet and Chauncey Barker were enticed to migrate by the opportunity to acquire land in the Union Company purchase. The brick structures that Kilbourn wanted for this community required a local brickyard, and Amos Maxfield soon developed facilities for burning brick on a clay bank a little east of the village. This was one of the residual banks of a much larger river that had once carried glacial melt waters. Jedediah Lewis was persuaded to settle in Worthington rather than in Granville, and to construct a second sawmill just south of the village.

The Worthington Academy subscription list is an excellent source of information about which materials and skills were available in the pioneer community and which had to be imported. Several residents subscribed boards that could be cut at one of the two local sawmills, and Samuel Wilson, who was operating the one north of town, pledged "$5 in sawing."[11] Others subscribed bricks, which could be fired at Amos Maxfield's brickyard, and Maxfield himself pledged five thousand bricks worth twenty-five dollars. Several subscribers pledged shingles, which they could cut themselves or hire them to be produced locally. Ebenezer Welch pledged one hundred bushels of lime, "if the whole is bought of him." Aaron Strong pledged forty dollars, Alexander Morrison, Jr., pledged twenty dollars, and Noah Andrews pledged fifteen dollars worth of carpentry work. All three were primarily farmers with some carpentry skills that probably provided a bit of supplemental income. The real "carpenters and joiners" in town, however, were "Barker and Goodrich" who were hired to make the window and door frames, lay the shingles, and make "126 feet Madilion Cornice at $63.00." The total contract with Barker and Goodrich for $205.00 was settled by providing them a mare valued at $65.00, crediting them $10.00 against their academy subscription, and paying the balance in cash.[12] When Chauncey and Peter Barker were hired two years later for additional work, the more experienced Chauncey was paid $1.50 per day while Peter received $1.25.[13]

There were numerous chores to be done, and several young men subscribed unskilled labor for the academy construction. Receipts show one-half day chopping wood for the brick kiln was credited at 37½¢. Maxfield's records for work at the brickyard include payment on Tuesday, November 7, 1807, to "Black Daniel," suggesting that African-Americans were already working in the community.[14] It is likely that they had come north from Chillicothe, where a number of Virginians and free blacks had settled.

Asahel Hart pledged thirty dollars in "bricklaying." His experience working on his uncle James Kilbourn's home was evidently not sufficient to build an academy of the quality the trustees desired, but he very likely served as a helper. On September 29, 1808, the trustees contracted with Daniel Bishop of Franklinton "to erect the Brick Walls of an academy" according to their plan. Scaffolding was to be prepared by Worthington residents, and bricks, lime, and sand were to be delivered "within a convenient distance." Bishop agreed that the work would be "done in a neat, Strong, & Workmanlike Manner agreeable to the materials furnished." He also agreed to complete the walls and chimneys for this fifty-three by twenty-seven foot, two-story building by the first of December. He was to be paid $3.00 for each one thousand bricks laid, $1.50 for each brick arch over the windows and doors, and $20.00 for "painting and penciling said walls." Two hundred dollars of this was to be paid by deeding him one hundred acres of land in the section of the military district for which Kilbourn was agent; he was also to be paid fifty dollars in cash, fifty dollars in "Meat, grain & Vegetables for the purpose of his boarding expenses While said Walls are in building," and "the remainder Whatever it May be in boards at one of the saw-mills in said Worthington."[15]

It was the last time Worthington would have to import a brick mason, for not only was young Hart gaining skill, but Arora Buttles had begun learning the trade. His contract with the academy trustees called for work as a "turnover in the brickyard or in tending Mason."[16] Buttles was hired at fifty cents per day, or thirteen dollars per month, "with usual board & Lodging (not Washing) . . . [and] one gallon of Whiskey pr Month. . . ."[17] He was sixteen years old when this agreement was signed, but he was to receive a man's whiskey ration and to be paid three dollars a month more than William Robe's initial contract to teach at the Worthington Academy. Buttles soon developed into Worthington's most skilled brick mason, partially because Hart died while on a trip back to New England, shortly after completing Ezra Griswold's new tavern. For this Hart was paid $153.30 for laying 102,200 bricks, exactly half of Bishop's rate three years earlier. His total bill from the "underpinning" to the cornices was $250.55.[18]

The academy was built at approximately the same time that Kilbourn constructed a commercial building on Main Street for his own enterprises. Shortly before her death, Lucy wrote her mother about Kilbourn's plans for both the academy and his own building.[19] The latter was slightly smaller, at fifty-six by twenty-two feet, and stood just south of the Kilbourn home. All of these early brick structures were the "I" buildings so popular in New England. Kilbourn's building had three commercial spaces on the ground floor, for his surveyor and land-agent businesses, his store, and the newspaper he planned to begin publishing as soon as possible. The second story contained sleeping rooms for his expanding family, and the "Worthington Hotel" that the family operated after his second marriage. This building has continued in commercial use largely unchanged to the present day.[20]

Kilbourn's appointment as surveyor for the U.S. Military District opened doors to speculation and profit for him as it had for so many others. One of the "towns" he surveyed was Norton, approximately twenty-six miles north of Worthington; Kilbourn named it no doubt hoping the name would attract support from his financial backer, Jedediah Norton. While he was surveying this, he encountered Nathaniel Brundige, who had recently arrived with his family and was looking for land to purchase. Kilbourn offered him "a fine piece of land" for four hundred dollars, which Brundige paid. Kilbourn returned to Chillicothe, had it recorded in Brundige's name, and cleared two hundred dollars on the deal for himself.[21] They must have maintained good relations, however; several years later one of Brundige's descendants managed the Worthington Hotel for Kilbourn.

Another purchaser in Norton was William Drake, who was migrating west in 1810 when he encountered Kilbourn on his way east. On inquiring and being told that Drake was headed for a site called Norton near the Whetstone River, Kilbourn congratulated him for "going to a perfect Eden." When Drake finally arrived at the single cabin on the Norton site, he laughed at himself for his grandiose expectations and confessed to the cabin owner, "I must say that if this satisfies Kilbourn's ideas of Eden, I never want to hear his conception of h- -l."[22]

Kilbourn frequently served as the agent for General Jonathan Dayton in selling military district land, and several records suggest his enthusiasm sometimes led him to commitments for which he did not yet have clear title. This was not uncommon at the time.[23] Evidence that Kilbourn apparently made every effort to straighten out misunderstandings is found in a letter from brick mason Daniel Bishop, in which Bishop refused to do business with Kilbourn because he had been told of a land transaction in which General Dayton's land was apparently in his wife's name and there was no clear title. Bishop asked, "How can an agent carry away or take from a woman her right of Dower if the husband cannot. . . ." Bishop refused to conduct any business with Kilbourn because "I am very much opposed to Law controversies and very little acquainted with Law."[24] They must have worked out their misunderstanding, however, for this letter was written six months *before* Bishop contracted to do the brick work for the academy and accepted one hundred acres of Dayton's land in partial payment.

The land speculators of the early nineteenth century in some ways resemble the stock market speculators of the late twentieth century, who invest for potential capital growth. Kilbourn served both as the real estate agent for major speculators and as the developer who was laying out prospective town sites. However, he had arrived late for Ohio's development boom, and his holdings never compared with early surveyors such as Lucas Sullivant of Franklin County who by 1810 owned 41,459 acres, Duncan McArthur of Ross County who owned 33,968 acres, or Kilbourn's mentor Thomas Worthington who owned 5,443 acres.[25]

Kilbourn was deeply involved in so many business interests that it sometimes took a while for them to become reality. Although he had planned space for a newspaper office when his commercial building was constructed and had had a press shipped from Pittsburgh, he

Fig. 15. The Kilbourn Commercial building, built ca. 1808, with ground floor rooms for Kilbourn's retail store, land office, and *The Western Intelligencer*, as well as second story sleeping rooms for his adjacent home and "Worthington Hotel," is believed to be the oldest commercial building in continuous use in Ohio. (Photograph by the authors)

had difficulty in acquiring an editor and printer. A prospectus was issued by James Kilbourn, proprietor; R. D. Richardson, editor; and George Smith, printer—but the first issue of *The Western Intelligencer* on July 17, 1811, contained R. D. Richardson's explanation for declining to serve and James Kilbourn's assurance that "an editor shall arrive from the eastern states . . . a gentleman of much experience as an editor, and justly ranks among those of the first scientifical acquirements."

It is not known why no such editor arrived, but by August 21, Joel Buttles, editor, and George Smith, printer, had "purchased the office and establishment of the *Western Intelligencer*." Once more it had become necessary to rely on home-grown talent; nevertheless, Worthington, through Kilbourn's efforts, had established the first newspaper in central Ohio.[26] Buttles defined the paper's purpose for its readers, stating their "determination to render the *Intelligencer* pleasing and instructive, by laying before their readers the most interesting foreign and domestic intelligence, literary and moral essays,

select and original poetic effusions, with occasional geographical &
historic sketches on the western country."²⁷ Its masthead quoted Benjamin Franklin, "Where Liberty Dwells, There is MY Country." The
new owners promised to publish this weekly paper "on the most suitable day for the arrival and departure of the mail" for "two dollars per
annum if paid in advance," two dollars and fifty cents if paid at the
end of six months, or three dollars if paid at the end of the year.

Like most printing establishments, the newspaper office did a variety of other business, advertising "Horse Hand Bills—neatly executed, on handsome paper with an Elegant Cut, and at reasonable
terms" or "Book binding—executed on a short notice." It also dealt in
trade, advertising that "writing paper will be exchanged for any quantity of rags." It even planned to publish at least one book, a school
geography written by John Kilbourn, the new Worthington Academy
principal. The prospectus described the textbook as containing two
hundred pages and costing fifty cents per copy, and it warned readers
that without a knowledge of geography "a person cannot understandably read even the common newspaper of the day and without a correct knowledge of what we read in these vehicles of public information, we shall be unable to acquire that degree of political knowledge
which our national institutions require. . . ." Worthington residents
were indeed on the western frontier, but they considered themselves
very much a part of the new American democracy.²⁸

There may have been some who doubted that young Buttles would
succeed as a newspaper editor, for after six months of operation he
editorialized that "The impotent slanders of a malicious few, predicting its downfall, have proved fallacious. . . . We have the satisfaction
of experiencing a daily increase of the list of subscribers. . . ." In fact,
the paper quickly became a convenient means of communication for
local advertisers. The job opportunities it advertised attest to a booming economy: Hector Kilbourn sought "an apprentice to the Mason's
Business, of about 17 or 18 years of age . . . of steady deportment and
industrious habits"; John Whitford wanted to employ "1 or 2 Journeymen Hatters, who are well acquainted with the business"; Levi
Pinney wished for "an apprentice to the blacksmith business . . .
a Boy between 14 and 17 years of age will be preferred . . . liberal
terms and advantages"; James Kilbourn advertised for an "industrious young man 15 to 20 to assist about a public house and tend
upon a stable"; and the paper itself sought "An apprentice to learn the

Art of Printing. An active boy with a tolerable English education and from 13 to 16 years of age."[29]

There were no advertisements for female help, but such arrangements were made privately. Denman Coe indentured his fourteen-year-old daughter, Betsey, to "live with & labour faithfully" at Griswold's Tavern "untill she is eighteen years of age." Griswold promised to treat Betsey well and give her "good instruction, council & advice, a plenty of good & wholesome food, lodging, & clothing," and six months of schooling. At the conclusion of her service, she was to receive a feather bed worth ten dollars, two pillows and cases, cotton sheets, and a bed quilt. She was also to receive one pair of every-day shoes and stockings, two new every-day gowns, a pair of fine shoes and stockings, two fine gowns ("suitable to ware at church & in the best of company"), two checkered aprons, one shawl, and a bonnet. Coe and Griswold each pledged a $200.00 bond for the completion of the contract.[30] This is an interesting arrangement in several respects. Betsey was essentially working four years to receive some education and a respectable wedding dowry. One hopes that she and Ruth Griswold, who was doubtless the supervisor of her work, were consulted regarding the terms.

A new addition to the town, once Griswold's new brick tavern was completed, was the "Physic & Medicinal Store" of Dr. Hills and Dr. Case, located in a room built especially for that purpose. It offered a varied mix of medicines, medical equipment, herbs, and spices including, among other things, borax, blue vitriol, cloves, cinnamon, calomel, essence of lavender, elixir of paregoric, ipecac, juniper berries, liquorice balls, resin, saffron, sponges, syringes, and wine.[31] This must have been a welcome addition because individual and family health reports were part of nearly every letter, and death was an ever-present possibility. Despite the presence of a doctor in the community from the beginning, five company members, two wives, several children, and unknown others died before the war with England. Infants were particularly vulnerable to infections, consumption was rampant, and accidents could always be life threatening when any cut might lead to fatal infection.

Local residents, though, had faith in their physicians. In 1805, Joel Allen described Dr. Lamb as having "studied Physic in the State of New York and is generally approved of as a man of sense and judgment and appears to be very kind and humane."[32] In 1811, during the visit of an eastern friend, Dr. Hills was described as "much engaged on acct of a sick child in the neighborhoud."[33] But there was little even this physician, who trained at prestigious Yale College, could do. One writer has described early nineteenth-century medical practice as appearing by modern standards to be uncomfortably close to astrology or magic.[34]

It would be extremely difficult to say that the skills of the physician, or the work of any one person, was absolutely essential to the community. Many people contributed to the daily needs of life. Kilbourn's gristmill played a key role under several managers. When Roswell Wilcox took it over, he advertised that he had been "from early life almost constantly employed in building and tending of mills." He promised to keep it in good repair and give customers "every attention in his power . . . and flatters himself that he can do the work . . . expeditiously and to their entire satisfaction."[35] William Vining and Ebenezer Brown were tinners specializing in the tin pails, cups, candlesticks, and baking pans needed in every home. Jeremiah Curtis brought seeds from Connecticut and established the first orchard in the area, a boon to every home which relied on apple cider. Joab Norton was a tanner who was urged to "bring with him all his tools for shoemaking and a quantity of dressed calf-skins."[36] James Russell was a talented mechanic, in either wood or metal, whose accounts reveal that he could make chairs or bedsteads, repair spinning wheels and plows, or make a new hoe handle.[37]

Within a few years Worthington was actually exporting products, as shown by an agreement between Levi Pinney and Franklinton merchants Lucas Sullivant and Lynn Starling. In June 1810, Pinney contracted to deliver "between the 20th day of November and the 1st day of December next . . . Sixteen Dollars & Thirty-eight Cents in good merchantable Fall Hogs which shall weigh at least 150 lb. each. . . ." These were to be delivered to Sullivant & Starling's Franklinton store "at the Cash price of Pork at that time."[38] This contract is remarkably similar to the futures contracts made by contemporary farmers, and it testifies to the raw products traditionally exported by an underdeveloped agricultural society.

The economy of the frontier village relied heavily upon handmade goods and home production; but within a decade Worthington achieved a remarkable degree of self-sufficiency and was approaching the interdependent reliance on outside markets that these families had known in New England.[39] Cayton and Onuf use the term "commercial capitalism" in reference to the economic and social order in which the primary activity is the private, competitive production of goods for profit.[40] It was achieved rapidly in the frontier communities of the early republic.

Pioneer Worthington demonstrated Frederick Jackson Turner's thesis that westward migration required "a return to primitive conditions on a continually advancing frontier line. . . ."[41] This community, however, illustrates a concept that has received far less scrutiny: the dramatic compression of time necessary for western settlers to move from frontier conditions to a market economy. Worthington's frontier period was real, but compared to the colonies of their seventeenth-century New England ancestors, its brevity was remarkable.

Boom and Bust,
1812–1821

— ❖ —

❖ CHAPTER II ❖

If Elected I Shall Not
Disappoint Your Confidence
or Shame Your Favor

— ❖ —

T HE FIRST SETTLERS in Worthington arrived in family groups. In times of crisis, they relied exclusively upon relatives and neighbors; however, they soon found that there were issues of social welfare that called for community responsibility—just as in the New England towns they had left behind. After the justice of the peace, one of the most elemental needs was for "overseers of the poor," who provided for those who could not care for themselves and had no family able to do so. In early Worthington, "the poor" included illegitimate children, persons too ill to work, elderly persons, and sometimes orphaned children. In the early nineteenth century, the plight of such persons was already an issue with a long history; some colonial towns had been known to solve it by encouraging indigent persons to move elsewhere.

English travelers often found Americans publicly straitlaced about sexual matters, insistent on "purity" and reluctant to admit to bastards.[1] Yet, illegitimate children were born. In Worthington, Justice of the Peace Glass Cochran ruled in February 1814 on a case brought by Overseers of the Poor Obediah Benedict and Ezra Griswold. It involved Columbus Cooper, "a poor boy born of Martha Pinney . . . [an] illegitimate child aged about four years" who was bound to the "care, instruction & bringing up of Tracy Willcox . . . untill he shall be twenty-one." Wilcox was to provide "a plenty of good & wholesome food, rainment & Lodging" and "use his best endeavors to have the said child [lead] a moral and christian life."[2] At twenty-one, Cooper was to receive thirty dollars in cash and a horse worth seventy dollars, supposedly to begin an independent, adult life.

In this case, the father was clearly known locally and his name was given to the child, but Mr. Cooper had apparently left the community without marrying the mother of his child or providing for the child's support. Martha was a thirty-three-year-old spinster when Columbus Cooper was born. Her parents had died, and evidently none of her six married brothers and sisters in the community were willing or able to raise the child. The birth of this boy was a shame that the family ignored completely when descendants published their genealogy a century later.[3] The community coped by placing the child with a respected local family, in a situation that was something between an adoption and an indenture. The official record ends with the assumption that this boy would work for his room and board, but readers can hope that he was treated kindly as a family member.

At the far end of life, there was the problem of the elderly, of a widow without family support. In 1820, a "court of enquiry" was brought by John Goodrich and Ozias Burr, the overseers of the poor, regarding Hannah, widow of Joseph Lewis. After hearing their testimony, Justice of the Peace Stephen Maynard ruled that "on mature Deliberation we Do Consider that she is much out of her mind or Insane and that there is Danger of her Wasting or Destroying her property but Do not think there is Danger of her Destroying her own Life or the Life or property of Others and She ought not to be put in Confinement."[4] Goodrich and Burr were directed to make an inventory of her estate and report it to the county court, which the following day named Ozias Burr as her guardian.

Goodrich and Burr were leaders in the Episcopal church, and one assumes that this case was a benevolent attempt to care for a senile old woman who was unable to manage her own affairs. The brief hearing before a local justice of the peace does, however, emphasize the potential ease with which malevolent relatives might conspire to deprive elderly persons of their own property.

The law was much more explicit in protecting the property of children, and a male relative or local justice of the peace was usually appointed as a guardian until they reached their twenty-first birthday. Unless a man's will specifically assigned his property to his wife and named her guardian of their children, Ohio law provided that the widow would receive one-third of the estate and that the remaining two-thirds would be divided equally among the surviving children. In the case of farm or business property, this forced the widow to cooperate with the court-appointed guardian in all decisions affecting the economic affairs of her minor children, even as to their clothing and schooling. Orphans, of course, not only had their fiscal affairs managed by their guardians, but usually made their home with this person.

Relatives such as uncles or brothers-in-law frequently served as guardians, but a significant number of orphans in early Worthington were entrusted to the care of local justices of the peace. Most of the time this appeared to be an amiable relationship, but a lawsuit by the local heirs of Miranda Topping illustrates how difficult the position of a public official could become.

Miranda Topping was an infant when her father died and was thirteen when she was orphaned, at which time she was entrusted to the guardianship of Worthington resident and Franklin County Associate Judge Recompense Stanbery.[5] Miranda lived the last six years of her life in the Stanbery home, dying—probably of consumption—before she reached her twenty-first birthday. This was not an unusual situation. In fact, three orphaned daughters of Jonah Bidwell, aged six to ten, joined the Stanbery household two years after Miranda.

At her death, Miranda was the sole heir of her father's two-hundred-acre farm. This reverted by law to her father's heirs: five aunts and one uncle, who did not live in the Worthington area, and seven cousins, who were the children of a deceased uncle in Worthington. These cousins sued Stanbery, claiming that he had not "rendered a just and accurate account" of the profits from this real estate and of Miranda's expenses while living as a member of the Stanbery household.

Although Stanbery's guardianship was eventually vindicated, a series of hearings before local justices of the peace present a detailed picture both of the relationship between a guardian and an orphan and of the daily life of a teenage girl in early Worthington. Itemized expenses for Miranda's benefit during these six years included regular clothing purchases, such as "morroco shoes for $2.25, lace for ruff 27½ cents, calico for bonnet 25 cents, three combs of Johnson 37½ cents, great coat $15.00, pair of woolen stockings $1.00, black lace ribbon 37½ cents, eleven yards red flannel $4.00, pair bone gloves 50 cents, handkerchief 37½ cents, parasol $2.00, frock of Chapman $1.72." The total expenditure of $358.66 included her doctor's bill and medicines, as well as the making of her coffin and the digging of the grave. The largest single item was $22.57 for her school tuition.

Her Worthington cousins contested the value of the work Miranda performed in the Stanbery home and whether this had been credited against her expenses. Everyone expected that an orphan living with a guardian would be treated as one of the family and would work around the household as other family members did, but the question was whether Miranda had been well enough to do sufficient work for her board. Neighbors who testified at the court hearing agreed that Miranda was a sickly girl, but this apparently varied as her condition worsened. Potter Wright testified that he had seen her milking and working around the Stanbery house, as well as passing by on her way to school. Elias Lewis saw her washing dishes and doing "light work such as knitting for the family." Piram Hunt saw Miranda getting dinner and judged, "I should say she did enough to pay for her board." Salome Russell saw Miranda baking and milking and said that Miranda attended a ball till nine o'clock on the Fourth of July before her death, although she did not dance. Moses Maynard described her as "very feeble, scarcely able to walk from the house to the gate which is perhaps four or five rods."[6]

Those who lived or worked in the Stanbery home saw the situation even more closely. Mary Bidwell, another of the orphans in the Stanbery home, said that she frequently heard Mrs. Stanbery "request her [Miranda] not to work for it would injure her health." Almeda Barker, who worked for the Stanberys two years before Miranda's death, testified that Miranda attended school and "worked for herself," but "did nothing of consequence for the family." David Ingham, who lived with and worked for the Stanberys the autumn before Miranda's death, described her as "quite unwell, had chills, and was unable to work." He indicated he frequently harnessed the horse and took her in the gig to the doctor. He considered her "a good deal of trouble," requiring "considerable waiting upon," as did Priscilla Weaver, who was paid ten dollars to nurse Miranda during her final illness.

Several neighbors testified regarding Stanbery's stewardship of Miranda's farm. Samuel Abbott described its status at Miranda's death as being "in much better condition than when he [Stanbery] took charge of it." Abbott recalled Miranda as always appearing well dressed when she rode out in the Stanbery carriage for her health.

The detailed picture of Stanbery's guardianship is one of responsible property management and of kindness toward a sickly girl, who probably unknowingly endangered his entire family with her contagious disease. If Miranda or her mother had legally been able to dispose of their property as they wished, perhaps they would have chosen to designate Miranda's widowed aunt and seven cousins in Worthington as beneficiaries, rather than include all of the New England aunts and uncles. Although Stanbery's stewardship of Miranda's assets was upheld, this legal challenge clearly reveals the responsibilities that accompanied any prestige or economic benefit a justice of the peace received from an appointment as the legal guardian of orphaned children. Officials were expected to be accountable for their public actions, and a leadership role in the community did not offer protection from a challenge to one's public stewardship.

Within a few years Sharon Township, which included Worthington, elected a variety of public officials in addition to justices of the peace and overseers of the poor. Governance was in the hands of three elected individuals: two township trustees and one township clerk. The trustees' task was to establish any necessary rules or regulations, to collect and account for the use of township property taxes, and to supervise the work of other township officials. These included the treasurer, two overseers of the poor, two appraisers of estates and stray animals, two fence viewers, three constables, and five road supervisors.[7] The last were usually geographically distributed to facilitate supervising work crews, since most property owners chose to satisfy their road tax by working themselves or having someone who owed them a debt work for them. Such work was credited at one dollar per day.

Local justices of the peace were responsible to the county court of common pleas, and there is no evidence that their decisions relating to Worthington residents were ever overturned by that body. The county court was granted jurisdiction by the first Ohio constitution for all "common law and chancery" cases, including criminal as well as all "probate and testamentary matters," such as administrations and guardianships.[8] The common pleas court had a president and two or three associate judges. In practice, the president was a legally trained lawyer while the associate judges were usually respected, former justices of the peace.

These were appointed positions, and some measure of their perceived honor is the fact that the title of "Judge" took precedence over
militia officer rank as a form of address. William Thompson was the
first Worthington man selected as a county associate judge in 1808,
but after him the community was then continuously represented
until the mid-1830s by Alexander Morrison, Jr., Recompense Stanbery, and Arora Buttles.[9]

The other official position in the village during this time period
was the postmaster. When Worthington was granted a post office
by the federal government in 1805, Nathaniel Little served briefly
as postmaster. William Robe was appointed postmaster at the same
time that he became the teacher in the academy. This was a political appointment by the postmaster general in Washington based on
local recommendation, but there is no evidence that political patronage became an issue locally until James Kilbourn was elected to
Congress.

This happened in the autumn of 1812, after Ohio's representation increased from one to six congressmen based upon the census of
1810. The Fifth Congressional District, which included Franklin
County, encompassed much of northwestern Ohio, including Lancaster and Newark to the southeast, Eaton and the Indiana boundary
to the west, and the area of present-day Sandusky to the north. It was
a geographic area larger than the state of Connecticut, but was Ohio's
most sparsely settled area.

James Kilbourn announced his candidacy as a Democratic-
Republican whose primary issue was an "ardent desire that a greater
degree of energy should be applied in the present condition of the
nation than has been hitherto manifested for the prosecution of the
present war."[10] This was a position far more popular on the western
frontier than in the New England environment of his youth. Kilbourn
elaborated on his belief in a message to voters the day before the election: "I am fixed in the opinion that the cheapest mode of conducting
a war . . . is with an overwhelming force for an army, a flowing abundance of all the provisions and munitions of war, and the most rapid
movements to every point required."[11]

These sentiments placed him among the most hawkish of the
western war hawks; however, this was what the voters wanted to
hear in the Fifth District, which bordered on and sometimes included
the battle lines. What was more controversial was Kilbourn's ques-

tionable loyalty to the county seat at Franklinton and to the new capital to be built at Columbus. His strong advocacy of Worthington, especially as a site for the state capital and as the location of post roads, had created opponents in the surrounding area. Kilbourn was himself ready to let bygones be bygones and had already established a retail store in Franklinton and was planning one for Columbus. He promised the voters that he was concerned with the prosperity of the entire district and that if elected "shall not disappoint your confidence or ever shame your favor."[12] The argument was evidently persuasive because he won Franklin County, defeating his closest opponent, Joseph Foos, the district's representative to the Ohio Senate, by more than one hundred votes.[13] He also won the whole district and traveled to Washington to take his seat at the opening of the Thirteenth Congress on May 24, 1813.

But even before he attended his first session, Kilbourn was concerned about the conflicting demands of his business affairs and his responsibilities as a congressman. In January, he wrote to Senator Worthington to seek his opinion on whether there would be an extra session in 1813 and, if so, when and how long. He explained that "The situation of my own affairs & the concerns of the Worthington Manufacturing Company, make it particularly desirable for me, that I should not be absent much of the next summer season, or in case it should be necessary, to obtain such previous notice, as will enable me to make the necessary arrangements, that the business may not materially suffer."[14]

Kilbourn was, however, present for the election of Henry Clay as Speaker of the House of Representatives, in what later become known as the War Congress.[15] Much of the debate in the Thirteenth Congress centered on war issues, and Ohio's two senators and six representatives usually voted unanimously to support President Madison's war policies. Kilbourn found himself directly opposing Congressman Timothy Pitkin, a Yale-educated lawyer who had represented the Farmington, Connecticut, district since 1805 and had become a leading spokesman for the Federalist party.[16] Kilbourn had become a westerner, not only geographically but philosophically.

Kilbourn took lodgings at Mrs. Hamilton's boardinghouse on Capitol Hill with a group of six others that included no Ohioans or New Englanders.[17] This was unusual since most congressmen sought lodgings with like-minded individuals from their own region. As few as

15 percent lived in lodgings that had the regional diversity of Kilbourn's boardinghouse during his first two sessions in the capital. The federal city was still being carved from the wilderness, and Washington's isolation rendered congressional boardinghouses the basic social unit of the city. James Young has gone so far as to compare them with modern fraternities.[18] Kilbourn was very much a Washington outsider despite his long acquaintance with Senator Thomas Worthington. Kilbourn had less education than many eastern representatives, but his credentials were as strong as many from the West. He was accustomed, however, to playing the leadership role in his community and was ill-suited to the collegiality and years of committee work that led to leadership roles in Congress.

Kilbourn, however, was not intimidated by more experienced members of Congress. Within a month he rose to offer a resolution requesting a committee be appointed to provide more "protection of the Northwestern frontier against the incursions of savages and other enemies, by granting donations of land to actual settlers . . . ."[19] He was named chairman of a select committee to study this issue and proposed a bill that died on the floor as the House rushed to adjourn by August 2 to avoid the worst of the ague season which plagued the nation's capital. Kilbourn may have departed early to tend to other business, for his last recorded vote was on July 20.

When Congress reconvened on December 6, Ohio's two senators and five of its representatives were present, but James Kilbourn did not arrive until December 22. On January 5, he introduced a resolution to take up his bill that had died in the previous session. Five days later he was joined by Representative Jennings of the Indiana territory in presenting petitions from "sundry inhabitants" praying for donations of land to actual settlers. These petitions suggest Kilbourn had learned an important lesson about the political process, that it is often the loudest constituent voices which receive attention. Much of this session, however, was consumed by debates relating to the war. More than a month was spent considering the pros and cons of what eventually became a bill for a $25 million loan to finance the war. Even issues as important as a proposal for a national bank "slumbered on the table."[20] When Kilbourn attempted to bring his bill to the floor five days before adjournment, a hearing was rejected by a vote of seventy-one to thirty-six.[21]

It was an extraordinary session, where orators like Daniel Webster and John C. Calhoun used their wit to attack or defend the administration's war policies. Washington socialite Mrs. Samuel Harrison Smith wrote her sister that "The debates in congress have this winter been very attractive to the ladies"—and the presence of ladies, in turn, influenced the performance. One gentleman was described as having finished his argument "and was just about seating himself when Mrs. Madison and a train of ladies enter'd, — he recommenced, went over the same ground, using fewer arguments, but scattering more flowers."[22]

One can imagine how this atmosphere must have affected a man of Kilbourn's temperament. Floor votes suggest that he was sometimes absent for three to five days at a time, perhaps attending to other business. He did speak in favor of the House proposal to encourage volunteer enlistments by awarding bonuses of fifty dollars at enlistment, fifty dollars at muster, and eight dollars to every person procuring a recruit. This prevailed over a Senate proposal to cut these bonuses in half.[23]

The third session of the Thirteenth Congress was called into meeting early by President Madison because of the burning of the capital by the British forces. Again, all Ohio senators and representatives were present on September 19, 1814, except Kilbourn, who arrived October 22.[24] Daniel Webster and John Calhoun had arrived only a few days earlier, but a quorum had been conducting business, thus Kilbourn missed the discussion of whether to rebuild or move the seat of national government. Every public building except the post office had been destroyed, and the House of Representatives took up crowded quarters there, appalled by the blackened walls of their former chamber.[25] Mrs. Smith described the capital's destruction to her sister: "Who would have thought that this mass so solid, so magnificent, so grand, which seem'd built for generations to come, should by the hands of a few men and in the space of a few hours, be thus irreparably destroy'd. Oh vanity of human hopes!"[26]

Soon after his arrival, during a debate relating to volunteer enlistments, Kilbourn proposed an amendment "to extend to privates killed during the service, the same provisions for the relief of their widows and children, as is provided in the bill for officer's families." Kilbourn's heart was in the right place, but the measure was defeated because of its broad scope. A few days later Kilbourn presented a memorial from 729 persons, praying that public lands be sold at 12½¢ per acre to actual settlers on the northwest frontier. A request to refer this to the committee on public lands was narrowly defeated by a vote of fifty to forty-eight.[27] Kilbourn had made two changes in his proposal. He now recommended a nominal charge of 12½¢ per acre rather than free land, and he was treating this matter as public-land policy, rather than simply as a war measure for public defense. Two years earlier such a modified proposal might have prevailed, but as the danger on the northwestern frontier diminished there was less need to offer inducements for settlement. There is no evidence that Kilbourn consulted Senator Morrow about his public-land proposal, yet Morrow had chaired the House Committee on Public Lands while serving as Ohio's only congressman until 1812, and he now served on the Senate committee. His support would certainly have been crucial to Kilbourn's proposition.

Kilbourn actively participated in the extended debate regarding a national bank, supporting the measure and at one point offering an amendment to make Chillicothe rather than Pittsburgh a site for taking subscriptions. When the House of Representatives defeated the project, Kilbourn took the floor the next day to offer a new proposal with varying amounts of capitalization. The speaker ruled this out of order for being of the same substance as the rejected bill.[28] Kilbourn understood the issue, but not the legislative process.

The final session of the Thirteenth Congress was heavily devoted to the subject of taxes, seeking means to pay for the war. Kilbourn supported the administration's proposal for personal property taxes on such items as carriages, furniture, and gold watches. Despite his own business, he supported duties on various manufactured goods such as iron, nails, candles, leather and silk hats, umbrellas and parasols, paper, playing cards, saddles, boots, beer and ale, tobacco, cigars, and snuff. He even offered a resolution that the Ways and Means Committee be directed to present a bill for an income tax on those who have "capital vested in public or any kind of stock, or in private loans, or in any other way yielding profits to the owner; and on those who are engaged in professional or other employments, producing an annual income exceeding a certain amount" to be set by the committee. This innovative proposal was defeated by only six votes; it would be another century before such a tax became law.[29]

Kilbourn's first term in Congress reflected support for, and loyalty to, the Madison administration's conduct of the war. Like most congressmen, he was regional in his biases and devoted himself almost exclusively to his proposal for free land for settlers on the northwest frontier. He exhibited true democratic principles in proposing the same relief for the widows of privates as for the widows of officers. He supported taxes on property and manufactured goods, and proposed an income tax, which he evidently considered fair, although both a property and an income tax would have been costly to him personally. There is much in the record of this congressional term that illuminates the strengths and weaknesses of Worthington's founder, and suggests why the community developed as it did.

Kilbourn was a man of creative ideas and liberal instincts, but he was a business entrepreneur whose temperament was ill-suited to the deliberations and negotiations of the legislative process. Congressional power was vested in its committee chairmen, chosen for their tenure and for their expertise on a specific subject or for their oratorical skill. Kilbourn lacked the patience for developing an area of committee expertise and, while he might have relished a role as the Webster or Calhoun of the west, he lacked the education and legal experience that made their rhetoric so effective. Although his attendance was the poorest of any Ohio senator or representative, nevertheless he was officially present—though not always voting—83 percent of the time during the three sessions of his first term in Congress. It is hard to believe that Kilbourn found this a satisfying role, and in light of his commitments with the Worthington Manufacturing Company, it is somewhat surprising that he did not choose to retire at the end of his first term.

The election process, however, required Kilbourn to declare his candidacy before returning for the third session of the Thirteenth Congress. When he addressed the electors on September 8, 1814, the war was essentially over on the northwestern frontier, but the federal capital lay in ruins and there were dangers from Lake Champlain to New Orleans. Kilbourn still had high hopes for his proposal of free land for setters in the northwest, and this was his primary appeal to the voters. He won reelection with a plurality of 2,175 votes, his five challengers splitting the remaining 2,619.[30]

When the Fourteenth Congress convened, Kilbourn missed the entire four-month first session. He claimed this was due to ill health, but one strongly suspects that his business affairs and lack of patience with the legislative process were somewhat relevant. Seven years later he was bitterly attacked for claiming to be ill during this session, and his critics asserted more than one hundred persons were prepared

to state under oath that he had never done more Worthington Manufacturing Company business than during these five months. Dr. Hills,
the Kilbourn family physician, defended his illness and maintained
that he continued to conduct business against his doctor's wishes.[31]
Kilbourn did present his credentials at the second session on January 29, 1817, nearly two months after it convened; and although he
was present and voting during the remaining five weeks, he played no
significant role.[32]

Kilbourn did, however, master the political patronage system.
Within a month of his first arrival in the capital, he secured the appointment of Matthew Mathews, the young man who operated his
retail store at Franklinton and who had recently married his daughter Lucy, as deputy postmaster for the new city of Columbus. He
advised him to move the store to Columbus and to consult with William Robe, the Worthington postmaster, about conducting the postal
business "in the best possible manner." Kilbourn acknowledged that
"This office may give you a little trouble at first, but will be a handsome thing [financially] eventually, and now was the only time to
secure it for years to come."[33]

When Mathews moved from Columbus to Worthington the following winter to assume responsibility for developing the Worthington Manufacturing Company property, Kilbourn advised him to
submit his resignation from the Columbus position quickly so that
"I may deliver it and get Mr. Buttles appointed to the office before
I leave here. There is so much confusion and rascality practiced in the
General Post Office, that I calculate on getting nothing done except
what I attend to personally on the spot." Though Joel Buttles was
awaiting Kilbourn's return to Ohio to marry his stepdaughter Lauretta Barnes, it was not only his prospective son-in-law's welfare that
was in Kilbourn's mind. He assured Mathews that "It will be important to our business to keep the office at the north end of Columbus,
and it will aid our business in many respects . . . to have Mr. Buttles
appointed when you resign."[34]

Ezra Griswold's eldest son, Ezra Jr., had recently moved to Columbus and was actively seeking the postmaster appointment from his
father's friend. Buttles wrote his prospective father-in-law with some
anxiety: "I shall say now as I have often before, that I will not solicit
appointments. Business is, however, greatly increasing and the Post
Office in a couple of years would be of use to a man, and on that ac-

count I should like to have it." In the next sentence he subtly referred to their coming relationship, inquiring how long Kilbourn's business might detain him in the east and expressing the "wish to hasten as far as propriety would allow the day so important to me and to Lauretta."[35] It was quite an appeal from a man claiming not to be soliciting appointments. Kilbourn did attend to the nomination personally before he left Washington, and Buttles remained the Columbus postmaster until he was displaced by the Jacksonian Democrats fifteen years later.

Political patronage has perhaps changed only slightly since Kilbourn's day, but one aspect of a congressional career was certainly quite different. Congressmen in the early nineteenth century did not view service in Washington as a career. In choosing not to run for reelection, Kilbourn was among the two-thirds of his congressional colleagues who did not serve more than two terms.[36] One might justifiably argue that he was saving himself the embarrassment of almost certain defeat over the issue of his poor attendance.

Kilbourn advanced neither his own nor Worthington's political fortunes by serving in Congress. It was an environment ill-suited to his talents. He might have been disillusioned with the legislative process and ineffective as a congressman, but he was in tune with the new political forces in the Republican party that were becoming more entrepreneurial and interventionist as politics turned to issues of economic development.[37] Kilbourn was returning home to devote full time to his business affairs.

As a businessman, Kilbourn was accustomed to making rather than negotiating decisions, and for this he was highly regarded locally. When the Franklin Bank of Columbus, the county's first bank, was chartered in 1816, four of its thirteen elected directors were Worthington men: James Kilbourn, Chester Griswold, Alexander Morrison, and Joel Buttles.[38] They were men who exemplified Curti's finding that above average economic status was closely associated with public leadership roles.[39]

With the end of the war and with Thomas Worthington in the governor's chair at the new capital nine miles south, Worthington businessmen turned their focus to the rising tide of prosperity Ohio was experiencing.

CHAPTER 12

From Reading, Writing, and Arithmetic to Greek, Latin, and Moral Philosophy

— ❖ —

NOTHING MORE VISIBLY marked Worthington's transition from a wilderness settlement to a prospering western village than the completion of the elegant, two-story, brick academy building. Worthington was prepared for a major expansion in the courses of instruction that were available to students. Fortunately, James Kilbourn knew just the man to serve as principal. His nephew, John Kilbourn, had recently received his A.B. degree from "Vermont University," and the Worthington Academy trustees offered him the position at $350.00 per year, to be paid quarterly beginning January 1, 1811.[1] They were eager for this academy to acquire the prestige of the New England classical grammar and preparatory schools upon which it was modeled.

The prospect of four quarters of schooling to be offered annually and taught by a college graduate was almost unheard of in a frontier community only seven years old. It was far more than was available anywhere else in central Ohio. By comparison, the first statistics for common schools in Ohio, nearly thirty years later, showed an average school term of four months and an average teacher's salary of $13.43 per month. As late as 1848, primary teachers in Columbus were paid $160.00 and secondary teachers $200.00 per year.[2] Public school teaching certificates were granted to persons without a college degree well into the twentieth century.

William Robe, who had been teaching the grammar school for five years, became assistant principal of the enlarged academy and continued to teach the grammar school subjects. By summer, the community had a newspaper in which the Worthington Academy course of instruction was advertised. Small children "who do not write" were admitted for $1.50 per term at the discretion of the board of trustees. The basic grammar school curriculum of spelling, reading, writing, and common arithmetic cost students $2.00 per quarter. A course of study including geography, history, English grammar and composition, surveying, and navigation was offered at $3.00 per quarter. An advanced curriculum of higher mathematics, Latin, Greek, rhetoric, logic, natural and moral philosophy, and astronomy was taught for $4.00 per quarter.[3] It was a broad curriculum for what was certainly initially a small student body, but Worthington was already planning to attract students from well beyond its borders.

As Wade has pointed out, subscription schools were one of the first marks of a developing community, easily established with a rented room, a teacher, and a few paying students.[4] Worthington Academy, however, quickly established itself as an educational institution competing for boarding scholars from a large geographic area. Not everyone, of course, shared in this opportunity. In Worthington, as in other communities with subscription schools, a significant number of the local youth were not served at all or only briefly because their parents were unable to pay. This was a critical problem in rapidly growing frontier communities. By 1820, 48 percent of Sharon Township's population—471 of the 983 enumerated residents—were under sixteen years of age, and there were no public schools.[5]

A public exhibition marking the end of the academy's school year on March 19, 1812, opened and closed with instrumental and sacred music and a prayer. Student presentations included an "introductory Latin oration, declamation on the happiness of the United States, oration on eloquence, declamation on the wonders of nature, scene from Shakespeare, declamation on the existence of God, dialogue on dueling, scene from Addison Cato, declamation on American independence, dialogue on city fashions, declamation on the dignity of human nature, dialogue on dancing, declamation on the starry heavens, and several original compositions on various subjects."[6] The crowd was so large that some found it hard to hear, but, apart from that, the newspaper editor awarded both instructors and students "a high degree of commendation." The diversity of presentations was certainly the most elaborate exhibition of culture the frontier community had yet experienced.

John Kilbourn's responsibilities as principal evidently included everything from supervising the rental of the school farmland to collecting unpaid subscriptions and supervising finishing work by carpenters. His report to the trustees in the spring of 1813 suggests that there was a dispute with Solomon Jones, who had leased the farm. Jones contested the number of bushels of corn he owed because the trustees "were to keep the fence in order, which they did not." Another problem was that the carpenters laying the floor had mistakenly used several hundred feet of boards which were the private property of Recompense Stanbery, but which had been delivered to the site along with other boards meant to fulfill Stanbery's subscription. John Kilbourn evidently considered this fiscal management more than he bargained for and billed the trustees five dollars for "my trouble and expense of time" in reconciling the accounts of the "present pecuniary situation of the Worthington Academy."[7] It would appear that there were still unpaid subscriptions and that the institution's financial situation was so fragile that the principal's salary might have been in arrears.

A decade later, the level of learning had been raised, and the title of the institution had been changed. The annual public exhibition at the end of the 1821 school year, by the "young gentleman of the Seminary," took place the day after examinations before an audience of the institution's trustees and the clergy of the Episcopal diocese. The younger students, some as young as eleven or twelve, recited memorized extracts from classical works such as "Scott's Lochinvar, Enoch's Prophecy, Scotts' Helvellyn, Dialogue between Brutus and Cassius, [and] Death of Adam and Eve."[8] More advanced students presented original compositions such as Mortimer R. Talbot's "It is easier to bear misfortune than prosperity," Bezabell Wells, Jr.,'s "Original and fortuitous reputation," Elisha Belcher and John W. Mattoon's "Classical and Mathematical Literature compared," and William Morehead's "The Character of a true Gentleman, and of a Dandy compared." The most advanced students demonstrated their classical language skills: Allen C. McArthur with a Latin dissertation, "De utilitate Lingua Latinae," and Salmon P. Chase with a Greek oration, "De rationibus scribendi, Joanniet Paulo propries." Chase was only thirteen at the time, but he had benefited from classical studies with a private tutor from an early age.[9]

The advanced level of learning exhibited to the public in 1821 had resulted from several changes in the Worthington Academy. John

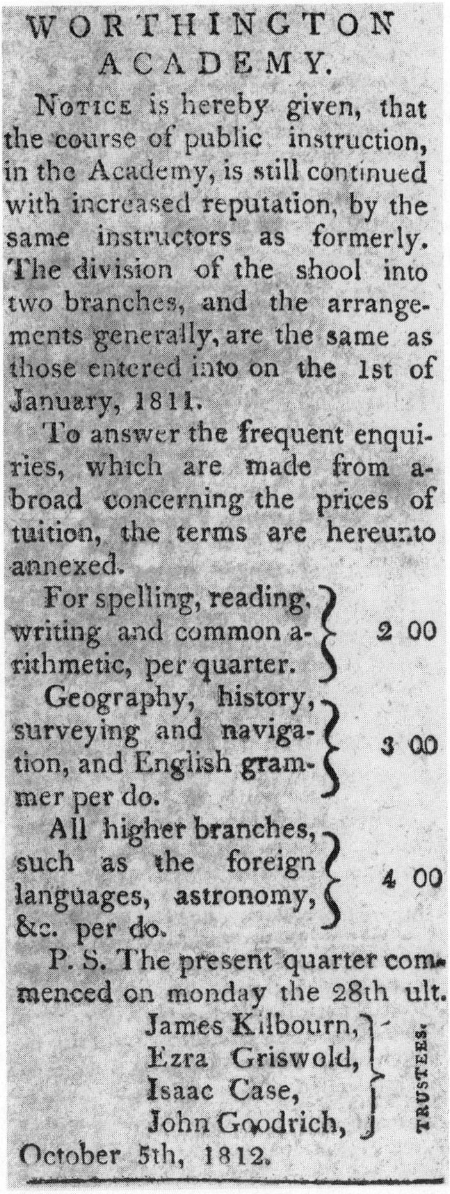

WORTHINGTON
ACADEMY.

NOTICE is hereby given, that the course of public instruction, in the Academy, is still continued with increased reputation, by the same instructors as formerly. The division of the shool into two branches, and the arrangements generally, are the same as those entered into on the 1st of January, 1811.

To answer the frequent enquiries, which are made from abroad concerning the prices of tuition, the terms are hereunto annexed.

For spelling, reading, writing and common arithmetic, per quarter.	2 00
Geography, history, surveying and navigation, and English grammer per do.	3 00
All higher branches, such as the foreign languages, astronomy, &c. per do.	4 00

P. S. The present quarter commenced on monday the 28th ult.

James Kilbourn,
Ezra Griswold,
Isaac Case,
John Goodrich,
} TRUSTEES.

October 5th, 1812.

Fig. 16. An October 5, 1812, advertisement describes the courses of study and the rates of tuition at the Worthington Academy, chartered in 1808. (Taken from *The Western Intelligencer,* Ohio Historical Society)

Kilbourn and William Robe had both moved to Columbus, the former to become the publisher of an Ohio gazetteer and the latter to serve as a clerk in the state auditor's office. There is no record whether John Kilbourn and William Robe left the institution of their own volition to accept opportunities in the growing capital city or whether the arrival and appointment of Rev. Philander Chase displaced them. Rev. Chase moved to Worthington in 1817 to become the rector of St. John's Episcopal Church, a role which will be discussed later, but his relationship to higher education in Worthington deserves special attention.

Chase wrote his son George, "I received from the trustees of Worthington academy the appointment of principal, to oversee the destinies of that institution."[10] His wife was somewhat more frank about both the status of this appointment and Rev. Chase's vision for the institution in a letter to a Connecticut friend: "Mr. Chase is appointed the principal of the academy, an office at present merely nominal, as the foundation of its future fame and usefulness is yet to be laid."[11]

The actual contract between Chase and the academy trustees appointed him "*Principal* or *President*," with powers to direct the course of instruction, the teachers employed, and the students enrolled. Rev. Chase was "in person to teach those who Shall be placed in the Said institution to study the Learned Languages and other Classical pursuits" and was to receive the tuition bills of such "Greek and Latin Scholars."[12] The intent seems to have been both to upgrade the quality of education being offered at the academy and to put together a package of responsibilities sufficient to induce Rev. Chase to settle in Worthington. His income from the academy position was directly related to the number of students he recruited and taught.

Rev. Chase dreamed of an institution west of the Alleghenies that would prepare an educated clergy to serve Episcopal churches throughout the west. It is significant that by 1821 the former "academy" was referred to as the Worthington Seminary; the students were all male, and several were boarding students from outside the Worthington area. This resulted from a new charter granted by the Ohio legislature in February 1819, creating "Worthington College" to offer instruction and award degrees "in all the liberal arts and sciences, in virtue, religion and morality. . . ."[13] Two-thirds of the trustees were still from Worthington, but one-third were from Columbus and Delaware, where Rev. Chase also served as rector of Episcopal congregations. The Worthington Academy was subsumed under the charter of the new Worthington College, and the community again united to raise subscriptions to construct a large, brick wing on the south side of the academy building to serve the college with a "spacious hall for speaking and recitation."[14]

One of the boarding students was Bishop Chase's nephew Salmon P. Chase, who lived with his uncle and attended classes taught by his cousin Philander, Jr. For the most part, young Chase would recall this as a disagreeable experience: "I was simply a farmer's boy doing all kinds of farmer's boy's work. . . . I used to count the days and I wished I could get home, or go somewhere else and get a living by work."[15] His uncle was, by then, feeling the effects of the country's economic depression. The bishop complained that "there was not a dollar left, after satisfying the hired man for the past, wherewithal to engage him for the future." The farm he had purchased at the height of the boom, in the hope that it would support his family, now forced him to "do what the [hired] man would have done; i.e. thresh the grain, haul and cut the wood, build the fires, and feed the stock. . . ." The bishop compared himself to the apostles, who as fishers of men were forced to feed the multitudes, but chafed that he had been forced to leave the higher duties of his calling to serve not tables but *stables*.[16] One has the distinct impression that the bishop escaped such onerous chores by offering his fatherless nephew a home and an education, but that he expected the boy to do extensive farm chores in return for his board.

The young boys attending the seminary were not prepared for college-level studies, and the institution continued to offer primarily the same preparatory work as the former academy. Girls continued to attend, but they were in a separate subscription school with its own teacher and course of study. A sampler made by twelve-year-old Huldah Bull was dated August 19, 1819, and identified Cynthia Barker as preceptress of the Worthington Academy. Mrs. Barker was a thirty-one-year-old widow with two small children, and the courses she offered girls—beyond basic reading, writing, and spelling—concentrated on feminine arts such as needlework and on moral sentiments like those Huldah embroidered on her sampler:

> Jesus permit my gracious hands to serve
> As the first effort of an anxious hand,
> And while her fingers o're the sampler move,
> Engage her tender heart to seek thy love.[17]

While Rev. Chase devoted his aspirations to a seminary for Episcopal clergy, a coeducational subscription school, the Grosvenor's Grammar School, was established in the village to provide schooling for younger children. Many students did not go beyond this level, and Grosvenor's closed its first term with a challenging address to the young scholars and their parents: "It is noble to aspire after the highest degree of excellence. Expect great things, attempt great things . . . Our favored country stands unrivalled in the annals of empire. The population of these states is progressing on a ratio almost unexampled, and it is not improbable that some of you may live to be the legislators and guardians of the future interests of more than fifty millions of souls. How important the duties that will devolve on you!"[18] If one changed the numbers, these could be the stirring words of any contemporary high school commencement speaker. But this address continued with a remarkable challenge to the girls:

And those who are to become mothers of this free born race; how exalted your station amongst the most favored successors, on whom it devolves to perpetuate our civil and religious institutions. That you may be qualified for your high vocation, a correct knowledge of the Grammar, of our language is necessary. Indeed you would be inadequate to the instruction of those infant intelligents, who must derive their first accents from maternal lips, without a thorough English education. I commend your judgement, which prefers useful, to shining accomplishments; and congratulate you, that you are destined to become partners, rather than play things in conjugal life. . . .[19]

The sexist assumption of this challenge, that girls are destined only to be mothers, reflects the nineteenth-century society which endowed men with all legal responsibilities from property ownership to voting rights; yet it is remarkably candid in defining a maternal role that teaches the basic moral values and the foundations of language necessary for democratic citizenship. Frontier women certainly did the work of a partner, but one senses that this community and this grammar school must have been unusually progressive in publicly praising educated married women as "partners rather than play things."

Both Worthington Academy and Worthington College were closely identified with the Episcopal church in terms of the trustees elected to governance, the selection of the principal and faculty, and the content of the course of instruction. This was not unusual, since ministers were often the most educated men in the community and frequently performed dual roles as teachers. Although Rev. Chase's contract called for him to teach the "learned languages and other classical pursuits" in person, he was more frequently absent than present in Worthington due to his responsibilities as bishop of the Ohio diocese. In March 1820, he was joined by his son Philander, Jr., who "took charge of the school." The younger Chase was a well-educated young man who had taught a country school in Connecticut before attending Harvard and had then served as chaplain-teacher on the ship *Guerriere*, whose captain was a friend of his father. Before arriving in Worthington, he had traveled to many of the European capitals from Moscow to Rome.[20] Although he was in ill health, his brief presence in Worthington brought a cosmopolitan perspective to the community and the school.

Academy advertisements during his tenure featured a beginner's curriculum of "reading, spelling & common Writing - $2.50"; a more advanced course of study including "English Grammar, Geography and Arithmetic - $3.00"; the same with "Penmanship, and the higher branches of Mathematics - $4.00"; or classical studies, "Latin - $5.00; or Latin, with Greek or French - $6.00." Bishop Chase's travels throughout the Ohio diocese made the school widely known and attractive to students from several other towns. The fact that "students may board in any respectable family or families in the town (except in taverns)" was an economic benefit for nearby households. Advertisements promised "The price for boarding, lodging, washing, lights and fuel, will not exceed one dollar and fifty cents per week, in cash . . . a principal part if desired may be made in various articles of produce and manufactures."[21]

It is perhaps unfair to assume that the presence of boarding students affected the peaceful atmosphere of the village—the culprits may, in fact, have been homegrown. A letter to the newspaper revealed problems in this time period: "Within two or three weeks past the repose of our citizens has been frequently disturbed, late at night, by a number of profligate, ill-bred boys. . . ." The editor acknowledged, "We do not believe with the writer that there has been any intention to encourage pilfering of fruit or to molest any other property, but a wanton disposition to set at defiance the operations of law . . . has certainly been manifested."[22] College towns have often developed a reputation for ill-advised pranks from their young-adult population, and Worthington seems to have been no exception.

It was not unusual for covenanted communities to take the lead in forming academies and colleges, and Worthington too went into the education business.[23] It was attracting students from the larger cities of Columbus and Delaware to the south and north, but it was facing competition with Granville, which did not aspire to prepare ministers, but was earning an excellent reputation for the preparation of teachers, an occupation for which there was an increasing need throughout the rapidly growing west.[24]

The orations at the close of each school year were popular with the public, but by 1820 Worthington presented a variety of cultural enrichment opportunities for adults as well as youth. Atherton has noted the role of circuses and theatrical entertainments in bringing outside culture to remote towns and villages.[25] Worthington was too small to attract much of this enriching entertainment, but it did rate as a stop for traveling curiosities such as the African lion that was exhibited in an iron cage at Kilbourn's hotel in 1819[26] or the "African Tiger and East India Monkey" presented at Griswold's tavern two years later. This tiger was advertised as "the only one of the kind ever exhibited in this country," but the detailed description of its black spots and yellow color suggests what would today be called a leopard or cheetah. It is curious that such a caged animal was considered an attraction to a citizenry not far removed from forests that still contained occasional bears or bobcats. But advertisers could be sensational, then as now, in describing an exotic beast: "Its ears are short and pointed; its eye is restless, and its whole aspect fierce and cruel."[27] Such sinister words may be tame by modern standards, but they catered to the same audience as the advertisements for a modern monster movie. The animal was obviously a family attraction, with a price of 12½¢ for adults and half price for children.

By 1820 there were also a variety of organizations in the community providing both social interaction and intellectual stimulation. That year the Masonic Lodge, the community's oldest organization, began construction of a building, measuring fifty-four by twenty-four feet, for their meetings. This two-story, brick structure was almost identical in size to the original academy building, but the gabled end facing Main Street was handsomely accented by a brick arch and Masonic emblems. This landmark building survives today as the Ohio Masonic Museum.[28]

When the cornerstone was laid with public ceremony on July 24, it was set in place "with solemn musick" and Grand Master John Snow "applied the square, level, and plumb to the stone in their proper positions and pronounced it well formed, true and trusty." He then, according to ancient custom, scattered corn and poured wine and oil upon the stone and addressed those present. A copper plate listed the five members of the building committee and identified local carpenter Chauncey Barker as the "Architect" and Arora Buttles as the "Principal operative Mason."[29] Lodge members provided the sleepers, joists, and window and door frames as needed, and Buttles's contract called for him to be paid eight dollars for every one thousand bricks laid, and four dollars for every perch of stone.[30] The exterior was completed in four months, and it not only served for Masonic Lodge meetings, but was for a time rented by a subscription school and by the Presbyterian congregation.

Of course the Masonic Lodge was open only to male members, but printer Ezra Griswold, Jr., handled subscriptions for the *Masonic Miscellany and Ladies Literary Magazine* at the newspaper office. This monthly, forty-page publication cost three dollars per year; Griswold recommended it not only to Masonic brothers, but "The ladies also, are especially invited to patronize it; for its secondary object, as the title indicates, is their edification and amusement."[31]

Another organization arose among the craftsmen attracted to the Worthington Manufacturing Company. James Kilbourn's nephew, Arius Kilbourn, was secretary when he announced, "The regular meeting of the Farmers and Manufacturers' and Mechanic Society of Worthington and parts adjacent, are holden on the Friday next preceding every full moon except when the moon fulls on Friday in which case the meeting is on the day of the full moon at 6 o'clock."[32] Although this curious announcement has the hint of a mystic cult, it was apparently a working man's guild that met regularly at the factory boardinghouse.

For those seeking a higher level of culture, the community offered both a philological society and a literary society. While the study of literary works was apparently the purpose of both, nothing is known of the former except that it met at Kilbourn's Worthington Hotel.[33] Perhaps it was open to both women and men or attracted an older clientele than the literary society that met at Griswold's Tavern.

Fig. 17. The 1820 Worthington Masonic Lodge, as it appeared late in the nineteenth century, is now an Ohio Masonic museum. (Courtesy of the Worthington Historical Society)

The Worthington Literary Society, though, is known by a letter to the newspaper, defending its membership and purpose publicly in a controversy that occurred in the spring of 1821. "The Worthington Literary Society is composed mostly of young men of twenty-one years old and under, of good talents and cultivated morals and manners. . . ." Readers were assured that "Numbers of them are members of the first families in town; and the others young gentlemen, whose enterprising spirit has brought them here from various parts, and whose industry, talents and good conduct, have gained for them esteem and general confidence, and a welcome reception and countenance, in the best society here."[34] In fact, the writer concluded that the literary society included most of the respectable young men of the village. Their meetings were described as being chiefly devoted to the study of geography, literature, original compositions, "writings necessary to business," and proposing and discussing questions of common interest. For variety and to perfect public speaking

skills, they had decided to "commit to memory and pronounce publicly some orations." This led to several dialogues and "four or five
full comedies and tragedies having some cheap-made scenery." Step
by step this proceeded and, "in two or three instances, they have received 12½ cents each, from persons attending, towards defraying
their little expenses. . . . It happened unfortunately, that in the form of
their notice for these public exhibitions, they used the word Theatre
which mightily affected the nerves of some few persons. . . ." Ah,
it was the word "theatre" that raised the moral ire of this religious-
based community.

But even more offensive to the strict moral code of some Worthington residents was the practice of gambling, and it was the ac-
cusation of card playing at one of the literary society's theatrical
productions that created furor within the community. The writer explained the incident in detail: "After the citizens were principally
assembled, and seated in the room, there was a short interval of time,
before the exhibition commenced; during which, the society, being
all behind the scene which separated them from the audience . . . a
man took from his pocket a pack of cards, and with three others, one
a stranger, the others some time residents here, to their dishonor,
commenced playing with them." No doubt hoping to redeem the
group in the eyes of the community, the letter writer assured his readers that "This was instantly discovered by the member of the Society
on the outside of the scene; the keeper of the house was notified and
it was instantly stopped. This reprehensible act was done in the back
part of the room, continued but two or three minutes, and was seen
but by a few of the audience; and those few witnessed the prompt
manner in which it was disapproved and suppressed."

It is a scenario that brings to mind the musical-comedy interpretation of early twentieth-century "Trouble in River City,"[35] when the
potential sins of the youth alarmed the town elders in Iowa. The
moral code of early Worthington expected residents to participate in
numerous alcoholic toasts for every celebration and allowed them to
enjoy dancing at community balls, but it frowned on theatrical productions and absolutely condemned card playing and its attendant
gambling. But more importantly, Ohio law specifically prohibited
"cock fighting, horse racing, bullet playing, billiard playing, card playing . . . any other species . . . of gambling . . . for any sum of money,
or other article of value."[36] Every person committing such an offense

was to be fined not less than two nor more than twenty-five dollars. It was a serious charge that could have cost Griswold his tavern license. But the Worthington Literary Society survived this incident and the subsequent turmoil, for records of its meetings continued to mid-century. One suspects, however, that members may have confined future meetings more to discussion of members' papers than to theatrical productions.

Hine has noted the extent to which a campaign for a specific institution or civic improvement tended to unite a community,[37] and to a large degree this was true of the Worthington Academy during the first two decades of the town's existence. Moreover, the nature of this unifying institution established a reputation for the community in the education business and an image of the village as a cultured place to settle.

All Kinds of Manufacturies
which Experience May Advise

— ◈ —

FRONTIER NEWSPAPERMEN were wont to report the mythic marvels of their particular towns, each describing his own prospering
Main Street in detail. Daniel Boorstin acknowledges the characteris-
tic American boosterism of such descriptions and expresses some
appreciation for those writers who resented having their rosy accounts challenged simply because the objects or events had "not yet
gone through the formality of taking place."[1] Surely Boorstin would
sympathize with James Kilbourn, whose enthusiasms frequently ran
some distance ahead of actuality; Kilbourn's redeeming virtue was
his unwillingness to be defeated by failure, and he repeatedly committed all of his resources to make his newest dream a reality.

In February 1812, within days of the defeat of Worthington's bid
for the state capital, Kilbourn advertised that he was closing all of
his existing store accounts and would take legal action against any
creditors failing to pay promptly.[2] Within weeks, "The Worthington
Manufacturing Company, James Kilbourn, Agent" advertised that
it had received from New York a large store of "European and India
Goods" in addition to a great variety of domestic goods from Kentucky, Tennessee, and Pittsburgh. All were available at "their store-
house (late the store of James Kilbourn) in Worthington."[3] When Kilbourn decided to focus on the expansion of his business operations,
his first move was to assume a broadly based company name that
would accommodate his long-range vision. Although the Worthington Manufacturing Company was at this point nothing more than

Kilbourn's retail store, he already visualized a chain of retail stores from central to northern Ohio that would be supported by a variety of manufacturing enterprises operating in Worthington.

Kilbourn did not have a monopoly on commercial business in Worthington. Alexander Morrison, Jr., advertised an "elegant assortment of merchandize" from Philadelphia at his store north of Griswold's Tavern.[4] His stock included medicines, clothing, groceries, and household furnishings such as queensware. Perhaps most interesting, was the fact that Lemuel Kilbourn was advertising his fulling mill on Salt Creek, south of Chillicothe, and was offering his product at Morrison's store in Worthington rather than through his brother.[5] This adds to the suspicion that some disagreement between the brothers had led to Lemuel's move from Worthington several years earlier.

James Kilbourn attempted, without success, to have the Worthington Manufacturing Company incorporated by the Ohio General Assembly. The house of representatives objected to the first article, which defined the company's purpose—perhaps because of its breadth and the vagueness of the proposed manufacturing and retail operations, or perhaps because Kilbourn was seeking to include out-of-state investors.[6] The legislature had just passed a comprehensive act regarding the incorporation of manufacturing companies, and it is not clear what special dispensation Kilbourn might have sought for his Worthington company.[7] The proposed articles of association may, however, have been printed locally and circulated to local and eastern investors by Kilbourn and his representatives.[8]

In April the company opened a retail store "at William Domigan's" in Franklinton that advertised the same assortment of imported and domestic goods as the Worthington store.[9] A chain of retail stores was not a new idea to the Ohio frontier. Marietta merchants, Backus and Woodbridge, had successfully established a series of stores in towns north of their Marietta base, and Kilbourn was undoubtedly well acquainted with these former Connecticut men.[10] Within a few years the Worthington Manufacturing Company moved its Franklinton store to Columbus and added retail outlets in Delaware, Sunbury, Norton, and Sandusky.[11] As population moved north after the war, the Worthington Manufacturing Company stores were there to serve their needs. The future looked rosy indeed.

On May 7, 1812, "James Kilbourn, George Fitch and Associates" bought fifty-two acres, including the "lower sawmill," southwest of

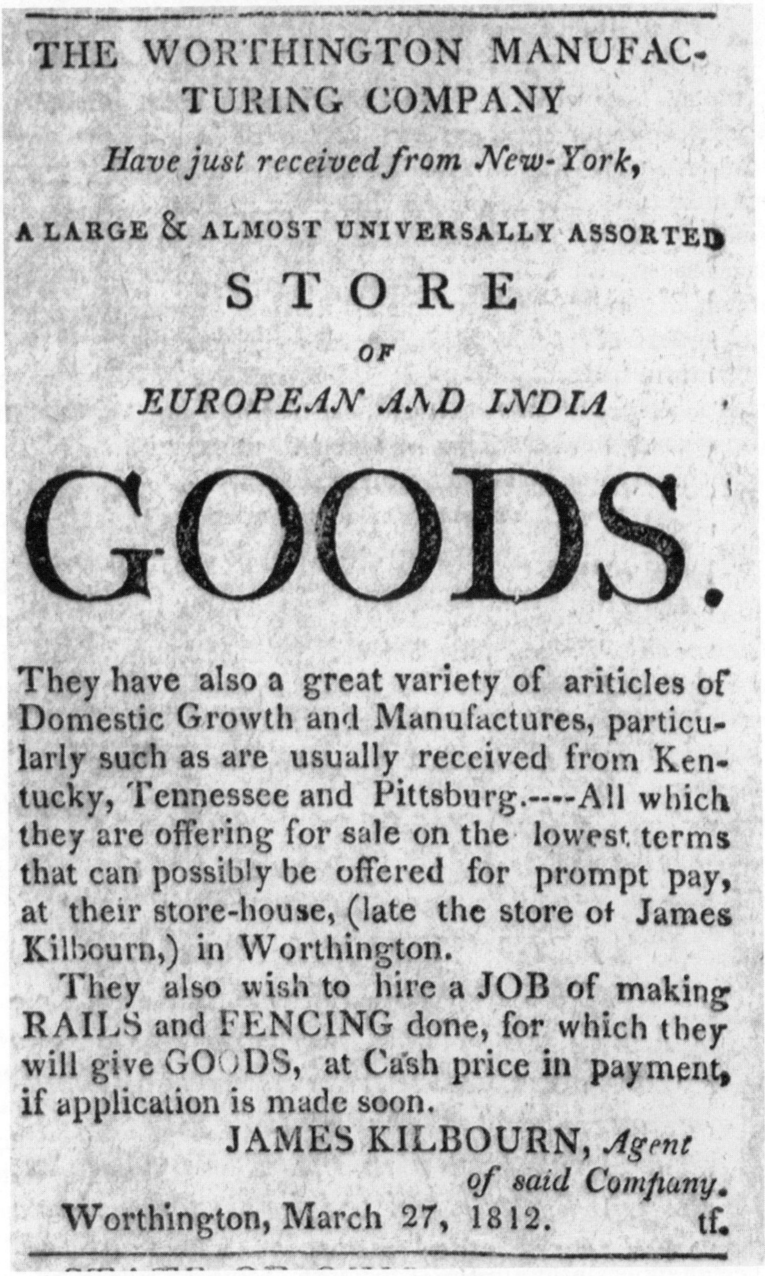

THE WORTHINGTON MANUFAC-TURING COMPANY

Have just received from New-York,

A LARGE & ALMOST UNIVERSALLY ASSORTED

STORE

OF

EUROPEAN AND INDIA

GOODS.

They have also a great variety of ariticles of Domestic Growth and Manufactures, particularly such as are usually received from Kentucky, Tennessee and Pittsburg.----All which they are offering for sale on the lowest terms that can possibly be offered for prompt pay, at their store-house, (late the store of James Kilbourn,) in Worthington.

They also wish to hire a JOB of making RAILS and FENCING done, for which they will give GOODS, at Cash price in payment, if application is made soon.

JAMES KILBOURN, *Agent*

of said Company.

Worthington, March 27, 1812.   tf.

Fig. 18. This March 27, 1812, advertisement describes goods available at the retail store that James Kilbourn was expanding into the Worthington Manufacturing Company. (Taken from *The Western Intelligencer*, Ohio Historical Society)

the village on the banks of the Whetstone River, as a site for manufacturing operations.[12] This was platted by Kilbourn into forty-three
lots plus a large "Mechanic's Square" and "Garden Square" on either
side of Factory Street, the main road between the mill and the southwestern corner of the village (see fig. 19).[13] Kilbourn immediately
advertised to hire "an active and stout Young Man, as a common
laborer . . . from one to six months, one who is acquainted with
making Rails & Fencing. . . ."[14]

By July he had acquired a shipment of 103 Merino sheep, the breed
so prized for their fine wool that it might sell for five to six times the
price of common wool.[15] Thirty-six of these were bucks, and Kilbourn
advertised that all but three, which were retained for the Worthington Manufacturing Company flock, were available "to let to ewes
for half the increase." He also promised a "manufactory in complete
operation the coming year," which would pay $1.00 per pound for
half-blood merino wool, $1.50 for three-quarter, $1.75 for seven-
eighths, and $2.00 for pure merino wool.[16] Kilbourn was planning to
draw on his early experience in the Connecticut woolen mill to establish a similar facility in Worthington; the long, staple merino wool
was essential for the premium woolen cloth he hoped to produce. He
realized few farmers could pay cash for a merino ram, but a number
might be willing to upgrade their flock on shares—particularly if they
were promised a market for premium wool. The merino shipment
from the east evidently arrived ready for shearing, for Kilbourn advertised that hatters could be supplied within one month with "full
blooded merino lambs wool at a reasonable price."[17]

It is important to remember that this business enterprise was
being launched during the same months that the United States declared war against England. Kilbourn was then a major in the Ohio
militia with responsibilities for a battalion, and it was during this
same period that he decided to run for a seat in Congress.[18] Nevertheless, all Worthington Manufacturing Company advertisements were
signed by James Kilbourn as agent, and there is every indication that
he had sole decision-making authority for the company. The first evidence of an expansion in the scope of the company was an advertisement in January 1813, between Kilbourn's election and the opening of the congressional session, which promised workman a share
of company stock. This advertisement solicited journeymen "of temperance and steady application to business" as blacksmiths, tanners,

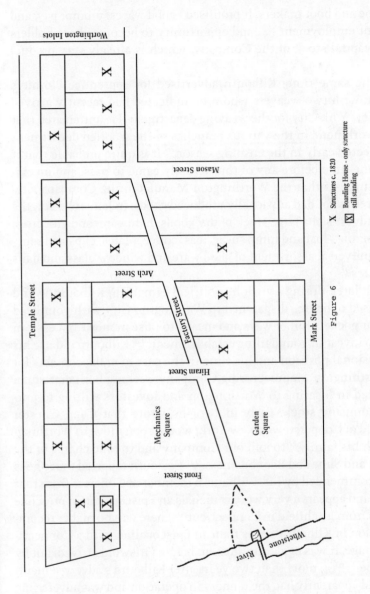

Fig. 19. Worthington Manufacturing Company Plat

Worthington Inlots

Temple Street

Mechanics Square

Garden Square

Front Street

Hiram Street

Factory Street

Mark Street

Arch Street

Mason Street

River

Whetstone

X   Structures c. 1820

⊠   Boarding House - only structure
     still standing

Figure 6

and shoe and boot makers. It promised "good wages, prompt pay, and constant employment . . . and opportunity to become share-holders in the capital stock of the Company, which is already very productive."[19]

At the same time, Kilbourn advertised for apprentice clothiers to work with two weavers whom he indicated had recently arrived from New York City for the weaving department. He anticipated that other workmen "in the various branches of the woollen department are expected early in the ensuing season." It is quite probable that it was some time before any of this actually came to pass, and no evidence suggests that the Worthington Manufacturing Company's retail stores as yet had any locally produced goods. In January 1813, the stores advertised a large stock of dry goods, hardware, and groceries, emphasizing "loaf and lump sugar, teas, coffee, plates, cups and saucers, an universal assortment of glass ware and window glass and nails of all sizes."

Much later, during a vitriolic political campaign, Kilbourn would be accused of being "dispatched to Washington City with your head and your pockets full of ways and means to raise money from eastern funds to invest in your darling establishment."[20] Kilbourn did use his congressional position and his time in the east to make contacts for the Worthington Manufacturing Company, seeking both craftsman interested in locating to Worthington and investors willing to purchase company stock. Early in 1814 he wrote that Capt. Chester Griswold of Cooperstown, New York, would soon move to Worthington with his family, "to join our Company and to take charge of the tanning and Shoe and Boot business."[21] Kilbourn reported that "he is well recommended by Mr. Williams a member of Congress from that district and appears a very worthy man. is an Episcopalian in principle and was from Litchfield in Connecticut." There was no higher recommendation in Kilbourn's eyes than an Episcopalian with a Connecticut heritage. It was evidently autumn before Griswold arrived, but by December 1814, more than two years after Kilbourn's advertisement, Griswold apparently had the tannery in operation and was advertising for four or five journeymen boot and shoemakers at the Worthington Manufacturing Company shop. He also offered "CASH for hides and skins and for good Tanners Bark."[22] Ironically, by the time the western frontier was secure and craftsmen were again willing to move west, the army's demand for material such as boots had nearly evaporated.

Young Matthew Mathews, who married Kilbourn's daughter Lucy in 1813,[23] became the on-site manager for the Worthington Manufacturing Company development, but Kilbourn was micromanaging everything about the project from Washington. In February 1814, Kilbourn expressed concern for Mathews's ill health "owing to your building the dam. You must purge your blood of the impurities imbibed while at work in the river and about the old dam. . . . I am glad to hear that the work on the mill is progressing, but I have not been able to obtain a bolt of cloth in all Philadelphia that I would like to purchase."[24] Clearly the woolen mill had not been built as quickly as Kilbourn had hoped because of the need for rebuilding or enlarging the existing dam. His unsuccessful search in Philadelphia for cloth to be used as a model for the new mill's product probably explains his absence from congressional votes for several different weeks during February and March.

Though Kilbourn anticipated a busy spring, no detail was too small for his attention:

Is the nail shop in operation and how is it doing? Did you get the Waggon & Guns from Mr. Avery? Did you obtain the deed from Zophar Topping? How is Capt. Barker and Mr. Weaver doing relating to finishing the rooms in the House & in preparing material for building in the Spring and Summer? I have heard that Capt. Barker has the Rheumatism is he laid by much of the time? Has Mr. Stansbery got the sheep in keeping? How is the lower saw mill doing & who attends it? Has all the iron come on from Pittsburgh yet & if not, how much & what sort has come? Is Mr. Maxfield informed as I requested him to be, that we shall want many bricks next summer? Has he examined the clay on the factory lots & how does he find it & where the best? We shall want the brick work due from Leut. A. Buttles, as soon as it can possibly be done in the Spring; of this you will advise him. Have you engaged any hands to work at making brick & if so how many? & if none, have you any in prospect?

Kilbourn's micromanagement from Washington must be viewed in light of his absentmindedness during his exploratory trip with Nathaniel Little in 1802, when he forgot his watch or luggage. Kilbourn felt a need to control all decisions, but he frequently became responsible for more details than he could handle. In the same letter he assured Mathews that "I am not able to tell you where the notes can be found which you mention, but they are safe somewhere; present my compliments to Capt. Sage & to Mr. Case & tell them that I will find & forward them as soon as I come home."

Kilbourn certainly had difficulty in delegating authority, and his record-keeping methods could be charitably described as "casual." He was undoubtedly a difficult man to work for, but he knew how indispensable young Mathews was to him. Lucy Mathews gave birth to their first son that spring, and Mathews expressed a desire to start farming on his own. Kilbourn responded, "if you do, I cannot think of living, or if I do, I might as well not. It will be impossible for me to go on with business without your assistance every day. Furthermore, it will be best for yourself, I am confident, however it may now appear to you." This is dramatic testimony in Kilbourn's own words of his ability to make friends and family feel guilty if they did not accept his wishes, and at the same time it illustrates his absolute confidence in his own knowledge of what was best for his family and friends.

When Congress adjourned, Kilbourn traveled to New York City and New England to seek investors for the company and artisans interested in migrating west. In June, he wrote to Mathews in a jubilant mood from his old hometown of Berlin, Connecticut: "Have suceeded in my business here beyond my most sanguine expectation. Have obtained a very handsome addition to the stock of our Company. One gentleman at whose house I was sick in Rhode Island and where I received the kindest attention has taken ten thousand dollars of our stock. I have with me a draft on New York and Philadelphia for the whole amount."[25] Money in hand was welcome indeed, but Kilbourn had, knowingly or unknowingly, sold his soul to James DeWolf, a merchant and shipowner who had made a fortune after the Revolutionary War as the captain of a slave-trading ship. During the recent war with England, his armed brig "Yankee" operated as a privateer, capturing more than $5 million of British property. He built a cotton mill at Coventry, Rhode Island, but was left with abundant funds to seek investment opportunities.[26] Kilbourn convinced DeWolf to purchase considerable land in central Ohio as well as to invest in the manufacturing company.

Land was one of the inducements that Kilbourn regularly used to attract not only investors but craftsmen who might migrate west. That summer the company advertised for apprentices: two "at the scyth & axe & other blacksmith business," two at "shoe & Bootmaking," one at "morroco shoes," one at the "Hatters Trade," and one at the "clothier's trade." There were a variety of jobs available at different levels of skill. Journeymen were wanted in the "Cabinet and Chairmaking business"; a "good brick moulder" and six "hands at common labor" were promised "good wages and prompt pay." But everyone was assured that "valuable land and well situated, may be had in payment for labor, if desired." The opportunity to become a landowner was still the greatest attraction the west had to offer, and Kilbourn was still in the lucrative surveying and real estate business.[27]

Kilbourn's vision for the Worthington Manufacturing Company operations extended north to Lake Erie and a site at the entrance to Sandusky Bay where he proposed a city that would become the lake's principal commercial harbor. This site was part of the "Firelands," in the western portion of the Connecticut Reserve, set aside for those who had suffered property losses in the Revolutionary War.[28] About 1811, Kilbourn persuaded Zalmon Wildman, a Danbury, Connecticut, merchant who was one of the owners of this site, of its potential for a port city that would provide access to central Ohio and the state capital.[29] While in Congress, Kilbourn sought federal support for a road linking the site to Columbus, but he was hampered by the facts that the city of Sandusky was no more than a paper plan and that some of the projected road would be forced to cross territory reserved by treaty for the Indians. Wildman replied that "if peace should not be obtained, the road would be indispensible, and if it goes through the land reserved for the savage enemy, I do not think that his title is so holy that I would regard it in time of war."[30] Despite Wildman's cavalier dismissal of Native American claims, the peace settlement made the road less urgent, and the city of Sandusky was slow to develop.

Kilbourn wasn't the only Worthington businessman interested in this site. Lake fish were a prized commodity in central Ohio. In 1814, eight Worthington subscribers led by Dr. James H. Hills put up the funds to build "a fishing net to be eight rods long and 12 feet wide and made of hemp for the purpose of fishing at lower Sandusky. . . ." The fishing net company's expenses for the year were $45.11, but the quantity of their catch is unknown. Several notations of expenses for salt, help to clean fish, and "halling" fish attest to the fact that the project had at least some success.[31]

The close of the war increased the flood of migration into Ohio and Indiana, and inflation ran rampant as land speculators purchased on credit and hoped for quick profits from resales. The Worthington Manufacturing Company grew to include a variety of artisans and was rapidly attracting others. Besides tanner Chester Griswold and others, it enticed Orange Johnson, a hornsmith and combmaker who quickly became one of the community's most prosperous businessmen.[32] Potter Wright, who came west to run a cotton mill that failed to materialize, founded a weaving card and machinery factory which prospered under the motto "Flourish ye western manufacturers."[33] Likewise, John Snow, a Rhode Island jeweler who moved west to manage the Worthington retail store, became an important leader in both the local and the state Masonic Lodges. Numerous young men found work in various company operations, crowding the company boardinghouse near the river and bringing vigor and vitality to the local economy.

In December 1816, the Ohio General Assembly extended the existing law regarding the incorporation of manufacturing companies. The "Articles of Association of the Worthington Manufacturing Company" were signed by thirteen subscribers on April 11, 1817, before local Justice of the Peace Recompense Stanbery and were filed the next day with the Franklin County Court of Common Pleas and the next week with the secretary of state.[34] This was the procedure specified in the 1812 law, and the company articles followed the state law item by item. It is not clear why Kilbourn waited five years to take this step or whether any changes were made from the articles that the company had been informally using since 1812. It is possible that he unsuccessfully sought authority to include out-of-state stockholders in the Ohio incorporation and to increase the amount of capital funding. There appear to have been several eastern investors who do not appear on the 1817 articles of association whose combined investment may have been as great or greater than the local subscribers, which would have brought the company's stock well above the $100,000 limit imposed by the Ohio legislature on manufacturing incorporations in Ohio.[35]

Article I of this incorporation defined the Worthington Manufacturing Company's purpose to establish "an extensive Manufactory of the various kinds of Woollen Cloth; with Wool Carding and Cloth dressing; of Fur and felt Hats; Leather; and the various manufactures of which Leather is a part; Blacksmithing in its various branches; a manufactory of Pot and Pearl ashes and generally any and all kinds of manufactories which experience may advise, and the company think fit and profitable for them from time to time to establish. . . ." Beyond manufacturing, the company was "to purchase, export and sell any and all kinds of the Country productions which we shall judge profitable . . . to divide into as many branches [retail stores] as we shall think expedient; and to purchase and hold, or sell, exchange and convey any property or estate real, personal or mixed which the Company or their officers and agents duly authorized may deem useful and expedient." This was apparently the article that the Ohio legislature found objectionable. Kilbourn clearly believed in the broad vision and rejected any attempt to narrow the company's focus. It was intentionally broad enough to include his land office as well as his original store.

Other sections of this agreement placed the company headquarters at Worthington, authorized $100,000 of capital stock in 1,000 shares worth $100 each, vested control in a board of five annually elected trustees who would appoint a president and secretary from their group, and specified stockholder meetings held semiannually or otherwise at the discretion of the president. The thirteen subscribers who signed these articles represented exactly 1,000 shares worth $100,000. Of these, James Kilbourn held or represented 171 shares worth $17,100, Chester Griswold 83 shares, carpenters Chauncey Barker and John Goodrich 147 shares between them, Matthew Mathews 65 shares, and the same for brickyard manager Amos Maxfield, sawmill operator Samuel Baldwin, blacksmith Levi Pinney, and cooper Moses Brown. It is not known how much actual cash any of these local shareholders invested or whether they received any dividends prior to 1817. No doubt some, and perhaps all, of the above shares were acquired in return for services rendered, as Kilbourn had promised in his January 1813 advertisement. All evidence suggests that local shareholders contributed labor "in kind," and that cash for capital improvements and stocking the retail stores was provided by eastern investors.

In his history of banking in Ohio, Huntington has referred to the prosperity of this speculative period following the war as "the golden age of the western country."[36] In 1815, under pressure from eastern banks that had suspended specie payments, Ohio banks followed suit and the legislature passed the famous "bonus law" which increased the number of bank charters dramatically and made the state a 20 percent stockholder. The Franklin Bank in Columbus, with four Worthington men on its board, was one of those chartered under this law in October 1816. The suspension of specie payments encouraged unauthorized notes by unchartered and unregulated institutions and eventually the complete collapse of citizens' confidence in paper money. But for the moment the boom continued, and the Worthington Manufacturing Company was one of those issuing its own notes for the payment of goods and services.

The company established "mercantile houses" in New York and Baltimore and was shipping goods from New York City up the Hudson River, across the lakes, and by wagon to its chain of stores from Sandusky to Columbus. It was also using wagons to bring goods from Baltimore and Kentucky to the same stores and boasted that customers would find "the most reasonable prices . . . which have ever been offered in the state of Ohio."[37] Utter cites this as the first evidence of the opening of trade between central Ohio and New York City by way of the Hudson River, anticipating the Erie Canal.[38] It was all part of Kilbourn's plan that Sandusky should be the major port on Lake Erie and that it would be connected to the state capital through Worthington. Calvin Case, another Kilbourn son-in-law, was persuaded to leave Worthington to start the company store at Norton, but died while on an eastern business trip in 1819.[39]

By 1818, however, it was no longer necessary to import all of the store goods. From their own factories at Worthington, the company now advertised leather goods "such as Saddles, Bridles, Boots, Shoes, &c.; Iron Tools, of almost every description, for Farmers' and Mechanics' purposes; Hats of all sorts and sizes; Woolen Goods of almost every description, from superfine broad cloth to the most common cloth, Blankets, &c."[40] There was plenty of competition in the booming economy, with at least five other merchants advertising a similar line of goods in Columbus, but none had the local manufacturing base of Kilbourn's enterprise.[41] It had taken only six years to convert his dream to reality—but with this achievement in Kilbourn's hand, the western economy crashed. In July 1818, the Bank of the United States suddenly reversed itself by restricting credit and requiring state banks to redeem their paper notes. Many of the western debts involved mortgages on inflated land that now could not be sold at any price, and certainly not for specie. As one writer concluded, "The [U.S.] Bank was saved and the people were ruined."[42]

Kilbourn had already lost a $124.38 judgment for defaulting on a note to John Walker, and the recent incorporation may have been an attempt to divert lawsuits from himself to the company.[43] Throughout 1818 and 1819 suits were filed by several creditors of the Worthington Manufacturing Company, involving hundreds or even thousands of dollars.[44] But the most serious threat was a lawsuit from its major eastern stockholder, James DeWolf, seeking to recover his investment.[45] Kilbourn, and perhaps others, evidently persuaded DeWolf to withdraw this suit by deeding him some of the company property as surety.[46]

The Worthington Manufacturing Company was, in modern terms, a "highly leveraged" operation. Like all merchants, its stores carried customer accounts on the books for months or even years. Clark describes one New England ledger in which three-fifths of the accounts showed no evidence of ever being closed. Outstanding debts ranged from four months to over thirteen years, with many not repaid until administrators sorted out the estates of the deceased.[47] The rapid growth of the Worthington Manufacturing Company's stores and the frequent changes of young managers left record keeping and collection methods open to question; however, money was in short supply everywhere, and Kilbourn was, no doubt, correct in complaining that the company was owed thousands of dollars that it had not been able to collect. Many of its eastern suppliers refused to extend more goods on credit, and without specie to repay its debts or to purchase goods for its retail stores, the company was forced to take the distressing step of closing stores. In January 1819, Christopher Ripley, clerk of the Columbus store, announced that its stock had been sold, "must close the business there as soon as practicable," and requested that all accounts be settled. John Snow dissolved his partnership with the company and purchased the stock of the Worthington store. R. W. Cowles, company cashier, refused to redeem a counterfeit twenty dollar note and reminded the public that "The Worthington Manufacturing Company has never issued notes larger than ten dollars."[48]

Thomas Webb, a New England Masonic brother who had met Kilbourn while in Worthington on lodge business in 1816, committed some of his eastern assets to purchase 150 shares in the company and purchased a house and farm in Worthington with the expectation of establishing a cotton factory at the company site.[49] It seems likely that the association of Masonic leaders Webb and Snow accounts for street names such as Mason, Temple, Arch, Mark, and Hiram on the company plat filed in 1819 (see fig. 19). Snow had purchased a house from Kilbourn and a partnership in the manufacturing company's store when he came west in 1817.[50]

Webb expressed approval when he learned from Snow of the retrenchment: "You know that it has always been my opinion that the business was too much scattered and that it never could succeed until many of the *Branches* were lopped off, and the *body, roots,* and limbs cleansed from the ravages of rust and sloth."[51] Webb was apparently urged by some of the eastern investors to take over management of the company, and he was en route to Worthington to consider the prospects of operating both a cotton factory and the entire company when he died unexpectedly of "apoplexy" at Cleveland.[52]

But retrenchment was not enough. Kilbourn's son-in-law, R. W. Cowles, who was serving as the company cashier, wrote his father in New England quite frankly: "The times are now of the most difficult, money is so scarce that a great many are troubled to pay who owe money & perhaps have plenty property . . . ." The majority of people in Ohio were land poor, and as Cowles explained, "The Worthington Company have more debts than they can pay . . . they have a great many unsettled accounts due them . . . Col. Kilbourn is employed in closing their concerns in the best manner he can."[53] Recent historians acknowledge reasonably good prospects for upward mobility on the frontier, but all too reasonable was also "the possibility of going broke."[54]

Each failure caused another; in what must have been the irony of ironies, the Franklin Bank was forced to sue James Kilbourn and his associates, the same man who had just the previous year led its slate of elected directors.[55] How humiliating it must have been for Kilbourn to be sued for $4,000 by his fellow bank directors. The court sold "80 head of sheep, 4 cows and 1 waggon," but there were no bidders for real estate.[56] Kilbourn was personally liable for the amount of company stock he owned or had guaranteed, and all of his assets were at risk. It was a problem afflicting all levels of society. In Cincinnati, Martin Baum reportedly liquidated more than $200,000 in assets to meet debts, and the famous physician Daniel Drake was forced to move into a log cabin that he dubbed "Mount Poverty."[57]

The Columbus newspaper, like others throughout Ohio, was full of advertisements for sheriff's sales. One of them, on June 9, 1821, had a special poignancy for the village of Worthington for it included Kilbourn's farmland and lots in the village, including his 1804 brick house, the "Worthington Hotel," and the commercial building that originally housed his retail store, his land office, central Ohio's first newspaper, and more recently the Worthington Manufacturing Company store.[58] Fortunately, Kilbourn's brother-in-law, Lincoln Goodale, and two step-sons-in-law, Joel Buttles and Cyrus Fay, were prosperous enough to purchase the Kilbourn home and allow James and Cynthia and their five children still at home to continue living there.[59]

Years later Kilbourn described this unfortunate period with wry humor: "On finding myself again totally without means except some physical strength and a mind not greatly discomposed, and concluding not to hang, drown or get drunk, I took up the compass again and went into the woods."[60] At the time, his son-in-law R. W. Cowles painted a much grimmer picture: "Col. Kilbourn is much harassed by debts of the Company, & has his property all executed though he retains possession of considerable yet—he has spent his time surveying in the lands purchased above for the last three or four months & has not dared to remain at home lest he should be imprisoned." But Cowles cautioned his father, "this last matter you will not mention as he has many friends & acquaintances in your Country & might hurt him."[61]

The most significant problem was James DeWolf's lawsuit against the Worthington Manufacturing Company, whose only remaining assets were the land and buildings on the Whetstone River.[62] The local craftsmen working there had lost the company retail stores as outlets for their products, and prices for all commodities had dropped dramatically in the cash-starved western economy. Local shareholders might have weathered the depression by depending on barter, but there were no means to repay eastern investors who had no stake in the future welfare of the community and were only concerned about recouping their investments.

By 1822 DeWolf was angry, and his suit against James Kilbourn, Chester Griswold, Benjamin Gardiner, and Ezra Griswold was clearly aimed at the persons with property assets. His attorney argued that DeWolf had made a loan to James Kilbourn, who was personally liable "as the said W. M.Company was not incorporated . . . when the original debt was contracted."[63] In essence, the $10,000 that Kilbourn had considered a purchase of company stock was being interpreted by DeWolf as a personal loan that was long overdue. In October 1818, DeWolf had received promissory notes backed by deeds to certain manufacturing company properties, but his attorney claimed a "mistake" had been made by Justice of the Peace Ezra Griswold in drawing the deed. The suit, for a debt that now totaled $14,896.92 with interest, was satisfied by an execution against all of the company property west of Front Street, which included the woolen mill, sawmill, the dam's water rights, and the company boarding house; the three-acre Garden Square; and the two lots in the northwest corner of Arch and Factory Streets, and the buildings thereon. These were appraised at a total value of $8,760.00, and DeWolf's $8,000.00 bid was the only one received. DeWolf achieved vengeance, but the vacant buildings he acquired soon deteriorated and must have been an empty reward. The only survivors were the few craftsmen who were able to go into business for themselves.

Although the depression of 1819 was hard on farmers, with prices a fraction of their levels two or three years earlier, they did not suffer the shocks as severely as did the manufacturing centers unless their land was heavily mortgaged.[64] Most farmers raised diverse products that could be consumed by the household, exchanged with neighbors, exchanged for credit at local stores, or shipped to market.[65] The 1820 census recorded 116 men engaged in manufacturing in Sharon Township, no doubt nearly all in Worthington, and 184 employed in agriculture.[66] It was these farms surrounding Worthington, as well as the barter and credit systems that the community had employed from the beginning, which largely sustained the village during these hard times.[67] Typical of most small businessmen, Moses Brown ran accounts at his cooper shop for regular customers. From September 1817 to March 1821, Orange Johnson's bill was $8.61, mostly for repairs: "set four hoops, 25 cents; repairing two tubs, 50 cents; repair churn, 25 cents; well bucket, 75 cents. . . ."[68]

Merchant Caleb Howard routinely took materials on consignment from local craftsmen. A typical receipt showed he "Received of Sylvester Hough fifty Grass Scythes & three cradle Scythes & twenty-three hoes, all of which I am to sell or return when called for."[69] Grass scythes were to sell for $2.50, cradling scythes for $3.25, and hoes for $1.12½ each.[70] Howard was to receive 25¢ commission on each scythe and half that for each hoe sold.

Some intrepid souls even dared to start a new business in the face
of the depression. When Smith and Hor opened a store in Worthington
in 1820, they advertised that they would accept "notes from the bank
of Cincinnati, J. H. Piatt, Urbana paper and Griswold's notes of Worthington."[71] No one was willing to accept paper money unless they
were close enough to the issuing institution to know its integrity personally. It is worth noting that by 1820 neither Franklin Bank notes
nor Worthington Manufacturing Company notes were acceptable
locally. Tavern keeper Ezra Griswold was one of many throughout
the state who issued local "shinplasters" that were redeemable at his
tavern. These were small in value, in this case in denominations of
6¼¢, 12½¢, 50¢, $1.00, and $2.00.[72] The amounts were purposely
small, but sufficient to keep a few local transactions moving.

Another new business was the *Franklin Chronicle,* a newspaper
published by Ezra Griswold, Jr., and Joseph Spencer from a room at
the Griswold Tavern. Worthington had been without a paper since
Buttles moved the *Western Intelligencer* to Columbus in 1814, but
returning to Worthington was actually a retrenchment for young
Griswold, who had been working as a printer in the capital city. The
partners managed to maintain the business for two years, mostly by
accepting trade goods in payment for newspaper subscriptions, advertisements, and items for sale such as writing paper. In 1821 their rates
of exchange credited "Good sweet Butter 10 cts. per lb., Wheat Flour
200 per cwt., Bacon hams 8 cts per lb., Pickled pork 7 cts per lb., Wool
50 to 75 cts lb., Flax 12½, Country linen 25 to 50 cts yd., Wheat 67½
bushel, Rye 44, Oats 25, Corn 37½, Barley 100, Chickens 100 doz.,
Eggs 8 cts [doz], Sugar 10 cts per lb., Beeswax 25, Tallow 16, Lard 10
cts per lb., Molasses 62½ gallon, Honey 75, Whiskey 37½ to 44, Hops
44 per lb., Dried Sage 75, Dressed Deer Skins 50 to 150 each."[73] There
was obviously a wide variety of produce available locally, and the
publishers apparently accepted anything that they could use themselves or barter to others.

Neither of these new enterprises survived. When Smith and Hor's
partnership dissolved, Leonard Smith retained the store and established a new distillery where he advertised that he would "exchange Whisky for Corn and Rye, on liberal terms." He also started
a "Wheelwright Business, where Waggons and Carriages of any description will be made new, or repaired on reasonable terms." In hard
times, diversity was a necessary asset. When Griswold and Spencer
dissolved their printing partnership, Spencer also went into the

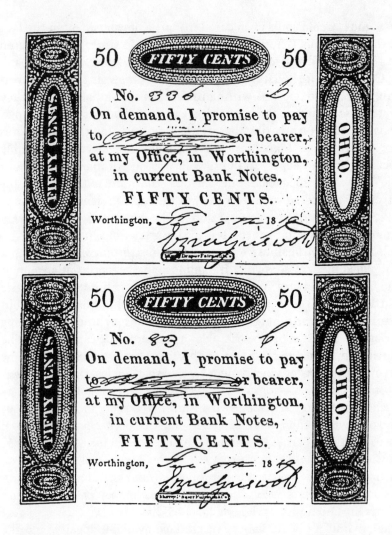

Fig. 20. Worthington tavern owner Ezra Griswold issued "shinplasters" redeemable at his tavern to facilitate commerce on the cash-starved western frontier. (Photograph by the authors)

wheelwright business, advertising "1, 2, 4, or 6 horse waggons made on the premises—Dandy or Dearborn Waggons made to any pattern wished for."[74]

Surprisingly, the collapse of the economy and the Worthington Manufacturing Company did not bring a complete halt to new employment or construction in the community. Samuel Baldwin advertised for "a sober & industrious man to attend saw mill & assist in boarding house." This was the manufacturing company sawmill and boardinghouse that Baldwin apparently continued to operate until they were attached in DeWolf's lawsuit. Arora Buttles, the principal brick and stone mason in the community, advertised for a "young man 17 or 18 to learn mason's trade."[75]

Although the Worthington Manufacturing Company dominated the Worthington industrial scene during the postwar economic boom and collapse, small-town business life went on. Worthington might be compared to a modern town that attracted a manufacturing company or government defense plant, which doubled the town's work force, but was forced to close in less than ten years. Historian Page Smith has pointed out that towns which did not succeed in becoming industrialized remained small towns,[76] and this now appeared to be Worthington's fate. Surely, if Kilbourn's dream had succeeded, the community's course would have changed dramatically. A growing industrial complex on its border would have eventually subsumed and destroyed the village planned by the original New England settlers.

Kilbourn was both the victim and the cause of the Worthington Manufacturing Company's collapse. In many respects it was a grand plan. He was ahead of his time in creating an "industrial park" where a variety of small entrepreneurs could benefit from proximity to each other. He was innovative in linking manufacturing production and retail marketing and thereby potentially maximizing profits. He had studied the geography and created a logical plan for utilizing the cheapest and quickest transportation routes through Lake Erie. He had political influence at the local, state, and national levels that might have been helpful in launching this venture. Ohio's population was growing at a phenomenal rate, and the Worthington community had developed an early base from which it could offer products and services.

But this was a man with a large ego and an enthusiasm for *everything*. Kilbourn found it impossible to eliminate any potential product or venture and focus on specific, and perhaps achievable, goals. His ego and ineffective management style made it difficult to delegate authority or attract experienced managers. This was the same man who kept forgetting his belongings on his original trip to Ohio to view possible settlement sites, and it is noteworthy that none of the Scioto Company members who came west with him a decade earlier became company stockholders. The death of Jedediah Norton in March 1812 deprived him of his most significant financial backer. Kilbourn was hopelessly overcommitted not only in his responsibilities to this company, but in his role as a congressman and in local responsibilities such as being the major of a militia battalion and president of the Worthington College trustees. His eastern stockholders were recent acquaintances who were more concerned with profitable investments than with establishing a corporation that could become the economic base of a developing region. He had a naivete that allowed him to conclude business agreements with a handshake and put the details on paper later—sometimes, like with the manufacturing company incorporation, *much* later.

Of course, the timing also was bad. There were factors in the national and state economy over which Kilbourn had no control. He blamed political acquaintances for encouraging him to set up an establishment to provide clothing and boots for the military, but he should have had enough business experience to predict the time needed to reach production, and he should have realized that no war would last forever. He blamed inexpensive foreign goods for flooding the market for woolen goods after the war, and that was true. But ultimately it was Kilbourn's treatment of capital assets as operating assets that doomed the venture. The Worthington Manufacturing Company was the saga of an optimistic visionary who was unable to attract and utilize skilled management to implement the plan. When it collapsed, Kilbourn himself perhaps suffered the most severe loss; however, some people had uprooted families to move west, and many people who had invested significant amounts of time, labor, and money were also left with nothing.

CHAPTER 14

Main Street Wide and Free of Mud and Many Buildings Handsomely Built with Brick

— ❖ —

THERE IS A UNIQUE opportunity to view Worthington in this period through the eyes of Appleton Downer, a New Englander, who in 1815 explored western sites as potential locations for establishing a law practice. He spent time in Zanesville, Newark, and Granville, and found the road from Granville to Worthington, "dreadfully muddy and obstructed with logs and brush. A few log houses scattered along the way."[1]

He was favorably impressed, however, by the Worthington site. "The town has a beautiful situation on a rising ground from which there is not a mountain or hill to be seen. . . . All rich without a foot of waste land but it is covered with woods." The tidiness of the village was equally impressive to this traveler accustomed to New England towns. "The street is wide and free of mud and beautifully green. Say 30 houses within one mile. Clear of woods for 50 or a 100 rods on each side. Good brick houses and a brick academy." That was a significant number of brick buildings for a site which little more than a decade earlier had been virgin wilderness, but it is worth noting that despite the elaborate town plat, the town had a single, grass-covered Main Street linking about thirty buildings. The forest had been cleared on either side to a distance approximating two to five modern football fields.[2]

While in Worthington, Downer stayed with the family of Dan Case, a farmer and distiller south of the village, whose son Calvin married James Kilbourn's daughter, Harriet. Downer had doubtless stayed in a number of modest taverns in the course of his travels, and he appreciated the fact that the Case lifestyle was above average for the western country. "Their table &c all in the nicest order in the very best Connecticut style. A thing very grateful, but very unusual in this loghouse country." Downer evidently concluded that Worthington was too small to support a legal practice. He also visited the emerging state capital in Columbus, which he found in a very rough state, and decided to return to Zanesville.

Downer apparently talked with many people, and the observations he expressed to his brother were quite frank. They are unusually analytical, perhaps because of his legal training in examining various perspectives: "Those who come here from the Atlantic make a thousand dear sacrifices and subject themselves to years of severe hardship. Many live a life of sorrow, longing for the native country. Others better their circumstances in time. Many are woefully drained but can't get back. Such a remove should not be made in haste by a person who has anything to loose. It is generally better to come and view first." Having done just that, young Downer concluded, "The practice of law is poor in this state, but it is probable I shall remain here and rely partly on some other business." This was a realistic assessment, and it was, in fact, common for professionally trained men to seek multiple sources of income. Lawyers frequently began by also teaching school or by becoming newspapermen; as they gained experience they often relied upon public office for additional income.

The same was true for ministers and physicians. The position as principal of the Worthington Academy was an important inducement to attract Philander Chase as the first rector of St. John's Episcopal congregation, but he also purchased a farm in the area, intending that it would become his family's primary source of income. Drs. Hills and Case opened an apothecary shop to supplement their medical practice; Calvin Case soon became a merchant instead of a physician.

Although Downer settled in Zanesville, and Worthington missed its first opportunity to attract a lawyer, the community grew dramatically in the postwar boom. John Kilbourn's *Ohio Gazetteer* of 1819 described Worthington as having "64 dwelling houses, stores and workshops, many of which are large and handsomely built with brick, four mercantile stores, and a building for an academy." As James Kilbourn's nephew and the former principal of that academy, John Kilbourn was not an unbiased recorder, but it does appear likely that the village nearly doubled in size during this brief period of frenzied speculation. And this did not include the buildings of the Worthington Manufacturing Company that Kilbourn's gazetteer described as "an extensive manufacturing establishment" on the river about three-fourths of a mile from the public square.[3]

Gazetteers naturally emphasized each town's road access. Worthington was described as being "on the great road leading from Kentucky by way of Chillicothe, Columbus, etc. to Lake Erie. In the middle of the public square, in the center of town, the post road leading from Zanesville to Urbana and Greenville crosses the former." As all western migrants well knew, in 1819 these were the principal north-south and east-west arteries through Ohio. Worthington residents referred to their town as being about one hundred miles from Lake Erie and the same to what had recently been the frontier line at Greenville. The next year proposals were requested and donations solicited to build the first bridge across the Whetstone River, both to improve the east-west road and to make it easier for local citizens who faced a difficult barrier when high water made it impossible to ford the river.[4]

But as rapid as Worthington's growth was, the new state capital of Columbus—which was only one-third of Worthington's age—was by 1819 reported to contain "200 houses and 1500 inhabitants."[5] In addition to the statehouse and penitentiary, Columbus contained "ten mercantile stores, a bank, two printing houses, and a market house." Both towns were growing, but Columbus was growing more rapidly, and this growth frequently came at Worthington's expense.

From the beginning, some individual settlers had stayed briefly and moved on. Worthington's first significant exodus, however, occurred during the western struggle to attract and retain new migrants during the war years, and shortly after the site for the new capital was established at Columbus.

Worthington residents were not immediately aware of its effect and did not realize that the Battle of the Thames, which defeated the Indians in the northwest and resulted in the death of their chief Tecumseh, essentially ended the war in Ohio.[6] Settlers were still nervous several weeks later when Joel Buttles wrote his sister Julia, who was spending the winter with relatives in New England, that "The Indian murder that seemed to come the nearest home, happened this fall while I was at Urbana . . . two men residents of that place were

found the next day eighteen miles north of there where they had en-
camped for the night, murdered, scalped, and butchered shockingly."[7]

By the spring of 1814, fears had subsided and migration from the
east resumed, but the new capital city was enticing some of Worthington's most capable young people. Not only did James Kilbourn
open a Worthington Manufacturing Company branch store in Columbus, but Joel Buttles, who edited the newspaper, moved the *Western
Intelligencer* to that city.[8] Buttles was in a gloomy mood as he wrote
his sister while he prepared to leave. "Worthington seems to me an
almost desolate place so many have moved away & married &c. Mr.
Barker, Cynthia & your going [east for the winter] . . . Nancy & Gregory forever gone—Dolly gone—Capt. Barker's & G. Case's families
now on the road to New England. Louisa away keeping school—All
our folks away & the house occupied by strangers . . . . The printing
office coming down here next monday & with it Ezra, Philo & some
boys."[9]

Buttles clearly hated the change, but the paper immediately established its position in the capital city, proclaiming its intention that
"party broth must not be expected to be wrought through the medium
of this paper . . . no infatuation or party animosity, shall ever mark the
character of our paper." Such sentiments were easy to espouse in an
environment dominated by the Democratic-Republican party. The
capital city at that time actually had no two-party political dialogue.
The partnership of Olmsted, Buttles, and Griswold had lofty ambitions of attracting a diverse readership. "The mechanics may find new
and useful invention . . . the farmer discoveries in agriculture . . .
admirers of poetry shall be occasionally delighted."[10] This was apparently the right mixture, for the paper thrived and evolved into
the *Columbus Gazette,* under the editorial leadership of Philo Olmsted and Ezra Griswold, Jr. Buttles soon left the newspaper business to
devote himself to his mercantile interests and to his new responsibilities as Columbus postmaster. When the first bank was chartered
in Columbus two and a half years later, his prosperity placed him
among the four current or recent Worthington residents who were
elected as directors. Although Worthington was exporting some of its
best talent, ties between the two communities were close.

Worthington, too, was receiving a flow of new immigrants as war
fears receded, and the Worthington Manufacturing Company began
to attract craftsmen and laborers. One immediate effect was an increase in the number of taverns, for these were the social centers of

Fig. 21. Joel Buttles came west with his family to Worthington in 1804 and edited the area's first newspaper, *The Western Intelligencer*, before moving to Columbus in 1814 and becoming a leading citizen of the capital city. (Courtesy of the Ohio Historical Society)

the community. During these boom years, at least seven men were licensed tavern keepers in Sharon Township.[11] In addition to the boardinghouse at the manufacturing-company site, two new hostelry establishments joined Griswold's Tavern and Kilbourn's Hotel in the village. The most elaborate was a Greek Revival-style building on the east side of Main Street, a block north of Griswold's. Built for Isaac Hor, this elegant frame structure was a lavish example of the skills of local house joiners, probably under the direction of the community's master carpenter, Chauncey Barker. Its symmetrical facade featured north and south wings two stories in height, each with four windows facing Main Street. The three-story center section was highlighted by a fanlight entry, flanked by two windows, and the whole was topped by columned tripartite windows with a fanlight accenting the gable.[12] It was easily the most elegant building erected in the nineteenth-century village.

Directly across Main Street from the Hor House, John Goodrich established a tavern in a plain, Federal-style building, which he probably built himself. Like the others during the boom period, it accommodated boarders, mostly laborers and blacksmiths at this establishment. Land speculators and new arrivals for the manufacturing company often stayed for a time at Kilbourn's hotel, but Worthington attracted few travelers except those who had business in the community. In the spring of 1815, James Allen, son of Scioto Company member Joel Allen, who had returned to New England, spent two weeks at the Griswold Tavern while attending to business affairs regarding property he owned just north of the village. He paid $4.00 for two weeks' board, $4.00 for two weeks' "horsekeeping" in Griswold's stable, and his itemized expenses for gin, wine, brandy and whiskey totaled $2.75½.[13]

Its central location assured the Griswold Tavern a continuing role at the heart of community affairs. At Christmas the large, second-floor room in the front was claimed by the young people for a ball. Julia Buttles's invitation bid her

> To rendezvous
> At Griswolds house
> On Christmas next advancing;
> Your company
> Will wanted be
> To spend the night in dancing.[14]

Dancing was not just for holidays, however. George Griswold bragged to one of his young lady friends that "We have a cotillion party here once a week."[15] From the beginning Worthington had attracted more single men than women, but the advent of the manufacturing company made marriageable young women a prized commodity. After the 1820 census, the local paper noted in some jest that

Fig. 22. The Griswold Tavern, 1811–1964, occupied a key position on the public square and was for many years the center of Worthington community life. (Courtesy of the Worthington Historical Society)

Ohio had an excess of 5,995 males aged twenty-five to forty-five, "a most cheering prospect this for old maids." Noticing that Connecticut had an excess of 7,601 females of the same age, the editor suggested, no doubt with tongue in cheek, that the Connecticut legislature purchase "a tract of our territory, in some of the new counties to the northward, and plant a colony of old maids. We could immediately man about six thousand, and the odd sixteen hundred, after the exercise of a little patience, might be furnished with husbands."[16]

The noise and bustle of people constantly coming and going at the tavern were exhausting to Ezra and Ruth Griswold as they approached their fifties. They built a new home across the street, anticipating that their son George would soon marry and take over the tavern. After the U.S. Bank curtailed credit and the economy collapsed, Ezra deeded his entire property to George for $3,579.56¼.[17] Confronted by DeWolf's lawsuit charging him with an error in drawing the deed for part of the Worthington Manufacturing Company property, Ezra Griswold did exactly as he had in 1802 and made a "paper transfer" of his property assets to a relative.[18] He had now served as township justice of the peace for more than a decade, and this carefully crafted document transferring all of his assets to George gave a complete inventory of the tavern property.

The tavern business required a substantial stock of liquor, including "five barrels of whiskey, one barrel of gin, one keg of F. [French] brandy, one barrel of cherry bounce," and "eight hundred segars." Brandy and cigars were, of course, imported from the east, but whiskey was available from a number of local distillers. Basic household supplies included "one barrel of sugar & some loaf sugar, one vinegar tub, two preserve potts, three meat tubs, three tea boxes, some sheet teas, four bushel hickory nutts, three barrels of fish partly full, 100 lbs of salt pork, one barrel of soap."

The tavern kitchen, which also served the family, was equipped with "two kitchen table, one kitchen cupboard, three iron sugar kettles, one grid iron, one jug & blacking, one tin bake oven fork, one pair of shears, one set of tin measures, one set of wooden measures, one wire sieve, two Iron pots, one bake oven, one iron spider, two skillets, eighteen tin bread pans, one griddle and frying pan, two pair of flat or smoothing irons, eight earthen pots, eight tin pans, one bread tub, one coffee boiler, one iron bason, one pounder, six brooms, four wooden bowls, two pepper boxes, one nutmeg [box], five pitchers, one cullender, one tin suet tub, one tin sugar box" and a wide variety of bottles, casks, trunks, boxes, baskets, sacks, and tubs for storing things. It is a list that suggests a bustling scene around the cooking fireplace of the busy main room in the tavern.

Serving ware and utensils included "eight goblets, one Dozen of spoons, eighteen silver teaspoons, four sets of knives & forks, two dozen of large plates, two dozen common plates & two dozen of small ones, two setts of china cups & saucers & two sets of common ones, four bowls, one large platter, two teapots, three coffee potts, two dozen of glasses, two dozen of wines [glasses], three quart decanters, four pint decanters." There were apparently far fewer knives, forks, and spoons than plates and glasses, unless wooden or iron utensils were available but not itemized.

The tavern's availability for justice of the peace hearings and dinner parties is reflected in the large number of chairs, which were probably made locally, "five sets of plank bottom and Windsor chairs, five sets of common kitchen chairs." For sleeping there were "Eight beds & bedding including underbeds, bedsteads & ropes & two other bedsteads, a number of Canopies, six pair of sheets, eighteen blankets, seven bed quilts." This suggests that most beds were equipped with canopies for warmth and privacy and had trundle beds to be pulled out. Most of these beds probably accommodated two adults or several children, and some may have been used with blankets without sheets. Other furnishings included "one clock and case, two looking glasses, three pair of andirons, one writing table, one long dining table, one grog table, one bottle case, one chest, six waiters, ten iron candlesticks & two brass ones, one glass & one tin lanthorn, four bells, dozen of tin sconces, seven tablecloths, six brown towels, two sets window curtains." This is the earliest mention of curtains in village records, and they were probably more for privacy than adornment. The image of this inventory is of a nicely furnished main room with a dining table, Windsor chairs, writing table, clock, looking glass, andirons at the fireplace and a couple of brass candlesticks. Bedrooms must have been sparsely furnished with little beyond the beds and bedding, a chamber "mug," a few pegs on the wall to hang clothing, and perhaps a tin sconce for candlelight.

Like all households, the tavern included a stable and essential livestock, in this case "one pair or yoak of oxen, two cows, one sorrel stud horse, one sorrel yearling, one mare, four hogs & ten pigs or shoats, forty-four swarms of bees." These were probably sufficient to provide milk and butter, as well as honey and pork for the tavern table, but one suspects that someone forgot to inventory the poultry. The stable equipment included two wagons, two sleds, one ox yoke, a saddle, bridle, martingales, and spurs.[19] There was no mention of a carriage, for in 1819 the roads to Worthington were still too poor to accommodate anything more than sturdy farm wagons or carts.

The crops on hand, when the inventory was made in August, included twenty bushels of corn, forty of oats, four stacks of hay in the meadow, and "all the hay in the two barns annexed to the tavern stand." The small farm tools included "six rakes, five pitchforks, one iron shovel, one mattock, one log chain, one keg nails, two iron wedges, four axes, one cream pail, three sickles, three scythes, three hoes, three curry combs, one dung fork, two steel yards, two hammers, one two-foot rule, one sand box, one grind stone, one plow clovis & pin, one pigeon nett."[20]

A pigeon net may seem to be a curious possession to anyone unacquainted with the midwestern frontier and the fall migrations of passenger pigeons that were attracted to the plentiful beech and oak mast. In the fall of 1821, the newspaper described one such migration: "For nearly an hour last Tuesday evening the horizon was darkened with them as far as the eye could extend in every direction." The flocks preferred to roost about two to three miles southeast of the village where "they make a noise resembling a distant waterfall, & which may be distinctly heard more than two miles." The editor reported that "Many of the citizens of the neighborhood of this ground amuse themselves by shooting them at night, and as many as from 500 to 800 have been brought in of a morning—as many as 20 have been brought down at one shot."[21] It was a sport that rapidly eliminated these huge migrations, but the pigeons were considered a delicacy and citizens feasted during the season.

The temporary log homes that the pioneers had built were dismantled so their timbers could be reused, or in some cases the entire cabin was removed to the rear of a lot to serve as a stable. The homes that were built in Worthington during the postwar era, both frame and brick, were of a quality comparable to or better than those most of the settlers had owned in New England. Shortly after his marriage to Achsa Maynard, Orange Johnson purchased the six-room, brick house just north of the village that Arora Buttles was completing when he went to war. Johnson built a shop adjacent to this for his comb-making business. In 1819, the Johnsons more than doubled the size of their home with an Adam-style addition that faced Main Street and was highlighted by a fanlight central entry.[22] Its five-bay facade, with single rooms on either side of the central hall on both floors, was fairly typical of the many "I-houses" in the village. Brick masonry, however, now featured Flemish-bond construction on the Main Street facades, rather than the common bond of the early years.

Across the street the home of Peter and Zilpha Barker was frame, relying on the carpentry skills of the Barker brothers. Just north of Isaac Hor's tavern, Arora Buttles built a large brick home with its gable end facing Main Street, making it suitable for a shop in front and family living quarters in the rear, a popular style in the village.[23] Like many modern contractors, Buttles built this home to sell, but lived in it himself until he did so. Because Worthington property was not marketable during the depression, this was where Buttles lived for several years after his marriage to Harriet Kilbourn Case, Kilbourn's widowed daughter. Its style is very similar to another home

Fig. 23. This elegant Federal-style home, built in 1819 for Orange and Achsa Johnson in front of the 1811 Buttles house, is now operating as a Worthington Historical Society lifestyle museum. (Photo by the authors)

on the southern edge of town occupied by Christopher and Julia Ripley, a merchant who worked at the manufacturing company store and who later had a leather-goods shop facing Main Street.[24]

One of the largest frame residences in the village was the Georgian-style home on the west side of the public square with four rooms on each floor.[25] Demas Adams, who married Kilbourn's stepdaughter Susan Barnes, lived there and operated it as a boardinghouse for Worthington Academy students and overflow guests from Kilbourn's Worthington Hotel.[26] The symmetry of the Georgian style was much admired, and the central entry that provided access to all rooms without going through one to reach another was considered a mark of gentility.[27]

The building boom, which accompanied the Great Migration after the War of 1812, saw the construction in Worthington of numerous two-story I-houses with gabled roofs.[28] The best ones, both brick and frame, incorporated features of the Adam style so popular in colonial New England.[29] The dentilated cornice and the entry with its elliptical fanlight and sidelights in the Johnson home and the Palladian window of the Hor House typified the best of this design.

The largest residence built in town during this period was the new home of Ezra and Ruth Griswold on the west side of Main Street north of the public square. It was built in 1817, at the height of the speculative boom, and was rented until they were ready to turn the tavern over to their son, George. Its imposing seven-bay facade was anchored by large chimneys on the north and south ends.[30] In the mid-1820s this home was valued at $1,480.00, compared to $1,000.00 for the Johnson home, $850.00 for the Adams residence, $688.00 for the Buttles home, and $600.00 for the Ripley house.[31] There were many smaller homes in the village and township, and a few that had a comparable value, but the Griswold home was the largest and most modern at this time.

Describing this building as "the house in which I now reside," Ezra Griswold transferred the house and all of its furnishings to his son George to protect them from creditors.[32] It was nicely furnished with "thirteen Windsor chairs, eight kitchen & two rocking chairs, six bedsteads ropes beds & bedding, one fall-leaf dining table & two square tables, one looking glass, one large kitchen cupboard, one book cupboard, two square stand tables, three chests, twelve window curtains." It would appear that the Griswolds kept the better quality items for use in their own home rather than in the tavern. The usual assortment of kitchen utensils and dining ware included sets of tea and coffee cups and "twelve large & twelve small blue or green edged plates, and fifteen silver tea spoons." The Griswolds had more space to seat and entertain family and guests than other homes in Worthington, but this was primarily a matter of quantity. The items in their home were representative of those in estates of the time period.[33]

It is interesting to compare the Griswold home and tavern inventories in 1819 with the Pinney and Buttles estates in 1805 shortly after the pioneer settlers arrived. Between the two times there was little difference in technology, particularly among the tools and farm equipment; however, the Griswold inventories reveal a dramatic difference in the household furnishings. Though one must remember that this listing reflects the possessions of one of the most affluent families in the village, the quantity of bedsteads, tables, chairs, and chests that the Griswolds owned testifies to the community's skilled craftsmen.[34] Multiple sets of cups and saucers, china plates, goblets, and decanters testified to a thriving trade in imported goods. Twelve sets of window curtains speak to the availability of fabric and a home-maker's time to sew, as well as to a sense of gentility.

The Griswolds had "one large & one small spinning wheel," but much of their clothing was made from commercially woven cloth. Since estate inventories rarely showed women's clothing, it is especially helpful to know that Ruth Griswold had "one womans great coat, two mantle, two silk gowns, two white muslin & cambrick gowns, twelve women's shirts, one paresol," and silk, cotton and woolen stockings. Clearly, the better class of people in the village had separate gowns for everyday wear and for dressy occasions.

This had probably been true from the beginning, with the settlers generally bringing work clothes and at least one outfit suitable for church. A newspaper advertisement in 1813 offered a reward for the return of "a cotton cross-barred handkerchief" lost between Worthington and Sunbury in which the following articles had been tied up: "One black cambric gown, One dove colored [gown], white and black gown, One green calico gown, One white muslin petticoat, One large leno shawl, Two pocket handkerchiefs, One pair of scissors, and several other articles."[35] How distressing this loss must have been to the seamstress who had spent hours of hand labor producing such garments. There is no clue to the age or social status of the owner—or owners, for these may have been the garments of two or more family members. It does, however, provide an interesting view of one method for transporting clothing when traveling short distances on horseback.

A more modest, but probably more typical, wardrobe was itemized in the David Bristol estate in 1820. Bristol was one of the original Scioto Company pioneers who farmed south of the village. At his death, he owned "one strait body coat, one old coat, one Great coat, pr. velvet pantaloons, three linen pantaloons, one tow pantaloons, one tow vest, one silk vest, one old vest, two linen Shirts, one Frock, two pr. old stockings, two old Hats, one pocketbook."[36] The appraisers evidently neglected to itemize his boots, but they valued his entire wardrobe at $25.02. As an elderly widower, perhaps Bristol saw no need to keep up with fashion.

Worthington in the postwar period no longer exhibited the rawness of a frontier settlement. It was one of only forty-eight towns and villages in Ohio with more than one hundred residents, and it probably ranked about twentieth with more than five hundred citizens.[37] Of

course, life was still difficult in many ways. The gravestones continued to accumulate in the churchyard on the east side of the public
square. Some of the most commonly feared perils were the bilious
fevers so prevalent in late summer and fall. Entire families could be
destroyed within days, as happened in the last week of August 1821,
when the Case family north of town lost four members—Eunice,
Norman, John, and Abiel—within five days.[38]

Cholera morbus was quite common, inflicting sufferers with
cramps and diarrhea but rarely proving fatal to adults. The contami-
nated food and water that caused it were little understood, but home
remedies abounded. The newspaper promised a remedy, "which has
never yet been known to fail of complete success in any stage of the
disease":

> Take a half grown chicken strip him of his feathers and intrails as quick
> as possible after killing him and while he is yet warm put him in a
> gallon of boiling water, add a little salt, and continue boiling half an
> hour; take of the liquer and give to the patient half a tumbler full and
> repeat it as often as he can bear it; an almost immediate effect will be
> produced. This has been known to produce a complete cure, after the
> patient had become so much exhausted that articulation had ceased.[39]

Homes were becoming more comfortable but ailments abounded, and
chicken soup was evidently valued as highly along the Main Street of
1820 as it is among modern mothers of sick children.

CHAPTER 15

To the Dough Faces of
the Last Congress

— ❖ —

AFTER THE BATTLE OF THE THAMES, military activity in the northwest devolved to garrison forces who manned the forts on the frontier. Local militiamen returned to their jobs in the booming economy months before the British burned Washington. The regular army was still seeking enlistments in Ohio by appealing to the patriotic spirit of the western men, but such entreaties were not sufficient for most men when the homes and lives of their loved ones were not endangered. The only enticements that succeeded were economic ones. While the advertisements of local recruiters challenged men not to "indulge yourselves in lethargic sleep when your country calls you to a vindication of her injured rights," the headlines promised "124 DOLLARS BOUNTY, 160 ACRES OF LAND" for every able-bodied man eighteen to forty who volunteered for the army.[1] The few Worthington men who enlisted found their responsibilities tedious and their units afflicted by morale problems. More than once, Captain Pinney was forced to advertise for deserters from the 27th Regiment, offering a "$10 reward" for Peter Miller, a twenty-seven-year-old carpenter born at York County, Pennsylvania, and described as six feet tall with dark hair. The same amount was offered for Nathan Williams, a deserter born in Hartford, Connecticut.[2] Perhaps these men enlisted for the bounty and then deserted, or maybe they became bored and discouraged by the lack of action.

Even prisoners of war were exchanged before some of the garrison companies were released. Worthington shoemaker William Hall probably had both business and personal reasons for being anxious to get home. He was realistic about his chances, however, when he wrote his friend Arora Buttles from Fort Shelby near Detroit, "Their is a poor chaunce for me at presants I see that plainly. The whole trouble of discharging the company will involve on me."[3] But even Hall had come home, married, and settled north of Worthington before the peace treaty was signed.[4]

The signing of the peace treaty was something of an anticlimax in Ohio, where the fighting had long been over; but Andrew Jackson's victory at New Orleans brought rejoicing throughout the northwest. Philo Olmsted, who was a partner in the *Western Intelligencer* both before and after it moved to Columbus, described his private celebration to his friend George Griswold: "I am alive and glad of it but I like to have killed myself last night eating bread and cider. Lt. A. Buttles and myself purchased a quart of cider and a loaf of bread and with the addition of sugar and water it made a most sumptuous dish I assure you." He encouraged Griswold to let him know if his Worthington friends had plans to celebrate the New Orleans victory and the war's official end: "If you should have a passover on account of the glad tidings of peace be so good as to send me word."[5] The nine miles between Worthington and the capital city were a short distance for a young man in search of a celebration.

Peace and prosperity brought Worthington a golden period that was highlighted by the most elaborate celebration in the community's nineteenth-century history. The occasion was an official visit by President Monroe on August 25, 1817, the first and last time an incumbent president officially visited Worthington. Elected the previous autumn and inaugurated in March, Monroe embarked during the congressional recess on a tour through the eastern and northern states with the stated purpose of inspecting coastal and frontier fortifications.[6] This took him along Ohio's northern border as far as Detroit, the area that was on the front lines through much of the recent war and a region with an increasingly significant voice in the national political debate.

The president, traveling on horseback, "generally in a canter," was accompanied by Generals Brown and Macomb and Governor Cass of the Michigan Territory. They stopped for the night at Delaware and rode south in the morning, the president in civilian dress with an "old-fashioned three-cornered hat," his face ruddy from days in the summer sun.[7] This was an image appropriate to the task, but far different from the chief executive in powdered wig and buckled breeches at a public reception in the nation's capital.[8] The presidential party was met six miles north of Worthington by several of the community's leading citizens and the Franklin Dragoons, a handsomely equipped local militia cavalry unit, which escorted them into the village.[9] A triangular bower had been erected on the public square. This was supported by three columns representing agriculture, manufacture, and commerce, which were connected by arches draped with green boughs. Worthington was emphasizing the tripartite foundation of its economy.

To the accompaniment of the militia band, the president was escorted to this bower, "proceeded by young Ladies and Misses who were all dressed in white, and their Heads adorned in the most tasteful style with wreaths and garlands, having in their hands flowers of every hue collected from the gardens, the meadows, the wilds, strewed them in the way before him. . . ." Worthington was flaunting its cultural awareness. This might be a community recently carved from the forest, but there were a number of persons present who had studied Greek and Latin literature and had firm ideas about how to stage a celebration in the classical style.

The president and the crowd of several hundred persons were greeted by the chairman of the day, Col. James Kilbourn. It is interesting that the newspaper referred to Kilbourn by his militia title, rather than as the congressman who had known James Monroe while he served President Madison as secretary of state and later as secretary of war. As might be expected, Kilbourn's welcome praised the president's recent role of directing "the energies of a brave and free people to *Victory, Glory* and *Peace.*" Monroe addressed the crowd of local citizens in equally flowery rhetoric, explaining his desire to see the northern border personally and emphasizing that his impressions of the country and the people had "exceeded his expectations."

Following the speeches, the presidential party dined with leading citizens of the community, including the recently arrived Rev. Philander Chase, who served as the chaplain of the day. President Monroe offered a toast to "The town of Worthington, and its worthy citizens,"[10] and chairman Kilbourn responded with toasts to the president and the generals in his party. This was a friendly crowd. Worthington was almost universally a Republican community, and it had supported Monroe's policies during the war. By three in the afternoon, the presidential party embarked for Columbus and arrived in the state capital that evening.

This may have been the most elegantly classical celebration that President Monroe encountered during his tour of the northwestern frontier. Worthington residents certainly demonstrated that they were cultured people. Kilbourn no longer held any position on the national political scene, but one of the key issues of the Monroe administration would be the respective roles of federal and state government in initiating and financing internal improvements such as roads and canals. Worthington boosters had high hopes that their town would have a place on the improved east-west "National Road" across Ohio and on a road or canal linking Lake Erie and the state capital.

The atmosphere of President Monroe's reception was noticeably more elegant and decorous than Worthington's annual celebrations of "the glorious 4th." Annual Fourth of July celebrations were always the community's largest and most boisterous holiday. Lacking saluting cannons, but possessing abundant patriotic pride, Worthington pioneers celebrated their first Fourth of July in 1804 by felling seventeen large trees on the public square, one for each state of the union at that time.[11] In succeeding years, the day of national celebration was always commemorated with speeches and toasts, but none exceeded the celebrations of July 4, 1820 and 1821. Historians have noted the significance of militia muster days and Independence Day celebrations in maintaining the classless unity so essential to small-town society.[12] Perhaps the economic depression that swept the western country in 1819 and the ensuing collapse of the Worthington Manufacturing Company dictated a "rally round the flag" spirit which would demonstrate the community's determination to survive.

In 1820, "a numerous body of patriotic citizens" assembled at "Smith & Hor's Hall" and marched in procession to the "College Chapel" for "divine services" celebrated by Bishop Chase. The Declaration of Independence was read by James Kilbourn, an oration was delivered by R. W. Cowles, and President Washington's valedictory address was read by Edward Mallory. Many of the audience then retired to Smith and Hor's tavern for "a suitable repast" that concluded with twenty-two toasts.[13]

A year later, editor Ezra Griswold, Jr., noted in the paper that July 4, 1821, was celebrated with "more gladness, cordiality of spirit and American feeling" than he had ever seen before.[14] The weather was "exceedingly fine," as though God himself had blessed this national jubilee. Festivities began early, when "A select party of about forty gentlemen, Merchants, Manufacturers and Mechanics, assembled at the Woolen Factory, at an early hour and accompanied by music, preceeded to the Hotel, where they joined the ladies, orator of the day, and citizens, when they marched in procession, under charge of the marshal of the day Capt. Isaac Hor, to the Academy. . . ." A contingent of forty workers, marching from the Worthington Manufacturing Company grounds on the river, was testimony to the extensive activity that was continuing at the woolen factory even though the retail stores had closed two years earlier. But this was less than half the number of persons the census reported engaged in manufacturing the previous year. Some of those men were, of course, located in the village proper, but one must still conclude that workers were gradually giving up and leaving town.

At the academy, "after divine service, an appropriate oration, replete with American sentiments, was delivered by the Rev. Philander Chase, Jr." The image of religious services coupled with an official public holiday is more in keeping with modern Thanksgiving Day observances than Independence Day. Rev. Chase was both the principal of the academy and, in his father's absence, the minister of St. John's Episcopal Church. He was, no doubt, recognized as the most capable orator in the community; nevertheless, the annual inclusion of divine services in the Fourth of July celebration clearly illustrates the close linkage between church and state in early Worthington.

In 1821, the pride of the community was a new flagpole erected on the public square by a committee headed by carpenter Milton Greer. The newspaper bragged that such a staff "has never been equaled in this state, or perhaps in the western country. Its dimensions are, in height 120 feet, and 18 inches diameter at the base; the main mast of White Oak, 73 ft. with a cap and cross trees, shipped with a top mast 47 ft. from which waved an elegant star-spangled banner. . . ." The flag was described as the gift of a "patriotic gentleman," but no mention was made of the lady or ladies who did the sewing. If patriotism was to be measured by the height of the flagpole, Worthington clearly intended to be a contender.

After these ceremonies, many of the citizens adjourned to Griswold's Tavern, where dinner was served at "37½ cents for Gentlemen and 25 cents for Ladies." The meal concluded with twenty-two "official" toasts, including ones to Independence Day, the Constitution, present and past presidents of the republic, various officers and soldiers of the army and navy, "the rising generation," and "The American Fair."[15] It was the series of volunteer toasts that followed the official ones, however, which most clearly revealed the sentiments of village citizens. Chester Griswold's toast, "To the dough faces of the last congress—Instead of disgracing another congress, they ought to serve a seven year's apprenticeship to the Cotton planters of the south," indicates quite specifically where this community placed the blame for the disastrous economic conditions. It is ample evidence that blaming Congress for the country's problems has a long history. Philo Burr's toast, "Agriculture—May the hardy cultivators of the soil soon find a more liberal reward for their labors," no doubt expressed a widely shared sentiment among local farmers whose market prices had dropped drastically. It would appear that the language became more colorful as the number of toasts wore on. H. R. Adams toasted "The enemies of our National rights and liberties—May they be lathered with a cannon sponge, and shaved with a hand saw."

Across the public square, the official party, which included the planning committee, marshals of the day, and Rev. Chase, dined at "Mr. Adams Hotel." Kilbourn's son-in-law Demas Adams was now managing the hotel along with his adjacent boardinghouse, and it is difficult to discern whether the two separate dinners represented a social class or age division or simply a separation based upon available space. The rhetoric of the toasts was certainly similar in both places. "To Agriculture, Manufactures and Commerce—United they stand, divided they fall" reflected the sentiments that had been expressed in the community from its beginning. The toast "To American Manufacturers—Now engaged in an unequal competition, may our government equalize the contest, by revising the Tariff, and give them 'fair play'" stated a recently perceived problem and the desired solution. The westerners considered it past time for government tariffs to be raised against foreign woolens and other manufactured goods that were flooding the market.

Although the community respected President Monroe, the U.S. Congress was reviled by all. One toast expressed it succinctly, "To the Congress of the U.S.—266 members—163 Lawyers! and 3 Me-

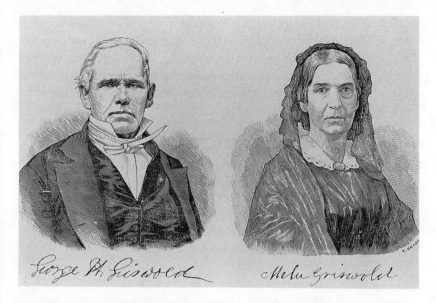

Fig. 24. George H. and Mila Thompson Griswold owned and operated the Griswold Tavern in Worthington for more than fifty years. (Taken from *History of Franklin and Pickaway Counties*)

chanics! ! Fewer Lawyers and better laws." Worthington certainly felt that Congress was out of touch with the common workingman and his problems. Mahoney has linked a local community's success or failure with the ability of local leaders to understand and adjust to the regional changes affecting it.[16] Most persons in Worthington, however, clearly felt that they were enmeshed in economic problems not of their making, and that there was little they could do personally to resolve them.

That did not mean that local citizens were not keenly aware of some of the larger social issues of the day. Sentiments against slavery were particularly strong in this New England community, and S. M. Frothingham, the vice-chairman of the day, addressed the issue in his toast, "To the enemies of Liberty—Slave holders, Tyrants. May all the plagues sent upon Pharaoh, fall on them, & trouble them much, until they let the dark coloured Sons of Africa go free." There was certainly nothing equivocal in that position.

Dinner concluded with everyone joining in singing an ode to freedom which had been composed by James Gardiner for the celebration in Columbus and shared with Worthington. It was sung to a familiar tune so that the entire company could join in the numerous verses. Perhaps the final stanza best symbolized both the community's memory of the men in the nearby cemetery who fought in the Revolution and the sentiments of men around the table who marched off with Hull's army in 1812.

Where late the scene was wild and rude,
And nature smiled in solitude,
Nor bark had press'd Missouri's flood,
    Save that of savage, fierce and brave;
Behold the march of FREEDOM'S car!
How bright, o'er western climes afar,
Now beams the splendor of her star,
    And lights Pacific's silver wave.
Her FREEMEN plough the trackless deep,
Her FREEMEN climb the rugged steep,
Her FREEMEN through the deserts sweep,
And lo! the golden harvests smile;
Here all the arts of Peace shall bloom,
And here the exile find a home;
Proud Independence rear her dome,
And FREEMEN guard the sacred pile.

Freedom was a tangible and treasured possession to these citizens. They had boundless faith in the advancing western frontier and in their ability to tame the wilderness. Even when times were bad, patriotism for the American ideal ran deep in Worthington. Everyone remembered what they and their fathers had fought for during the Revolution, and they were proud of the country they were developing.

The entire day was one of leisure and joyous visiting. The midday meal stretched to half past six before the company parted, "pleased with each other and with the rational entertainments of the day." What a comforting statement that is. What a deep sense of community it conveys. But this was simply the conclusion of the official celebration. For the young adults of the village, the highlight of the occasion was an evening ball, "where, on the light fantastic toe, all care appeared to be forgotten; glee and mirth reigned, heightened by the smiles of beauty and cheerfulness." There is an idyllic quality to the newspaper's description of the Fourth of July in Worthington. There is also every reason to believe that it accurately portrayed a specific time and event—but the community faced serious problems that had only temporarily been set aside.

In 1820, Smith and Hor's Hall was the celebration headquarters, but by 1821 the tavern was inoperative and for sale. In 1820, James Kilbourn, as always, played a significant role in the celebration by reading the Declaration of Independence. In 1821, he was not mentioned in the newspaper, and we have already noted from his son-in-law's letter that he was surveying in the northern part of the state and was avoiding his home lest he be imprisoned for debts. The county court was filled with lawsuits against the Worthington Manufacturing Company that threatened its very survival and the jobs of those workers who marched into the village to celebrate. It remained to be seen whether optimism was sufficient to sustain this town, which had built so many substantial buildings, created educational and cultural institutions, and attracted a diversified agricultural, manufacturing, and commercial workforce.

It was not uncommon, as the frontier moved west, for border towns to become devitalized. Populations frequently shrank as communities settled down to living off the surrounding farms.[17] Worthington was at a critical juncture. From the beginning it had been unified by its drives to found an academy, to be the state capital, and to develop a manufacturing and retail network. The failure of these institutions threatened the social fabric of the community.[18]

Within months, the trend became apparent. Griswold and Spencer announced that they were dissolving their printing partnership by mutual agreement. The last issue of their newspaper, on September 24, 1821, explained that the paper was moving to Delaware and invited its subscribers to continue with the *Delaware Patron and Franklin Chronicle*. The editors explained, "The reasons, which have induced us to remove, are many, but the most important one is the fact that our business in this place has been so small, that we do not realize money enough from it to purchase the paper on which we print, and have been compelled to draw from other sources, a considerable portion of the expenses of the establishment. We expect, by blending it with other business, to proceed with less embarrassment in Delaware."[19] Ezra Griswold's tavern and rental farms had evidently been subsidizing his son's newspaper venture, and his own economic reverses probably rendered further support impossible.

For the second time, Worthington lost its newspaper to a larger and more prosperous community. As Wade has pointed out, a newspaper was the most important unifying element of urban culture. While a town is many things as a cultural, social, and political center, it is above all the place where people earn a living.[20] One of the main reasons the editors were unable to meet expenses was that many of their subscribers had the same financial problem. By the end of the year, Dr. James Hills announced that he, too, was moving his family and his medical practice from Worthington, and that effective January 10, 1822, patients could consult him at Griswold and Howard's tavern in Delaware.[21] Once again, Worthington was losing some of its brightest and most capable young men, though Ezra Griswold, Jr., Caleb Howard, and James Hills all maintained close ties with friends and relatives who remained in Worthington.

Chester Griswold, however, left Worthington a bitter man. He had lost everything he had in the lawsuits that included the Worthington Manufacturing Company tannery, and he returned to New York State disillusioned. One of the saddest situations was that of Leonard Smith, who fled the town, leaving Worthington friends and business colleagues to face his creditors. Smith was expelled from New England Lodge No. 4 for "unmasonic conduct," and a newspaper notice alerted other lodges. "Smith has been a Merchant in this place, which he left about the 21st day of January last. He is about 26 years of age, five feet eight inches high, light complexion, speaks slow, and most of his gestures and actions are marked with moderation. It is probable that he has located himself in some of the states bordering on the Mississippi."[22] Local Masons could post a description that treated Smith like a criminal and warned other Masonic brothers, but there was little recourse for his creditors and friends like Arora Buttles, who was forced to sell his home because he had signed as surety for some of Smith's notes.[23]

During the postwar economic boom, Worthington had much to celebrate. It had doubled in population, and the new residences and commercial structures were elegantly constructed even by New England standards. Its academy-college offered the most advanced education available in central Ohio. As the seat of the Episcopal bishop for Ohio, it hosted annual meetings of the diocese; it had also become a center of Masonic activity with its new lodge building. It had, moreover, established a manufacturing and retail network that attracted a significant number of talented craftsmen to the community. But the banking crisis of 1819 brought an economic disaster that threatened its very existence. Worthington had reached a turning point.

A Pleasant and Thriving Post Town, 1821–1836

— ❖ —

❖ CHAPTER 16 ❖

Runaway Negro Taken Near
This Place and Set at Liberty

— ❖ —

LITTLE MORE THAN thirty years after the first settlers reached the
site, Worthington was described in Jenkins's *Ohio Gazetteer and
Traveler's Guide* as "A pleasant and thriving post town . . . on the
great northern turnpike," surely a location worthy of inclusion on
any western traveler's itinerary.[1] There was no local chamber of commerce in the nineteenth century nor a state department of tour-
ism, but editors of gazetteers did not hesitate to perform the same
function.

Actually, the greatness of the "northern turnpike" was a matter
of perception. By 1825, there was a mail and stage coach route from
Columbus north through Worthington, operating twice a week to
Delaware and once a week to Lake Erie at Portland, the present city of
Sandusky.[2] From the port of Sandusky this route essentially followed
Indian trails along the Sandusky River and then went south through
the current towns of Tiffin, Upper Sandusky, Marion, Delaware, and
Worthington to Columbus.

A year later McDowell and Neil advertised that their stages would
run three times weekly from Cincinnati to Portland through Columbus, making the trip from the Ohio River to Lake Erie in four days.
How often this projected schedule was actually accomplished is unknown, but a new era of business and leisure travel had definitely
arrived. Prospective travelers were informed that there were four
steamboats on Lake Erie "plying between Buffalo and Detroit." This
presented an opportunity for "ladies and gentlemen who may wish to

retire from the Southern States, during the sickly seasons, to spend a few months in the Northeastern States and on the Atlantic seaboard." En route they could view "some of the most beautiful parts of the state of Ohio," as well as Lake Erie, Niagara Falls, the New York canals, and "those celebrated places of fashionable resort, the Ballston and Saratoga Springs." Passengers were allowed 25 pounds of baggage or charged the rate of one passenger ticket for each additional 150 pounds.[3] Newspaper advertisements in subsequent years suggest this was a seasonal operation, running only during the summer months when the lake was free of ice and the roads were somewhat more passable; but stagecoaches and lake steamers meant that travel standards for tourists had improved significantly in central Ohio.[4]

Improved roads also meant that Worthington families now had an alternative to walking, riding horseback, or traveling in farm wagons. Carriages and buggies could now be used on the road to Columbus or Delaware, and by 1830 several of the more affluent families in Worthington owned them.[5] There was apparently a rental market as well, for in 1827 Asa Gillet's estate included a "hack" valued at fifty-five dollars, suggesting he had a vehicle to hire for short distances such as to Columbus or perhaps Delaware.[6]

After the collapse of the Worthington Manufacturing Company, James Kilbourn increasingly turned his attention to the development of Sandusky, attempting to make a profit from land transactions there.[7] When he was elected to represent Franklin County in the Ohio House of Representatives in 1823, Kilbourn still pressed for a canal route linking Sandusky and Columbus. Everyone agreed on the economic benefits of canal transportation. Farmers could get cheaper transport, merchants could extend their trade, laborers could increase their employment opportunities, landowners could enhance property values, and manufacturers could reach a wider market.[8] When the federal government determined that funding for such internal improvements would largely be the responsibility of the states, site contenders turned their appeals toward Columbus. When the Ohio General Assembly authorized a canal commission and engineer to study the situation in 1822, flour was selling for $3.50 a barrel in Cincinnati, compared to $8.00 a barrel in New York City.[9] Western farmers were desperate. The canal committee reported that "Crops in the finest and most productive parts of the state, are left to waste on the fields that produce them, or be distilled to poison and brutalize society."[10] Ohio's needs were critical, but the route was controversial.

After a year of study, the canal commissioners and engineer reported five potentially practical routes: the Mahoning and Grand Rivers, the Cuyahoga and Muskingum, the Black and Muskingum, the Scioto and Sandusky, and the Maumee and Great Miami Rivers.[11] To Kilbourn, the Scioto and Sandusky River route through the center of the state was the most logical and practical, but to the politicians of the general assembly the solution was to "embrace portions of all three natural routes but all of none of them."[12] In February 1825, to secure the greatest development of Ohio lands and the necessary number of votes, the legislature authorized *two* routes. An eastern canal from Cleveland to Portsmouth was to link the population centers in northeastern and southern Ohio, and a canal from Dayton to Cincinnati would serve the populous southwestern part of the state.[13] Some historians have compared the canal-construction projects of the early nineteenth century to mass-transit projects today. Most never produced great profits and many even lost money, but they nevertheless served the public welfare.[14]

North-central Ohio was sparsely settled, but those residents felt betrayed. Moses Beach, the postmaster of New Haven, angrily expressed the reaction that Kilbourn and other supporters of the central route no doubt shared: "this event incites a general spirit of resistance and alarm among the people."[15] But the decision was firm, and both Worthington and Sandusky lost the potential for industrial growth and urban development that the canal routes established.[16]

James Kilbourn, however, never accepted defeat. He was already campaigning for election to the Ohio General Assembly, advocating the construction of a turnpike between the lake port and the state capital.[17] He promoted a route that would cut the distance from Columbus to Sandusky to 106 miles, passing through Worthington, Delaware, Norton, Claridon, and Bucyrus, all of these except Delaware being communities that he had platted.[18] Not only was Kilbourn's son Hector involved in surveying and developing Sandusky, but Kilbourn had secured the appointment as postmaster at Claridon for his son Byron and was counting on him to develop family business interests there.[19] In Bucyrus, which would become the major town on this route, Kilbourn's agreement with the landowner, Samuel Norton, granted him "one equal half part thereof" for surveying fifty acres into streets and lots for a city.[20] It was a handsome settlement for Kilbourn, and far more than surveyors normally received. To many citizens of Bucyrus, Kilbourn was a local hero and a congenial host at the local tavern. For the first public sale of lots, he composed a "Song of Bucyrus," to extol its virtues:

> Then hear my friend, your search may end,
>   For here's a country to your mind,
>   And here's a town your hope's may crown,
>   As those who try it soon shall find . . .[21]

For ten stanzas the bad poetry continued, but lubricated with whiskey the tune was apparently good local politics.

A plan for a privately owned toll road from Columbus to Sandusky was consistent with the times. Utter emphasizes the significance of private turnpike companies in building Ohio's system of highways, contending that by the 1820s and 1830s the best roads in the state were operated for private profit.[22]

The Columbus and Sandusky Turnpike Company was incorporated on January 31, 1826, by the Ohio legislature with twenty-six investors including Columbus stagecoach owners, McDowell and Neil, as well as numerous farmers with land along the projected route.[23] One hundred thousand dollars of capital stock was authorized in one hundred dollar shares, but the most significant contribution was a successful appeal to the United States Congress that granted 31,840 acres of land along the route to be sold to help finance construction. Worthington was represented by James Kilbourn as the surveyor and Orange Johnson as the superintendent of construction.

The projected cost was $81,680, or a little more than eight hundred dollars per mile including bridges. By July 1827, Orange Johnson advertised for bids to construct the forty-eight-mile section from Sandusky to Bucyrus, the northern portion of the route being the least developed and the most in need of the new road. Specifications required that "Thirty-six feet in the centre of the road must be grubbed; sixteen feet on each side, low cutting, and sixteen feet high cutting . . . . In low and wet ground the centre of the road to be raised four feet above the bottom of the ditches, in other grounds three and a half feet."[24] This turnpike was planned as a dirt road.

There were financial problems from the beginning. Some persons subscribed for stock beyond their ability to pay, and land sales did not produce the expected revenue because there were few inducements for settlement in this flat and poorly drained country. Between 1828

Fig. 25. Worthington businessman Orange Johnson served as superintendent for the construction of the Columbus and Sandusky Turnpike. (Courtesy of the Worthington Historical Society)

and 1833, the company borrowed money to keep construction moving, but there were insufficient funds to construct a "Macadamized" surface like the National Road, which was being built east to west across Ohio at the same time.[25] This process of compressing layers of broken stone to form a smooth road surface was named for its inventor, Scottish engineer John Macadam. In the terrain that the Columbus and Sandusky Turnpike crossed, its use might have made the difference between success and failure.

Nevertheless, by October 1833, a seventy-mile section from Sandusky south was completed and accepted for toll. Four-wheeled vehicles drawn by two horses or oxen were charged 25¢, two-wheeled vehicles paid 18¾¢, a sled or sleigh drawn by two horses or oxen cost 12½¢, a horse and rider was charged 6¼¢, and there were varied rates for livestock being driven or led on foot. There was no charge for militiamen going to and from muster, for mail coaches, or for any person going to and from Sabbath service.[26] This was consistent with state laws relating to toll roads and their rates.

A year later the last thirty-six miles were completed to Columbus, making the total cost of the 106-mile road $74,376. The Columbus and Sandusky Turnpike was completed under budget, but sacrifices had been made to adjust to less-than-projected income. The result was a road quality that satisfied no one. The clay surface became a network of impassable ruts and mud holes during much of the year, and at times it was so bad users refused to pay the toll. One minister, crossing the swampy plain south of Sandusky complained, "We left the turnpike, for the aggravation of this miserable track was greatly enhanced by the sight of a gate with rates of toll in glaring black paint every ten miles, and took the old road. . . ."[27] Bucyrus residents, who had no road to the lake prior to its completion, were somewhat more tolerant and considered it a "splendid road when dry." But even they admitted it was impassable when wet and indignantly refused to pay the toll. One enraged traveler "hitched the [toll]gate behind his wagon and dragged it several miles."[28] Faced with competition from the canal, which was now completed south from Cleveland, and with prospects for a recently incorporated Mad River and Lake Erie Railroad, the turnpike's financial situation was precarious.

In fact, the stagecoaches continued to use the old route from Columbus to Sandusky even though it was approximately twenty miles longer. The best description of this journey is one written by

Charles Dickens after he traveled this route April 22–23, 1842.[29] Wishing to leave Columbus on an unscheduled day for the tri-weekly stage, Dickens hired an "exclusive extra" coach with four horses to be changed at the same stops as the regular stage. Carrying a hamper of "eatables and drinkables," his party left Columbus at seven in the morning, "stopped in the wood to open our hamper and dine" about two in the afternoon, and arrived at a "rough log house" that served as an inn at Upper Sandusky about ten o'clock that night. He passed through but made no mention of Worthington. He described the first day's travel over this sixty-two-mile section of the route as "a track through a wild forest, and among the swamps, bogs, and morasses of the withered bush." Where logs had been thrown into swampy ground to provide a corduroy road surface, he found the ride like "going up a steep flight of stairs in an omnibus." One must presume that the stagecoaches chose to follow the better of the two routes north to the lake. If so, "The great northern turnpike" must have been a catastrophe by any traveler's standards. As the Indians had known years earlier, the shortest distance between two points was not necessarily the quickest.

Although there was a tollgate north of Worthington, the Columbus and Sandusky Turnpike did not materially affect travel to and from the village. As soon as the canal was completed to central Ohio, Worthington residents who traveled to New York or New England preferred to go some thirty miles east to Hebron where they could take a canal boat to Cleveland and connect with a steamboat across the lake to Buffalo. It was apparently a safe and respectable journey, for twenty-year-old Mary Case, a schoolteacher who had attended the Granville Female Seminary, used this route to travel east with her mother and grandmother to visit relatives. Mary was not impressed with "the hot crowded dirty noisy canal boats with their impure air and their impositions," but the ladies apparently suffered no ill effects from being confined with passengers sick with ague. For grandmother Sarah Buttles, then in her seventies, this was evidently the first trip to New England since she came west in 1804 and was widowed. What an adventure. Her daughter noted, "Mother is almost astonished at herself sometimes that she ever started to come so far off."[30]

From the early days of settlement, there was a surprising amount of travel between Worthington and New England. Nevertheless, the arrival of stagecoaches and canal boats in central Ohio and the advent of steamboats on Lake Erie and the Ohio River brought a degree of speed and comfort that residents found exhilarating. This era, which followed the economic depression after the banking collapse of 1819, has been described by historians as a transportation revolution created by turnpikes, canals, and railroads, transforming the market economy from local to national dimensions.[31]

The road that became the most famous route in nineteenth-century Ohio, however, wasn't a road at all. Much has been written about the Underground Railroad, that system of safe houses that provided a means for enslaved African-Americans to travel north to freedom.[32] Ohio was a key state in this movement because of its geographic location between the Ohio River and Canada, and Worthington had several known "conductors" on this system; however, the story of free blacks in Worthington began long before the Underground Railroad.

The New Englanders who settled Worthington were opposed to slavery, but there were few African-Americans either in early Ohio or in the Worthington settlement. It is not known whether the one "colored" person recorded in the 1820 census of Sharon Township was the same "Black Daniel" who was paid for working in Amos Maxfield's brickyard in 1807.

Free black males in Ohio were very nearly granted voting rights by the state constitutional convention of 1802,[33] but the more the state's population grew, the more restricted the position of African-Americans became. The infamous "Black Laws" passed by early legislative sessions made it difficult for them to obtain bond to enter the state and made it necessary for them to carry a certificate of freedom in order to be employed. They were also barred from militia service, jury service, testifying against whites, or sending their children to white schools.[34]

Despite such laws, an event occurred in Worthington in 1821 that marked this community as a safe place for free blacks to live. The only contemporary record of this incident was an advertisement by a Louisville, Kentucky, plantation owner named Robert Turner, who offered a five-hundred-dollar reward for a runaway slave named Isham who had been apprehended by a "slave catcher" and was being returned to Kentucky, but "was taken a few days since, near this place [Worthington] and was set at liberty. . . . he is supposed to be still in

Fig. 26. Julia Buttles Case came to Worthington as a child in 1804. Her letters provide glimpses of return visits to New England before marrying and later in life. (Taken from *Old Northwest Genealogical Quarterly*)

the neighborhood or gone towards Lower Sandusky and Canada & is well known to some in the vicinity."[35] Ohio was a free state and Worthingtonians most certainly were not going to allow someone to ride through town with a black slave in tow or to apprehend a black man living locally as a free man.

Worthington was far from alone in opposing the fugitive-slave law that required local officials in free states to return slaves to their masters. A riot a couple of months earlier at New Albany, Indiana, between local citizens and Kentuckians who attempted to seize an African-American who was in court attempting to prove his freedom, was widely reported in local newspapers.[36] This, no doubt, was in the minds of local residents when they were confronted with a "slave catcher" in their own town. Nevertheless, a five-hundred-dollar reward was astronomical. A few newspaper editors, such as James Wilson of the Steubenville *Western Herald*, refused on moral grounds to carry advertisements for runaway slaves, but most Ohio papers did.[37] Advertisements in Columbus newspapers typically offered ten- to twenty-dollar rewards and described the fugitives in some detail: "ANTHONY is of a yellow complexion, with a singular mark on the bridge of his nose; about five feet eight inches high, round shoulders, very pert when spoken to, and is fond of spirits; about 25 years of age."[38]

The five-hundred-dollar reward offered for the black who was freed from a "slave catcher" in Worthington indicates that Turner was incensed by the action and was relying upon one of the many participants or spectators to provide information. It must have been tempting in a depressed economy where such a sum would have purchased a one-hundred-acre farm with good buildings. The implication that Isham was "well known to some in the vicinity" suggests that he may have been working in the Worthington area or was known to free blacks who lived in Worthington, but the absence of any record of his recapture speaks strongly of the cohesiveness of the Worthington community in opposing slavery. It did not mean that blacks were treated as equals to whites there—or anywhere else in Ohio—but it did mean that Worthington was a community where they could feel secure.

The 1830 census recorded three hundred "colored" persons in Franklin County; of these, the families of Benjamin Lee and John Lee and the bachelors David Spillman and Henry Gurlo were in Sharon

Township.[39] Because Benjamin and Nancy Lee remained in the community until 1850, when they listed their place of birth as Virginia, it is likely that they were born as slaves and were given their freedom by masters who moved to Ohio. They did not own real estate, and there is little evidence to judge how these families interacted with the community. However, on August 19, 1830, and in September 1831, two infant children of Benjamin Lee died and were buried in the southeast corner of St. John's Episcopal Church burying ground, which at that time served the entire community.[40] One child was recorded as being a patient of Dr. Kingsley Ray, which indicates that this black family had access to the services of a white physician.

Although there is no record of any Worthington resident being a member of the American Colonization Society, Cynthia Goodale Kilbourn's brother, Columbus merchant Lincoln Goodale, was an active leader of the organization in Columbus and in the whole of Ohio. It is quite likely that some Worthington citizens supported its stated purpose of "repairing a great evil in our social and political institutions" by "colonizing the free people of color."[41] In 1827, the Columbus newspaper enthusiastically reported the landing of ninety-three "colonists" on an island off the Liberian coast.[42] There were some persons, in the north as well as the south, who felt manumission was inhibited by the fact that many people were troubled by the presence of free blacks in their community.[43] Although modern society finds removal a repugnant solution to the slavery issue, there were many in 1830 who considered it an enlightened viewpoint, designed to restore freedom and provide redress to those who had been forcibly taken from their African homes.

In 1835, the Ohio Methodist conference commended the American Colonization Society and expressed regret for the extremist activities of eastern abolitionists who were advocating the immediate abolishment of slavery. The conference considered that "to encourage inflammatory lectures . . . in favor of immediate abolition is injurious to Christian fellowship, dangerous to our civil institutions, unfavorable to the privileges and spiritual interests of the slaves, and unbecoming any Christian Patriot or Philanthropist, and especially any Methodist."[44]

The means for ending slavery was obviously a controversial issue in this denomination, as in others, for all three Worthington congregations were represented among the group of citizens who on

March 28, 1835, at the home of W. S. Spencer, organized the Worthington Anti-Slavery Society. This group was affiliated with the Ohio Anti-Slavery Society and adopted a constitution that stated their objective of achieving not only the emancipation of slaves from their masters, but "the emancipation of the colored man from the oppression of public sentiment and unjust laws and the elevation of both [slaves and free blacks] to an intellectual and moral equality with whites." It is a thought-provoking statement of purpose, made powerful not only by the simplicity of its language but by its direct attack upon the "oppression of public sentiment," an issue that continues to divide this country 160 years later.[45]

Members of the Worthington society pledged their own efforts "to do this by endeavoring to convince all our fellow citizens by arguments addressed to their understanding and consciences that slave holding is a heinous crime in the sight of God and that the safety and best interest of all concerned require its immediate abolition." They went so far as to pledge themselves to "endeavor in a constitutional way to influence Congress and our State Legislature to relieve the colored people where they have the power of legislation." This was a strong statement, but one clearly intended to operate within existing law and political process.

This constitution was circulated within the community for signatures and was subscribed to by sixty-six persons, the only requirement being that "Any person who consents to the principles of this Society may become a member." Curiously, in view of the stated purpose, there were no persons of color among the original members. There is no evidence whether free blacks were offered the opportunity to join or whether they were afraid to do so.[46] The Worthington Anti-Slavery Society did include twenty-four females, the only organization in the village, other than churches, known to have included both men and women. That same year, two of the charter members, W. S. Spencer and A. H. Pinney, were elected as trustees of the first village council, so they obviously reflected community leadership.

Subsequent minutes of the society do not reveal when members began taking an active part in assisting blacks to move north on the Underground Railroad, but they do disclose an increasingly militant opposition to any politician who did not support, both in word and action, the concept that "*All* Men are created equal." Worthington was establishing itself not only as a community that would help runaway slaves move toward freedom, but more importantly as a place where African-Americans could feel reasonably secure in living and working. In that respect, it was indeed a "pleasant and thriving post town."

◆ CHAPTER 17 ◆

Leghorn Bonnets, Horn Sided
Corsets, and German
Silver Teaspoons

— ◆ —

SQUIRRELS ARE BECOMING so numerous in this county as to
threaten serious injury if not destruction to the hopes of the
farmer during the ensuing fall."[1] A civilized environment solved
some problems, but it created others. As more and more land was
cleared for fields of corn and as some of the larger natural predators
like bobcats retreated deeper into the woods, the squirrel population
escalated. Residents responded with a county-wide squirrel hunt
which produced 19,660 scalps, not counting those from hunters who
failed to turn theirs in. The Columbus newspaper gloated, "We challenge any other county in the state to kill squirrels with us."[2]

But squirrels weren't the only beneficiaries who were profiting
from the bounty of Ohio farms. Utter contends that the immigrants
who flooded the state provided a significant market for farm produce during their first year of residence, but that after the second
year these same immigrants became successful producers who contributed to the surplus of crops seeking a market.[3] After two decades
of clearing and cultivation, the farms surrounding Worthington were
prosperous producers desperate for a profitable means of reaching
beyond the local market. Village residents were, of course, consistent
consumers for local farmers. The 1822 estate of Nathaniel Little, who
worked as a saddler, included a bill from Moses Maynard for "a pig
weighing 21¾ [lb.] $1.25, a half bushel of peaches 25 cents, a half
bushel of apples 50 cents."[4] Such transactions between local farmers
and villagers were fairly typical.

Before the advent of the canal, however, the costs of transporting grain to eastern markets were prohibitive. It was much cheaper and more profitable to transport whiskey or hogs when it required about fifteen bushels of corn to fatten a hog or to produce about forty-seven gallons of whiskey.[5] The inventory of Selah Wilcox's estate in 1824 illustrates the value of farm produce in this pre-canal era: "60 bushel corn at 12½ cents a bushel, 35 bushel wheat at 37 cents, 50 lbs. cheese at 6 cents a pound."[6] After harvest the following summer, wheat had dropped to 25¢ per bushel and rye was worth only 13¾¢ per bushel.[7]

It is quite clear from estate inventories that local farmers relied upon a diversity of crops to become as self-sufficient as possible. Laurinda Case's share as the widow of Israel P. Case included "4 fat hogs in the pen $16, hay in barn $8, oats in bundle $3, corn in cribs $14.06, cheese in house $3, potatoes in field $3, rye in the grannery $2."[8] In this period local farmers commonly produced corn, wheat, rye, oats, hay, flax, potatoes, apples, and peaches; they cut wood from their woodlot and often produced either sorghum molasses, honey, or maple sugar. All of these were consumed by the household and sold or traded in local markets. Livestock was also diversified. Farmers usually had at least one or two horses and frequently a colt, usually at least one or two cows and calves, often a yoke of oxen and some steers or yearling heifers, always two or three sows and pigs, and occasionally a few sheep.[9] Sheep were vulnerable to a variety of predators, even domestic dogs, and their presence in the area declined as commercial woolens became more readily available. Diversified crops and livestock were, however, the standard for nineteenth-century "family farms."[10]

Inventories suggest that the basic farm equipment used in this community did not change dramatically during the first two or three decades of settlement. Everyone still had wagons and plows, but the Selah Wilcox inventory in 1824 portrayed one of the more prosperous farm estates valued at $493.23. It included one "bull plow" and two "patent plows" worth seven dollars each.[11] The presence of both types of plows in this estate illustrates the transition then taking place in soil cultivation technology and the speed with which the new technology was being adopted in Ohio. Most of the farmers during this time had a "fanning mill" worth about four dollars, clear evidence that grain was being cleaned on individual farms.[12] Most had at least two scythes and two or more sickles, proving that these were widely available from local blacksmiths and that most farms counted on more than one man working at the same time.[13] Several inventories contained "flax breakers," showing that the home production of linen fiber was quite common.

The farm tools of the American colonies on the eastern seaboard were little changed from Roman times, with simple hoes, spades, plows, sickles, scythes, rakes, and flails representing the hand labor necessary for planting and harvesting. But change was beginning to occur, particularly as iron began to replace wood and as manpower shifted to horsepower.[14] Worthington farmers were definitely interested in testing and acquiring the latest technological conveniences.

Peter Barker actually designed and patented a "thrashing machine" that he advertised as "much superior to any heretofore in use." Testimonials from neighbors who used it during the July 1827 harvest were glowing. Levi Pinney stated, "The machine is propelled by one horse with ease and from the experiment which I made of it, I am led to the conclusion, that properly attended it will thrash in one day from 250 to 300 bushels of wheat, allowing ten working hours to the day." John G. Miller said it was "worked by one horse with perfect ease, requires but two men in immediate attendance upon it (one to feed and another to remove the straw), will cost but from 30 to 40 dollars, and will thrash, I think, three hundred bushels of grain per day, without any other than ordinary exertion." Ebenezer Washburn saw it "thrash forty-five sheaves in five minutes of which it was said that every sixteen would make a bushel." Moses Trumbull "assisted in thrashing, cleaning and measuring the wheat, and found that it thrashed the wheat very clean, at the rate of 36 bushels an hour."[15]

This was one of the first threshing machines in the state. Such performance was certainly a giant step forward from the hand flailing method of separating grain from straw, but Barker's marketing success apparently did not equal his inventive genius. The invention brought him no fame or fortune, but testimonials from farmers who spoke of threshing three hundred bushels of wheat per day only twenty-three years after they settled this wilderness is dramatic evidence of both productive soil and much hard work in clearing and cultivating fields. Such farms were the base that sustained the Worthington community when the manufacturing company collapsed.

Many of the local farmers were landowners, but a significant number were tenants. Due to an untimely death, one of these land-lord-tenant agreements was preserved in detail. In 1827, Asa Gillet died as a result of "slipping from a hay mow onto a pitchfork." It was a death that shocked the community for "he survived the accident about a fortnight [before] death then put an end to his sufferings."[16] The strong suggestion of a tetanus infection is grim testimony to the vulnerability of a man in the prime of life in the era before antibiotics.

The 235-acre Gillet farm was north of town, bounded on the west by the river and traversed by the road to Delaware. It was advertised by his executors as containing 100–150 acres "well improved and suitable for meadow or plough land." This suggests that approximately one hundred acres were still wooded. The farmstead was described as being elevated and healthy with "a good Barn, comfortable dwelling house, and out houses, and a good bearing orchard."[17]

The agreement signed on April 1, 1826, between Gillet and his tenant, William Dunton, was for three years. Dunton was to have the use of all of the land and "tenements" and was, in turn, to provide the "labor necessary for the growth and increase of the stock," which included "horses, neat cattle, and hogs."[18] Proceeds from any increase in the livestock were to be divided equally. In the dairy, expenses for rennet and for marketing cheese were to be defrayed and taken against the profits, which were to be divided equally. Dunton was responsible for repairing fences by making "three hundred rails each and every year and lay them in fence where they were the most wanted." Gillet was to pay the real estate taxes.[19] The fact that no crops were mentioned in the rental agreement suggests that this farm was growing corn, hay, oats, and pasture that were consumed by the livestock on the farm, from which were obtained marketable pork, beef, butter, and cheese.

Many farmers had skills or specialized products that were used to supplement their cash income. The Stephan Maynard farm was one of the most prosperous in the area with an estate appraised at $665.89. The inventory included "500 hogshead staves, 160 barrel staves, 10 hogshead headings," and a "rope and pulling block." Either Maynard was a cooper or he was providing materials for one who was employed on the farm. The inclusion of thirteen cherry logs suggests that timber was being selectively cut on the Maynard farm south of town and dried for sale to local cabinetmakers.[20] Some farmers produced a specialty product. The seventy sap buckets sold in the Israel P. Case estate auction were probably typical of a farm with a sugar maple grove.[21]

The receipts in both farm and village estates reflect the diversity of services available in this community, which was now a thriving agricultural market town. Orange Johnson was producing and selling combs, Laughlem McLean was tailoring coats, Christopher Ripley's saddle shop was selling whips made by Eri Bristol, Charles Mills was making vests and pantaloons, and Samuel Brown was selling bridle leather.[22] Potter Wright provided carding, and Levi Pinney offered blacksmith services.[23] There is little evidence regarding the financial value of women's work, but the regular trade in butter and cheese from dairy operations, which wives normally conducted, reveals the value of such products. There was also regular production of linen and wool cloth in a number of homes. Emily Maynard reported to her sister, "I have wove fifty yards of cloth on Father's loom and should have wove as much more if I had not been sick. . . ."[24] She suffered from pleurisy that winter, which evidently hampered her ability to work, but her statement reflects a large loom and a skilled operator. This product may have been for family use; but considering that her parents were approaching their seventies, that their children were all adults, and that Emily had been married for several years, this sounds much more like the "outwork" that clothiers contracted from rural households.[25]

Men like carpenter/cabinetmaker Joseph Greer were responsible for much of the increased quantity and quality of the furnishings in local homes. When Greer died in 1829, he left his family with few resources, but his estate reflected a well-equipped craftsman. His estate contained a handsaw, sash saw, dovetail saw, compass saw, a hand drill, a pair of nippers, a candling mallet, and an iron square. It also contained several shaves, including a round one; several chisels, including a "duckbill" one; clamps, including a "smith's vise" and a saw clamp; and an assortment of rasps, hammers, files, gauges, "callipers," a bass winder, a screw cutter, a "turning lathe and two rests" valued at sixteen dollars, and a "large turning lathe" appraised at ten dollars.[26] Lathes were valuable pieces of equipment, owned by few craftsmen. Greer's possession of two lathes for turning spindles, chair legs, or balusters for stairs, placed him among the cabinetmaking elite.[27]

Specialized workmen like cooper Sidney Brown marketed their wares from Columbus to Chillicothe and Sandusky. G. R. Butler bought twenty butter firkins. Burr, Gregory and Co. in Columbus ordered cheese casks from thirteen to seventeen inches in diameter, sugar barrels, ten-gallon kegs, five-gallon kegs, twenty-five kegs in assorted sizes, bacon casks, and twenty flaxseed firkins.[28] Much of Brown's trade, however, was in making and repairing the salt, sugar, vinegar, cider, and whiskey barrels and the pickle and soap tubs that were now common in nearly every Worthington household.[29]

Even after the collapse of the Worthington Manufacturing Company retail chain, including the original store in Worthington, the town continued to support four or five merchants throughout the 1820s and 1830s. All of these ran credit accounts for regular customers and conducted a significant portion of their business by trading in goods and services rather than in cash. R. W. Cowles was probably typical in offering a 25 percent discount on most items if they were paid for in cash.[30]

Comstock and Cowles, and later Cowles alone, had the largest general store in Worthington during this period, and practically every estate settled during this time included a bill from there. An inventory taken two months before Cowles's death in 1842, valued the merchandise on hand at $4,996.08 and sales during the sixty days prior to his death at $950.70.[31] The size of the inventory, the volume of sales, and the variety of goods all suggest that Worthington attracted customers from several miles around.

One of Cowles's largest departments was the dry goods section, which featured over three hundred varieties of yard goods of varying fabrics, colors, and quality. Prices varied considerably depending on the quality of the material. Some of the more luxurious and costly fabrics were "innis green" valued per yard at $2.84 to $5.30, "Casimer" in black or blue-black at $1.90 to $2.25, "cadet" cloth at 56¢ to $2.25, "urban cloth" at 62¢, "beaverteen" at 58¢ to 75¢ cents, "Orelan Deflora" at 83¢, "Moris DeLane" at 19¢, figured saxony at 49¢ to 72¢, and "bombagin" at $1.00.

The variety of colors available might have been influenced by Cowles's teenaged daughters and their friends. "Satinet" was offered in black, blue, drab, or figured; velvet in purple, green, brown, drab, or red; "mersails" in buff, purple, or white; chintz in light blue, pink, buff, striped, or "spotted"; flannel in red, green, white, or checked. Calico—in brown, black, green, pink, blue, figured, or checked—could be purchased for 8¢ to 27¢ a yard; or plaid gingham for 37¢. "Painted" lawn or muslin ranged from 26¢ to 40¢. Checks, plaids, polka-dot, and prints clearly represent access to the fabrics of a sophisticated weaving industry.

Cowles carried both domestic and imported fabrics, and the range of the latter suggests that Worthington women had access to the latest eastern and perhaps even European fashions. Prices, including "original cost and carriage," were 54¢ to 88¢ per yard for "English marino" in brown, green, blue-black, or black; French merino wool was more expensive at $1.00 to $1.20; and German was less expensive at 50¢ a yard. Swiss muslin, either plain or flowered, ranged from 27¢ to 66¢, and French chintz was 48¢ a yard.

Vesting was available in black silk, in white or black satin, and in several stripes. Pink crepe, black lace, and "sliper shally" imply the suggested presence in the village of some rather elegant party dresses, as do a variety of ribbon trims ranging from dark purple to plaid to "Chinese." The latter were so expensive at $2.50 to $3.91 per yard that one suspects seamstresses used them very sparingly, for accent.

The dry goods department also included a variety of items for the home. Sheeting was available in "coarse linen, Coddington, or Russian." Customers could find canvas, bed padding, several colors and weights of drilling, and A.C.A. or Manchester "tick" at 20¢ a yard. A lady could purchase a plain or damask tablecloth from $1.25 to $1.75. Oil cloth could be purchased in several grades from 63¢ to $1.75 per yard, and Cowles carried several varieties of wallpaper priced from 17¢ to 25¢ per yard. Technological innovations, such as wallpaper, were changing the appearance and comfort of the home, just as equipment such as threshing machines were affecting the farm.

Cowles carried a variety of woolen and cotton knitting yarns, but he also had ready-made stockings, gloves, and mittens, no doubt from New England mills. Stockings in black or white, cotton or worsted, cost from 16¢ to 75¢ a pair. In gloves, ladies were offered a choice of "elastic wrist," black or flesh-colored silk, wool, white or flesh-colored cotton, black net, or white kid for prices ranging from 8¢ to 40¢ a pair. For men there were "good black" and "coarse woolen" gloves. Handkerchiefs were available in linen, chenille, gauze, gingham, red worsted, or plaid. Fans cost 5¢ each. Cotton or worsted suspenders were priced from 10¢ to 27¢. A variety of ladies shawls cost from 55¢ for worsted to $3.70 for "leghorn."[32]

Of course there was also a wide variety of sewing thread. Pins were expensive at $1.00 per package, as were needles at $1.65 per paper. Silver thimbles cost 29¢ each, and "eyelotts" were 37¢ per gross; there was a wide variety of buttons, ranging from iron, horn, "black coat," velvet, "satin vest," to "figured gilt."

Many residents, of course, patronized a local milliner or made their own bonnets, but Cowles offered leghorn bonnets from $4.40 to $5.00 each, straw ones at $1.37 to $1.65, children's bonnets at 90¢, "Tuscan" bonnets at 75¢, cloth caps at $1.00, fur caps from $2.32 to $3.25, hoods at 28¢, and an assorted variety of twenty-two hats valued at $1.50 each. It would appear that industrialized manufacturing was poised to replace home production in everything except home-sewn garments.

Although many villagers undoubtedly patronized local shoemakers for boots and shoes and repairs, Cowles offered a wide variety of "ladies slippers, misses boots," and ladies', men's, and children's shoes, priced from 40¢ to $1.25 per pair. He also carried "sole leather" at 18½¢ per pound, sheep skins for 53½¢, or "Morrocco" skins for 81¢ each—for those with the time and skill to resole boots or craft purses and small leather items.

As befitted any town specializing in education, Cowles's store had a section devoted to books and school supplies. He stocked a variety of geography, mathematics, grammar, history, and scientific texts, as well as spelling and copy books and several dozen "toy books." Dictionaries were priced at 37¢ each, almanacs at 31¢, Bibles at 46¢, testaments at 11¢, and hymnbooks at 25¢. Paper was valued in the inventory at $4.00 per ream, but it was sold by the sheet. Black, blue, or red ink was 6½¢ to 8½¢ per bottle, and quills were two for 1¢. Candles could be purchased at 10¢ per pound.

There were merchants in the village who specialized in groceries and fresh meat, such as the Tuller brothers, but Cowles had a section in his store where the aroma of spices undoubtedly predominated. This aroma was a mix of mustard, nutmeg, pepper, pimento, clove, saffron, and ginger—as well as coffee (at 14¢ a pound) and various imported teas (at 33¢ to 83¢ a pound). In this same area customers could find lump sugar, loaf sugar, or "Orleans" sugar by the barrel. Dyes and fixatives such as madder, indigo, cochineal, French yellow, and alum attested to the survival of a home weaving-and-knitting industry. Red, white, and venetian red lead were available for mixing paint. In this same area one found glue, starch, rosin, epsom salts, borax, gum shellac, sulfur, castor oil, snake root, gum camphor, bayberry, cough syrup, and boxes of "Jewetts pills." A bag of pipes for smokers apparently rested near gallon jugs of wine and gin and not far from a keg of gunpowder. Tobacco was for sale at 25¢ to 40¢ per pound, black or Scotch snuff at 19¢ to 25¢.

In one section of the store, pocket and side combs of horn, small iron combs, and wooden pick combs accompanied clothes brushes, toothbrushes, shaving brushes, razors and razor strops, boxes of boot blacking, and cakes of shaving or brown soap. A bunch of false hair was priced at 37¢ and several other "artificials" at 28¢.[33] "Horn sided corsets" were 40¢ to 82¢, and spectacles were 16¢ a pair.

There was an extensive housewares section that offered a German silver coffeepot for $1.66 and several "Britainia" teapots from 73¢ to 88¢ each.[34] Cowles carried glass salts, peppers, and mustards; sugar and creamer sets; a variety of pitchers, platters, edged soups, sauce dishes, dining plates, oval dishes, and tumblers; and a complete set of china priced at $5.34. There were several sizes of glass knobs for bureaus and doors, cupboard and chest locks, brass candlesticks at 36¢ each or iron ones at 1½¢, and "taper lamps" at 8¢.[35] Iron teaspoons were 2½¢ each, "Britainia" teaspoons at 6¢, and "German silver" teaspoons at 7¢. Knives and forks were valued from 67¢ to $1.55 per set.

The hardware section was filled with boxes and kegs of nails, screws, gimlets, bolts, martingale rings, and fish hooks—all of diverse sizes and varieties. There was also a variety of grain shovels, spades, manure forks, stone crocks, buckets and pails of various sizes, axe handles, brooms, bushels and pecks, wash basins, chamber pots, sad irons, whitewash and paint brushes, steelyards, rolls of wire, nail and shoe hammers, and several sizes of rope. Mousetraps cost 10¢ each, whips 50¢ to 75¢, sheep shears 47¢, and padlocks 19¢. There was a wide variety of small items such as sieves, awls, files, augers, butcher knives, chisels, and such.

The most expensive items in the store were a "large brass kettle," inventoried at $14.95, and a clock, valued at $10.00. Trunks were available at $2.00 each, two large mirrors were priced at $3.25 each, and umbrellas sold at 84¢ each. The overwhelming impression made by this inventory is the amazing speed with which the residents of this village had acquired access to the goods of mass production. What began modestly when the Worthington Manufacturing Company wagons started hauling eastern goods, shipped west on lake steamers, had become a cornucopia of products by the 1830s, when canal boats competed with the wagons of the National Road. There were, of course, persons in the village and on the surrounding farms who preferred to make their own soap or candles, but this was now a matter of economic choice or of perceived quality rather than of availability. The same was true for home spinning and weaving. By the 1830s, even tools and cooking utensils were frequently imported rather than individually crafted by local blacksmiths.

This did not mean that Worthington did not appreciate craftsmanship. It was at this same time that one of the most ingenious Yankee craftsmen ever to inhabit the village brought it national and even international attention.[36] James Russell had migrated west from Massachusetts, and, as early as February 1808, he was billing Ezra Griswold for "repairing a big wheel."[37] His carpentry and cabinetmaking skills provided steady work. That year he completed for Griswold alone two bedsteads, a plow handle, a hoe handle, and six chairs.[38]

Russell apparently had a creative mind, a mechanical aptitude, and a passion for astronomy that was widely shared in the early nineteenth century. By the 1830s, he was Worthington's most famous citizen, being described in the Ohio gazetteer as "the ingenious inventor of Russel's new and improved Planetarium or Columbian Orrery."[39] Orreries were mechanical models of the solar system, named for the earl of Orrery who sponsored the first one in England early in the eighteenth century. Russell's project evolved over several years with the assistance of several interested young men, such as Ralph Hills and George Topping, and the facilities of Potter Wright's machine shop.

Even as the orrery continued to grow, its fame spread and people traveled some distance to view it. Dorcas Cary, whose father had been a member of the Scioto Company, asked her husband whether he had seen it as he traveled from their home in Crawford County to Columbus for the session of the state legislature. She confessed, "My mind has been quite excited with a wish to behold the ingenuity of man, displaying the Beauteous movements of the Heavenly Bodies."[40] For some, the sight was apparently almost a religious experience.

In its final form, the "great Zodiac" of planets orbited a sun represented by a revolving, gilt globe approximately fifteen inches in diameter. The inner planets of Mercury, Venus, the Earth, and its moon rotated in a circle forty-eight feet in diameter, while Jupiter,

Saturn, and Herschel—now known as Uranus—were separate little orreries that extended the rotation to sixty-six feet. The planets were represented by "beautiful glass globes, made opaque, with some attention to their relative magnitudes and telescopic appearance."[41]

The entire imposing device contained "about 500 cog wheels, large and small, principally of brass." The whole mechanism—composed primarily of wrought iron, cast iron, and brass—weighed approximately one and a half tons. Planets, satellites, and moons revolved on their axes in appropriately inclined orbits, and all together totaled eighty-one separate motions.

It was too magnificent a creation to be limited to a western village the size of Worthington, and it was eventually taken east by a wagon and four-horse team to be displayed across New York State on its way to New York City.[42] There it was exhibited at the American Institute, accompanied by the astronomy lectures of a Parisian professor who pronounced it superior to any astronomical machinery he had seen in London, Paris, Hamburg, Berlin, or St. Petersburg.

One New York reporter admitted that he had expected an interesting lecture on astronomy but that "we had no idea of being transported so unexpectedly beyond the limits of the entire planetary system . . . but there we were viewing with perfect astonishment the most brilliant, finished piece of mechanism, illustrating the position, revolution and varied changes of all the great planets of the universe . . . which proved to us that the ingenuity of man, in constructing such a wonderful piece of mechanism, was capable of accomplishing his most complicated designs."[43] Russell's orrery was definitely the "Omnimax" planetarium extravaganza of its day, and it briefly placed the name of Worthington on the national scene.[44]

By the 1830s, Worthington had become not only a thriving market town for a diversified agricultural community, but it had nurtured creative genius that was appreciated well beyond its borders.

❖ CHAPTER 18 ❖

So Much Boast of Succession
Handed Down from the Apostles

— ❖ —

By 1821, Worthington was a community with three thriving religious congregations, but without church buildings. A decade later all three had their own buildings and a strengthened sense of individual identity that persisted throughout the nineteenth century.

The organization of St. John's Episcopal Church on February 6, 1804, was a remarkable achievement for a group of recently arrived pioneer settlers. The desire to organize a church was far from a universal priority in frontier communities. Sweet quotes a missionary to the Western Reserve who found, though many people there came from "a land of bibles and Sabbaths and ministers and churches," that "now they act like freed prisoners."[1]

The leaders of the Worthington settlement, however, were determined that their community would, from the beginning, have regular Episcopal services. The keynote speaker for St. John's sesquicentennial celebration noted that the original "articles of agreement" had a strange duality. On a secular note, they established a society that intended to seek incorporation under Ohio law, which would be administered by a moderator, a recording clerk, three trustees, and a treasurer. On a sacred note, they created an ecclesiastical establishment with two church wardens, a reading clerk, a tithing man, and "sufficient" choristers.[2] The word "parish" did not appear in this document, and the brief mention of "the Clergyman or other officiating person" did not describe this position or its duties. The pioneer congregation apparently assumed that James Kilbourn, as an ordained deacon, would conduct services when he was available and that a lay reader would serve in his absence.

Kilbourn, however, was frequently absent on business affairs, and the congregation desperately wanted a regular clergyman. As early as 1810, trustees Ezra Griswold, John Goodrich, and Alexander Morrison solicited the assistance of the national Episcopal convention to attract an ordained minister. Rev. Baldwin responded, assuring them that "every Member expressed an anxious desire that some person would visit you: but the distance and the difficulties attending such an undertaking, prevented the few Clergymen unemployed in this State [Connecticut] from accepting your proposals."[3] The Episcopal Church was not strong enough to place a high priority on western missionaries.

In 1816, James Kilbourn and Joseph Dodridge, an Episcopal minister in western Virginia who also served at Steubenville, Ohio, made the bold move of inviting delegates from all Episcopal congregations west of the Alleghenies to convene at Worthington "for the purpose of constituting a regular diocese in the western country and selecting a suitable personality for the bishop thereof."[4] Although some forty persons arrived for the preaching, Kilbourn and Dodridge were the only clergymen, and they restricted themselves to another appeal to eastern bishops for rectors to serve congregations in the west.

The following spring, Roger Searle, an Episcopal clergyman on the Western Reserve, carried a request from Kilbourn to the general convention. It was a passionate plea comparing the status of the Episcopal church in Ohio to the western country itself, "a soil rich and luxuriant in natural productions . . . yet a wilderness and in that state incapable of sustaining our people." For Christian ministers Kilbourn considered "the space for action like the Country is wide and ample, but like the Wilderness unproductive until it shall be rendered productive by his own exertions."[5]

A clergyman was, however, already on the way. Perhaps he had heard of and been attracted by Kilbourn and Dodridge's attempt to organize a western diocese and select a bishop. In any event, Rev. Philander Chase visited Ohio that spring and preached at several locations on the Western Reserve and at Zanesville. The first Sunday in June 1817, he preached at Worthington and soon afterward was persuaded to become the rector of St. John's parish in Worthington, the Trinity congregation in Columbus, and St. Peter's in Delaware.[6]

There was no salary attached to the rector's position, although donations were undoubtedly contributed from time to time by members of these congregations. Chase expected to earn a living from his concurrent appointment as principal of the Worthington Academy and from the farm he purchased south of town which he expected to operate with hired help.

A year later, in convention at the Worthington Academy in June 1818, five Episcopal ministers and lay delegates formed the Episcopal diocese of Ohio and elected Rev. Chase as their bishop.[7] It was a move that placed Worthington at the center of the Ohio Episcopal organization and that made it the convention site for the diocese during the first six years of its existence. His responsibilities as bishop caused Rev. Chase to be often absent from Worthington, but Chase's services were a memorable experience. Elnathan Maynard, son of Stephan Maynard, one of the church leaders during Rev. Chase's tenure, recalled the academy room on the second floor where services were held as "very plainly furnished. I think the seats were only boards or slabs." A morning service at 10:30 and an afternoon service at 1:00 were separated by an hour at noon, which the Maynard family frequently spent at the Chase home, where "No luncheon was served, but sling (whiskey and water sweetened) was passed."[8] This was a standard courtesy of the day, which Maynard compared to offering someone a chair.[9]

Chase initially found the Worthington residents "remarkable for civil and moral deportment." His tenure in Worthington might have been quite different had his wife Mary Fay Chase not succumbed to tuberculosis within a year of her arrival—for it was Mary Chase who wrote the constitution and opened her home for the organizational meeting of the Worthington Female Tract Society. Such groups were formed in a number of places at this time to provide Christian readings, usually reprinted from other publications as free pamphlets for local families. Dues were twenty-five cents annually. Cynthia Kilbourn was the first president, and Ruth Griswold was the vice-president. Former teacher Clarissa Thompson would be treasurer for twenty-four years. The group's first pamphlet was a reprint of an old English bishop's "Rules for Christian Children and Youth." Sometimes the women met for prayers and to read potential materials for publication. Other times they met for work, such as to "repair garments for indigent children who could not attend Sunday school

Fig. 27. Rev. Philander Chase was the first rector of St. John's Episcopal Church at Worthington, the first bishop of the Episcopal Diocese of Ohio, and the founder of Kenyon College. (Courtesy of the Ohio Historical Society)

for want of decent clothing."[10] The Worthington Female Tract Society was a classic example of the moral role assigned to nineteenth-century women in developing and maintaining the moral values of the family and, through it, of society.

The death of Mary Chase and her husband's being called on to travel widely as bishop coincided with the economic collapse of 1819, which doomed both the Worthington Manufacturing Company and the projected evolution of the Worthington Academy into Worthington College. These would all seem to have been troubles enough for Chase's ministry in Worthington, but serious animosity also developed between Chase and Kilbourn. Both were men with substantial leadership qualities, but both had large egos and were accustomed to having things done *their* way. Chase won many friends outside his immediate circle, but those who worked directly with him were regularly alienated by his dictatorial manner and by his inclination to identify Philander Chase's will with God's will.[11]

The Ohio diocese adopted a canon at its 1819 convention that a clergyman could be brought to trial for "disorderly and immoral conduct, neglect of duty, disregard to the Constitution and Canons of the Church, or disseminating, or countenancing opinions which are contrary to its doctrines."[12] This was apparently directed specifically toward Deacon Kilbourn, who had evidently clashed with Chase over his business and political affairs. The following year, Kilbourn was called before the diocese for trial, "on charges affecting his moral conduct."[13] Chase made a scathing address at the 1820 convention, which Kilbourn attended as a deacon, regarding proper and improper ministerial behavior. There were others in the St. John's congregation who shared his concern. Chester Griswold, embittered by Kilbourn's faulty management of the manufacturing company that resulted in lawsuits against everything Griswold owned, was an elected St. John's trustee and a delegate to the 1821 convention. But someone, perhaps his mentor Alexander Viets Griswold, persuaded Kilbourn to resign rather than to face trial. On June 6, 1821, Bishop Chase informed the delegates that he had received a letter from James Kilbourn which "declared his intention no longer to be a minister of the Church of Christ." Chase indicated, "I have agreeably to the aforesaid Canon displaced him from the ministry."[14]

It was a sad conclusion, but in truth Kilbourn had neither the theological training nor the time to devote himself to a ministerial role.

There was also a history of disaffection with Kilbourn. Some in the congregation, like William Thompson, had been alienated at least a decade earlier; and some, like the Beaches and Bristols, had pointedly left the Episcopal church for the Methodist congregation. Unfortunately, Rev. Chase was not the man to unite the troubled congregation. He was rarely in Worthington after 1820, and he entrusted his responsibilities as rector first to his son Philander, Jr., and later to his nephew Intrepid Morse and to two other theological students, Marcus Wing and William Sparrow, who were afterward associated with Kenyon College.[15]

When Chase resigned as rector of St. John's Episcopal Church to accept a teaching position in Cincinnati in 1822 and traveled to England the following year, he was actively pursuing his dream of developing an Episcopal seminary in the west. To attract financial support in England he offered to donate his Worthington farm as the seminary site, provided he and his family could retain occupancy of the "mansion house" as part of his salary as superintendent of the school.[16] Although neither Chase nor the Ohio diocese was satisfied with Worthington as a site for this seminary, he began to offer instruction at his home in 1824 and had as many as fifty students there before moving to new quarters in Knox County and opening Kenyon College in 1828. It is noteworthy that during this time Chase had no association with the Worthington College facility. Chase was very pleased to leave Worthington and was particularly happy that his second wife, Sophia, would no longer be disturbed by "the viper-like hissing of envy and toad-like croakings of malice and atheism."[17] Chase's alienation from Worthington was shared by Worthington's feelings for Chase. His early supporters were deceased, removed from the community, or estranged.

In 1817, St. John's Episcopal Church had attracted Rev. Chase as its rector with visions of a bright future; however, after a decade of dissension and neglect, its prospects only caused Rev. Sparrow to look apprehensively at the growing Methodist and Presbyterian congregations and complain, "Our people seem very dead. You seldom find a truly zealous man among them. They will talk about the Church and about the dissenters; of churches, wood, brick, and stone, of pulpits, desks, chairs and organs, of Methodists and Presbyterians, but have not a word to say about religion. May the Lord open their eyes."[18]

Ironically, it was these people, whom Rev. Sparrow found apathetic and concerned only with their physical surroundings, who soon began constructing the church building that allowed the congregation to remove their services from the college premises and gave them more of a sectarian focus. Like earlier public buildings in the village, St. John's Church required contributions of materials and labor. Arora Buttles, George H. Griswold, and Stephan Maynard, Jr., were the trustees in 1830 who sold the twenty-acre woodlot, presumably to raise funds to build a church. Griswold hauled stone for the foundation. Maynard, together with his brother Elnathan, cut walnut trees on their farm, dragged the logs to the sawmill, and had them sawed into lumber for the pews. Buttles, the only mason in town who is known to have mastered Flemish-bond construction, undoubtedly laid the brick. By 1829, Rev. William Preston was able to report to the convention that Worthington had "completed the outside of a beautiful brick church"; however, progress was slow, and the first service in the new building was not held until January 23, 1831.[19]

Although St. John's Episcopal Church was the third building for worship to be constructed in Worthington, it had an elegance of design and construction that surpassed the other two and survived longer. Its Gothic Revival style was accented by a pointed-arch entry and windows, a stepped-gable facade, and a square tower with the belfry topped by a balustrade and finials. The design was probably inspired by Gothic churches Rev. Chase had seen in England; it is remarkably similar to the 1823 St. Mark's Episcopal Church in Lewistown, Pennsylvania, designed by Rev. Norman Nash.[20] By 1828 Nash was working with Chase on the design and construction of Kenyon Hall at Gambier, and although Chase was alienated from some members of the Worthington Episcopal congregation, he continued to visit in the Buttles home and may well have shared Nash's Gothic design. In New England, Anglican churches were traditionally considered more genteel in their architecture than Congregational churches, and the evangelical congregations most popular on the frontier pointedly avoided fashionable elegance.[21] One senses that the Episcopal congregation was presenting a visible answer to the competition they were feeling from the rapidly growing Methodist and Presbyterian congregations. They were using their church building to define themselves as people of refinement.

Historians have noted the unifying effect of revival meetings that frequently brought converts to all local religious societies, but the more churches there were in a community, the greater the social cleavage.[22] There is ample evidence that this was true in Worthington. There was an upsurge of democratic hope among ordinary people that made the more populist congregations, like the Methodists, very attractive.[23] Competition, and even hard feelings, developed as the Methodist congregation grew quite rapidly in the years following the War of 1812. This tension was accentuated by several families who had been active in the formation of the Episcopal Church, but had transferred their membership. Most left without official comment. Samuel Beach, Jr., however, maintained that it is "my duty to turn away from all such as practice breaking any of the precepts of the bible, and to join such as come nearest to making the bible the rule of their faith & practice."[24]

Such sentiments may have been widely shared. Methodism had Episcopalian roots; in fact, John Wesley never resigned his position as a minister in the Anglican Church. Wesley's church in America referred to itself as the Methodist Episcopal Church, but it defied the Anglican culture of patriarchalism.[25] Sometimes the local feud turned bitter. Methodists held regular "class meetings," led by lay leaders, for Bible reading and discussion of religious beliefs. Apparently one such discussion considered the theological distinctions between Episcopalians and Methodists. Amos Hawley, in response to Ezra Griswold's criticism of the harsh feelings between the two congregations, challenged the Episcopalians, "as you make So much Boast of your Authority and line of Sucession handed down from the Apostols, I think that it is high time that you bring forward your witnesses and prove your Claim . . . if I am rightly informed it has been peased patched and vampt over & over very much like my Great Grandfathers Jack knife which had a number of new blades & handles added and yet it was my great Grandfathers knife."[26]

Such folk wisdom illustrates the early Methodist belief that preaching did not require a theological education to be effective. One Methodist minister wrote in 1821, "We believe it to be a universal principle, that people adhere more to the man who teaches from his own experience and knowledge of things, than he who attempts to teach from books only or the experience of others."[27] Even such a noted Methodist cleric as Bishop Francis Asbury reportedly said, "I

Fig. 28. St. John's Episcopal Church was dedicated in 1831 by the first Episcopal congregation in Ohio, organized in February 1804. (Photograph by the authors)

presume a simple man can speak and write for simple, plain people, upon simple truths."[28] By carving a life from the wilderness, western pioneers had gained great confidence in their personal abilities, and many of them trusted their own common sense to determine the difference between right and wrong. The founders of the Methodist congregation in Worthington expressed their disdain for persons who were ordained to preach the word of God, but who practiced a lifestyle that they themselves found inconsistent with the Bible.

It was men of such simple faith who, in 1823, erected the first church building in Worthington for the Methodist congregation. It was an unpretentious brick building at the southeastern corner of the village, facing south toward the barns and the groves of trees that had sheltered the congregation in its beginnings. There were two large doors in the front of this church; on the interior wall between the doors, there was a large pulpit, rounded like a bowl, which had the words "Preach Christ" painted inside. Light came from four windows on either side, another above the pulpit and two at the opposite end. When needed, this was supplemented by candles in tin sconces between the side windows and by four oil lamps that hung from the ceiling.[29] Two aisles led from the two front doors, and each had a large tinplate stove approximately one-third of the way back that was surrounded by wood in season. These aisles divided the pews into three sections. Women occupied the middle benches and men the sides.[30] Entrances to the two aisles leading to separate seating for men and women was a common pattern in pioneer communities, and all three local churches limited congregational leadership roles to men.[31]

Like all Methodist congregations in small western villages, the Worthington Methodists were part of a circuit and enjoyed regular visits from a circuit-riding preacher for a number of years before they could support a minster of their own. These circuits were united in an Ohio conference, which in 1816 resolved "That it is inexpedient and imprudent for a traveling Preacher to dishonor himself by associating with the Free Masons in their Lodges."[32] This was another wedge between Methodist beliefs and the values of Worthington leaders who had constructed a Masonic Lodge in the community even before any church building. In 1817, the Methodist conference strengthened this stand, declaring "We are decidedly & sentimentally opposed to the practice [Masonic] & are determined . . . to set our Faces & lift our hands against it."[33] It was a position that directly opposed the beliefs of Masonic leaders, such as John Snow and Thomas Webb, who were taking an active interest in the management of the Worthington Manufacturing Company—at the same time that many of its employees were becoming involved in the Methodist revivals and class meetings. Historians have identified both religious and political roots in the anti-Masonic movement of the 1820s and 1830s, but in Worthington it was additional evidence of the social cleavage between Episcopalians and Methodists.[34]

Not all, however, were divided between denominations. At his death in 1827, Asa Gillet's will "bequeathed two hundred and fifty dollars to the Episcopal Society in this town, the same amount to the Methodist." Actually, this was a codicil to the will written on his death bed two weeks earlier; he had originally given the entire five hundred dollars to the Methodists.[35] Either he had second thoughts or someone persuaded him this was more appropriate. Since he was deceased, this could not be interpreted as a move to earn favor for himself from either group; and since he made no bequest to the Presbyterians, he was not supporting every church in town. It would appear most likely that Gillet was raised in the Episcopal faith and converted to, or was at least attending, the Methodist congregation prior to his death.

The Presbyterian congregation was the third religious society with a substantial presence in early Worthington. There were families of the Presbyterian faith in the Carpenter settlement north of Worthington when the Scioto Company settlers arrived, and they were apparently visited by recently licensed "missionaries" before they organized themselves as the Liberty Presbyterian Church in 1810.[36] This was the typical Presbyterian strategy for serving members of their faith who had moved west. They first formed a nucleus for regular preaching, and when they could afford to contribute to a minister, they organized a congregation.[37] The Liberty congregation was close enough that some Worthington families may have occasionally attended preaching in that neighborhood, but it was in June 1816 that a group of eleven persons met in the home of Peter and Zilpha Barker, just north of the village, to form the Worthington Presbyterian congregation.[38]

They soon received preaching on alternate Sundays from Rev. Ebenezer Washburn, who also served a congregation at Berkshire. On December 13, 1821, at the home of Daniel Upson, twenty subscribers incorporated themselves as the Presbyterian Society of Worthington and elected Job W. Case, Arius Kilbourn, and Edward Mallory as trustees, Daniel Upson as treasurer, and Samuel Baldwin as clerk.[39] James Kilbourn's nephew, Arius, was a leader of this society, but it should be remembered that the Kilbourn family in Connecticut were members of the Congregational Church and James had converted. None of these subscribers are known to have had any prior affiliation with the Episcopal church in Worthington, and apparently there was distinctly less animosity from this direction than was exhibited between the other two congregations.

In fact, the Presbyterians initially shared the Academy building with the Episcopalians for services; then, after the construction of the Masonic Lodge, they met there before constructing their own church building. In regard to ministers, there was certainly more affinity between the Presbyterians and the Episcopalians than between the Presbyterians and the Methodists. Presbyterians placed high priority on an educated ministry, and in some locations their scorn for uneducated Methodist preachers approached persecution.[40] In 1826, Worthington acquired its first resident Presbyterian minister, Rev. Highland Hulburd.[41] With his instigation and leadership, the congregation began planning their first "meeting house," and Hulburd himself traveled east to raise subscriptions. The resulting frame building, on the west side of the public square adjacent to Samuel Baldwin's blacksmith shop, was so unpretentious that one letter writer described it as "small and plain, without any steeple and looks like a barn."[42]

The first services in this building were held on April 17, 1830. The church was similar in design to the Methodist church, with the pulpit on the interior wall between two front doors. Across the rear of this building, a "gallery" seat, several steps higher than the floor, was designed for singers but became a favored spot for the young people. The growth and strength of the congregation under Rev. Hulburd's leadership was attested to by the formation of seven neighborhood groups containing the names of eighty-four members who met weekly for "conversation meetings."[43] This is consistent with the congregational self-government of this denomination.

Most early churches maintained strict discipline for their membership, but in no denomination was censorship by peers more strict than among the Presbyterians. In 1835, one woman repented to the session for arguing with a sister member and, as a result of her confession, was restored to the right of communion. Members, however, could be and were suspended if they had "absented themselves with design from public worship and the Lord's supper." One member, with whom the elders labored in vain, publicly "avowed himself a Universalist" and was suspended "till he give evidence of repentance and reformation."[44]

People expected their church to dictate the morality of their behavior, particularly if they had publicly committed themselves as "saved." Emily Maynard reported to her sister that "brother Darius has become serious with regard to religion insomuch that he has refrained from swearing."[45] Pledging to reform behavior was the most visible method of demonstrating an internal change of attitude, and it was the result most sought at the camp meetings and revivals that were so prevalent throughout this period. One local letter writer reported in 1828 that the Methodists, Universalists, and Presbyterians were all having camp meetings "every day for about two weeks, sometimes seven meetings a day."[46]

Closely associated with the religious revivals, and taking its methods from their success, was the growing temperance reform movement. Leaders of this movement believed that intemperance marked persons as unfit for salvation, and that it was immoral for church members to derive profits from the liquor trade. Such themes were the new gospels of reform.[47]

It was not uncommon for taverns to be located directly across the street from a church, as they were in Worthington after the construction of the Episcopal building. Such juxtaposition had been true from colonial days. The early years of the nineteenth century, however, saw an alarming rise in the consumption of alcoholic beverages and other undesirable changes in drinking habits. Between 1805 and 1830, annual alcohol consumption peaked at approximately nine gallons of liquor, thirty gallons of cider, and one quart of wine per person aged fifteen and older.[48] In the colonial era in the east, alcoholic beverages were commonly consumed in small amounts in the home throughout the day and in communal binges such as the Fourth of July celebrations, on election days, and at militia musters. By the 1820s, there was a marked rise both in communal and in solitary binges.[49] Much of this same pattern occurred in Worthington between 1804 and 1830.

Alcoholic beverages were a part of everyday life in early Worthington. It was expected that officers would buy the whiskey for militia muster day and that candidates would provide a keg on election day. The Fourth of July celebration regularly included twenty or thirty toasts, and the Episcopal minister offered members of his flock sling between sermons. Doctors prescribed whiskey for various ailments, and children were given diluted alcoholic beverages to drink as being more healthy than river or rain water. Whiskey and cider were cheap and plentiful, and they were a tasty accompaniment to diets heavy on fatty meats and bland cornbreads and puddings. One observer described drinking as "sort of a panacea for all ills, a crowning sheaf to all blessings."[50]

Early churches considered the use of liquor to be legitimate and healthy as long as it did not visibly impair the drinker's ability to think and act rationally.[51] Temperate consumption was evidently the position Rev. Chase espoused. His account with Ezra Griswold from the time he arrived in Worthington until he moved to his own farm in early December 1817 shows that he regularly purchased a quart of whiskey for thirty-one and a half cents approximately once a week, and from time to time purchased some gin or cider.[52] From the Puritans on, no one had seriously objected to the temperate use of alcoholic beverages.

But in Worthington in the 1820s, as elsewhere, problems from excessive consumption of alcohol were rising. No record of deaths in the community and their causes exists prior to 1825 when George Griswold was appointed sexton of St. John's cemetery. Moreover, his records did not include the cause of every death; however, even judging by these partial records, in a town of approximately five hundred persons, four deaths attributed to intemperance in less than a decade was sufficient to be alarming. Griswold noted on May 21, 1827, that John Sherman, "about 35 or 36 years old . . . his death was occasioned by intemperance"; I. P. Case died September 22, 1832, of "intemperance"; Dr. Wyley "died in a drunken fit"; and a "drunken man died at Kilbourns," perhaps a traveling man who was not well known in the community.[53]

The estate of Israel P. Case included accounts for the purchase of $86.56 worth of whiskey from local distiller Hiram Andrews between October 1825 and May 1832. With whiskey usually selling at thirty-seven and a half cents per gallon, this amounted to thirty-five and a half gallons annually. The amount Case spent to purchase cider from several neighbors was almost as high. Case was fifty-one years old at his death, and he was survived by a widow and seven children who were from two to nineteen years of age.[54] Even if one accounts for some liquor consumption by family and friends, it is clear that Case was regularly consuming a prodigious amount of alcohol. Case was a respected member of the community who was a member of the Scioto Company advance party in 1803, one of the incorporators of St. John's Episcopal Church in 1807, and a militia captain during the War of 1812. His estate contained expenses for medicines from Daniel Upson and for visits from physician Kingsley Ray that totaled $65.33 during the last two years of his life. There is no record of the social costs, which might have included abusive relationships with his wife and children or with relatives and neighbors, but intemperance could clearly ruin a life and affect a family.

Deaths caused by intemperance were a tragic extreme, but many people were beginning to see and experience the negative effects related to the consumption of alcoholic beverages. Joel and Arora Buttles purchased the house where Adna and Lura Bristol lived to prevent their brother-in-law "from sacrificing the house by way of the foolish bargains which he in the latter part of his life was frequently making."[55] It was no coincidence that evangelists began viewing intemperance as a wicked depravity and preaching sobriety as a requisite step for conversion. Rowdy young men who interrupted camp meetings were a visible demonstration of the need for reform.

For most religious denominations, their position supporting temperance developed gradually. In 1816 the Methodist conference barred ministers from distilling or selling liquor; in 1828 it praised the temperance movement; by 1832 it urged total abstinence. The Presbyterian church in 1812 urged ministers to preach against intoxication; in 1827 it pledged support for the temperance movement; in 1829 it urged members not to distill, retail, or consume spirits; finally, in 1835, it too recommended total abstinence.[56]

As the temperance movement progressed from "temperate" usage to voluntary and total abstinence, its popularity grew rapidly. Many who have studied the temperance reform movement have commented on the relationship between total abstinence and evangelical theology. Converts who pledged abstinence made an immediate tangible change which symbolized spiritual rebirth. Ironically, some who drank out of anxiety and to reach a state of euphoria found that sermons about the devil's brew produced anxiety that could only be relieved by an abstinence pledge and that their newly found salvation produced a similar state of euphoria. Page Smith even sees public temperance meetings with public confessions as part of an attempt to recapture the shattered covenanted community.[57]

It was in this climate that some members of local churches promoted the formation of a temperance society in Worthington. A general meeting was called on February 25, 1834, to discuss the reasons for and against joining a temperance society and to circulate a paper for membership. The only surviving record of this meeting is George Griswold's notes on sixteen objections to such a society, perhaps a reflection of his own opinion as a tavern owner.[58] Mr. Lazelle undoubtedly spoke for many in saying, "I can drink or not as I please and control myself without any special pledge." He also felt that temperance societies were not particularly effective because they did not exclude the use of cider and wine from their pledge.

Dr. Ray expressed himself as being unwilling to pledge himself "to entire abstinence from ardent spirits, because it is sometimes necessary to my health." Mr. Abbott saw no need for a temperance society because "the [Presbyterian] church to which I belong is a temperance society." Mr. Ladd objected on the grounds that such societies were secular, and he felt that their aim was an improper union of church and state. Mr. Mallory saw temperance societies as a money-making scheme, and Mr. Cowles was concerned about their political influence. Mr. Spencer and Mr. Comstock each indicated, "I can't carry on my business effectively without ardent spirits." Dr. Morrow objected to the curtailment of personal liberties that such societies imposed, maintaining that "This is a free country and I have a right to drink." Mr. Highy cited the scriptures as sanctioning the use of strong drink. Cowles expressed a moderate position that was probably held by many local citizens when he indicated, "I have no particular objection to temperance, but I am not yet ready to join." But Mr. Jackson may have been the most honest when he expressed publicly what more than one undoubtedly felt privately: "I will not join the Temperance Society because I love to drink."

Those who voiced objections to the formation of a temperance society included two local physicians and members of all of the three established churches. Although many of the influential men of Worthington were opposed to a temperance society in 1834, the community may not have been far from the national norm in terms of personal practice. Temperance reformers claimed that one in ten persons were voluntarily abstaining from alcoholic beverages by the 1830s.[59] There was certainly more recorded objection to the formation of a "temperance society" than there was disagreement with the belief that temperate use of alcoholic beverages was a virtue. There seems to have been considerable sentiment for believing that this was a moral issue that could best be controlled within the churches.

It would appear that Worthington defied national trends in one respect. In the overlapping temperance and slavery reform movements of the 1830s, most reformers considered temperance more crucial, regarding "the chains of intoxication heavier than those which the sons of Africa have ever worn."[60] In Worthington, however, the formation of an anti-slavery society preceded a temperance society.

❖ CHAPTER 19 ❖

Correct Mental and Moral
Habits and Amiable Manners

— ❖ —

DURING ITS FRONTIER period, Worthington—like most Ohio communities of the early nineteenth century—offered educational opportunities through subscription schools in which the parents of all scholars paid a fee. While it was advantageous to have a lot set aside by the Scioto Company for a school building and helpful to receive support for school expenses from the rental of school-owned farm property, these sources of fiscal support were not sufficient to provide education for all children in the community. The situation in Worthington was consistent with the conception established in Ohio law when the state was admitted to the union, that Section Sixteen in each township would be reserved for the use and support of a school.[1]

It was never intended that this arrangement would be completely sufficient to support a system of public schools. In fact, early Ohioans opposed the centralization of education and considered it an infringement of a property owner's rights for the state to take his money to educate his neighbor's child.[2] It was 1821 before the general assembly passed legislation outlining a method to organize public school districts and permitting local districts, if they wished, to establish a tax to support a school. To no one's surprise, few communities accepted this voluntary opportunity to tax themselves to erect a schoolhouse, or "for the purpose of making up the deficiency that may accrue by the schooling of children, whose parents or guardians are unable to pay for the same."[3]

Four years later, the legislature passed an act requiring support
and regulation of common schools. This became the basis for public
education in Ohio. This 1825 law specified the method for struc-
turing school districts and imposed a one-half-mill annual property
tax for the support of schools, which would provide "instruction of
youth of every grade and class without distinction, in reading, writing, arithmetic, and other necessary branches of a common education."[4] The law also provided that each county court of common
pleas would appoint three examiners, who would certify the qualifications of everyone wishing to teach in these common schools. The
Columbus newspaper admitted that, while the law might be defec-
tive in some details, it was still a landmark in the history of the
state. Within a year the paper noted proudly, "We never see a set of
little ragged urchins idling around our streets."[5]

Sharon Township was soon divided into school districts as the law
required, with the northern part of the village of Worthington becoming District Two and the southern part District Three.[6] District Two
directors Ansel Mattoon, James Clark, and Sidney Brown leased the
building that had formerly housed Grosvenor's subscription school
for one dollar per month.[7]

Worthington resident and Franklin County school examiner John
Ladd sold part of a town lot he owned, on the southwest corner of
what is now Oxford and New England streets, to District Three directors Ira Metcalf, Pirum Hunt, and Arora Buttles, who soon erected a
one-room brick building.[8] These small schoolhouses in the southwest
and northeast quadrants of the village had none of the prestige of the
academy on the public square, but they did ensure that any child in
the community could receive the "necessary branches of a common
education." No one seemed to remember in 1825 that the lot where
the academy building sat and the farm lot which provided it rental
income had been expressly reserved by the Scioto Company founders
"for the use and benefit of a Publick school."[9]

Actually young Worthington scholars were better off than many of
those enrolled in the nearby rural schools—which frequently began
offering classes in a log house donated by a farmer who had moved his
family into a better home. Both male and female teachers were employed in these public schools. Men taught more often in the winter
term, which tended to attract older boys who might become discipli-
nary problems; women taught more often in the summer term, when

the older boys were occupied with farm work. It was a practice that made thrifty use of local resources, and the first state commissioner of education recommended it to counties "who are in the habit of paying men for instructing little children, when females would do it for less than half the sum, and generally much better than men can."[10] At that time male teachers were paid on average $25.00 per month, and female teachers received $12.50.

In either case, common-school teachers, working with thirty or more students at several different levels of instruction, had little time to give individual attention to each pupil. It was a frustrating situation for those who would like to have done better. Nancy Clark, an experienced teacher employed for the summer term in a rural school just east of Worthington, wrote to a fellow teacher, perhaps in some jest, "I am again a prisoner with a group of little immortals committed to my charge." Actually she found this school, with an average attendance of twenty-six to twenty-eight scholars per day, one of the most pleasant "of any in which I ever engaged . . . a very kind neighborhood."[11] She was probably following the usual custom of boarding a week at a time in the homes of various scholars.

Since pupils remained in the same school for several years, local directors often felt there was an advantage to changing teachers frequently. In any event, young women often resigned to be married, and young men to pursue better employment. This concerned Samuel Galloway, one of Ohio's most respected early superintendents. He complained that "Men do not change their blacksmiths as frequently as they change their teachers—a fact which indicates that the feet of horses are treated with more consideration than the minds of children."[12]

Throughout the 1820s and 1830s, Worthington also offered several learning opportunities for adults. The literary society continued to flourish; and, like many communities, Worthington occasionally had a subscription singing school. One of these schools, for which records survive, was taught by Carlos Curtis of Kingston, in Delaware County, during the winter of 1825–26. For two dollars per session, he taught two evenings each week for three months.[13] This was apparently a school only for men, with more than thirty subscribers paying from fifty cents to one dollar for the privilege of attending. Curtis's primary role was probably to teach the words and tunes of some of the more popular songs of the day.[14]

The purpose of such "schools" may have revolved as much around social interaction as cultural enlightenment or personal development. Such a belief is reinforced by the presence of James Kilbourn's name on the subscription list, a man in his fifties who had been known for years to entertain his friends with some brandy and eggnog and to join in singing favorite ballads or those of his own composition.[15]

For parents who could afford it and who wanted more than a common school education for their children, Worthington still excelled in subscription schools for both boys and girls. The subscription list for the construction of the Worthington College building in 1819 included the usual commitments of materials and labor from nearly forty local residents, but there was a noticeable resolution to improve the library. Orris Parrish pledged five dollars "for books of history and poetry of standard authors," and Chester Griswold contributed "Hinnes History of England," a twelve-volume work valued at thirty-six dollars.[16]

But the economic depression and Rev. Chase's departure from the community doomed the projected Worthington College enterprise. These factors also had a negative impact on the established Worthington Academy, which relied upon Episcopal clergymen for leadership—although it continued throughout the 1820s to attract boarding students from some distance. These students included at least one or more Wyandot Indian boys from the mission near Upper Sandusky, whose fees were paid by sponsors. But there was a troublesome lack of integration of these Indian youth into the community. While visiting a student he was sponsoring, John Johnston expressed his concern that the boy "understands very little of what he reads, and this must continue to be the case so long as the scholars are kept so much of their time out of the society of the whites . . . there are many things to be learned to complete the character of man beside the knowledge of letters."[17] Such isolation is a telling criticism of a church-sponsored school.

When Rev. Chase moved the classes from his farm south of Worthington to Gambier and founded Kenyon College, the preparatory function of the Worthington Academy was threatened; but an interesting interim solution was reached in 1829, when the Columbus presbytery, under the leadership of Rev. James Hoge, received a charter to found an academy.[18] Classes commenced that fall in the

Worthington Academy building, but announcements of the new academy made it clear that there was competition for its ultimate location. "As to the place where it will be located, it is not yet determined. Worthington, Columbus, and Delaware have been spoken of, and there is but little doubt but it will be established at one of the above places."[19] Once again it was clear how vigorously communities competed for the education business.

This academy continued at Worthington for several years. By 1832, the Presbyterians were offering studies in the Worthington Academy facilities for both young men and young women. Rev. James Hoge continued as president of the board of trustees, but Rev. James Eells, Dr. Daniel Upson, I. G. Miller, and Dr. Kingsley Ray of Worthington played key leadership roles. The teachers in the Worthington Academy were Henry Eells, a graduate of Hamilton College in New York State, and Henry Ballentine, a graduate of Ohio University. Students were offered a five-month course of instruction in "various branches of Science and Literature," for fees from three to ten dollars per term depending on the level of instruction.[20]

Two innovative aspects of the curriculum were particularly noteworthy. Advertisements promised, "An opportunity will be afforded to any young man, who may desire it, to labor in the work shop, attached to the Academy, or on the lands belonging to it, in horticulture or agriculture, for the preservation of health, and to enable them to defray in part the expenses of their education." It should be noted that this was considered a health or economic choice, not a vocational learning experience. But special provisions were also designed for those "who may wish to qualify themselves as Teachers of Common Schools."[21] The passage of the Ohio public school law created an increased demand for qualified teachers.

At the same time, a twenty-four-week summer term of the Worthington "School for Young Ladies" commenced under the direction of Miss Eells and Miss Everest. Their qualifications were not stated, but probably included completion of a seminary program similar to the one they proposed to teach. The course of instruction offered reading, penmanship, geography, and plain needlework for two dollars per quarter; English grammar, arithmetic, ancient and modern history, rhetoric, and ornamental needlework for three dollars; natural philosophy, chemistry, botany, logic, and natural theology for four dollars; French and Latin for five dollars; Poonah or Oriental painting for two dollars; and an "improved method of painting on velvet" for four dollars. The trustees assured that "No pains will be spared, to make the young Ladies who attend this school, thorough in every branch of study, and to lead them to form correct mental and moral habits, and amiable manners."[22] Subscription schools under religious sponsorship had no qualms about teaching moral values. They saw it as a critical part of their mission.

This was an era that emphasized the finer moral nature of women, particularly educated women. The friendship book which Phoebe Ann Weaver received from Orrell Kilbourne in 1835 bore the wish, "May its pure pages be filled with chaste and lofty sentiments, worthy the character of a young lady and of those that ought to be her friends."[23] Worthington's reputation as an educational center for both young men and women continued under several changes of church sponsorship, with the largest and most successful institution becoming the Worthington Female Seminary chartered by the Methodists in 1839.[24] During the decade of the 1830s, education became the chief economic enterprise of the village, which provided an attractive environment for boarding students. As one advertisement succinctly phrased it, "The town is pleasant, rural and healthy; the society quiet and intelligent; and its proximity to Columbus, the metropolis of the State, quite desirable."[25] Worthington was far enough removed from the city to offer a protective moral environment, but close enough to the state capital to be convenient.

Such inducements, combined with a large, brick college building and a degree-granting charter from the state legislature, were the attractions James Kilbourn utilized to encourage Dr. Wooster Beach of New York City to establish an Ohio Reformed Medical College at Worthington in 1830.[26] Dr. Beach was a controversial figure in the medical profession, "convinced the present practice of Physic and Surgery . . . was absolutely a curse to society."[27] His emphasis on botanical treatment was revolutionary and unacceptable to most physicians of the early nineteenth century, and it is worth noting that the two physicians who served Worthington in 1830, Dr. Upson and Dr. Ray, were never connected with the college.

The projected opening of the college, in December 1830, emphasized an attached "Dispensary for analyzing and preparing vegetable medicine; and an Infirmary, where persons from the neighborhood, or a distance, laboring under Fevers, Consumption, Dyspepsia, Liver

complaints, Gravel, Ulcers, Fistulas, Cancers, &c. will be successfully treated, without *Bleeding, Mercury, or the Knife*, and from
which the student will acquire a correct knowledge of the nature, operation, and superior efficacy of vegetable agents in removing disease." Such statements were, in many respects, a declaration of war
upon medicine as it was being currently practiced in Ohio. In fact,
J. J. Steele, the college's first president warned, "Students and others,
had better beware of the slanders of the present physicians, who
know no more about our institution, than they do about Botanical
Medicine."[28]

Requirements for admission to the Ohio Reformed Medical College were "A certificate of good moral character" and "A good English
Education." Lectures, recitations, textbooks, and examinations were
promised in anatomy and physiology, reformed surgery, the theory
and practice of medicine, midwifery and the diseases of women and
children, materia medica with practical and general botany, medical
and botanical chemistry and pharmacy, moral and mental philosophy, phrenology, medical jurisprudence, and medical history. Tuition
for the course was a total of $150.00 if paid in advance, or $75.00 in
advance and $100.00 at the completion of the course. There was no
specified time required for completing the course of study; when the
faculty felt the student was qualified, he would receive a diploma—
"some will pass in one year, others will require more."[29] It was, of
course, assumed that all applicants would be male, and they were.

Dr. Steele was inaugurated as president of the college in December
1830 with great fanfare, but by March he was relieved of his duties for
"base and improper conduct" and replaced by Dr. Thomas Morrow.[30]
No records have survived that explain this, but it was a setback that
prevented the school from reaching full operation until the following
year. Dr. Morrow, a native of Kentucky, was a graduate of Dr. Beach's
college in New York, and he remained as president until the college
was closed in 1839.[31]

The institution quickly became successful, with a faculty of four
members and approximately forty students per term. The school year
was divided into a six-month fall and winter term, from October 1
through March 31, and a four-month spring and summer term, from
April 1 through July 31. Dr. Morrow lectured on the theory and practice of medicine, anatomy, physiology, and operative surgery; Dr.
Jones taught obstetrics and diseases of women and children; Dr. Terry

lectured on materia medica, pharmacy, and the principles of surgery; and J. R. Paddock, A.M., was the instructor in botany and chemistry. Boarding students could obtain "room, lodging, washing, firewood, and candles" at a cost of $1.50 per week during the spring and summer term and $1.62 weekly during the fall and winter term.[32]

There was a ten-dollar charge to receive a diploma; the institution's reputation became somewhat tarnished by one student who apparently paid this fee and received a diploma without attending classes.[33] Most students, however, worked diligently to develop their own notebooks of "recipes" to cure various diseases. "Brown's Pain Killer," for instance, was recommended as an excellent lineament. It combined "Oil of alcohol, oil of olibanum [frankincense], oil of hemlock, oil of sassafras, oil of peppermint, oil of cedar, oil of cloves, spirit turpentine, gum camphor, spirit stramoni [jimpson weed], afri capsico [African nightshade]." This was allowed to "digest 10 days" before being bottled for use.[34]

In the early 1830s, the medical school allowed Worthington to benefit from an abundance of practicing physicians; at the same time it provided the economic benefits of boarding students and the cultural diversity represented by the young men who were attracted to the institution. Several local young men attended, and James Kilbourne, Jr., was one of the eighty-eight graduates while the college was in Worthington. Only half of these graduates were from Ohio, the others came from states as diverse as Georgia, Iowa, Kentucky, Massachusetts, Mississippi, Missouri, New York, Pennsylvania, Tennessee, and Virginia.[35]

Such a wealth of educated young men provided the young ladies of the village with very attractive romantic opportunities and resulted in several marriages among both students and faculty. Dr. Morrow married Isabel Greer, Dr. Jones married Cynthia Kilbourne, and Professor Paddock married Julia Bristol. Emily Griswold married Benjamin Franklin Johnson, a student whose father became governor of Virginia.[36]

Although the medical college thrived through the mid-1830s, the depression of 1837 reduced enrollment, and it became necessary to economize by closing the infirmary. But a more important issue— and one that soon caused the college's demise—was a simmering local resentment regarding the procurement of cadavers for anatomical study. Such bodies were normally obtained from the potter's fields of larger cities, but in Worthington there were rumors of mysterious bodies being found and of cemeteries north of town being disturbed.

The situation came to a head in the fall of 1839, when a lady from Marietta died at the insane asylum in Columbus. When her relatives arrived to claim her body, it could not be found; rumors circulated that it had been taken to the medical school in Worthington. On December 23, a large meeting was held at Worthington "to adopt measures for the security of bodies in their graves." This was led by residents from Delaware County who expressed outrage toward the medical faculty and students for "disturbing the dead of their last repose."[37] A leader of the protest was Dr. Richard Catley, a graduate of the Worthington Medical College who had taught anatomy briefly at the school before becoming embittered and moving to Delaware.[38] Resolutions were adopted to demand the return of the Marietta woman's body, the return of the building to its original status as the Worthington Academy, the dismissal of the medical class, and the removal of the college's students from town within two weeks.[39]

When these demands were refused, a mob forced its way into the college building and into Dr. Morrow's residence. They did not find the body of the Marietta woman—whose relationship to Worthington was never more than a rumor—but they were incensed to discover the body of an African-American in a corn shock on the college property. Whether this was a furtive hiding place utilized by some anatomy students or simply the body of a poor man who had sought warmth and shelter is not known. The mob's outrage, however, led to the introduction of a bill in the Ohio legislature "making it a Penitentiary offence for anyone to disinter, or be found in possession of a human body, for the purpose of dissection." This alarmed the medical community throughout the state for it would have prevented both autopsies and education. Some physicians insisted that "the establishment at Worthington, does not belong to the regular profession . . . . The Physicians of the state are not therefore, accountable for the acts of unprofessionalism."[40]

Dr. Morrow responded that "from the commencement of this Institution, an unprincipled and reckless warfare has been carried on against it by a few prejudiced and interested individuals in this vicinity, who have evinced a determination to put it down."[41] The state legislature compromised by amending the act that had chartered Worthington College, repealing the section which "may be construed to authorize the trustees of said college to confer medical degrees."[42]

The truth of the situation may have been most clearly revealed by a schoolgirl's letter a few days after the December riot: "There is a great confusion among them [medical students] now, they have been mobbed, subjects have been taken away from them, and the old school, and the Presbyterians are making great threats against them."[43] The key is the last phrase. Dr. Kingsley Ray and Dr. Daniel Upson, the primary physicians in Worthington for a number of years prior to the establishment of the medical college, were leaders of the Presbyterian church, and Dr. Ray was the clerk of its session. About 1838, he left Worthington to establish a practice at Delaware. The conflict about principles of medical practice was one that would not be easily resolved; however, a moral issue about the use and procurement of bodies for anatomical study would quickly mobilize public opinion. There may well have been abuses in the procurement of bodies at Worthington, and it was certainly too small a community for this to be an anonymous issue, but the root of the medical college's problem was its challenge to prevailing medical theory.

The Scioto Company founders had placed a high value on education. This was evident in their action to set aside two inlots in the village and one hundred acres of farmland for the support of a school. The original proprietors were successful in establishing a common school during the first winter of their settlement in Worthington; they followed it with an academy within the first decade, an abortive attempt to found a college, and the creation of a short-lived medical school. Throughout its early years, Worthington sparkled as an educational mecca, but twice it burned itself out in the heat of conflict, once between Rev. Chase and Worthington Episcopalians and once between botanical physicians and the prevailing medical establishment. The result was an economic and cultural loss, but one whose impact was cushioned by the concurrent development of the Worthington Female Seminary by the Methodists. The village was still in the education business.

❖ CHAPTER 20 ❖

That Dead Animals or Nuisances
of Any Kind Be Buried
in Some Vacant Place

— ❖ —

Worthington boarding schools may have been able to
describe their town to potential scholars as "pleasant, rural
and healthy," which it was indeed relative to many western towns in
the first half of the nineteenth century.[1] But everyday life was neither
as pleasant and healthy as contemporary promoters suggested nor as
quaint and pristine as modern historical interpretations often imply
to visitors.

The most frequent topic and the most detailed descriptions in
nineteenth-century letters between relatives and friends were the
illnesses and deaths in the community, particularly the deaths of persons at an early age. Today too we greet each other with "How are
you?" and often proceed to discuss our own symptoms and the health
or illness of others with an enthusiasm surpassed only by our interest
in the weather. But modern discussions do not communicate the
sense of mortality and the inevitable futility regarding illness, even
among the young, that underscored the psychological burden which
was an integral part of nineteenth-century life.

Julia Strong, an academy student, wrote her sister that "poor Emily
Griswold is now lying at the point of death. She is afflicted with a
most distressing disorder in the head which entirely baffles the Physicians skill."[2] When Julia paid a last visit to her seventeen-year-old
classmate, her friends "were all standing round the bed weeping and
wringing their hands," and Rev. Chase "prayed with her, asked her
some questions, exhorted her to put her trust in God . . . ." After the
funeral, Julia lamented, "O! Cynthia will it be for us and every other

young person if we follow the bright example which this young lady has set for us. Emily, though so young that she could scarcely be said to have commenced living, has shown by her death that she lived sufficiently long in this world to do the great work for which she was sent into it, that is to prepare for another."[3]

As sad as the belief may seem that life has no purpose except to prepare for a better existence after death, it has been observed across many cultures that in times of insecurity the appeal of life after death is enhanced. A number of researchers have studied the effect of religious belief and religious practice on a person's anxieties regarding death. Recent findings suggest that religious beliefs can both induce and attenuate death anxiety, and that it is regular religious participation—perhaps because of its accompanying social interaction—which is more significant than religious orthodoxy in alleviating death anxiety.[4] This illuminates the psychological weight that nineteenth-century theologians placed upon terminally ill individuals or upon the parents of dying children. Belief in eternal damnation for everyone who had not personally experienced and accepted God as their savior placed a particularly heavy burden upon young people seeking salvation for their immortal souls.

When death was an experience shared by family and close friends, rather than an event concealed in a remote hospital room, fatalistic attitudes among survivors were commonplace. This was particularly true for women anticipating childbirth. Larkin quotes a letter describing a mutual acquaintance who "died as she had expected to," in the agony of a difficult childbirth.[5] Even the establishment of a medical college, which included a course in obstetrics, failed to protect Worthington women. It was less than two months after Israel P. Case's death from intemperance that his oldest daughter, Laura Delano, was buried about four feet away and sexton George Griswold noted cryptically, "child bed."[6]

Consumption was one of the most devastating killers in the early nineteenth century, particularly among young adults. It was not an unusual occurrence when eighteen-year-old Miranda Topping, who had been orphaned by the disease, succumbed herself in 1827. Before the contagious properties of tuberculosis were understood, it often swept through families for several generations. Women and children who lived and worked indoors were more vulnerable than men, such as farmers, who spent much of their time in uncontaminated open air.[7]

Griswold's sexton records provide some perspective on the accidents and illnesses that were life threatening. Within months of Asa Gillet's previously mentioned pitchfork wound, John Lawson suffered and died from "a fall from the roof of his house which broke his leg."[8] Since broken limbs could be successfully set and bound with a splint, the probability is that he perished from either internal injuries or a blood clot that went unnoticed and unrecorded and were, in any event, beyond treatment by contemporary medical practitioners.

Despite the dangers inherent in frontier life, fatalities were far more often caused by illness than accident. Patty Spooner, wife of William, died of typhus fever and pioneer William Thompson of "typhus pleurisy," both forms of an infectious disease whose transmission from insect bites was not then understood. But when Malinda Weaver died in July 1833 from the dreaded cholera, she was buried the same day.[9] Everyone knew cholera was contagious, and deaths that summer had begun with an outbreak at the Ohio penitentiary that had spread throughout the vicinity and had caused fifty-six deaths in the Columbus area in little more than a month. The newspaper recommended that chloride of lime and soda be diluted in water and used to disinfect the clothing and bed linens of afflicted persons. Residents were urged to "purify the apartments of the sick" and to "disinfect sewers, cess-pools, & privies."[10] People were beginning to learn about the causes and prevention of disease.

Young children who had not developed mature immune systems were, of course, most susceptible to the germs that pervaded frontier society. Sexton George Griswold provided a poignant record of parents left to grieve: the year-old child of Warren Wilcox who died of "bowel complaint"; the year-old son of R. W. and Laura Cowles who died of dysentery; the son of Moses Maynard, Jr., who died of "hooping cough" before his second birthday; four-year-old Caroline Maynard and nine-month Emily Goodrich who succumbed to "malignant scarlet fever"; Griswold's own two-year-old son, Worthington, who died of "worms &c."; Charles Burr's nine-month-old son, Henry, who died of dysentery; six-month-old George Andrews who died of croup; three-year-old Granville Cowles who was stricken with both whooping cough and dysentery; and Nelson Rolp who died of measles at the age of eight.[11] During the decade from 1825 to 1835, Giswold's sexton record contains the burials of seventy-three children under the age of eighteen. It was a tragic loss for a village with a population of only three to four hundred persons.

Even deeply religious parents found it difficult to accept the death of a child as God's will. Cynthia Strong was so affected by Mrs. Griswold's grief at Emily's death that she wrote, "O! how fresh did her distress bring to mind that of my dear mother's when she wept over her little Son . . . ."[12] The death of a child was an experience many families had shared, and one most parents deeply feared; but it is difficult to comprehend the level of grief that was endured by Rensselear and Laura Cowles, who buried six children in St. John's Cemetery within seven years. The last was five-year-old Gertrude, who died of the same scarlet fever that several years earlier had killed her three-year-old brother. Something of the family's anguish is revealed in a letter her nineteen-year-old sister wrote to a friend:

> Death with his sure arm has . . . snatched one from among us, & that one our brightest ornament, Our dear little Gertrude. She was very suddenly & violently attacked with scarlet fever . . . had a raging fever, without cessation for six days, then sunk into a stupor from which it was impossible to rouse her . . . You can't imagine her sufferings during the whole of her sickness . . . I never witnessed such a dreadful death . . . It did seem impossible to bear it, but we must be resigned to the will of him who orders all things for our good. He does not afflict us willingly, but who he loveth, he chooseth.[13]

Despite the ever-present psychological burden of such early deaths, daily life in Worthington had improved noticeably as the village entered its third decade. Stoves for heating and cooking were now common among the better homes of the village, and they were regularly advertised for sale by foundries in Columbus. The inventory of R. W. Cowles's estate revealed that the family had five stoves in their home, primarily wood-burning models made of cast iron, although one "box stove and pipe" relied upon coal, a barrel of which was recorded in the inventory.[14] As nearby woodlots were cut over and firewood became more scarce, people increasingly turned to stoves that consumed approximately half as much wood as a cooking fireplace.

The better homes were also acquiring such comforts as carpeting, curtains, and a wide variety of furniture. The Cowles home included a "parlor carpet, hall carpet, stair carpet & rods, bedroom carpet, front chamber carpet, stripe carpet, a home made carpet, two old carpet," as well as a "hearth oil cloth." Window coverings included "4 white curtains & valances, 5 calico curtains, 2 paper curtains, and 4 grass blinds." Both the quantity and variety of furniture had increased because of products that were available from local cabinet- and chairmakers. For seating the Cowles family had six red, six black, six yellow, six "old kitchen," and seven cane-bottom chairs, as well as a red rocking chair, an old rocking chair with a cushion, four "small children's chairs," a settee and cushion, and two footstools. Clearly, large gatherings of family and friends could be accommodated in comfort. With six candle sticks, two "snuffers" and trays, a glass lamp, and a glass lantern the quantity and quality of artificial light available to extend the evening hours had increased substantially.

But Worthington was still a village, and residents were beginning to feel some inferiority when they compared their lifestyles to those of friends and relatives in the rapidly growing city of Columbus. Julia Buttles Case wrote her daughter Mary while she was attending the female seminary in Granville, "sometimes I think of going to C—— to stay a week but our folks are so much like kings and queens there I do not feel equal to it."[15] The Cases were prosperous farmers south of Worthington, but Julia's brother Joel had become one of the leading merchants and bankers in Columbus and had recently moved into an elegant brick home built by his brother Arora on the east side of the capitol square. It is likely that Julia's wardrobe would have left her feeling somewhat shabby during a round of visits among her Columbus siblings, nieces, and nephews.

The disparity between the two communities, which had been increasing for some time, is consistent with the geographical dimension of refinement described by Bushman. Fashion and refinement were associated with city life while simplicity and rudeness categorized the country.[16] This was illustrated by the wardrobe of William Robe, the early Worthington postmaster and academy teacher who moved to Columbus to work as a state government clerk. At his death in 1823, his clothing included seven pantaloons, six vests, eight shirts, three coats, an overcoat, a pair of suspenders, six pairs of stockings, two pairs of boots, one pair of shoes, two pairs of pumps, one pair of slippers, a flannel muffler, four handkerchiefs, two money purses, two pocketbooks, a walking stick, a hat, and a silver watch valued at fifteen dollars.[17] Robe was a dwarf who may have compensated for his short stature by taking particular pride in his appearance, but the number and variety of items in his wardrobe is approximately triple those in any Worthington estate inventory near that time.

It was not only the quality of the residents' personal lifestyles that was causing inferiority feelings in Worthington. Ever since its founding, the village had relied upon James Kilbourn's leadership, and the collapse of the Worthington Manufacturing Company dramatically reduced his political power. Although he again ran for Congress in 1822, he not only failed to win the district, but he finished third among voters in his home county.[18] The following year, Kilbourn did run successfully for the Ohio legislature, where his primary effort was the unsuccessful attempt, discussed earlier, to influence the location of the Ohio Canal in favor of a central route from Sandusky through Worthington to Columbus; he failed to win reelection. Although Daniel Upson was elected to a term in the legislature in 1828 and although Arora Buttles became an associate judge of the county court in 1824 and Rensselear Cowles a county commissioner in 1830, Worthington's political influence at the county and state levels grew progressively weaker as the central Ohio population increased.[19] This was an era that at least one historian has described as the "golden age of state authority," and Worthington was finding its political voice eclipsed at the state capital by surrounding county-seat towns.[20]

In the initial settlement of Worthington, the same proprietors owned town lots and farm lots, and the New Englanders considered both village and farm residents as Worthington citizens—even though local government in Ohio was based upon townships rather than towns. By 1830, Sharon Township, which included the village of Worthington, had 910 inhabitants. Three hundred and sixteen of these, one-third of the total, were recorded within the village, while the remaining two-thirds occupied the adjoining township farms.[21] The minority population in the village apparently felt that self-government was necessary if Worthington was to continue to be a safe and healthy environment that protected moral and cultural values as its founders had envisioned. In 1835, the village's citizens successfully sought to have Worthington incorporated by the Ohio legislature.[22]

This act vested corporate authority in an elected mayor, a recorder, and five village council trustees who had the power to appoint a treasurer, a marshal, and other officers as needed. Justices of the peace continued to serve both the village and township, and the township maintained its own elected officials. The Worthington incorporation took effect the following year when James Kilbourn was elected as mayor, George Griswold as recorder, and William Bishop,

Ira Metcalf, Henry Pinney, and William Spencer as trustees. They proceeded to appoint R. W. Cowles as treasurer, Abner Putnam Pinney as marshal, and Homer Tuller, George Snow, and D. W. Huntington as fire wardens.[23] It is noteworthy that despite his business failure and his removal as an Episcopal deacon, James Kilbourn was still respected as a political leader in the village he had founded, as was his son-in-law Rensselear Cowles. Two sons of original proprietors, George Griswold and Abner Putnam Pinney (whose wedding had been the first in the village) were now joined in their leadership roles by the next generation, Henry Pinney being Abner Putnam's oldest son.[24] Pioneer families still played an important role in village life, but they were now joined by an equal number of leaders who represented later arrivals. More importantly, all of these positions were voted on annually and changed frequently. Prior to his death in 1850, Kilbourn was elected four times to an annual term as mayor, though the position had more honor than power. Village ordinances were now made by the elected village council, and Kilbourn never had authority in the incorporated village like he had held as agent for the Scioto Company.

The first village ordinance, passed on February 20, 1836, was a detailed document that was surely engendered by the sentiment which led to the incorporation. Citizens of Worthington were anxious to clean up their village. The council decreed that "any person having any dead animal in a putrid state, or liable to become so . . . shall cause the same to be immediately removed beyond the bounds of the town, and not left in any road or street connected therewith, or shall bury the same in some vacant place, so that no part thereof shall be less than two feet below the surface. . . ."[25] The marshal was empowered to fine offenders five dollars and the cost of removal if they failed to comply. One wonders whether this solved the problem to the satisfaction of all, or whether dead livestock were simply dumped in the countryside, much like unwanted kittens or puppies might be today.

Worthington was not being innovative with such an ordinance. Nearby Delaware had put a similar law into effect more than a decade earlier, and Worthington citizens may have felt competitive pressure to improve the image of their town.[26] But dead animals were not the only nuisance. The Worthington ordinance prohibited placing "manure, lumber, firewood, material for building, shavings, chips" in any street of the town. Firewood was allowed to "be laid in the street . . . a reasonable time for the same to be sawed and piled away." It was then to be stacked evenly in line with the front of the building and allowed to extend no more than three feet from a building's walls. Building materials were allowed to occupy twenty feet on the front of a lot where a building was being erected, and scaffold poles were permitted "for a reasonable time," but all rubbish and scaffolding were to be removed when no longer necessary. If such materials were not removed within twenty days of a complaint to the marshal, the owners were again subject to a fine and the cost of removal.[27]

The image of a village whose main street was strewn with manure piles, with uncut firewood and heaps of chips and brush, with mounds of stones and bricks for construction, with a litter of scaffolding and lumber is not the picture commonly portrayed in schoolchildren's history books. However, towns in the early part of the nineteenth century not only contended with such rubbish, but also with a variety of free-ranging livestock and their manure. Worthington's first attempt to control animals was a law enacted that same year restraining sheep and swine from running at large within the limits of the village.[28] Perhaps there was a connection between such laws and the establishment of the medical college, for Worthington made valiant efforts during the 1830s to clean up the village, and it soon required owners of lots along Main Street and around the public square to build sidewalks of brick, plank, or gravel so that pedestrians might be spared the mud and manure of the streets.[29] Increased wagon, stagecoach, and carriage traffic had reduced the grass-covered Main Street of 1815 into a wheel-rutted roadway that was either muddy or dusty in season.

Beyond such physical conditions, Worthington was anxious to ensure that an appropriate moral character was associated with any public exhibitions held in the community. Within weeks of its organization, the town council passed an ordinance that required any person who wished "to exhibit for gain, price or reward, any natural or artificial curiosity, or exhibition of horsemanship in a circus or any public show . . ." to obtain a permit from the mayor or recorder. The amount that would be charged for each license was left to the mayor's discretion, but failure to obtain a permit was subject to a fine of not less than twenty nor more than forty dollars.[30] Such a severe penalty suggests the community was attempting to prevent the exhibition of human or animal freaks, which were sometimes carted from town to town, or to discourage feats of horsemanship, which were associated with gambling—long an anathema to the Worthington community.

When the village was incorporated, the population of Worthington was extremely youthful. In the 1830 census, 77 percent of the village population was thirty years of age or younger, and the township had a similar age distribution.[31] Elected officials no doubt felt they had a public duty to protect the physical health and moral attitudes of their youth. Westward migration was by now flowing through central Ohio to new frontiers in Indiana, Michigan, Illinois, and Missouri. To retain its place as an educational center and to be attractive in retaining its own young people, the village needed to appear healthy and prosperous. Bartlett maintains that self-promotion was as much a part of the scene for nineteenth-century towns as the flamboyant high-pressure sales of retirement communities have become in the twentieth century.[32]

With the creation of official village government, Worthington began taking steps to establish a neat and orderly village, which provided a safer and more healthy environment for its citizens. It was consistent with the type of community that the Scioto Company had planned prior to leaving New England, and it began to establish a pattern for the later residential development and twentieth-century suburban city that evolved.

Epilogue

— ❖ —

TRAVELING INTO THE American interior in the period before the Civil War has been described as traveling into the future, to a new style of society being formed by a mobile population on an unfamiliar landscape.[1] As Americans moved west, they created environments of social equality that were sometimes uncomfortable or even alarming to many of the eastern and international travelers who could afford leisure travel. The society that immigrants created was not the same as the society they left behind—no matter what their expectations. This was true of the seventeenth-century English colonists who settled in America, and it was true of New Englanders who settled the trans-Appalachian frontier at the beginning of the nineteenth century.

In the narrowest sense, the members of the Scioto Company who became the original proprietors of Worthington, Ohio, admirably accomplished their stated purpose "to make a settlement in the Territory of the United States Northwest of the Ohio." Although the current city boundaries extend well beyond the 164 lots of the original village that was planned back in Connecticut, these original boundaries now define "old Worthington." The New England character of this area is protected by an Architectural Review Board that was established in 1967 and authorized "to promote the stability of property values and to protect real estate from impairment or destruction of value for the general community welfare. . . ."[2] The public square created by the pioneers has become a treasured "Village Green," which is the site of community-wide market days, festivals, band concerts, and patriotic ceremonies. The Worthington Historic District established in 1980 includes twenty-six properties listed in the National Register of Historic Places.[3]

One suspects that if the Scioto Company pioneers could attend a reunion in the city of Worthington nearly two hundred years later, they might be quite pleased with the town they had planned. But the modern city is a result, not only of their careful planning, but of the western environment that modified and shaped the plan to its own image. The irony is the extent to which failure, as much as success, determined the course of this development.

Without James Kilbourn's entrepreneurial spirit and charismatic leadership, the Scioto Company would never have been organized and Worthington would not have been settled. But the dominance of his leadership was also the weakness that prevented the fledgling village from becoming a great city. Kilbourn did not have the financial resources and, even more importantly, he lacked the negotiating skills to form the political alliances necessary to acquire the state capital site. Yet its proximity to the capital guaranteed Worthington a supporting role. Ironically, it was this role as a market town for an agricultural community, rather than development as an industrial city, that preserved the essence of the community's New England character.

As a self-made man, Kilbourn perhaps lacked the confidence to delegate leadership responsibilities. He spread himself thin by attempting to manage everything himself and by relying upon the loyalties of members of his extended family. Whether it was this aspect of Kilbourn's leadership style or the wealth of opportunities that were available on the western frontier, it is a fact that the Worthington settlement quickly lost the presence of men such as Nathan Stewart, Nathaniel Little, Thomas Phelps, and Alexander Morrison, Jr., who initially held positions of responsibility. The untimely death of Levi Buttles removed him from the leadership roles he had quickly assumed; yet even if he had lived, his talented family would likely have settled in the Granville, Ohio, community he was organizing. James Kilbourn was always the undisputed leader of pioneer Worthington, and he outlived all but one of his Scioto Company contemporaries.[4] The faithful Ezra Griswold, and later his son, George, could be counted on to implement the details of Kilbourn's vision and to record the progress of St. John's Episcopal Church, the Worthington Academy, and the village council. The town was shaped to Kilbourn's image, both by the success of his ventures and by his failure to attract the state capital or the canal route or to establish an institution of higher education.

The importance of the Episcopal church as a bond for organizing this company of emigrants cannot be overemphasized. It certainly provided the linkage between the Connecticut and Massachusetts contingents. However, Kilbourn's intention to make the western settlement predominantly Episcopalian by setting aside a town lot and farm lot for church use was doomed to failure. The concept of religious freedom was a cornerstone of the federal Constitution, and those who settled on the democratic frontier were quick to reject any elitism in religious belief or practice. The rapid growth of Methodism created a divisive, rather than a unifying, religious environment in early Worthington, for the original community leaders quickly found themselves members of the minority congregation.

The Episcopal, Methodist, and Presbyterian congregations that were formed during Worthington's initial population boom survived throughout the nineteenth century, and animosities gradually faded as they united on issues such as slavery and temperance. Twentieth-century growth brought congregations of many faiths, including Jewish, into the modern city; however, Protestant Christianity continues to be predominant, and the denominations of the nineteenth century maintain a strong presence. Currently, two significant religious organizations are the Grace Brethren congregation and the Seventh Day Adventists, both of whom operate private schools affiliated with their churches.

Religious diversity was but one reflection of population diversity. Persons whose origins were outside of New England were initially accepted into the total community, but as ethnic minorities grew there was a greater tendency for newcomers to develop visible identities and organizations of their own. This was typified by the small number of African-Americans who lived and worked in the community from its pioneer period. Some of the earliest were apparently associated with the brickyard east of the village, and several had homes in that area. Some probably attended the Methodist church, which before the Civil War had members who were active in the Underground Railroad, and loaned money to local blacks who wished to

purchase a home.[5] It was no accident that the African Methodist Episcopal Church was the fourth congregation in the community to build
a house for worship or that it would be located just east of the village
where several of these families lived.

Worthington's growth in population, like that of many developing towns, was neither a straight linear progression nor a series of
peaks and valleys. Perhaps it can best be characterized by population
surges followed by plateaus of stability. Worthington's initial population growth was the product of the boosterism of James Kilbourn
and others, followed by a population explosion during the economic
boom that followed the War of 1812. Gazetteers suggested that the
village contained nearly six hundred persons by 1820, with several
hundred more who identified with the village on surrounding farms.
This was Worthington's nineteenth-century population peak. Economic depression, the collapse of the Worthington Manufacturing
Company, the lure of cities like Columbus, and open land to the west
caused a population exodus during the 1820s.

From its incorporation in 1835 until the twentieth century, Worthington was a "sleepy market town," with a stable population between 400 and 450 persons.[6] The advent of the electric street railway
linking Worthington to Columbus in the 1890s and the growth of the
"fresh air movement" early in the twentieth century brought slow
but persistent growth that nearly doubled the population by 1920; it
doubled again to reach a total of approximately 1,500 persons by the
outbreak of World War II. There was modest growth in new subdivisions immediately following the war, but the population exploded
from 2,000 to 9,000 persons during the 1950s. The village officially
became a city in 1956, and rapid annexation of land increased its
physical size. Development of this land brought the population to
approximately 15,000 persons by 1970. By then, Worthington was a
landlocked suburb surrounded by the city of Columbus, and the city's
population has remained stable for the past twenty-five years.

But the Worthington City School District of approximately twenty
square miles is significantly larger than the city itself, and its current population of approximately 55,000 persons identify themselves
with Worthington. Geographically the school district is about three-
fourths the size of the original Scioto Company purchase, but its relationship to Worthington is similar to the pioneer residents of the
outlying farm lots who identified themselves with the original village

of Worthington. Both the pioneer village and the present city contain affiliated populations outside their official boundaries that are two to three times larger than the number of their legal residents.

During growth surges, both the village and the city have been ready to sacrifice their physical entity to achieve progress. The subscribers seeking the state capital in 1812 stood ready to provide considerable acreage and the academy building as a temporary home for the legislature. The growth following World War II caused the demolition of a number of significant nineteenth-century buildings to accommodate a variety of commercial structures from banks to filling stations. Periods of population stability during the last three-quarters of the nineteenth century allowed the preservation of many of the early structures of the village, and the stable population of the past twenty-five years has brought an increased appreciation of the community's heritage and a concern for its preservation.

The kinship networks that were so significant during the migration and early settlement of the community gradually faded as intermarriages with new arrivals dispersed kinship ties. Kinship networks appear to have been most closely identified with change, and they continued to be an important factor for both inward and outward migration. The Kilbourn nephews who arrived to play key roles at the Worthington Academy and the Worthington Manufacturing Company were examples of the former. The departure of the Glass Cochran family for Indiana in 1817 was only the first of what would become a tide of westward migration by successive generations. About 1840, merchants and innkeepers Edward and Dayton Topping, sons of Scioto Company member Zophar Topping, together with their sisters and brothers-in-law William Andrews and Charles Barrickman, moved west to establish Worthington, Indiana. About the same time, Azariah and Charles Pinney, sons of the pioneer Azariah, moved their families to farms near Iowa City, Iowa, and followed their father's trade as coopers. Two of the early marriages in Worthington were between Charlotte Beach and Levi Pinney, and Samuel Beach, Jr., and Violet Case. Before mid-century, five of their children—brothers, sisters, and cousins—moved together to Iroquois County, Illinois.[7] Such moves were typical of the times.

Although kinship continued to play a role in the life of Worthington, like many small towns throughout the nineteenth century, its significance did not compare to the importance it assumed during migration. There are still several descendants of Scioto Company pioneers in the Worthington area, as well as in nearby communities such as Columbus and Delaware. But the heritage of the founding New Englanders that influences the modern city is not genealogy, it is the village plan and the architectural style of the buildings the pioneers constructed during the boom of the first two decades.

Geography was a key factor in the community's development. The establishment of the state capital nine miles south of Worthington was the most critical factor in restricting the town's development. A new county had already been created on the northern boundary of the Scioto Company purchase, with Delaware as its county seat. Worthington was too close to both Columbus and Delaware to become a regular stop on the stagecoach route; yet it was too far away to play an important role in either county or state government.

Often, change comes so gradually that defining moments can only be recognized long after the fact. But in Worthington, July 7, 1893, was unquestionably an historic day. The village council granted the Columbus Electric Street Railway a right of way in the center of Main Street from the southern edge of the village to the center of the village square. Within months electric streetcars were linking the state capital and the New England village, and Worthington's future as a residential suburb was ensured.

Actually, the town's orientation had already changed several times, and it was destined to do so again. The road south from the public square to Franklinton and the erection of James Kilbourn's commercial building south of the public square dictated that the initial mercantile center of the village would flow south from the public square. This was reinforced by the initial industrial development— the sawmill and later the Worthington Manufacturing Company complex on the river southwest of the village. Although this industry failed to survive, the commercial area south of the public square was reinforced by the improvement of Main Street as part of the Columbus and Sandusky Turnpike, by the east-west post road crossing at the public square, and by the era of the Worthington Academy, Worthington Medical College, and Worthington Female Seminary.

In the mid-nineteenth century, when the route of the Columbus and Cleveland Railroad passed about a mile east of the village, Worthington attracted industries such as sawmills, which were no longer dependent on water power. The railroad also encouraged a somewhat premature promise of residential growth, and the first subdivision was platted in 1856 along the east side of the village. But it was the interstate highways of the 1960s and 1970s that dramatically changed Worthington's commercial center. The completion of I-270, the Columbus outerbelt, not only defined Worthington's northern boundary, but it attracted a shopping mall and office parks that reinforced the city's role as a residential and "white collar" business suburb. For many of the residents of the Worthington school district, the Worthington Mall adjacent to I-270 is perceived to be the city center.

But the commercial center south of the public square, which languished during the latter part of the nineteenth century and early years of the twentieth century, never died. Though grocery and hardware stores were gradually driven out of business by the competition of chain and discount stores, a slow and gradual transition to specialty stores and food-service establishments coincided with the community's revived appreciation of its New England heritage. Today, the "Old Worthington" business district south of the Village Green thrives with retail activity—its limited area inviting pedestrian traffic as conveniently as any recently planned mall.

One of the first priorities of the pioneer settlers, quality education, despite some interesting detours along the way, continues to be a factor that sells real estate in the Worthington area. The successful establishment of the Worthington Academy launched the community's reputation as a center for quality education. Residents who are attracted by such a feature can be expected to maintain and enhance it, but Worthington failed to establish an institution of higher education in the first half of the nineteenth century when many Ohio towns were doing so. This was largely because of the Worthington Academy/College's governance by the Episcopal church and the weakness of this denomination both in the community and throughout the west, and because of the conflict between James Kilbourn and Rev. Philander Chase that led Chase to move to Gambier to establish Kenyon College.[8]

However, the Worthington Medical College, the Worthington Female Seminary established by the Methodists, and the Ohio Central Normal School (which later occupied the seminary building) maintained a level of education beyond grammar school in Worthington for most of the nineteenth century. It was the commencement of the normal school in 1870 that led to the establishment of a model school in the Worthington community for teacher training, and it was the effort of James Wright, the first lawyer to live in Worthington, that culminated in an act by the Ohio legislature to return the town and farm lots set aside by the Scioto Company proprietors for school usage to the *public school* board. The academy/college building was razed in 1873, and an impressive two-story building was constructed for the "model" school. It accommodated elementary students on the ground floor and Worthington's first public high school on the second floor, which also served tuition students from the surrounding township.

It was fortunate indeed that, before the twentieth-century growth in population, the principle was clarified and that it was reestablished that the community's founders had set aside property for the support of *public education*. As increasing school enrollment crowded the buildings on the town lot, a new high school was built in 1915 on the eighty-acre school farm lot beside the river. This has since been joined by an elementary building and a new high school complex, complete with auditorium, theater, athletic fields, stadium, and swimming pool. The community received a valuable educational legacy from its founders—both in attitudes about education's significance and in property for its support. Although the public school system currently enrolls nearly 11,000 students, representing more than fifty nationalities, and operates two high school campuses, four middle schools, and twelve elementary schools, both residents and school personnel take pride in their system's educational quality.

Another valued heritage from the nineteenth century is the village-council form of government that was established at the 1835 incorporation. The modern city budgets approximately $10 million to provide the police and fire protection, maintenance of streets and sewers, park and recreation facilities, and trash-collection services that modern urban residents expect. Although a city manager and a paid staff administer these services, decision-making is still vested in an elected city council that appoints appropriate boards and commissions for issues such as zoning, parks, and architectural review.

Just as individuals may trace characteristics of physical appearance or personality to their genetic heritage, planned communities such as Worthington, Ohio, can trace aspects of their town design, historic buildings, and religious and educational heritage to their founders. This may be particularly true for towns settled by New Englanders who organized themselves into companies for the express purpose of migration and settlement. It is important, however, to recognize the unanticipated results that regional and national events such as war and economic depression bring to bear upon such plans. Even subtle differences in leadership styles and geographic sites can result in towns such as Worthington and Granville, Ohio, developing distinctly different characters—although they were founded by New England neighbors who organized themselves in a nearly identical manner.

An understanding of this heritage can enrich our perception of these towns, which have survived and changed from pioneer settlements to modern suburbs, and provide a unified identity for communities that continue to absorb immigrants from diverse cultures around the world.

Appendix A

— ❖ —

Land Ownership of Worthington Proprietors, by Residence

Proprietor	Residence	Inlots	Farm lots (acres)	Outlots (acres)
D. Bristol	Barkamsted	4	182	201
S. Beach	Barkamsted	4	232	—
L. Humphrey	Barkamsted (⅓)	4	149	—
J. Kilbourn	Berlin	4	347	—
R. Attwater	Blandford	12	439	748
G. Cochran	Blandford	10	390	608
N. Little	Blandford	8	299	473
A. Morrison	Blandford	5	209	275
A. Morrison, Jr.	Blandford	9	317	559
S. Sloper	Blandford	2	123	67
N. Stewart	Blandford	4	199	276
W. Thompson	Blandford	10	406	589
J. Norton	Farmington	17	583	965

Proprietor	Residence	Inlots	Farm lots (acres)	Outlots (acres)
L. Buttles	Granby	5	212	309
J. Case	Granby	5	214	269
L. Hayes	Granby	3	154	134
T. Phelps	Granby	3	150	108
E. Street	Granby	2	126	65
Jon. Topping	Granby	2	122	67
Jos. Topping	Granby	2	122	66
Z. Topping	Granby	3	149	134
I. Plumb	Hartford	1	93	—
M. Andrews	Montague	2	116	65
J. Stanbery	New York	1	93	—
J. Gould	Russell	2	192	65
A. Case	Simsbury (⅓)	4	149	134
I. Case	Simsbury	4	193	233
I. P. Case	Simsbury (½)	2	93	—
E. Griswold	Simsbury	5	209	272
J. Mills	Simsbury (⅓)	4	149	134
Ab. Pinney	Simsbury	8	232	505
A. P. Pinney	Simsbury (½)	2	93	—
Az. Pinney	Simsbury	1	93	—
W. Vining	Simsbury	4	198	200
R. Wilcox	Simsbury	1	93	—
J. Allen	Southington	3	107	154
J. Curtis	Southington	2	123	67
L. Kilbourn	Southington	1	93	—

Source: Scioto Company partition deed, 11 Aug. 1804. Franklin County deed record A:14–23; Delaware County deed record A:161–65.

Appendix B

— ◈ —

Scioto Company Extended-Family Networks

New England Relation[1]	Scioto Company Member[2]	Worthington Relations[3]
—	<u>Joel Allen</u>	—
—	**Moses Andrews**[4]	dau-in-l., R. Griswold
		son-in-l., C. Pinney
—	Russell Atwater	—
—	**<u>Samuel Beach</u>**	son-in-l., L. Pinney
		dau-in-l., V. Case
—	**<u>David Bristol</u>**	dau-in-l., L. Buttles
bro-in-l., T. Phelps	**<u>Levi Buttles</u>**	son-in-l., A. Morrison, Jr.
		son-in-l., A. Bristol
		dau-in-l., L. Barnes (Kilbourn)
		dau-in-l., H. Kilbourn
		son-in-l., J. W. Case
sister, D. Humphrey	Ambrose Case[5]	—
bro-in-l., L. Humphrey		

New England Relation	Scioto Company Member	Worthington Relations
son, I. P. Case	**Israel Case**	son-in-l., S. Beach, Jr.
bro-in-l., J. Case		dau-in-l., L. Morrison
father, I. Case	**I.P. Case**	fath-in-l., A. Morrison
		moth-in-l., M. Morrison
bro-in-l., I. Case	**Job Case**[6]	dau-in-l., J. Buttles
—	Glass Cochran	—
—	Jeremiah Curtis	—
—	John Gould	—
sis-in-l., L. Topping	**Ezra Griswold**	son-in-l., N. Andrews
		dau-in-l., M. Thompson
sister, M. Topping	Levi Hayes	—
bro-in-l., J. Topping		
bro-in-l., A. Case	Lemuel G. Humphrey	dau-in-l., B. Pinney
brother, L. Kilbourn	**James Kilbourn**	son-in-l., J. Buttles
		son-in-l., A. Buttles
brother, J. Kilbourn	Lemuel Kilbourn	—
—	Nathaniel Little	fath-in-l., W. Thompson
		moth-in-l., A. Thompson
—	Joel Mills	—
bro-in-l., W. Thompson	**Alexander Morrison**	dau-in-l., S. Buttles
son, A. Morrison, Jr.		son-in-l., A. P. Pinney
		son-in-l., I. P. Case
		son-in-l., C. Thompson
father, A. Morrison	Alex. Morrison, Jr.	moth-in-l., S. Buttles
—	Jedediah Norton	—
sister, S. Buttles	Thomas Phelps	—
bro-in-l., L. Buttles		

New England Relation	Scioto Company Member	Worthington Relations
son, Az. Pinney	**Abner Pinney**	dau-in-l., P. Morrison
son, A. P. Pinney		dau-in-l., C. Beach
son-in-l., W. Vining		dau-in-l., C. Andrews
		dau-in-l., L. Thompson
		son-in-l., L. Humphrey
father, A. Pinney	**Azariah Pinney**	dau-in-l., E. Sloper
brother, A. P. Pinney		sis-in-l., P. Morrison
bro-in-l., W. Vining		sis-in-l., C. Beach
		sis-in-l., C. Andrews
		sis-in-l., L. Thompson
		bro-in-l., L. Humphrey
father, A. Pinney	**Abner P. Pinney**	fath-in-l., A. Morrison
brother, Az. Pinney		moth-in-l., M. Morrison
bro-in-l., W. Vining		sis-in-l., C. Beach
		sis-in-l., C. Andrews
		sis-in-l., L. Thompson
		bro-in-l., L. Humphrey
—	Ichabod Plumb	—
—	**Samuel Sloper**[7]	son-in-l., A. Pinney
—	Jonas Stanbery	—
—	Nathan Stewart	—
—	Ebenezer Street	—
bro-in-l., A. Morrison	**William Thompson**	son-in-l., N. Little
		son-in-l., C. Pinney
		son-in-l., G. Griswold
		dau-in-l., L. Morrison
brother, J. Topping	John Topping	—
brother, Z. Topping		

New England Relation	Scioto Company Member	Worthington Relations
brother, J. Topping brother, Z. Topping bro-in-l., L. Hayes	Josiah Topping	—
brother, John Topping brother, Josiah Topping sis-in-l., R. Griswold	**Zophar Topping**	—
fath-in-l., A. Pinney moth-in-l., R. Pinney	**William Vining**	—
—	Roswell Wilcox	—

Source: Virginia E. McCormick, *Scioto Company Descendants: Genealogies of the Original Proprietors of Worthington, Ohio.* Worthington: Cottonwood Publications, 1995.

Notes:

1. Defined as parent-child or sibling relationships by birth or marriage.
2. Underlined names came to Worthington; bold names were in Worthington or had sons or daughters in Worthington in 1835.
3. Defined as father-mother or son-daughter relationships by marriage.
4. Remained in Massachusetts, but five children came to Worthington.
5. Sold Worthington property to his brother Isaac.
6. Migrated to Granville, but son settled on Worthington farm lot.
7. Died in Blandford, but his family came to Worthington.

Appendix C

— ❖ —

MIGRATION OF WORTHINGTON PROPRIETORS, BY RESIDENCE

Proprietor	Residence	Migration	1835 Tax List
D. Bristol	Barkamsted	1803 > Wor., d. 1820	Son, 6 lots
S. Beach	Barkamsted	1803 > Wor., d. 1815	Heirs, 129 acres
L. Humphrey	Barkamsted (⅓)	1807 > Del. Co.	—
J. Kilbourn	Berlin	1803 > Wor., d. 1850	Son, 4 lots
R. Attwater	Blandford	> New York State	—
G. Cochran	Blandford	1803 > Wor.> 1817, Ind.	—
N. Little	Blandford	1803 > Wor.> 1808, Del., Ohio	—
A. Morrison	Blandford	1803 > Wor. d. 1810	—
A. Morrison, Jr.	Blandford	1803 > Wor.> c. 1814, Urbana, Ohio	—
S. Sloper	Blandford	d. 1802, Hrs.> Wor. 1804	Heirs, 119 acres
N. Stewart	Blandford	1803 > Wor. > 1806, ?	—

Proprietor	Residence	Migration	1835 Tax List
W. Thompson	Blandford	1803 > Wor., d. 1830	Son, 210 acres
J. Norton	Farmington	d. Farmington, 1812	—
L. Buttles	Granby	1804 > Wor., d. 1805	Son, 2 lots, 100 acres
J. Case	Granby	1805 > Granville, Ohio	Son, 170 acres
L. Hayes	Granby	1805 > Granville, Ohio	—
T. Phelps	Granby	1803 > Wor. > 1805, New England	—
E. Street	Granby	d. New England	—
Jon. Topping	Granby	1803 > Wor., d. 1809	—
Jos. Topping	Granby	1803 > Wor. > 1820, Sand. Co.	—
Z. Topping	Granby	1803 > Wor., d. 1814	Heirs, 121 acres
I. Plumb	Hartford	1805 > Wor.> 1808, Del. Co.	—
M. Andrews	Montague	d. Montague	Heirs, 2 lots, 65 acres
J. Stanbery	New York	1814 > Zanesville, Ohio	—
J. Gould	Russell	d. New England	—
A. Case	Simsbury (⅓)	1837 > Logan, Ohio	—
I. Case	Simsbury	1804 > Wor., d. 1818	—
I. P. Case	Simsbury (½)	1803 > Wor., d. 1832	Heirs, 114 acres
E. Griswold	Simsbury	1803 > Wor., d. 1822	Son, 6 lots, 239 acres
J. Mills	Simsbury (⅓)	d. New England	—
Ab. Pinney	Simsbury	1804 > Wor., d. 1804	Heirs, 15 lots, 352 acres

Proprietor	Residence	Migration	1835 Tax List
A. P. Pinney	Simsbury (½)	1803 > Wor. > Del. Co.	Son, 6 lots
Az. Pinney	Simsbury	1804 > Wor., d. 1811	Son, 39 acres
W. Vining	Simsbury	1804 > Wor., d. 1867	203 acres
R. Wilcox	Simsbury	1804 > Wor.> 1810, Clinton Twp.	—
J. Allen	Southington	1803 > Wor.> 1806, Southington, Conn.	—
J. Curtis	Southington	1804 > Wor.> 1805, Del. Co.	—
L. Kilbourn	Southington	1803 > Wor.> 1806, Ross Co.	—

Source: McCormick, Scioto Company Descendants.

Notes

— ❖ —

Introduction

1. No historian has provoked more thought regarding the western frontier—and attracted more adherents and critics—than Frederick Jackson Turner, *The Frontier in American History* (New York: Henry Holt, 1953). As context for analysis, we found Ray A. Billington and Martin Ridge, *Western Expansion: A History of the American Frontier*, 5th ed. (New York: Macmillan, 1982) to be particularly useful.

2. More than fifty years ago, Stewart H. Holbrook, *The Yankee Exodus: An Account of Migration from New England* (New York: Macmillan, 1950), wrote of this phenomenon; quite recently, Ted Morgan, *Wilderness at Dawn: The Settling of the North American Continent* (New York: Simon and Schuster, 1993), treats it well.

3. Noteworthy examples are John Mack Faragher, *Sugar Creek: Life on the Illinois Prairie* (New Haven: Yale University Press, 1986), and Don Harrison Doyle, *The Social Order of a Frontier Community: Jacksonville, Illinois, 1825–1870* (Urbana: University of Illinois Press, 1978).

4. For elaboration refer to Bernard M. Bass, *Handbook of Leadership*, 3rd ed. (New York: The Free Press, 1990), and Carl F. Graumann and Serge Moscovici, eds., *Changing Conceptions of Leadership* (New York: Springer-Verlag, 1986). For the most complete biography of Kilbourn, see Goodwin Berquist and Paul C. Bowers, Jr., *The New Eden: James Kilbourne and the Development of Ohio* (Lanham, Md.: University Press of America, 1983).

5. David J. Russo, *Families and Communities: A New View of American History* (Nashville: American Association for the Study of State and Local History, 1974), provides context for such analysis. Virginia McCormick, *Scioto Company Descendants: Genealogies of the Original Proprietors of Worthington, Ohio* (Worthington: Cottonwood Publications, 1995), offers specific background.

6. This concept was introduced by Page Smith, *As a City on a Hill: The Town in American History* (Cambridge: Massachusetts Institute of Technology Press, 1966).

7. Andrew R. L. Cayton and Peter S. Onuf, *The Midwest and the Nation: Rethinking the History of an American Region* (Bloomington: Indiana University Press, 1990), provides helpful context regarding the development of communities in the early republic.

8. For context in this area, see Malcolm J. Rohrbough, *The Land Office Business* (New York: Oxford University Press, 1968); Benjamin H. Hibbard, *A History of the Public Land Policies* (New York: Peter Smith, 1939); and C. E. Sherman, *Original Ohio Land Subdivisions* (Columbus: Ohio Cooperative Topographic Survey, 1925).

9. We found Christopher Clark, *The Roots of Rural Capitalism: Western Massachusetts, 1780–1800* (Ithaca: Cornell University Press, 1990), particularly helpful both in analyzing the "transitions to capitalism" and in understanding the New England concept of land ownership as it related to independence.

10. For an Ohio perspective on this time period, we especially appreciated William T. Utter, *The Frontier State: 1803–1825* (Columbus: Ohio State Archaeological and Historical Society, 1942); Andrew R. L. Cayton, *The Frontier Republic: Ideology and Politics in the Ohio Country, 1780–1825* (Kent: Kent State University Press, 1986); and Eugene H. Roseboom and Francis P. Weisenburger, *A History of Ohio* (Columbus: Ohio Historical Society, 1986).

11. Our understanding of the significance of town development as land speculation was enhanced by Richard C. Wade, *The Urban Frontier: The Rise of Western Cities, 1790–1830* (Cambridge: Harvard University Press, 1959).

1. A COMPANY TO MAKE SETTLEMENT NORTHWEST OF THE OHIO

1. SCMB, 5 May 1802.

2. Berquist and Bowers, *New Eden*, 1–20; see also "Autobiography of Col. James Kilbourne," *Old Northwest Genealogical Quarterly* 6 (Oct. 1903): 111–21, which is actually an autobiographical letter from James Kilbourn, in Worthington, to Payne Kenyon Kilbourn on March 22, 1845, in response to a request for information, which the latter would publish in *The Family Memorial: A History and Genealogy of the Kilbourn Family* (Hartford: Brown and Parsons, 1850), 65–78, 102–4. The family name was consistently written without a final *e* until James's two youngest sons changed the spelling to Kilbourne and about 1840 their father began writing it the same. We have chosen to follow James and his contemporaries' spelling of this time.

3. Alexander Viets Griswold later became a bishop of the Episcopal Church. John S. Stone, *Memoir of the Life of the Rt. Reverend Alexander Viets Griswold, D.D., Bishop of the Protestant Episcopal Church in the Eastern Diocese* (Philadelphia: Stavely and McCalla, 1844).

4. William M. Vibert, *Three Centuries of Simsbury, 1670–1970* (Simsbury, Conn.: Simsbury Tercentenary Committee, 1970), 58–63; Albert E. Van Dusen, ed., *The Public Records of the State of Connecticut* (Hartford: State of Connecticut, 1953), 9:360–61.

5. Holbrook, *Yankee Exodus*, 10.

6. The boy was Alfred Avery whose family settled at Granville, Ohio, soon after the Scioto Company settlement at Worthington. "The Historic Settling of Granville," *Old Northwest Genealogical Quarterly* 8 (1905): 237.

7. Morgan, *Wilderness at Dawn*, 423.

8. Gary R. Teeples, *Connecticut 1800 Census* (Provo, Utah: Accelerated Indexing Systems, 1974).

9. Philip J. Greven, Jr., *Four Generations: Population, Land and Family in Colonial Andover, Massachusetts* (Ithaca: Cornell University Press, 1970), 268–75.

10. Kenneth L. Lockridge, "Land, Population and the Evolution of New England Society, 1630–1790," in *Colonial America: Essays in Politics and Social Development*, ed. Stanley N. Katz (Boston: Little, Brown, 1971), 466–91.

11. Turner, *Frontier in American History*, 153–54.

12. Ray A. Billington, *Frederick Jackson Turner: Historian, Scholar, Teacher* (New York: Oxford University Press, 1973), 125.

13. A model of the Fitch steam engine is in the possession of the Ohio Historical Society. "Mr. Fitch's 'Mysterious Machine,'" *Ohio Historical Society Echoes* 10 (April 1971). John Fitch's biographical sketch in *The National Cyclopaedia of American Biography* (New York: James T. White, 1929), 6:63–64, appears to have been written by one of James Kilbourn's grandsons and is subject to the bias commonly associated with biographical sketches contributed to county histories.

14. For discussion of this concept, see Billington and Ridge, *Western Expansion*, 220.

15. SCMB, 5 May 1802.

16. Morgan, *Wilderness at Dawn*, 410–37; Roseboom and Weisenburger, *History of Ohio*, 47–54; Sherman, *Original Ohio Land Subdivisions*, 51–56; and Cayton, *Frontier Republic*, 33–50.

17. Holbrook, *Yankee Exodus*, 13, 25.

18. Smith, *As a City on a Hill*, 3–16, 44.

19. SCMB, 14 Dec. 1802.

20. SCMB, 14 Dec. 1802. This group should not be confused with the ill-fated Scioto Company, an offshoot of the Ohio Company organized by William Duer and others, which attempted to attract French settlers. See "The Scioto Company and Its Purchase," *Ohio Archaeological and Historical Society Publications* 3 (1894): 109–40; Robert F. Jones, *"King of the Alley," William Duer: Politician, Entrepreneur, and Speculator, 1768–1799* (Philadelphia: American Philosophical Society, 1992), 118–25.

21. Sherman, *Original Ohio Land Subdivisions*, 108–16.

22. Edmund Dana, *Geographical Sketches on the Western Country: designed for emigrants and settlers* (Cincinnati: n.p., 1819).

23. Timothy R. Mahoney, *River Towns in the Great West: The Structure of Provincial Urbanization in the American Midwest, 1820–1870* (Cambridge: Cambridge University Press, 1990), 32.

24. *Debates of Congress, 1789–1856* (New York: D. Appleton, 1857), 651–54.

25. McCormick, *Scioto Company Descendants*, 266.

26. SCMB, 19 May 1802 and 17 June 1802.

2. To Explore Said Territory and Report to the Company

1. Unless otherwise noted, all quoted material in this chapter is taken from the "Journal of Nathaniel W. Little," *Old Northwest Genealogical Quarterly* 10 (1907): 237–45, and James Kilbourn's letter to his wife Lucy, 16 August 1802, Worthington Historical Society.

2. Archer Butler Hulbert, *Historic Highways of America* (Cleveland: Arthur H. Clark, 1903), 5:163.

3. Utter, *Frontier State*, 2:202.

4. This area, which they tentatively reserved with the land office upon their return, was township 10 in the Congress Lands, which is currently Madison Township of Pickaway County. Big Belly Creek is now Big Walnut Creek, and Walnut Creek is now known as Little Walnut Creek. The early town of Franklinton has become part of the city of Columbus.

5. Alfred Byron Sears, *Thomas Worthington: Father of Ohio Statehood* (Columbus: Ohio State University Press, 1958).

6. McCormick, *Scioto Company Descendants*, 242–43; Mary Anne Cummins, "The Stanbery/Stanborough Genealogy," typescript, Delaware County Historical Society, 34–35. Jonas Stanbery did bring his family west to Zanesville, Ohio, in 1814. He was the father of Henry Stanbery, Ohio and U.S. Attorney General, best known for his defense of President Andrew Johnson during his impeachment trial.

7. SCMB, 5 Oct. and 25 Oct. 1802.

8. Sherman, *Original Ohio Land Subdivisions*, 89–93.

9. Ibid., 98–101.

10. Various privately held property abstracts for the U.S. Military District, range 18, township 2.

11. The Virginia Military District, between the Scioto and Miami Rivers, was separate from the U.S. Military District because Virginia had originally claimed this western area and had received the district as part of the cessation settlement. See Sherman, *Original Ohio Land Subdivisions*, 12–20.

12. For a discussion of this issue, see Cayton, *Frontier Republic*, 55–56; and Timothy J. Shannon, "This Unpleasant Business: The Transformation of Land Speculation in the Ohio Country, 1787–1820," in *The Pursuit of Public Power: Political Culture*

in Ohio, 1787–1861, ed. Jeffrey P. Brown and Andrew R. L. Cayton (Kent: Kent State University Press, 1994), 26–27.

13. This incident is described by Morgan, *Wilderness at Dawn*, 465–66, quoting from Langham's complaint in *The Territorial Papers of the United States*, vol. 3, comp. and ed. by C. E. Carter (1934)

14. SCMB, 19 Dec. 1802.

15. Shannon, "This Unpleasant Business," 15–25.

16. For details on Congress and U.S. military land locations, see Sherman, *Original Ohio Land Subdivisions*, 89–94, 107–16. For background on government land policy at this time, see Rohrbough, *Land Office Business*; and Hibbard, *Public Land Policies*.

17. Allan G. Bogue and Margaret Beattie Bogue, "Profits and the Frontier Land Speculator," *Journal of Economic History* 17 (Mar. 1957): 1–24.

18. Ross County Deed Record, 2:336 and 556. Landowners are given in the Franklin County tax records for 1806–10 as compiled in Ronald V. Jackson, Gary R. Teeples, and David Schaefermeyer, *Index to Ohio Tax Lists, 1800–1810* (Bountiful, Utah: Accelerated Indexing Systems, 1977).

19. Daniel J. Ryan, "From Charter to Constitution," *Ohio Archaeological and Historical Society Publications* 5 (1900): 1–164; W. A. Taylor, *Ohio Statesman and Hundred Year Book* (Columbus: Westbote, 1892), 16–33; Roseboom and Weisenburger, *History of Ohio*, 64–70.

20. SCMB, 14 Dec. 1802. See appendix A for list of names, towns of residence, and acres subscribed.

21. Vibert, *Three Centuries of Simsbury*, 55–57.

22. John William Reps, *Cities of the American West: A History of Frontier Urban Planning* (Princeton: Princeton University Press, 1979), 8–13.

23. For elaboration of this concept, see Wade, *Urban Frontier*, 27–30.

24. Dr. Stanbery is not included in this figure. His nephew did, however, later settle in Worthington.

3. A Place Most Favorable for Our First Improvement

1. SCMB, 19 Dec. 1802.

2. SCMB, 22 Feb. 1803. For example, during 1802–1803 Ezra Griswold of Simsbury had three transactions in pounds and eleven transactions in dollars. Simsbury town records, 21:452–510 and 22:105–10.

3. "Report of James Kilbourne, Agent of the Scioto Company for the Summer of 1803," *Old Northwest Genealogical Quarterly* 6 (1903): 87–91. This was copied in 1903 by Frank T. Cole from the original manuscript, then in the possession of Kilbourn's granddaughter, Mrs. William G. Deshler.

4. James Kilbourn, Chillicothe, to Lucy Kilbourn, Simsbury, 13 May 1803, KFP, box 1, folder 3.

5. Merle Curti, *The Making of an American Community: A Case Study of Democracy in a Frontier County* (Stanford: Stanford University Press, 1959), 33.

6. Linear and square measures of land, inside of rear cover, *Ohio Lands: A Short History* (Columbus: State Auditor, 1989).

7. Israel Ludlow, original survey notes, U.S. Military District, range 18, township 2, 22 Nov. 1797, OHS.

8. GFP, box 18, folder 7.

9. Nathaniel Massie to Thomas James, 3 Feb. 1802, NMP, folder 9.

10. "Report of James Kilbourn," 7–10 May 1803.

11. Quoted in Virginia D. Anderson, *New England's Generation* (Cambridge: Cambridge University Press, 1991), 53.

12. "Report of James Kilbourne," 18 May 1803.

13. Utter, *The Frontier State*, 146.

14. "Report of James Kilbourne," 18 May 1803.

15. James Kilbourn to Lucy Kilbourn, 13 May 1803, KFP.

16. Kilbourn seems to be reverting to old English and early New England villages in thinking of outlots for pasture and hay. Most of the subscribers used these parcels as investments for resale.

17. James Kilbourn to Lucy Kilbourn, 13 May 1803, KFP.

18. Richard A. Bartlett, *The New Country: A Social History of the American Frontier* (New York: Oxford University Press, 1974), 180.

19. "Report of James Kilbourne." Tradition maintains that Lemuel Kilbourn brought his family with him in June and that, therefore, his wife Sarah Hastings Kilbourn was the first Scioto Company woman on the site of the new village. Kilbourn's report makes no mention of Lemuel's family, which included teenage children, but it seems unlikely that he would have been traveling alone.

20. E. G. Squirer and E. H. Davis, *Ancient Monuments of the Mississippi Valley* (1848; reprint, New York: AMS Press for the Peabody Museum of Archaeology and Ethnology, 1973): 83–84; Robert McCormick and Jennie McCormick, *Worthington Landmarks: Photo-Essays of Historic Worthington Properties* (Worthington: Cottonwood Publications, 1992), 8–11. Subsequent archaeological excavations have confirmed that the remaining mound contained burials.

21. Bartlett, *New Country*, 144.

22. Ibid., 182.

23. Diary of Harriet Thompson, 15-year-old daughter of proprietor William Thompson, quoted in *New England in the Wilderness* (Worthington: Worthington Historical Society, 1976), 13. Harriet Thompson married successively Nathaniel Little, William Pratt, and Reuben Lamb. The original diary was in the possession of her descendants into the twentieth century, but its location, if it still exists, is no longer known.

24. Signatures to Scioto Company articles of agreement, SCMB, 14 Dec. 1802.

25. Lee Soltow, "Inequality Amidst Abundance: Land Ownership in Early Ohio," *Ohio History* 88 (Spring 1979): 133–51.

26. Norton was a Farmington, Conn., businessman who married Elizabeth Kilbourn and had no children. In the partition of the Scioto Company land in 1804, he received 17 town lots and 1,539 acres of farmland, most of which was eventually sold by James Kilbourn as his agent. See McCormick, *Scioto Company Descendants*, 199.

27. Mody C. Boatright, "The Myth of Frontier Individualism," in *Turner and the Sociology of the Frontier*, ed. Richard Hofstadter and Seymour Martin Lipset (New York: Basic Books, 1968), 43–64. Although historians have discredited Turner's thesis of frontier individualism, the image continues in children's books, novels, and television and movie portrayals.

28. Clark, *Roots of Rural Capitalism*, 22–23.

29. Susan E. Gray, "Family, Land, and Credit: Yankee Communities on the Michigan Frontier, 1830–1860" (Ph.D. diss., University of Chicago, 1985).

30. Everett S. Lee, "A Theory of Migration," *Demography* 3 (1966): 47–67.

31. Ezra Griswold to Alexander V. Griswold, 13 Feb. 1802, Simsbury town record 22:105–7.

32. David Creasy, *Coming Over: Migration and Communication between England and New England* (Cambridge: Cambridge University Press, 1987), 107–29.

33. Simsbury town record 21:511.

34. Blandford deed record 47:467.

35. Billington and Ridge, *Western Expansion*, 248, reports that good New England farms at that time were selling from fourteen to fifty dollars per acre depending on improvements.

36. Blandford deed record 41:536, 538.

37. SCMB, 11 Aug. 1803.

38. Sears, *Thomas Worthington*.

39. Doyle, *Social Order of a Frontier Community*, 28–29. See also Smith, *As a City on a Hill*.

40. Turner, *Frontier in American History*.

4. If You Calculate for Smooth Roads Free from Hills You Will Be Disappointed

1. C. M. Storey, ed., *Massachusetts Society of the Cincinnati* (Boston: Society of the Cincinnati, 1964).

2. McCormick, *Scioto Company Descendants*, 259–60, 189–90, 256.

3. Ibid., 35–38.

4. On this point, see Cayton, *Frontier Republic*, 68.

5. McCormick, *Scioto Company Descendants*, 157–58, 118–19, 273, 266–67; obituary, George Hayes Topping, *Ashland Press*, 16 Oct. 1901.

6. McCormick, *Scioto Company Descendants*, 111–12, 187, 9.

7. This became the Licking Company, which will be considered in more detail later.

8. Of the thirty-eight Scioto Company members, seven (18.4%) were investors who did not come west, seven (18.4%) were single young men who married in Ohio, twelve (31.6%) were married men whose children were all born in New England, and twelve (31.6%) were married men who fathered children after the migration. The average husband's age was 39.7 years (N=22), and their wives averaged 35.6 years (N=19) and 5.3 living children. This compares with husbands averaging 37.4 years of age and wives averaging 33.8 years and 3.08 children during the Great Migration of the 1630s. Anderson, *New England's Generation*, 23.

9. Faragher, *Sugar Creek*.

10. Daniel Scott Smith, "All in Some Degree Related to Each Other: A Demographic and Comparative Resolution of the Anomaly of New England Kinship," *American Historical Review* 94 (Feb. 1989), 44–79.

11. Griswold family genealogy, *Old Northwest Genealogical Quarterly* 6 (Oct. 1903): 171.

12. Orrel Kilbourne Whiting died in Columbus in 1863, always proud to have been one of the pioneers of Franklin County.

13. James Kilbourn to Thomas Worthington, 7 Feb. 1804, TWP, roll 3, box 2, folder 6.

14. Samuel R. Brown, *The Western Gazetteer: or Emigrants' Directory* (Auburn, N.Y.: H.C. Southwick, Printers, 1817); William T. Utter, *Granville: The Story of an Ohio Village* (Granville: Granville Historical Society, 1956), 38.

15. Drake is quoted in Utter, *Frontier State*, 340.

16. Lura Ann Bristol, Worthington, to Levi Buttles, Gambier, 30 Sept. 1869, BFP. These were grandchildren, and Lura's mother was living with her and describing the Levi Buttles family trip she experienced from Oct. to Dec. 1804.

17. From the Edward Phelps account book, Windsor, Conn., March 1806, reported in "Settlement of Blendon Township," *Old Northwest Genealogical Quarterly* 10 (Apr. 1907): 128–30. Three years later this settlement was made just east of Worthington by Connecticut relatives and neighbors.

18. Utter, *Granville*, 45–52, describes the 1805 journey of New Englanders, one party of which was led by Scioto Company member Job Case.

19. Hulbert, *Historic Highways of America*, 23.

20. Ruhamah Hayes, Worthington, to Mrs. Elizabeth, wife of Capt. Job Case, Granby, 23 Aug. 1805, JBC.

21. Jane C. Nylander, *Our Own Snug Fireside: Images of the New England Home, 1760–1860* (New York: Alfred A. Knopf, 1994), provides an excellent basis for comparing the material artifacts in New England homes of this period with these estate items, which migrants apparently considered essential for the trip west.

22. Abner Pinney died on Nov. 23, 1804. Estate appraisal, 6 May 1805, OHS, GR 2795, 8–13. Levi Buttles died on June 14, 1805. Estate appraisal, 30 Sept. 1805, OHS, GR 2795, 24–31. These sources will be extensively quoted in the pages that follow.

23. When the land was partitioned on Aug. 11, 1804, the largest shareholder was Jedediah Norton of Farmington, Conn., with 1,548 acres of land and 17 town lots. The smallest shareholders were Israel P. Case and Abner P. Pinney, sons of proprietors and laborers in the advance party, who each had one-half interest in one town lot and a ninety-three acre farm lot.

24. Scioto Company partition deed, Franklin County deed record A:14–23.

25. A steelyard was a balance scale for weighing items. Gimlets were small hand augers with spiraled cutting points in various sizes for boring holes.

26. A surtout was a long frock coat. Nankeen was usually a buff-colored cotton cloth that originated in Nankin, China.

27. The silk nankeen vest was probably made from Chinese silk. Small clothes were underwear. Stockings were knitted and either had feet, like modern stockings, or did not have feet, like the leg-warmers often worn by modern dancers. A knaped hat had a top knot, while a castor hat was made from beaver or rabbit fur.

28. A hatchel was used to separate and comb flax fibers. It was composed of long iron teeth that were set into a board. This inventory suggests a supply of teeth was carried west to replace broken teeth or to make a new hatchel as needed.

29. Jack Larkin, *The Reshaping of Everyday Life, 1790–1840* (New York: Harper and Row, 1988), 25.

30. Christopher P. Bickford, *Farmington in Connecticut* (Farmington: Farmington Historical Society, 1982), 225–30.

31. Tinner Asa Andrews of Farmington was reportedly producing 10,000 articles of japanned ware annually by 1800.

32. R. Carlyle Buley, *The Old Northwest: Pioneer Period, 1815–1840* (reprint, Bloomington: Indiana University Press, 1978), 1:147.

33. Richard L. Bushman, *The Refinement of America: Persons, Houses, Cities* (New York: Alfred A. Knopf, 1992), xii and 406.

34. It is impossible to compare these two settlers with a larger group of central Ohio immigrants because the earliest surviving Franklin County tax list is a partial listing from 1806, after these estates were filed for probate. At that time, most of the property adjoining Worthington was held in quarter-township sections by nonresident land speculators. For analysis of the problem of estimating wealth distribution from probate records, see Carole Shammas, "Constructing a Wealth Distribution from Probate Records," *Journal of Interdisciplinary History* 9 (1978): 297–307.

35.   Percentage of Property, by Property Type

	Personal Apparel	Household Furnishings and Equipment	Livestock and Equipment	Tools
Pinney	13.0	37.2	26.7	23.1
Buttles	8.2	24.1	38.9	28.8

This is consistent with the distribution of wealth by class and age studied by Jackson Turner Main, *Society and Economy in Colonial Connecticut* (Princeton: Princeton University Press, 1985), 139–63.

36. Bushman, *Refinement of America,* 207–37.

37. Larkin, *Reshaping of Everyday Life,* 132–38.

38. Ruhamah Hayes to Elizabeth Case, 23 Aug. 1805.

5. In Perfect Health and Much Pleased with Our Situation

1. SCMB, 1 Dec. 1803.

2. Joel Buttles's Diary, written about 1842, recalled his family's arrival in Worthington, on December 4, 1804. Even then, a cabin twenty rods from the center of the settlement was described as being in the woods.

3. SCMB, 12 Dec. 1803.

4. Ibid., 13 Dec. 1803.

5. "Organization of Franklin County," *Old Northwest Genealogical Quarterly* 15 (July 1912). This source will be quoted in the passages that follow.

6. Ordering this report recorded was the equivalent of tabling the matter.

7. Caroline P. Ward, "History of the Worthington Public Library," typewritten Ms, 1931, Worthington Public Library. The bylaws were transcribed by Ruth Griswold from a yellowed paper labeled "Laws of Stanbery Library," which was found among the Ezra Griswold papers. The location of the original is no longer known.

8. George Knepper, *Ohio and Its People* (Kent: Kent State University Press, 1989), 197, cites several early Ohio libraries, including the famous one at Amesville that was financed by coonskins.

9. James Kilbourn, Worthington, to Thomas Worthington, Washington, 7 Feb. 1804, TWP, roll 3, box 2, folder 6.

10. Delaware County deed record A:161–65. James Kilbourn's survey chain and compass are now the property of the Worthington Historical Society.

11. SCMB, 14 Dec. 1803.

12. JBD.

13. SCMB, 19 Dec. 1803.

14. Ibid.

15. Nathaniel Massie to John Graham, 4 Apr. 1797, NMP, folder 9.

16. The Scioto Company Minute Book has a ledger of accounts for individual members in the rear.

17. James Kilbourn to Thomas Worthington, 7 Feb. 1804.

18. Ibid.

19. *History of Franklin and Pickaway Counties* (Cleveland: Williams Brothers, 1880), 425; Franklin County marriage record 1:5.

20. McCormick, *Scioto Company Descendants,* 26–27, 213–14.

21. Reference to Thomas Phelps as the first teacher is in *Shedding Light on Worthington* (Worthington: Woodrow Guild of the Presbyterian Church, 1931), 31. The receipt for the final $3.53 (probably with interest) paid by Nathan Stewart to Clarissa Thompson for teaching school in 1804 is in GP, 1802–1809.

22. James Kilbourn to Thomas Worthington, 7 Feb. 1804.

23. "St. John's Church," *Old Northwest Genealogical Quarterly* 6 (Oct. 1903): 147–49.

24. James Kilbourn to Thomas Worthington, 7 Feb. 1804.

25. G. W. Aldrich, "New England Lodge No. 4," *Worthington News*, 25 Oct. and 1 Nov. 1945.

26. Robert V. Hine, *Community on the American Frontier* (Norman: University of Oklahoma Press, 1980), 128.

27. James Kilbourn to Thomas Worthington, 7 Feb. 1804.

6. A Just and Legal Land Division

1. This acreage included the intersecting streets mentioned and a perimeter road in front of the lots facing the square.

2. Wade, *Urban Frontier*, 30–39.

3. Depending on the direction they faced, Worthington lots were either 126.12 feet by 269.36 feet or 134.68 feet by 252.25 feet.

4. Bid list for town lots, SCMB. [Dec. 1803.]

5. Franklin County deed record A:14–23; Delaware County deed record A: 161–65.

6. JBD.

7. SCMB, 23 Apr. 1804.

8. *New England in the Wilderness*, 13.

9. Articles of agreement, SCMB, 14 Dec. 1802.

10. SCMB, 23 Apr. 1804.

11. Franklin County deed record A:14–23; Delaware County deed record A:161–65.

12. SCMB, 8 Aug. 1804.

13. Deeds for these transactions burned in the 1879 Franklin County courthouse fire and were not rerecorded, but it appears from the surviving index that they occurred in the fall of 1804.

14. Electors for township clerk, GFP, box 15, folder 10. This list is not dated but it contains the name of Levi Buttles, who arrived on Dec. 4, 1804, and died on June 14, 1805. Since township elections normally occurred in March, this is presumed to be a March 1805 list.

15. Soltow, "Inequality Amidst Abundance," 133–51. The 1800 census estimated a population of 45,000 in the Northwest Territory that became Ohio. There were approximately 230,000 in Ohio in 1810.

16. *History of Delaware County, Ohio* (Chicago: O.L. Baskin, 1880), 430.

17. JBD.

18. In founding Delaware, Byxbe formed a partnership with Henry Baldwin, heir of Senator Abraham Baldwin who had acquired extensive land holdings in the U.S. Military District. See *History of Delaware County*, 312–13.

19. Utter, *Granville*, 25–30.

20. Jared Mansfield to James Kilbourn, 3 July 1804, reprinted in *Old Northwest Genealogical Quarterly* 6 (1903): 115.

21. Delaware County deed A:238, 268, 274–77, 7 Jan. 1806. This area includes the present city of Powell, which developed with the advent of the railroad. Early settlers

in this area north of Worthington related to Worthington or to the Liberty Presbyterian Church founded in 1810 by settlers of the early "Carpenter settlement."

22. James Kilbourn to the "Gentlemen of the Scioto Company," 29 Jan. 1805, transcription at Worthington Historical Society.

23. Bass, *Handbook of Leadership*, 184. This discussion is based on Max Weber, *Essays in Sociology* (New York: Oxford University Press, 1946). Although charismatic leadership was employed here for positive goals, the extent of its danger can be understood in M. Rainer Lepsius's application of Weber's model to the rule of Adolf Hitler. See Graumann and Moscovici, *Changing Conceptions of Leadership*, 53.

24. Scioto Company committee to Roswell Wilcox, 21 Apr. 1807; Delaware County deed record A:457.

25. Delaware County deed record A:171, 25 Aug. 1804.

26. Delaware County deed record A:341, 3 Dec. 1806.

27. James Kilbourn to James Allen, 30 Jan. 1807, *St. John's Banner* 1 (July 1900), 28.

28. Franklin County, Ohio, 1810 tax schedule, range 18, township 2, sections 2 and 3.

29. *Western Intelligencer*, 17 July 1811.

30. Ezra Griswold's notes on a letter sent to his brother Roger, 4 Jan. 1810, GFP, box 1, folder 1.

31. *Western Intelligencer*, 12 Aug. 1812.

7. An Elderly Gentleman Passed through with All His Posterity

1. James Kilbourn to Lucy Kilbourn, 16 Aug. 1802, WHS.

2. McCormick, *Scioto Company Descendants*, 26–34, 201–17, 280–83. Descendants of two branches of this family still live in the Worthington area, but a significant number of the grandchildren moved to Illinois together in the 1840s.

3. Clark, *Roots of Rural Capitalism*, 11–12; Doyle, *Social Order of a Frontier Community*, 28–29; Mody C. Boatright, "Myth of Frontier Individualism," in *Turner and the Sociology of the Frontier*, ed. Richard Hofstadter and Seymour Martin Lipset, 43–64; Faragher, *Sugar Creek*, 144–51.

4. Daniel J. Boorstin, *The Americans, The National Experience* (New York: Random House, 1965), 51–52.

5. Cynthia Barker, Montague, Mass., to Julia Buttles, Granby, Conn., 19 Sept. 1813, JBC. Cynthia does not mention her pregnancy, saying only "I shall not see Worthington this winter," but her son Cyrus was born early in 1814.

6. Byron Kilbourn, Milwaukee, Wisc., to his cousin Emma Jones, Columbus, Jan. 1890, quoted in *A State in the Making: Correspondence of the late James Kilbourne*, ed. Emma Jones (Columbus: Tibbetts Printing, 1913), 115.

7. Payne Kenyon Kilbourn, *Family Memorial*, 65–78.

8. McCormick, *Scioto Company Descendants*, 199.

9. Mary P. Ryan, *The Cradle of the Middle Class: The Family in Oneida County, New York, 1790–1865* (Cambridge: Cambridge University Press, 1981), 13.

10. Russo, *Families and Communities*, 224.

11. JBD. Arthur W. Calhoun discusses the importance of family ties in business and politics in *A Social History of the American Family* (New York: Barnes and Noble, 1945) 2:144–45.

12. *History of Franklin and Pickaway Counties*, 404.

13. See, for example, Robert E. Bieder, "Kinship as a Factor in Migration," *Journal of Marriage and the Family* 35 (Aug. 1973): 429–39, a study of Benzonia, Mich.

14. *History of Delaware County*, 469.

15. Lucy Kilbourn to James Kilbourn, 2 July 1805, KFP, box 1, folder 1.

16. James Kilbourn to Lucy Kilbourn, 10 Aug. 1805, KFP, box 1, folder 1.

17. Lura Ann Bristol to her cousin Levi Buttles, 30 Sept. 1869, BFP. At this time Lura Ann's mother, Lura Buttles Bristol, was living with her and talking about the family heritage.

18. Joel Allen to Ezra Griswold, Sept. 1806, GP, 1802–1809.

19. John Demos, *A Little Commonwealth: Family Life in Plymouth Colony* (New York: Oxford University Press, 1971), 183–84.

20. Since data on the total population or a random sample of the community is not available, a statistical analysis is not warranted. The relationship, however, is too obvious to be ignored. It is consistent with Bieder's data for Benzonia, Mich., which found 68.4 percent persistence for families with kinship ties and 25 percent for those without. Bieder, "Kinship as a Factor in Migration."

21. Doyle found the persistence rate in Jacksonville, Ill., over a decade normally hovered between 40 and 50 percent. Don Harrison Doyle, *Social Order of a Frontier Community*, 96–97. Doyle, Bieder, and others recognize that mobility is related to factors other than kinship such as occupation, age, property ownership, and number of dependents. See also Eugene Litwak, "Geographic Mobility and Extended Family Cohesion," *American Sociological Review* 25 (June 1960).

22. McCormick, *Scioto Company Descendants*, 111–12.

23. Calhoun, *Social History of the American Family*, 2:30.

24. Franklin County marriage records, Sharon Township, 1804–1814.

25. Larkin, *Reshaping of Everyday Life*, 65. Worthington had seven marriages each in Feb. and July; five in April; four in Jan. and Mar.; three in May, Nov., and Dec.; and two in June, Sept., and Oct.

26. N=14 for the New England generation; N=83 for the Worthington generation. All marriages that produced children were counted for both generations, but the shorter length of marriage and the smaller families in Worthington probably reflect the larger population. Those who migrated from New England were *survivors*. Readers may wish to compare these data with Robert V. Wells, "Demographic Change and the Life Cycle of the American Family," 85–94, and James A. Henretta, "The Morphology of New England Society in the Colonial Period," 191–210, both in *The Family in History: Interdisciplinary Essays*, ed. Theodore K. Rabb and Robert I. Rotberg (New York: Harper and Row, 1973).

27. Margaret Walsh, *The American Frontier Revisited* (London: The Economic History Society, 1981), 64.

28. Marriages of Scioto Company descendants from 1804–1835 for which month, day, and year of marriage and for which month, day, and year of first birth are recorded.

29. John D'Emilio and Estelle B. Freedman, *Intimate Matters: A History of Sexuality in America* (New York: Harper and Row, 1988), 23.

30. McCormick, *Scioto Company Descendants*, 261. William Platt's son by his first marriage married a sister of future president, Rutherford B. Hayes.

31. Franklin County Supreme Court record 2:372.

32. William Thompson estate #773, Franklin County, 2 Oct. 1830, Common Pleas Court, OHS, GR 1244.

33. Calhoun, *Social History of the American Family*, 2:147.

8. A TOLERABLY COMFORTABLE CABIN

1. H. Warren Phelps, "Some Historic Records from Franklin County Commissioner's Books," *Old Northwest Genealogical Quarterly* 7 (July 1904): 192–93; "Com-

mon Pleas Court Records from the Organization of Franklin County," *Old Northwest Genealogical Quarterly* 15 (July 1912): 61.

2. JBD, here and in passages to follow.

3. *History of Delaware County*, 430.

4. Buley, *Old Northwest*, 244–46.

5. Joel Allen to James Allen, *St. John's Banner* 1 (July 1900): 27. This is undated but would appear to be in 1804 because he referred to both Mr. Kilbourn's and Mr. Smith's compasses being out of order for surveying.

6. Ruhamah Hayes to Elizabeth Case, 23 Aug. 1805, JBC.

7. Ibid.

8. E. Griswold account with Stewart and Little, 1 Nov. 1804–Aug. 1805, GFP, box 16, folder 3.

9. John Hoffman advertisement, *Western Intelligencer*, 17 July 1812.

10. James Kilbourn to Ezra Griswold, 26 July 1806, GFP, box 1, folder 1. This must have taken about six weeks, for on September 4 Ezra Griswold sent a note via Alexander Morrison, Jr., authorizing him to pick this up at Chillicothe.

11. Kathryn Kish Sklar, *Catharine Beecher: A Study in American Domesticity* (New York: W. W. Norton, 1976), 156–57; D'Emilio and Freedman, *Intimate Matters*, 57.

12. Lucy Kilbourn to James Kilbourn, 8 Aug. 1806, Worthington Historical Society. Kilbourn was then in Washington and on his way to New York. Despite Lucy's plea, he probably also went to New England before returning.

13. Among six Worthington estates appraised between 1804 and 1811, there were eleven horses ranging in value from a $75 stud horse to a $15 yearling colt with an average value of $42. The personal property appraisal of these estates averaged $462.68. One must consider that this represented the elite of the community; laborers who owned no land and little personal property had no estate recorded.

14. John Topping estate appraisal, 6 Sept. 1809, OHS, GR 2795, 133–36.

15. Alexander Morrison estate appraisal, 23 Sept. 1811, OHS, GR 2795, 165–71.

16. Azariah Pinney estate appraisal, 3 Nov. 1811, OHS, GR 2795, 187–91.

17. David Freeman Hawke, *Everyday Life in Early America* (New York: Harper and Row, 1988), 55.

18. *Western Intelligencer*, 29 Dec. 1813.

19. *Western Intelligencer*, 28 Dec. 1811.

20. This museum provides a dramatic example of the low-ceilinged dark interior that Bushman associated with seventeenth-century colonial homes, contrasted with the light openness of eighteenth-century homes with higher ceilings and larger windows. It is important to note that in the Worthington pioneer community these changes occurred less than a decade apart, reflecting the 1811 Buttles home and the 1819 Johnson home. Bushman, *Refinement of America*, 8.

21. Jedediah Lewis estate appraisal, 26 Nov. 1807, OHS, GR 2795, 96–113.

22. JBD.

23. Ruhamah Hayes to Elizabeth Case, 23 Aug. 1805, JBC.

24. *Western Intelligencer*, 31 Jan. 1812.

25. Ethel Conrad, "Touring Ohio in 1811: The Journal of Charity Rotch," *Ohio History* 99 (Summer–Autumn 1990), 155. Dr. Hills may have considered leaving Worthington, but he did, in fact, stay in the community for another ten years.

26. *Western Intelligencer*, 21 Feb. 1812.

27. Worthington school committee, 31 Dec. 1804, GP, 1802–9.

28. Robert's teaching contract, 17 Nov. 1806, GP, 1802–9.

29. Solomon Jones contract with school trustees, 9 Apr. 1806, GP, 1802–9.

30. Academy Society resolution, 17 May 1805, GP, 1802–9.

31. Worthington Academy subscription list, 17 May 1805, GP, 1802–9.

32. William Thompson to Mr. [Michael] Baldwin, 4 Jan. 1808, GFP, box 1, folder 1. Thompson was seeking Baldwin's help as a lobbyist since he lived in Chillicothe and was well acquainted with legislative procedure.

33. Academy subscription record, 17 Nov. 1806, GP, 1802–9. This was evidently Griswold's copy and does not contain the names of subscribers other than Griswold and Kilbourn.

34. "An Act to incorporate the Worthington Academy," *Laws of Ohio*, OHS, FLM 249, 6:51–54.

35. "An Act to Incorporate St. John's Episcopal Church of Worthington and Parts Adjacent," *Laws of Ohio*, OHS, FLM 249, 5:56–60; officers from 1804 through 1807, "Early Records of St. John's Church," *St. John's Banner* 1 (Jan. 1901): 47–49.

36. Minutes of the Ohio Presbytery, 17 Oct. 1805, Office of History, Presbyterian Church U.S.A., Philadelphia, Pa.

37. William W. Sweet, *The Presbyterians*, vol. 2 of *Religion on the American Frontier, 1783–1840* (1936; reprint, New York: Cooper Square Publishers, 1964).

38. Louise Heath Wright, "The Methodist Episcopal Church of Worthington, Ohio," *Old Northwest Genealogical Quarterly* 7 (Jan. 1904): 28–32; "Methodist Church History to 1900," *Worthington News*, 12 Feb. 1942; John Young, ed., *Exploring Our Roots: A Story of the Worthington United Methodist Church, 1808–1986* (Worthington: United Methodist Church, 1986), 7–9.

39. Charles C. Cole, Jr., *Lion of the Forest: James B. Finley, Frontier Reformer* (Lexington: University of Kentucky Press, 1994), 15–25; Jean V. Matthews, *Toward a New Society: American Thought and Culture, 1800–1830* (Boston: Twayne Publishers, 1991).

40. John H. Wigger, "Taking Heaven by Storm: Enthusiasm and Early American Methodism, 1770–1820," *Journal of the Early Republic* 14 (Summer 1994): 167–94.

41. *Western Intelligencer*, 17 July 1812.

42. Thomas H. Rawls, *Small Places: In Search of a Vanishing America* (Boston: Little, Brown, 1990).

43. The third federal census recorded Philadelphia with 53,722 inhabitants and Washington with 2,208.

44. All of the 685 inhabitants in Sharon Township were in the 8,000 acres purchased by the Scioto Company, which was referred to by them as "Worthington." It appears that at least half of these residents were in the village and the remainder on farm lots within two miles of the public square. Harlan Hatcher, *The Western Reserve: The Story of New Connecticut in Ohio* (New York: Bobbs-Merrill, 1949), 68. Hatcher attributes the slow growth of the city surveyed by Moses Cleaveland for the Connecticut Land Company to overpriced city lots held by speculators.

45. "To Establish a Permanent Seat of Government," *Old Northwest Genealogical Quarterly* 15 (July 1912): 83. This proposal was dated 29 Jan. 1808.

46. Ibid., 84–85. These subscriptions were made 3 Feb. 1810.

47. *Ohio House Journal* 10 (1811–12): 298–300; *Ohio Senate Journal* 10 (1811–12): 192–99.

48. "To Establish a Permanent Seat," 81–87.

49. *Western Intelligencer*, 9 Oct. 1811.

50. Amos Maxfield receipt of Ezra Griswold, 8 June 1811, GFP, box 3, folder 3.

51. Samuel Henderson to Ezra Griswold, 5 Dec. 1806, GFP, box 3, folder 3.

52. *Western Intelligencer*, 4 Sept. 1812.

53. Ibid., 16 July and 23 Oct. 1811.

54. Ibid., 16 Oct. 1811.

55. Leland D. Baldwin, *The Keelboat Age on Western Waters* (Pittsburgh: University of Pittsburgh Press, 1941), 82.

56. *Western Intelligencer* 1, 24 Jan. 1812.

57. Joel Allen, Worthington, to James Allen, Southington, Conn., 8 Nov. 1805, printed in *St. John's Banner* 1 (July 1900): 27, when the original was in the possession of Mrs. Adaline Allen Roe of Piqua, Ohio.

58. *Western Intelligencer*, 18 Sept. 1811.

59. Ibid., 4 Sept. 1811.

9. Squires with Muskets and Rifles

1. J. P. Kenyon, ed., *A Dictionary of British History* (New York: Stein and Day, 1981), 203.

2. Franklin County marriage record 1:5.

3. *History of Franklin and Pickaway Counties*, 426. For election procedures and duties, see "An act defining the duties of justices of the peace and constables in criminal and civil cases," *Laws of Ohio*, OHS, FLM 249 (1809) 7:43–67, 208–13.

4. Franklin County marriage record 1:57, 5 June 1808.

5. Franklin County marriage record 1:95, 3 Jan. 1812

6. *Western Intelligencer*, 5 June 1812.

7. A. Buttles and Hector Kilbourn appraisal, 6 Jan. 1818, GP, 1810–20.

8. Orin Case complaint, 25 May 1811, GP, 1810–20.

9. Ezra Griswold to Sharon Township constable, 26 Nov. 1814, GP, 1810–20.

10. *Thomas Palmer* v. *James Russell*, 20 Sept. 1810, and Ezra Griswold to Sharon Township constable, 4 Jan. 1811, GP, 1810–20.

11. Joel Buttles, constable, regarding judgment against Benjamin Chapman to Reuben Carpenter, GP, 1810–20. The total appears to be seven cents short, but perhaps the plaintiff forgave the difference.

12. David Justice, jailor, to John Goodridge, Jr., constable, 1 Nov. 1815, GP, 1810–20.

13. Ezra Griswold to any constable in Franklin County, 27 May 1811, GP, 1810–20.

14. *Zophar Topping* v. *Isaac Bartlett*, n.d., GP, 1810–20. Ezra Griswold was married to Ruth Roberts and Zophar Topping to Lois Roberts, both daughters of Lemuel and Ruth (Woolford) Roberts of Simsbury. McCormick, *Scioto Company Descendants*, 118, 273.

15. Clark, *Roots of Rural Capitalism*, 38.

16. Allan R. Millett and Peter Maslowski, *For the Common Defense* (New York: The Free Press, 1984), 85, 128.

17. Adjutant general, militia officer elections, OHS, microfilm 6956, box 1, folders 18 and 19.

18. Militia roster, Capt. James Kilbourn's company, 24 Apr. 1806, GP, 1802–9. A militia company normally had a captain, a lieutenant, an ensign, four sergeants, four corporals, one drummer, one fifer, and forty or more privates.

19. James Kilbourn account with Ezra Griswold, 1805–10, GP, 1802–9.

20. The federal militia act requirements are in Russell F. Weigley, *History of the United States Army* (Bloomington: Indiana University Press, 1984), 93–94; "An Act for disciplining the militia," *Laws of Ohio*, OHS, FLM 249, 7:1–43, 14 Feb. 1809 (hereafter Ohio militia act).

21. Espontoons were short pikes carried by eighteenth-century infantry officers for signaling orders to the regiment. It is noteworthy that they were still being used on the frontier.

22. Capt. James Kilbourn's militia roll, 24 Apr. 1806, GP, 1802–9.

23. Capt. Ezra Griswold's muster roll, 14 May 1808, GP, 1802–9.

24. Zenas Kimberly, Warrentown, Ohio, to Nathaniel Massie, Chillicothe, 20 Dec. 1806, NMP, folder 6, discusses Governor Tiffin's message to the legislature regarding problems with the militia.

25. Ohio militia act, 1809, 7:3–43.

26. Major James Kilbourn to Capt. Ezra Griswold, 24 Mar. 1809, GP, 1802–9.

27. This occurred on May 25, 1812. Roseboom and Weisenburger, *History of Ohio*, 79–83.

28. *History of Delaware County*, 471. This uniform was evidently prescribed when Norton became captain in the fall of 1811.

29. Ohio militia act, 1809, 13.

30. Essentially the line established by the Greenville Treaty of 1795. Militia companies were called for service in order based upon their date of organization, presumably taking the most experienced and best trained companies first.

31. *History of Delaware County*, 472.

32. Arora Buttles, in camp near Detroit, to Joel Buttles, Worthington, 7 July 1812, JBC.

33. Arora Buttles, Detroit, to Harriet Buttles, 28 July 1839, BFP.

34. *Western Intelligencer*, 30 Sept. 1812.

35. Thomas Russell receipt, 13 Sept. 1812, GFP, box 3, folder 3.

36. William Henry Harrison papers, Ohio Wesleyan University microfilm ed., series 1, reel 1.

37. *Western Intelligencer*, 5 May 1813. For a description of this siege, see H. W. Compton, "The Siege of Ft. Meigs," *Ohio Archaeological and Historical Society Publications* 10 (1902): 315–30.

38. Capt. Chauncey Barker's company, 24 Aug.–15 Sept. 1812 and 4 May–27 May 1813; Capt. Israel P. Case's company, 24 Aug.–4 Oct. 1812 and 4 May–27 May 1813; Capt. Levi Pinney's company, 1 May–12 Dec. 1812; Capt. Aaron Strong's company, 7 Oct.–15 Dec. 1812; Arora Buttles, drum major on staff of Col. McArthur, 1st Ohio Militia Regiment, and lieutenant in Capt. George Sanderson's company, 27th U.S. Infantry, 1813–1814; Lt. Abner Pinney, Capt. Sanderson's company, 27th U.S. Infantry, in *Roster of Ohio Soldiers in the War of 1812*, Ohio adjutant general.

39. Authorization to recruit, James Kilbourn for Duncan McArthur and Lewis Cass, 12 Apr. 1813; Gen. Lewis Cass to Lt. Arory (Arora) Buttles, 18 Apr. 1813, BFP.

40. Franklin County estate file #162, testimony of service from 6 Dec. 1813 to 7 Sept. 1814.

41. *Western Intelligencer*, 1 Sept. 1813.

10. APPRENTICE WANTED—OF STEADY DEPORTMENT AND INDUSTRIOUS HABITS

1. Larkin, *Reshaping of Everyday Life*, 34–42.

2. Clark, *The Roots of Rural Capitalism*, 14, 95–100.

3. To Ezra Griswold from Lynn Starling, tavern license receipt, 28 Sept. 1810, Franklin County clerk, GP, 1810–20.

4. Ezra Griswold account with James Kilbourn, 1805–1810, GP, 1802–9.

5. Exhibition ball bill, 19 Mar. 1812, and Ezra Griswold daybook 6, 10 Jan. 1812, GP, 1810–20. Sling is whiskey that has been diluted with water and sweetened with sugar. Ezra Griswold account with James Kilbourn.

6. Phelps, "Some Historic Records," *Old Northwest Genealogical Quarterly,* 7:190.

7. Alexander Morrison, Jr., account with the Worthington Academy trustees, 6 June 1809, GP, 1802–9.

8. Patent beehive contract from Horace Wolcott of Granville, 11 Apr. 1810, GP, 1810–20.

9. Worthington Academy subscription list, 17 May 1805, GP, 1802–9.

10. *Western Intelligencer,* 12 June 1812.

11. Worthington Academy subscription list.

12. Memorandum between the corporation of the Worthington Academy and Goodrich and Barker, 11 Aug. 1808, GP, 1802–9.

13. Chauncey Barker's account with Worthington Academy, 26 Mar. 1810, GP, 1810–20.

14. Amos Maxfield account with Worthington Academy trustees, 11 Dec. 1807, GP, 1802–9.

15. Contract between trustees of the Worthington Academy and Daniel Bishop, 29 Sept. 1808, GP, 1802–9.

16. It is not clear whether this is the archaic term referring to an apprentice transferred from one tradesman to another or whether this referred to the job of turning the drying bricks.

17. Agreement between Worthington Academy trustees and Rory [Arora] Buttles, 17 Mar. 1808, GP, 1802–9.

18. Asahel Hart bill, 8 Jan. 1812, Ezra Griswold daybook 6, copy at WHS.

19. Lucy Kilbourn to her mother, brother, and sister, 23 Jan. 1807, KFP, box 1, folder 2.

20. McCormick and McCormick, *Worthington Landmarks,* 16–19.

21. *History of Delaware County,* 516.

22. Ibid., 517.

23. John Cleves Symmes was notorious for sales of land beyond the boundaries of his purchase in southwestern Ohio, and claims were filed in the U.S. Congress for years.

24. Daniel Bishop to James Kilbourn, 7 Apr. 1808, GP, 1802–9.

25. Soltow, "Inequality Amidst Abundance," 133–51.

26. Buttles moved the *Western Intelligencer* to Columbus in 1814, and it evolved into the *Ohio State Journal,* which was for many years the newspaper of record in the state capital.

27. *Western Intelligencer,* 21 Aug. 1811.

28. Ibid., 7 Feb. and 13 Mar. 1812.

29. Ibid., 17 July, 21 Aug. 1811 and 14 Feb., 27 Mar. and 8 May 1812.

30. Indenture between Denman Coe and Ezra Griswold, 15 Apr. 1813, GP, 1810–20.

31. *Western Intelligencer,* 1 Jan. 1812.

32. Joel Allen to James Allen, 8 Nov. 1805, *St. John's Banner* 1 (July 1900).

33. Conrad, "Touring Ohio," 155.

34. Larkin, *Reshaping of Everyday Life,* 90.

35. *Western Intelligencer,* 8 May 1812.

36. *History of Delaware County*, 195.

37. James Russell account with Ezra Griswold, 22 Dec. 1808, GP, 1802–9.

38. Levi Pinney contract with Sullivant and Starling for payment of his note, 31 June 1810, GP, 1810–20.

39. Christopher Clark, "The Household Economy, Market Exchange, and the Rise of Capitalism in the Connecticut Valley, 1800–1860," *Journal of Social History* 13 (Winter 1979): 169–90.

40. Cayton and Onuf, *Midwest and the Nation*, 127.

41. Turner, *Frontier in American History*, 2.

11. If Elected I Shall Not Disappoint Your Confidence or Shame Your Favor

1. Larkin, *Reshaping of Everyday Life*, 192.

2. Obediah Benedict and Ezra Griswold, overseers of the poor, 30 Feb. 1814, GFP, box 15, folder 5.

3. Pinney genealogy, *Old Northwest Genealogical Quarterly* 6 (1903): 186–87.

4. Hannah Lewis guardianship record #323, Franklin County Common Pleas Court, 16–18 Oct. 1820, OHS, GR 1241.

5. McCormick, *Scioto Company Descendants*, 265. Miranda Topping guardianship record #65, Franklin County Common Pleas Court, 17 Oct. 1821–8 Apr. 1829, OHS, GR 3280. These sources will be quoted throughout the following passages. Stanbery had been a Sharon Township justice of the peace before being appointed associate judge of the Franklin County Common Pleas Court.

6. Miranda Topping died 9 Jan. 1827.

7. A typical election report for these offices appeared in the *Franklin Chronicle*, 9 Apr. 1821.

8. Taylor, *Ohio Statesmen*; 1802 Ohio Constitution, article III, sec. 3–6.

9. Associate judges were abolished by the second Ohio constitution in 1851.

10. *Western Intelligencer*, 4 Sept. 1812.

11. James Kilbourn, "To the Independent Electors of Franklinton, Columbus and the Townships Adjacent" [12 Oct. 1812], and "Mr. Kilbourn's Congressional Career," *Old Northwest Genealogical Quarterly* 6 (Oct. 1903): 123–24.

12. James Kilbourn, "To the Independent Electors"; "Mr. Kilbourn's Congressional Career."

13. *Western Intelligencer*, 26 Oct. 1812. Franklin County returns were as follows: Kilbourn, 292; Foos, 172; Cloud, 123; and Irvin, 61.

14. James Kilbourn to Thomas Worthington, 19 Jan. 1813, TWP, roll 8, box 6, folder 1.

15. *The Debates and Proceedings of the Congress of the United States* 13th Congress, 1st session, (Washington, D.C.: Gales and Seaton, 1854), 106.

16. *Biographical Directory of the American Congress* (Washington, D.C.: Government Printing Office, 1971), 1548.

17. Perry M. Goldman and James S. Young, eds., *The United States Congressional Directories, 1789–1840* (New York: Columbia University Press, 1973), 57 and 61. The directory refers to Mrs. Hamilton, Sr., suggesting that this was perhaps the mother of Alexander Hamilton. Her other congressional boarders were from Tennessee, Pennsylvania, South Carolina, Kentucky, Louisiana, and Virginia.

18. James S. Young, *The Washington Community, 1800–1828* (New York: Columbia University Press, 1966), 98–108.

19. *Debates and Proceedings,* 13th Congress, 1st session, 21 June 1813, 311 and 434. The text of Kilbourn's bill was published in the *Western Intelligencer,* 12 July 1813.

20. *Debates and Proceedings,* 13th Congress, 2nd session, 5 Jan. 1814, 850, 855, 2023.

21. Ibid., 13 Apr. 1814, 2016.

22. Mrs. Smith to Mrs. Kirkpatrick, 13 Mar. 1814, in Mrs. Samuel Harrison Smith, *The First Forty Years of Washington Society,* ed. Gaillard Hunt (New York: Charles Scribner's Sons, 1906), 96.

23. *Debates and Proceedings,* 13th Congress, 2nd session, 1903 and 2749.

24. Ibid., 13th Congress, 3rd session, 10, 302, 438.

25. Constance McLaughlin Green, *Washington: Village and Capital, 1800–1878* (Princeton: Princeton University Press, 1962), 62–67.

26. Mrs. Smith to Mrs. Kirkpatrick, August 1814, *First Forty Years,* 110.

27. *Debates and Proceedings,* 13th Congress, 3rd session, 521, 547.

28. Ibid., 617, 635, and 692–94.

29. Ibid., 18 Jan. 1815, 1079.

30. "Mr. Kilbourn's Congressional Career," 132–35.

31. 1822 congressional campaign, *Columbus Gazette,* 12 Sept. and 3 Oct. 1822.

32. *Debates and Proceedings,* 14th Congress, 4 Dec. 1815–30 Apr. 1816, 2 Dec. 1816–3 Mar. 1817, 768. Kilbourn was present just 14 percent of the time during the two sessions of the Fourteenth Congress.

33. James Kilbourn to Matthew Mathews, 23 June 1813, in "The Columbus Post Office," *Old Northwest Genealogical Quarterly* 6 (Oct. 1903): 138. Matthew Mathews married Kilbourn's daughter Lucy on Mar. 13, 1813 at Worthington.

34. James Kilbourn to Matthew Mathews, 12 Mar. 1814.

35. Joel Buttles to James Kilbourn, 15 Apr. 1814, in Jones, ed., *A State in the Making,* 34. Much of Kilbourn's correspondence was destroyed after his death by his wife Cynthia, but his granddaughter Emma Jones published what she inherited.

36. James S. Young, *Washington Community,* 90–93. Forty-nine percent of the Thirteenth Congress did not return for the Fourteenth, and 63 percent of the Fourteenth did not return for the Fifteenth.

37. For elaboration of this concept, see Robert H. Wiebe, *The Opening of American Society* (New York: Alfred A. Knopf, 1984), 194–97, and James MacGregor Burns, *The Vineyard of Liberty* (New York: Alfred A. Knopf, 1982), 236–38.

38. *Columbus Gazette,* 8 Jan. 1818; Alfred Lee, *History of the City of Columbus* (Chicago: Munsell, 1892) 2:405.

39. Curti, *Making of an American Community,* 416–40.

12. From Reading, Writing, and Arithmetic to Greek, Latin, and Moral Philosophy

1. John Kilbourn's contract from Worthington Academy trustees, 30 Nov. 1810, GFP, box 6, folder 8.

2. Report of Samuel Lewis, commissioner of common schools, to the 36th Ohio General Assembly.

3. *Western Intelligencer,* 17 July 1811.

4. Wade, *Urban Frontier,* 136.

5. U.S. Census Office, *4th Census of the United States, 1820* (Washington, D.C.: Gales and Seaton, 1821). Sharon Township had 169 males under ten, 77 males from ten

to sixteen, 152 females under ten, and 73 females from ten to sixteen. This is a summary; the original schedules for Franklin County have not survived.

6. *Western Intelligencer,* 20 Mar. 1812.

7. John Kilbourn's report to Worthington Academy trustees, 14 Apr. 1813, GP, 1810–20.

8. *Franklin Chronicle,* 11 June 1821.

9. Frederick J. Blue, *Salmon P. Chase: A Life in Politics* (Kent: Kent State University Press, 1987), 1–3. Salmon P. Chase, nephew of the Worthington College president, Bishop Philander Chase, later became U.S. senator, Ohio governor, secretary of the treasury in Lincoln's cabinet, and chief justice of the United States Supreme Court.

10. Philander Chase to George Case, 10 July 1817, quoted by Philander Chase in *Bishop Chase's Reminiscences: An Autobiography* (Boston: James B. Dow, 1848), 1:134.

11. Mary Chase, Worthington, to Mary Tudor, Hartford, 20 Oct. 1817, quoted in Chase, *Bishop Chase's Reminiscences,* 143.

12. A verbatim copy of the contract between Bishop Chase and Worthington Academy trustees, 6 June 1817, which was in the possession of W. F. Griswold when it was published in the *Old Northwest Genealogical Quarterly* 3 (Jan. 1900): 44.

13. "An act to establish a college in the town of Worthington," *Laws of Ohio,* OHS, FLM 249, 17:154–60.

14. *Columbus Gazette,* 28 Oct. 1819, 3.

15. Blue, *Salmon P. Chase,* 4.

16. Chase, *Bishop Chase's Reminiscences,* 174–75.

17. Huldah Bull's sampler, 19 Aug. 1819, Worthington Historical Society. Cynthia Andrews Barker was the daughter of Scioto Company member Moses Andrews and the widow of carpenter Eliphalet Barker, who had worked on the academy building.

18. *Franklin Chronicle,* 19 May 1821.

19. Ibid.

20. Chase, *Bishop Chase's Reminiscences,* 163–70.

21. *Franklin Chronicle,* 25 Mar. 1822.

22. Ibid., 28 Aug. 1820.

23. For an elaboration of this concept, see Smith, *As a City On a Hill,* 238–45.

24. Utter, *Granville,* 152.

25. Lewis E. Atherton, *Main Street on the Middle Border* (Bloomington: Indiana University Press, 1954), 127–42.

26. *Columbus Gazette,* 2 Apr. 1819, 3.

27. *Franklin Chronicle,* 7 June 1821.

28. G. W. Aldrich, "New England Lodge No. 4," *Worthington News,* 25 Oct. and 1 Nov. 1945; McCormick and McCormick, *Worthington Landmarks,* 40–43.

29. *Franklin Chronicle,* 31 July 1820.

30. Construction contract, 3 June 1820, archives, New England Lodge No. 4, Ohio Masonic Museum.

31. *Franklin Chronicle,* 23 July 1821.

32. Ibid., 16 Apr. 1821.

33. Ibid., 28 Aug. 1820.

34. Ibid., 19 Mar. 1821. This source will be quoted throughout the following discussion of the Worthington Literary Society.

35. This refrain about trouble in River City is from the song "Ya Got Trouble!" in Meredith Willson's musical comedy, *The Music Man* (1957). It rallied small town Iowa parents of 1912 to guard the morals of their youth from the dangers of a pool hall.

36. "An act for the prevention of certain immoral practices," *Laws of Ohio*, OHS, FLM 149 (1809), 7:215–18.

37. Hine, *Community on the American Frontier*, 142.

13. All Kinds of Manufacturies which Experience May Advise

1. Daniel J. Boorstin, *Cleopatra's Nose: Essays on the Unexpected* (New York: Random House, 1994), 192.

2. *Western Intelligencer*, 28 Feb. 1812.

3. Ibid., 27 Mar. 1812.

4. Ibid., 1 Dec. 1813.

5. Ibid., 3 Nov. 1813.

6. Kilbourn's request for incorporation was entered into the *Ohio House Journal* on Feb. 15, 1812, brought up for discussion several times in both the House and the Senate, and rejected on Feb. 2, 1813. No full text of the incorporation is included in these deliberations since it did not pass.

7. "An Act for the incorporation of manufacturing companies," 11 Jan. 1812, *Laws of Ohio*, OHS, FLM 249.

8. Berquist and Bowers, *New Eden*, 116–24. We have not been able to confirm their contention that Kilbourn was elected president of the company in May 1812 and reelected annually by shareholders. Kilbourn always signed as "agent," rather than as "president," when he represented the company, and no evidence of company shareholder meetings has come to our attention.

9. *Western Intelligencer*, 8 May 1812. Domigan had a retail store in Franklinton that became affiliated with the Worthington Manufacturing Company.

10. James Backus and Dudley Woodbridge memorandum books, BWFP, OHS, MSS 128.

11. Worthington Manufacturing Company advertisement, *Columbus Gazette*, 14 May 1818. Although Kilbourn and Wildman referred to Sandusky city, most accounts of the period refer to the site as Portland. It is today the city of Sandusky.

12. Franklin County deed records 59:437 and 60:433. George Fitch was a resident of New York City and may have been connected to Kilbourn's first wife, Lucy Fitch.

13. The plat was reportedly surveyed in May 1812, but Kilbourn appeared before Sharon Township Justice of the Peace Recompense Stanbery on Mar. 5, 1819, to acknowledge signing it. It was apparently not recorded until then, and the streets may have acquired their Masonic names after the involvement of Thomas S. Webb in 1816. The plat is included in the property abstract of the residence at 25 Fox Lane, which encompasses the Worthington Manufacturing Company boardinghouse—the only surviving building from this period.

14. *Western Intelligencer*, 8 May 1812.

15. Utter, *Frontier State*, 166 and 250, reports that Wells and Dickinson at Steubenville were offering $2.75 per pound for merino wool in 1814, when common wool was bringing about 40¢.

16. *Western Intelligencer*, 24 July 1812.

17. Ibid.

18. Correspondence from Major Kilbourn is signed, "Comdt, 1st Battn, 4th Regt., 2 Brigd, 2d Division, Ohio Militia."

19. *Western Intelligencer*, 20 Jan. 1813.

20. "Richards," in *Columbus Gazette*, 12 Sept. 1822.

21. James Kilbourn to Matthew Mathews, 8 Feb. 1814, KFP, box 1, folder 2. Chester Griswold and Ezra Griswold did not consider themselves related, although they probably had a distant connection.

22. *Western Intelligencer,* 10 Dec. 1814.

23. Franklin County marriage record 1:115, 14 Mar. 1813 (Ezra Griswold, J.P.); McCormick, *Scioto Company Descendants,* 159. Mathews was twenty-four and had worked with Kilbourn about two years at the time he was overseeing the Worthington Manufacturing Company development.

24. Kilbourn to Mathews, 8 Feb. 1814. This letter will be quoted throughout the passages that follow.

25. Kilbourn, Berlin, Conn., to Mathews, Worthington, Ohio, 10 June 1814, quoted in Jones, *State in the Making,* 35–36.

26. Allen Johnson and Dumas Malone, eds., *Dictionary of American Biography,* vol. 8 (New York: Charles Scribner's Sons, 1930), 275.

27. *Western Intelligencer,* 13 Aug. 1814.

28. Sherman, *Original Ohio Land Subdivisions,* 80–82.

29. For a more complete discussion of this enterprise, see Berquist and Bowers, *New Eden,* 151–71.

30. Zalmon Wildman, Danbury, to Kilbourn, Washington, 12 Mar. 1814, quoted in Jones, *State in the Making,* 32.

31. Fishing Net Company contract, 5 Feb. 1814, and expenses from 21 June to 21 Dec. 1814, GP, 1810–20.

32. McCormick, *Probing Worthington's Heritage,* 59–63.

33. *History of Franklin and Pickaway Counties,* 432.

34. Rerecorded in Franklin County deed book H:33 after the original record burned. A copy is included in the property abstract of 25 Fox Lane.

35. Large eastern "stockholders" such as DeWolf, Webb, and Whittemore do not appear on this incorporation. As DeWolf's lawsuit later makes clear, he considered his investment a loan rather than a stock purchase. Webb and Whittemore may have pledged assets rather than cash and had not been included by 1817.

36. C. C. Huntington, "A History of Banking and Currency in Ohio before the Civil War," *Ohio Archaeological and Historical Society Publications* 24 (1915), 235–539. For further discussion of the financial disaster of 1819, see Utter, *Frontier State,* 263–95.

37. *Columbus Gazette,* 14 May 1818.

38. Utter, *Frontier State,* 221–22.

39. McCormick, *Scioto Company Descendants,* 160.

40. *Columbus Gazette,* 14 May 1818.

41. General merchants advertising regularly in the *Columbus Gazette* in 1818 included Delano and Fay, Samuel Barr & Co., Henry Brown & Co., Robert Russell (across the street from the Worthington Manufacturing Co.), and I. and R. W. McCory.

42. Huntington, "Banking and Currency in Ohio," 291.

43. *John Walker* v. *James Kilbourn,* Franklin County Common Pleas Court, complete record 1:47–48, Nov. 1817–Mar. 1818.

44. Franklin County Common Pleas Court, complete record 1:258–80; execution book 6:57.

45. Berquist and Bowers, *New Eden,* 142, refers to a copy of this suit in the possession of Thomas Aquinas Burke, but indicates it was withdrawn. It does not appear in the Franklin County record.

46. *James DeWolf* v. *The Worthington Manufacturing Company,* Franklin County Common Pleas Court, chancery record 1:33–38, Apr. 1822–June 1823.

47. Clark, *Roots of Rural Capitalism*, 34–35.

48. *Columbus Gazette*, 21 Jan. 1819.

49. Herbert Leyland, *Thomas Smith Webb: Freemason, Musician, Entrepreneur* (Dayton: Otterbein Press, 1965), 325–28, 360–61, 366–82, 393–96.

50. McCormick and McCormick, *Worthington Landmarks*, 28–29. This home is now owned by and operated as part of the Worthington Inn.

51. Thomas Webb to John Snow, 22 Mar. 1819, quoted in Berquist and Bowers, *New Eden*, 122, from the Snow papers in the Ohio Masonic archives.

52. Berquist and Bowers, *New Eden*, 122–24, and 143.

53. R. W. Cowles, Worthington, to Whitfield Cowles, Hartford, 15 May 1820, RWCP.

54. Lacy K. Ford, Jr., "Frontier Democracy: The Turner Thesis Revisted," *Journal of the Early Republic* 13 (Summer 1993): 144–63.

55. *Columbus Gazette*, 8 Jan. 1818.

56. *The President and Directors of the Franklin Bank of Columbus* v. *James Kilbourn, et al.*, Franklin County Court of Common Pleas, complete record 1:506.

57. Wade, *Urban Frontier*, 171.

58. *Columbus Gazette*, 17 May 1821.

59. Franklin County deed books H:30–32, and 4:52. Kilbourn never again owned real estate in Worthington.

60. James Kilbourn to Payne Kenyon Kilbourn, 22 Mar. 1845, printed as "Autobiography of Col. James Kilbourne," *Old Northwest Genealogical Quarterly* 6 (Oct. 1903): 120.

61. R. W. Cowles, Worthington, to W. Cowles, Hartford, 18 Oct. 1821, RWCP.

62. *James DeWolf* v. *The Worthington Manufacturing Company*, Franklin County Common Pleas Court, chancery record 1:33–38, Apr. 1822–June 1823.

63. Ibid.

64. Wade, *Urban Frontier*, 161-62.

65. Clark, *Roots of Rural Capitalism*, 85.

66. Sharon Township, Franklin County, Ohio, in United States Census Office, *Census for 1820* (Washington: Gales and Seaton, 1821). Readers should be aware of potential omissions and inaccuracies in this data. The published summary records no persons in Sharon Township engaged in commerce—suggesting that persons such as tavernkeeper Ezra Griswold reported himself as engaged in agriculture, since he received a major portion of his income from rented farmland. The Franklin County schedules were destroyed and data for known merchants such as John Snow cannot be checked.

67. For background on the relationship between merchants and farmers, see A. J. Reiss, "The Sociological Study of Communities," *Rural Sociology* 24 (1959), 118; and Clark, *Roots of Rural Capitalism*, 65–71.

68. Account between Moses Brown and Orange Johnson, 21 Mar. 1821, SBP, box 2, folder 1.

69. Receipt from Caleb Howard, 19 Oct. 1820, assigned to G. H. Griswold; presented for collection 6 Mar. 1823; paid in full 25 Aug. 1823, GFP, box 17, folder 1.

70. This is clear evidence that technological innovations such as cradling scythes for cutting grain had reached this western community by 1820. R. Douglas Hurt, *American Farm Tools: From Hand-Power to Steam-Power* (Manhattan, Kans.: Sunflower University Press, 1982), 40–41.

71. *Franklin Chronicle*, 10 Apr. 1820.

72. Richard G. Coakwell, *Coin World*, 24 Sept. 1980, 88.

73. *Franklin Chronicle*, 9 July 1821.
74. Ibid., 2 Oct. 1820 and 24 Sept. 1821.
75. Ibid., 26 Feb. 1821.
76. Smith, *As a City on a Hill*, 84–109.

14. Main Street Wide and Free of Mud and Many Buildings Handsomely Built with Brick

1. Appleton Downer, Worthington, to his brother Samuel M. Downer, Preston, Conn., 10 Nov. 1815, LAD. This letter will be quoted throughout the following passages. Appleton Downer returned to Zanesville in December, where he practiced law, married, and was elected to the Ohio Senate in 1831.
2. A rod, usually referred to as a "pole" or "perch" by nineteenth-century surveyors, was 5½ yards or 16½ feet.
3. John Kilbourn, *Ohio Gazetteer*, 6th ed. (Chillicothe: Builbache and Scott, Printers, 1819), 162.
4. *Franklin Chronicle*, 31 July 1820.
5. The *Columbus Gazette*, 26 Aug. 1819, had an article on John Kilbourn's recently published gazetteer. There is apparently some publishing exaggeration in these figures for the 1820 census summary by townships that showed Montgomery (including Columbus) with 1,631 residents and Sharon (including Worthington) with 983 persons. Allowing for persons living on farms in both townships, it would appear that the population of Columbus was almost double that of Worthington.
6. Utter, *Frontier State*, 111. The decisive battle occurred on Oct. 5, 1813.
7. Joel Buttles to Julia Buttles, 18 Nov. 1813, JBC.
8. For the evolution of the *Western Intelligencer* into the *Columbus Gazette*, see Stephen Gutgesell, *Guide to Ohio Newspapers, 1793–1973* (Columbus: Ohio Historical Society, 1974): 122, 138.
9. Joel Buttles to Julia Buttles, 25 Feb. 1814, JBC.
10. *Western Intelligencer*, 16 Mar. 1814.
11. "Licensed Tavern Keepers in Sharon Township," *Ohio Genealogical Quarterly* 2 (April 1938): 144.
12. This building was known locally as the Beers Tavern for the family that owned it for much of the nineteenth century. It was photographed and sketched prior to being destoyed by a fire early in the twentieth century.
13. James Allen account with Ezra Griswold, 30 May–13 June 1815, GFP, box 5, folder 2.
14. Printed in *Shedding Light on Worthington*, 19. This was probably in December 1814—correspondence shows Julia Buttles was in New England in 1813, and she was married in Franklin County on Feb. 8, 1815, when she was nineteen years old.
15. George H. Griswold to Prudence Lewis, 26 Feb. 1818, GP, 1810–20.
16. *Franklin Chronicle*, 23 Apr. 1821.
17. Agreement between Ezra Griswold and George H. Griswold, August 1819, GP, 1810–20. The inventories that follow are taken from this agreement.
18. Ezra Griswold had not yet become a party to the James DeWolf suit, but his own business may have been under pressure, and he may have signed as surety on notes of others. After his death, this transaction was challenged in the settlement of his estate. Franklin County Common Pleas Court, probate case #380.
19. Martingales were the part of the horse's harness that ran from the nose strap to the girth between the forelegs and were used to prevent the horse from rearing or throwing back its head.

20. A mattock was a flat-bladed tool used for digging roots from the soil, a dung fork was used for removing manure from stables, steelyards were a balance scale for weighing items, the grindstone was used for sharpening tools, a clevis was the U-shaped piece of iron used to hitch a plow or wagon to the double-tree a team of horses pulled.

21. *Delaware Patron and Franklin Chronicle*, 26 Nov. 1821.

22. McCormick and McCormick, *Worthington Landmarks*, 20–23. This is now a Worthington Historical Society museum. For a description of Federal-style homes with such entries, see Rachel Carley, *The Visual Dictionary of American Domestic Architecture* (New York: Henry Holt, 1994), 99.

23. McCormick and McCormick, *Worthington Landmarks*, 34–35. This currently houses the offices of the *Ohio Antique Review*.

24. McCormick and McCormick, *Worthington Landmarks*, 36–39. This birthplace of Confederate General Roswell Ripley is now a commercial property.

25. Carley, *American Domestic Architecture*, 84–88; John M. Baker, *American House Styles: A Concise Guide* (New York: W. W. Norton, 1994), 28.

26. McCormick and McCormick, *Worthington Landmarks*, 30–33. This has been in continuous use as a residential property.

27. Characteristics of refinement and comfort in homes are detailed in Bushman, *Refinement of America*, 250–72, and Larkin, *Reshaping of Everyday Life*, 118.

28. Virginia McAlester and Lee McAlester, *A Field Guide to American Houses* (New York: Alfred A. Knopf, 1990), 96–97.

29. Ibid., 153–61.

30. No longer standing, this home was pictured in the "Griswold Genealogy," *Old Northwest Genealogical Quarterly* 6 (1903): 172.

31. Sharon Township tax list, 1826, OHS, GR 2470. Homes were not listed for taxes until the law was changed in 1825. It is probable that all of these properties had a lower value than their actual construction cost during the speculative boom. By 1826 the Ripley house was owned by Silas Williams and the Buttles home by F. and C. Deming, and the value was probably lower because of their use as rental properties.

32. Bill of sale, Ezra Griswold to George Griswold, 16 Aug. 1819, GP, 1810–20. After Ezra Griswold's death in 1822, this transfer was protested in court by his creditors. The inventories to follow are taken from the 1819 agreement.

33. See, for example, Eliphalet Barker estate #148 (1815), Zophar Topping estate #162 (1815), William Thompson, Jr. estate #222 (1817), Israel Case estate #242 (1818), Samuel Sloper estate #243 (1818), Jonathan Park estate #304 (1819), and Bela M. Tuller estate #339 (1821), Franklin County Common Pleas Court, OHS, GR 1241.

34. The fall-leaf dining table owned by the Griswolds was made at the Worthington Manufacturing Company and has now been restored for use in the Worthington Historical Society museum.

35. *Western Intelligencer*, 15 Sept. 1813, advertised by Daniel M. Brown. Nylander, *Our Own Snug Fireside*, 149, provides perspective on the labor invested in home-sewn garments.

36. Estate file #307A, 13 June 1820, Franklin County Common Pleas Court, OHS, GR 1241.

37. Utter, *Frontier State*, 392. Utter describes eight (of forty-eight) as having more than 1,000 and eight as having 500 to 1,000. Franklin County census schedules for 1820 were destroyed; but the published summary showed Sharon Township with 983 residents, and tax duplicates suggest that perhaps half or more of these residents were in the village of Worthington.

38. *Franklin Chronicle*, 27 Aug. and 4 Sept. 1821.
39. *Franklin Chronicle*, 20 Aug. 1821.

15. To the Dough Faces of the Last Congress

1. Lt. Arora Buttles, 27th Infantry Reg., advertisement, *Western Intelligencer*, 14 May 1814.
2. *Western Intelligencer*, 2 June 1813 and 6 Apr. 1814.
3. Wm. Hall, Ft. Shelby, Detroit, to Lt. A. Buttles, 22 Apr. 1814, BFP.
4. McCormick, *Scioto Company Descendants*, 114. Hall was married 1 Jan. 1815 to Polly Curtis, daughter of Scioto Company member Jeremiah Curtis, who settled on Alum Creek in 1805 and established an orchard, saw- and gristmills, and a distillery.
5. Philo Olmsted to George H. Griswold, 1 Mar. 1815, GFP, box 1.
6. Harry Ammon, *James Monroe: The Quest for National Identity* (1971; reprint, Charlottesville: University Press of Virginia, 1990), 371.
7. Lee, *History of the City of Columbus*, 1:261.
8. Wiebe, *Opening of American Society*, 200.
9. A complete description of the day's events appeared in the *Western Intelligencer and Columbus Gazette*, 4 Sept. 1817. It is this account that is used in the passages to follow.
10. Alfred Lee, *City of Columbus*, 1:261.
11. *History of Franklin and Pickaway Counties*, 432.
12. Russo, *Families and Communities*, 31.
13. *Franklin Chronicle*, 10 July 1820. Smith and Hor's hall was the three-story frame tavern a block north of the public square that was described earlier.
14. *Franklin Chronicle*, 9 and 16 July 1821. These papers provide the descriptions of the festivities that follow.
15. This is a reference to ladies who were often spoken of as "The Fair Daughters of Columbia."
16. Mahoney, *River Towns*, 274–76.
17. Hine, *Community on the American Frontier*, 132, quotes Seth Humphrey's *Following the Prairie Frontier* and expands on the point that not all platted towns survived.
18. Doyle, *Social Order of a Frontier Community*, 62–63, elaborates on this point.
19. *Franklin Chronicle*, 24 Sept. 1821. The other businesses referred to were a tavern in Delaware and a paper mill at Stratford, about halfway between Worthington and Delaware.
20. Wade, *Urban Frontier*, 39 and 130.
21. *Delaware Patron*, 17 Dec. 1821. Dr. Hills married Beulah Andrews, daughter of Scioto Company member Moses Andrews. See McCormick, *Scioto Company Descendants*, 10–11.
22. *Delaware Patron*, 10 June 1822. The Masonic announcement is dated 9 May 1822.
23. Franklin County deed record 6:61.

16. Runaway Negro Taken Near This Place and Set at Liberty

1. Warren Jenkins, *The Ohio Gazetteer and Traveler's Guide* (Columbus: Isaac N. Whiting, 1841), 484–85. Publisher Isaac N. Whiting, Columbus's largest book dealer, married James Kilbourn's daughter Orrel in 1835.
2. *Columbus Gazette*, 30 June 1825, 3. Portland was the township that contained the present city of Sandusky, and the town was usually referred to as Portland until mid-century.

3. *Ohio State Journal*, 4 May 1826, 3. A. I. McDowell was the father of the Civil War general Irvin McDowell, and William Neil owned the farm that became the site of Ohio State University.

4. *Ohio State Journal*, 28 May and 31 May, 1827, 3. The stage and mail line was anticipating moving from thrice weekly to daily service between Cincinnati and Portland.

5. Franklin County auditor, Sharon Township tax records, 1832, OHS, GR 2471. The only property tax assessment that itemized carriages in Sharon Township was in 1832 and included seven families with carriages valued from twenty to seventy-five dollars: Job W. Case, George Griswold, Orange Johnson, John Johnson, Edward Mallory, Daniel Upson, and M. S. Wilkinson.

6. Asa Gillet estate #644A, 16 Feb. 1827, Franklin County Common Pleas Court, OHS, GR 1243.

7. Charles E. Frohman, *Sandusky's Yesteryears* (Columbus: Ohio Historical Society, 1968); Lewis C. Aldrich, ed., *History of Erie County* (Syracuse: D. Mason, 1889); W. W. Williams, *History of the Firelands, Comprising Huron and Erie Counties, Ohio* (1879; reprint, Evansville, Ind.: Unigraphic, 1973); Berquist and Bowers, *New Eden*, 151–71.

8. Carter Goodrich, ed., *Canals and American Economic Development* (New York: Columbia University Press, 1961), 252.

9. *Ohio House Journal*, 3 Jan. 1822, quoted in *History of the Ohio Canals* (Columbus: Ohio State Archaeological and Historical Society, 1905).

10. Micajah T. Williams, "Report of the Committee on Canals," Twentieth Ohio General Assembly, 1822, 4. This was a reference, of course, to the common practice of converting corn to whiskey.

11. Governor Trimble's message, 5 Dec. 1822, *History of the Ohio Canals*, 15.

12. *History of the Ohio Canals*, 18–19.

13. "An Act to provide for the Internal Improvement of the State of Ohio by Navigable Canals," 4 Feb. 1825, *Laws of Ohio*, OHS, FLM 249. This passed with overwhelming support, 58 to 13 in the house, 34 to 2 in the senate. The western canal was later lengthened from Dayton north to Maumee. See Harry N. Scheiber, "Urban Rivalry and Internal Improvements in the Old Northwest, 1820–1860," in *The Old Northwest: Studies in Regional History, 1787–1910*, ed. Harry N. Scheiber (Lincoln: University of Nebraska Press, 1969), 249–64.

14. Bartlett, *New Country*, 311.

15. Moses Beach to James Kilbourn, 28 Feb. 1825, KFP. New Haven was in southern Huron County, not the town on a current Ohio atlas.

16. Goodrich, *Canals and American Economic Development*, 247.

17. Kilbourn barely won this election with 372 votes; his three opponents split the remainder: Williams, 340; Laughty, 248; and McElvain, 195. *Columbus Gazette*, 16 Oct. 1823.

18. This route was reviewed in detail in the *Ohio State Journal*, 22 May 1828, when the land granted by Congress was auctioned to raise funds for construction.

19. Hector Kilbourn to James Kilbourn, 22 Dec. 1822, in Jones, *A State in the Making*, 48–49. Claridon did not prosper, and Byron soon moved to work on the construction of the Ohio Canal. He then moved west to become a founder of Milwaukee, Wisconsin.

20. Contract between Samuel Norton and James Kilbourn, 12 Feb. 1822, *History of Crawford County and Ohio* (Chicago: Baskin and Battey, 1881), 347. This was the town which benefited most from the completion of the Columbus and Sandusky Turnpike.

21. *History of Crawford County*, 349–50.

22. Utter, *Frontier State*, 212–13.

23. *Ohio Senate Journal*, 24 (1825–26), 299; Ohio House of Representatives, *Report of Select Committee on the Memorial of the Columbus and Sandusky Turnpike Company*, 24 Jan. 1844; Alfred Lee, *City of Columbus*, 1:314–16.

24. *Ohio State Journal*, 17 Aug. 1827.

25. The section of the National Road from the Ohio side of the river opposite Wheeling to Zanesville received a $150,000 appropriation from Congress in 1825, and additional funding the following two years. This route followed Zane's Trace part of the way. See Archer B. Hulbert, "The Old National Road—The Historic Highway of America," *Ohio Archaeological and Historical Publications* 9 (1901): 404–519.

26. "An Act to Incorporate A Company to Construct a Turnpike from Columbus to Sandusky City," section 9, *Laws of Ohio*, OHS, FLM 249, 24:66–72, 31 Jan. 1826.

27. Hewson L. Peeke, *A Standard History of Erie County, Ohio* (Chicago: Lewis Publishing, 1916), 1:168–69.

28. *History of Crawford County*, 340

29. Letter from Charles Dickens, 24 Apr. 1842, quoted by Hewson L. Peeke in "Charles Dickens in Ohio in 1842," *Ohio Archaeological and Historical Publications* 27:72–81; Robert Price, "Bos Reports on Ohio," ibid. 51:195–202.

30. Mary Case, Vermont, to Sophronia Morrison, Columbus, 16 July 1838; and Julia Buttles Case to Job W. Case, Worthington, 23 Sept. 1838; JBC. Mary Case and Sophronia Morrison were first cousins, both granddaughters of Sarah Phelps Buttles. Sarah Phelps married Amos Hawley in 1814 and was again widowed, but she is referred to here as Sarah Buttles to clarify her connection with Levi Buttles, the father of all of her children. She lived another six years after this trip.

31. James M. McPherson, *Battle Cry of Freedom: The Civil War Era* (New York: Oxford University Press, 1988), 11–12.

32. Wilbur Henry Siebert, *The Mysteries of Ohio's Underground Railroads* (Columbus: Long's Book, 1951); Byron D. Fruehling and Robert H. Smith, "Subterranean Highways of the Underground Railroad in Ohio," *Ohio History* 102 (Summer–Autumn 1993): 98–117.

33. Daniel J. Ryan, "From Charter to Constitution," 113–25; Utter, *Frontier State*, 19–23. This election provision was defeated by a tie-breaking vote by convention chairman Edward Tiffin.

34. *Laws of Ohio*, OHS, FLM 249, 2:63 (5 Jan. 1804) and 5:53 (25 Jan. 1807); Frank U. Quillin, *The Color Line in Ohio* (1913; reprint, New York: Negro Universities Press, 1969), 21–24.

35. *Franklin Chronicle* advertisement, several weeks beginning 4 June 1821. Oral tradition inaccurately attributed this incident to 1812, and these embellished details were reported by Wilbur Henry Siebert in "Beginnings of the Underground Railroad in Ohio," *Ohio Archaeological and Historical Society Publications* 56 (1948): 71–72.

36. *Franklin Chronicle*, 2 Apr. 1821.

37. Utter, *Frontier State*, 328.

38. One of four runaways advertised by Joseph Harrison of Green Spring Furnace, Ky., *Ohio State Journal*, 27 Oct. 1832.

39. U.S. Bureau of Census, 1830, Sharon Township, Franklin County, Ohio, OHS, GR 17.

40. "Sexton Records of George H. Griswold, St. John's Episcopal Cemetery," *Ohio Genealogical Society Report* 30 (1990): 193–204.

41. Memorial to the U.S. Congress, *Annals of Congress*, 14th Congress, 2nd session, 482–83. Slaves freed by their masters were to be offered free passage back to Africa to an area which became the country of Liberia.

42. *Ohio State Journal*, 18 Oct. 1827.

43. Louis Filler, *The Crusade against Slavery* (New York: Harper and Brothers, 1960).

44. Manuscript journal of the Ohio Methodist Conference, 19 Aug. 1835, quoted in Cole, *Lion of the Forest*, 132–33.

45. "Anti-Slavery Society of Worthington," copied 8 Dec. 1921, from a manuscript book in the possession of Miss Alberta Williams, OHS, #17457. This source will be quoted in the passages that follow.

46. Several years later, as slaves moved north through "underground railroad" safe houses in the Worthington area, several free blacks living in the area were reportedly "conductors."

17. LEGHORN BONNETS, HORN SIDED CORSETS, AND GERMAN SILVER TEASPOONS

1. *Columbus Gazette*, 29 Aug. 1822.

2. *Columbus Gazette*, 12 Sept. 1822.

3. Utter, *Frontier State*, 146.

4. Nathaniel Little estate #385, 1822, Franklin County Common Pleas Court, OHS, GR 1242. This is *not* the same Nathaniel Little who came west with Kilbourn to view prospective sites, but another man who was probably a relative, perhaps a nephew or cousin.

5. Jed Dannenbaum, *Drink and Disorder: Temperance Reform in Cincinnati from the Washingtonian Revival to the WCTU* (Urbana: University of Illinois Press, 1984), 25.

6. Selah Wilcox inventory, 2 Dec. 1824, estate file #500, OHS, GR 1242.

7. Simeon Wilcox inventory, August 1825, estate file #553, OHS, GR 1243.

8. Israel P. Case inventory, 10 Oct. 1832, estate file #877, OHS, GR 1244.

9. Stephan Maynard inventory, 24 Nov. 1822, estate file #381; Selah Wilcox inventory, 2 Dec. 1824, estate file #500; Simeon Wilcox inventory, Aug. 1825, estate file #553; Asa Gillet inventory, 16 Feb. 1827, estate file #644A; William Thompson inventory, 2 Oct. 1830, estate file #773; Charles Thompson receipts, 1832, estate file #795A; Israel P. Case inventory, 10 Oct. 1832, estate file #877, OHS, GR 1242, 1243, 1244.

10. Robert L. Jones, *The History of Agriculture in Ohio to 1880* (Kent: Kent State University Press, 1983), provides a topical study of early nineteenth-century agriculture in the state.

11. Selah Wilcox inventory. Bull plows were heavy instruments to be pulled by oxen, often used for breaking virgin sod. Patent plows were improved models, "patented" with a cast-iron blade, which were first introduced in New York State about 1819. Hurt, *American Farm Tools*, 7–10.

12. Fanning mills had a blower to separate chaff and dirt from grain. They became available in the early 1800s and were standard equipment by the 1830s. Hurt, *American Farm Tools*, 68.

13. Long-handled and long-bladed scythes permitted a man to walk across a field cutting grass for hay, and cradling scythes caught the cut grain and dropped it in clusters to be bound into sheaves. Short-handled sickles with a crescent-shaped blade were ancient hand tools that required the user to bend to the task, but they continued to be used in small spaces or rocky fields for cutting grain, grass, or weeds. Hurt, *American Farm Tools*, 40–41, 84.

14. Hurt, *American Farm Tools*, 4–6.

15. *Ohio State Journal*, 17 Apr. 1828. According to the *Annual Report of the U.S. Patent Office*, 1847 (cumulative), microfilm, Ohio State University, this patent to Peter Barker was dated 20 Aug. 1827. It may have been typical of the inexpensive local

versions of threshing equipment that Hurt says were developed during the 1820s and 1830s. Hurt, *American Farm Tools*, 69–70.

16. Dearing Cowles, Worthington, to Whitfield Cowles, Hartford, Conn., 24 Feb. 1827, RWCP.

17. *Columbus Monitor*, farm advertised from Nov. 1831 through Feb. 1832.

18. Neat cattle were raised for beef, as opposed to dairy cows raised for milk.

19. Agreement between Asa Gillet and William Dunton, 1 Apr. 1826, case file #644A, OHS, GR 1243.

20. Stephan Maynard inventory, 24 Nov. 1822, estate file #381, OHS, GR 1242.

21. Israel P. Case sale bill, 10 Oct. 1832, estate file #877, OHS, GR 1244.

22. Nathaniel Little estate receipts, 1820–1822, estate file #385, OHS, GR 1242.

23. Israel P. Case estate receipts, 1824–1830, estate file #877, OHS, GR 1244.

24. Emilia Maynard, Clinton Township, to Dorcas Carey, Tymochtee, Crawford County, 23 Mar. 1826, JCP. These were the married daughters of Scioto Company pioneer Roswell Wilcox, who at that time had a sawmill and tavern between Worthington and Columbus.

25. There is far more information on this practice in New England than in Ohio. See Clark, "Household Economy," 169–90.

26. Joseph Greer inventory, 21 Nov. 1829 and sale bill, 19 Dec. 1829, estate file #741, OHS, GR 1244.

27. Robert S. Woodbury, *History of the Lathe* (Cleveland: Society for the History of Technology, 1961), 13.

28. Receipt from G. R. Butler, 22 Dec. 1835, SBP, box 1, folder 4; receipt from Burr, Gregory & Co., 18 Feb. 1836, SBP, box 1, folder 1; receipt from Sherwood Gregory, 21 Jan. 1836, SBP, box 1, folder 3. Firkins were normally one-fourth the size of a barrel, but as barrel sizes varied depending upon the intended commodity, so did the size of firkins. Kegs were usually ten gallons or less in size.

29. Ledger book 1818–21, 1827–40, SBP.

30. This is indicated in the value of items listed in the store inventory taken on Mar. 1, 1842. R. W. Cowles inventory #1479, Franklin County Common Pleas Court, OHS, GR 3368, 202–27. This inventory is the source of the information to follow.

31. Ibid., sales 1 Mar. 1842 to May 3, 1842. The population of the village and the contents of estate inventories suggest that the store goods available in 1842 were not appreciably different than those available about 1835–36.

32. Leghorn was plaited straw, commonly used in bonnets, and derived its name from the originals that were imported from Leghorn, Italy.

33. It is not clear, but "artificials" perhaps referred to false teeth.

34. "Britainia" ware was an alloy made of tin, copper, and antimony.

35. Taper lamps had a wick and a source of fuel such as oil.

36. McCormick and McCormick, "James Russell's Magnificent Orrery," *Probing Worthington's Heritage*, 102–4.

37. This would have been a wooden spinning wheel.

38. GP, 1802–9.

39. Jenkins, *Ohio Gazetteer*, 1839.

40. Dorcas Cary, Tymochtee, to John Cary, Columbus, 10 Jan. 1837, JCP.

41. *Ohio State Journal*, 16 May 1842, 3. At this time the planet that is now called Uranus, but known in the nineteenth century for its discoverer William Herschel, was the outermost planet known.

42. Obituary of George H. Topping, one of the drivers, *Ashland Press*, 16 Oct. 1901.

43. *Ohio State Journal*, 10 Jan. 1843, 3, quoting a lengthy excerpt from the *New York Express*.

44. Russell's orrery was destined for exhibition across Europe, but this apparently never happened. One account says it was destroyed by fire and never rebuilt, while another says that it became the property of a New England college. Attempts to confirm either have been unsuccessful.

18. So Much Boast of Succession Handed Down from the Apostles

1. William W. Sweet, *Men of Zeal: The Romance of American Methodist Beginnings* (New York: Abingdon Press, 1935), 195.

2. Richard G. Salomon, "St. John's Church Sesquicentennial Address," 3 Jan. 1954, SJPR. Dr. Salomon was professor of history at Kenyon College. Much of this was published in Richard G. Salomon, "St. John's Parish, Worthington and the Beginnings of the Episcopal Church in Ohio," *Ohio Historical Quarterly* 64 (Jan. 1955): 55–76.

3. Ashbel Baldwin, Stratford, Conn., to Ezra Griswold, John Goodrich, and Alex'r Morrison, Worthington, 20 Aug. 1810, GP, 1810–20.

4. *Ohio Monitor*, 10 Sept. 1816, advertisement announcing the convention for 20 Oct. 1816.

5. Typescript photocopy of letter from James Kilbourn to the bishops, clerical and lay delegates of the Episcopal Church meeting in convention at New York City, 1 May 1817, Worthington Historical Society. The original letter is in the archives of the Episcopal Diocese of Ohio at Cleveland.

6. Chase, *Bishop Chase's Reminiscences*, 127–34.

7. Salomon, "Sesquicentennial Address"; Salomon, "St. John's Parish," 152. See also, the reports of the Ohio Diocese in William Stevens Perry, ed., *Journals of the General Convention of the Protestant Episcopal Church, U.S.A.*, vol. 2 (Claremont, N.H.: 1874). There was difficulty in having this decision accepted by the eastern leadership, but Rev. Chase was ordained in Philadelphia the following winter.

8. Elnathan Maynard, "A Few Personal Recollections of Bishop Chase," *St. John's Banner* 1 (July 1900): 16–19.

9. Larkin, *Reshaping of Everyday Life*, 285, contends that failure to offer visitors liquor was a breach of hospitality.

10. Salomon, "Sesquicentennial Address," quoting from the volume of handwritten records of the Worthington Female Tract Society, which in 1832 became the Female Missionary Society. These records are in the archives of the Episcopal Diocese of Ohio in Cleveland.

11. Salomon, "Sesquicentennial Address," 20.

12. *The First Ten Years of the Protestant Episcopal Church in the Diocese of Ohio, 1818–1827* (Columbus: Scott and Bascom, 1853).

13. Philander Chase to Joseph Dodridge, 16 Nov. 1820, in "The Rev. Joseph Dodridge Memoirs, Letters, and Papers," typescript manuscript in the archives of the Pittsburgh Diocese, quoted in Berquist and Bowers, *New Eden*, 178–83. Their account gives the most complete description of this incident.

14. *First Ten Years*, 54. This convention, like all between 1818 and 1823, was held at the Worthington Academy.

15. Salomon, "Sesquicentennial Address," 22.

16. Bishop Philander Chase, "Deed of Gift," 27 Nov. 1823, quoted by George Franklin Smythe in *Kenyon College* (New Haven: Yale University Press, 1924), 305–9.

17. Salomon, "Sesquicentennial Address," 19, quoting Chase, *Bishop Chase's Reminiscences*. It is worth noting that Chase would, within a few years, leave the Kenyon College presidency in a remarkably similar embittered fashion.

18. Ibid., 22.

19. National Historic Register, St. John's Episcopal Church, Worthington, Ohio, FRA-2170-A, 1 July 1975; 1829 convention report, SJCR, box 17; Richard N. Campen, *Ohio: An Architectural Portrait* (Chagrin Falls: West Summit Press, 1973), 206.

20. St. John's Episcopal Church stands on the present Worthington Village Green much as it appeared originally. The tower was changed for safety after the Civil War; however, prior to the building's 1931 centennial, the building was restored to the appearance shown in an 1859 photograph. The first Worthington Methodist Church was replaced in 1864, and the first Presbyterian Church was remodeled and enlarged in 1842 and replaced in 1927. Richard G. Saloman, "Philander Chase, Norman Nash and Charles Bullfinch: A Study of the Origins of Old Kenyon," OHS, PA Box 544, #14.

21. Bushman, *Refinement of America*, 335–48.

22. Hine, *Community on the American Frontier*, 145.

23. Nathan C. Hatch, "The Democratization of Christianity and the Character of American Politics," in *Religion and American Politics*, ed. Mark A. Nell (New York: Oxford University Press, 1990), 92–120.

24. St. John's Episcopal Church, first record book, 31–32.

25. Russell E. Richey, *Early American Methodism* (Bloomington: Indiana University Press, 1991), 56.

26. Amos Hawley to Ezra Griswold, 12 Aug. 1818, GFP, box 15, folder 7. Ironically, Hawley was married to widow Sarah Phelps Buttles, whose sons Joel and Arora were leaders in the Columbus and Worthington Episcopal congregations. Sarah's position in this dispute is unknown.

27. Thomas Hine, *Methodist Magazine* 4 (June 1821): 228, quoted by Cole in *Lion of the Forest*, 20–21.

28. T. Scott Miyakawa, *Protestants and Pioneers: Individualism and Conformity on the American Frontier* (Chicago: University of Chicago Press, 1964), 90–91.

29. Wright, "Methodist Episcopal Church," 28–32; C. J. Cummins, *Methodism in Worthington* (Worthington: Methodist Church, 1953), 5; John F. Young, *Exploring Our Roots*, 10–11. All of these rely on Louise Wright's personal account, based upon her memories as the daughter of Rev. Uriah Heath who served this church for several years.

30. After the establishment of the Worthington Female Seminary in 1838, these students occupied the west side and men the east and the corners.

31. Faragher, *Sugar Creek*, 168.

32. Cole, *Lion of the Forest*, 113.

33. Ibid.

34. Matthews, *Toward a New Society*.

35. Dearing Cowles to Whitfield Cowles, 24 Feb. 1827, RWCP (R. W. Cowles was a witness to the will and the executor of the estate); Asa Gillet will, Franklin County will record A:181–84.

36. Harriet Frye, "Liberty Presbyterian Church and the Liberty Community: 150 Years," typescript manuscript, 1960, Delaware County Historical Society.

37. Sweet, *Presbyterians*.

38. Julia L. Nelson, "The Presbyterian Church of Worthington, Ohio," *Old Northwest Genealogical Quarterly* 7 (Jan. 1904): 33–35. Julia Nelson was a granddaughter of Job W. and Julia Buttles Case, two of those original eleven members. There is no reason to doubt this information, but it should be noted that Peter Barker was *not* one of the subscribers when the society incorporated in 1821.

39. Record of incorporations, Franklin County clerk of courts, 1821–22, OHS, GR 2921, 5A.

40. Miyakawa, *Protestants and Pioneers*, 126.

41. Program of dedication, First Presbyterian Church, Worthington, Ohio, January 1927, Worthington Presbyterian Church records.

42. May 1829 letter, quoted by Julia L. Nelson in "Presbyterian Church of Worthington."

43. Ibid.

44. Ibid. There was a loosely organized Universalist group in the Worthington area that eventually built a meeting house about two miles north of the village at the present site of Flint.

45. Emilia Maynard to Dorcas Cary, 23 Mar. 1826, JCP.

46. Quoted in Julia L. Nelson, "Presbyterian Church of Worthington."

47. John Allen Krout, *The Origins of Prohibition* (New York: Alfred A. Knopf, 1925), 113–16.

48. W. J. Rorabaugh, *The Alcoholic Republic: An American Tradition* (New York: Oxford University Press, 1979), 233. This equated to about seven gallons of absolute alcohol.

49. Ibid., 149–69.

50. Henry Howe, quoted in Cole, *Lion of the Forest*, 116–18.

51. James Russell Rohrer, "Battling the Master Vice: The Evangelical War against Intemperance in Ohio, 1800–1832" (master's thesis, Ohio State University, 1985), 66.

52. Rev. P. Chase account, 30 July–25 Dec. 1817, GP, 1810–20.

53. Griswold sexton records, St. John's Cemetery.

54. Franklin County estate #877; McCormick, *Scioto Company Descendants*, 82–83.

55. 13 Oct. 1845, JBD, referring to the purchase made several years earlier.

56. Rorabaugh, *Alcoholic Republic*, 207–9.

57. Dannenbaum, *Drink and Disorder*, 22; Rorabaugh, *Alcoholic Republic*, 189; Smith, *As a City on a Hill*, 151.

58. "Objections to Temperance Society to be answered at general Meeting," 25 Feb. 1834, GFP, box 1, folder 3. This source is quoted throughout the following passage.

59. Ian R. Tyrrell, *Sobering Up: From Temperance to Prohibition in Antebellum America, 1800–1860* (Westport, Conn.: Greenwood Press, 1979), 5.

60. Rorabaugh, *Alcoholic Republic*, 214.

19. CORRECT MENTAL AND MORAL HABITS AND AMIABLE MANNERS

1. Edward A. Miller, "History of the Educational Legislation in Ohio from 1803 to 1850," *Ohio Archaeological and Historical Publications* 27 (1919): 1–271.

2. Utter, *Frontier State*, 321.

3. Ohio General Assembly, *Laws of Ohio*, 22 Jan. 1821, OHS, FLM 249, roll 6, 51–56.

4. Ohio General Assembly, *Laws of Ohio*, 5 Feb. 1825, OHS, FLM 249, roll 7, 36–41; Miller, "Educational Legislation."

5. *Ohio State Journal*, 11 May 1826, 3.

6. By mid-century, twelve Sharon Township school districts were regularly dividing tax funds, but it is not clear whether all twelve were established immediately after the passage of the 1825 law.

7. Receipt from Daniel Upson to district two school directors, 16 Oct. 1828, SBP, box 1, folder 13.

8. Franklin County deed record 12:163, 3 Oct. 1829.

9. Articles of agreement, SCMB, 14 Dec. 1802.

10. Samuel Lewis, "Third Report of the Ohio Commissioner of Common Schools," *Ohio Executive Documents* 17 (1839): 46; Samuel Lewis, "Location of School Houses," *Ohio Common School Director* 1 (1838): 92–93.

11. Nancy S. Clark, Worthington, to Martha J. Thomson, Delaware, 6 May 1838, WHS, Worthington Female Seminary folder.

12. Samuel Galloway, Secretary of State, *Report on the Condition of Common Schools, 1846* (Columbus: n.p., 1846), 11.

13. Subscription list for Worthington Singing School, 24 Apr. 1826, CCP.

14. Harry R. Stevens, "Folk Music on the Midwestern Frontier, 1788–1825," *Ohio Archaeological and Historical Quarterly* 57 (1948): 126–46.

15. *History of Crawford County*, 349–50.

16. Worthington College subscription list, 5 Feb. 1819 and 5 Mar. 1819, GP, 1810–20.

17. John Johnston, Worthington, to Rev. James Finley, 3 Dec. 1825, quoted in Cole, *Lion of the Forest*, 52.

18. Ohio General Assembly, *Laws of Ohio*, 12 Feb. 1829, OHS, FLM 249, 27:131.

19. *Delaware Patron*, 13 Aug. 1829, 1.

20. Ibid.

21. *Ohio State Journal and Columbus Gazette*, 21 Apr. 1832, 3.

22. Ibid.

23. Friendship book, PAW, 1835–44.

24. Ohio General Assembly, *Laws of Ohio*, 9 Mar. 1839, OHS, FLM 249, 37:141–43. This institution constructed an impressive three-story brick building and had over one hundred students per term, but closed in 1857 because of competition from Ohio Wesleyan, a coeducational institution established at nearby Delaware.

25. *Ohio State Journal*, 27 Mar. 1841, 4.

26. Worthington College records, 22 Sept. 1830, GFP, box 6, folder 6; Frederick C. Waite, "Second Medical School in Ohio, at Worthington 1830–1840," *Ohio State Medical Journal* 33 (1937): 1334–36.

27. *Reformed Practice of Medicine, by the Professors of the Reformed Medical Colleges of New York and Worthington* (Boston: 1831), vi.

28. *Ohio State Journal and Columbus Gazette*, 28 Oct. 1830, 3.

29. Ibid.

30. Dr. Steele's inauguration was reported in the *Ohio State Journal and Columbus Gazette*, 22 and 25 Dec. 1830; Dr. Wooster Beach to trustees of the Worthington Medical College, 16 Mar. 1831, GFP, box 6.

31. Johnson and Malone, *Dictionary of American Biography*, 13:237–38.

32. *Ohio State Journal*, 4 Oct. 1834, 3; 28 Aug. 1835, 3.

33. [Cincinnati] *Western Medical Reformer*, 8 Sept. 1845.

34. AHBL.

35. Harvey Wickes Felter, "Graduates of the Worthington Medical College, 1833–1838," *History of the Eclectic Medical Institute, Cincinnati, Ohio, 1845–1902* (Cincinnati: 1902). The Worthington college was recognized as the forerunner of the Cincinnati institution.

36. The Morrow-Greer marriage is recorded in "Parish Registers of St. John's Church," *Old Northwest Genealogical Quarterly* 2 (1899): 179; the Jones-Kilbourne,

Johnson-Griswold, Paddock-Bristol marriages are in Franklin County marriage records 3:60, 4:145 and 215, OHS, GR 898; see also Felter, *Eclectic Medical Institute*, 86–94.

37. *Ohio State Journal*, 31 Dec. 2, 1939.

38. Felter, *Eclectic Medical Institute*, 14–16.

39. *Ohio State Journal*, 1 Jan. 1840, 3.

40. Letter signed by thirty physicians, printed in the *St. Clairsville Chronicle* and reprinted in the *Ohio State Journal*, 18 Feb. 1840. The bill introduced in the legislature failed to be enacted into law.

41. *Ohio State Journal*, 7 Mar. 1840, 2.

42. Felter, *Eclectic Medical Institute*, 17.

43. Emma Carey, a student at the Worthington Female Seminary, to her sister Cinderella Carey, 18 Dec. 1839, JCP.

20. THAT DEAD ANIMALS OR NUISANCES OF ANY KIND BE BURIED IN SOME VACANT PLACE

1. Worthington Female Seminary advertisement, *Ohio State Journal*, 27 Mar. 1841, 4.

2. The cause of death in this case might have been anything from typhoid fever—which pioneers often referred to as brain fever—to a brain tumor.

3. Julia P. Strong to Cynthia Strong, 18 June, 21 June, and 26 June 1820, GP, 1820–29. Emily Griswold came west with her parents as a nine-month-old infant in the fall of 1803.

4. L. D. Nelson and C. H. Cantrill, "Religiosity and Death Anxiety: A Multi-Dimensional Analysis," *Review of Religious Research* 21 (Spring 1980): 148–57; Richard Lonetto and Donald I. Templer, *Death Anxiety* (Washington, D.C.: Hemisphere Publishing, 1986).

5. Larkin, *Reshaping of Everyday Life*, 78.

6. Griswold sexton records, 12 Nov. 1832.

7. Larkin, *Reshaping of Everyday Life*, 79–80.

8. Griswold sexton records, 21 Apr. 1827.

9. Ibid., 9 Oct. 1827, 23 Mar. 1830, 29 July 1833.

10. *Ohio State Journal*, 26 Aug. 1833.

11. Griswold sexton records, 12 Aug. 1828, 20 July 1830, 12 June 1831, 17 Aug. 1831, 5 Aug. 1833, 7 Aug. 1834, 16 Apr. 1835, 22 Sept. 1835.

12. Julia P. Strong to Cynthia Strong, 21 June 1820, GP, 1820–29.

13. Cynthia Cowles, Worthington, to Emma Carey, Tymochtee, 21 Nov. 1840, GP, 1840–49. For names and deaths of other children in this family, see McCormick, *Scioto Company Genealogies*, 160–61.

14. R. W. Cowles inventory and estate appraisal, 16 July 1842, OHS, GR 3368. This is the source of the inventory to follow.

15. Julia Case, Worthington, to Mary Case, Granville, 27 Dec. [1836], JBC. It is possible to date the year of this letter from the mention of the marriage of Julia Beach and Amasa Webster.

16. Bushman, *Refinement of America*, 353–54.

17. William Robe inventory, Feb. 1823, estate file #389, OHS, GR 1242.

18. The winner of the congressional seat was William Wilson, judge of the Licking County Common Pleas Court. Both he and Orris Parrish, a Franklin County lawyer, had more votes in Franklin County than Kilbourn.

19. *History of Franklin and Pickaway Counties,* 136–62.

20. Wiebe, *Opening of American Society,* 194.

21. U.S. Bureau of Census, 1830, Sharon Township, Franklin County, Ohio, OHS, GR 17. This is the earliest surviving Franklin County census so it is not possible to make comparisons with 1810 and 1820. Of the 910 inhabitants, 13 were "free colored," and 897 were white; 316 persons lived in the village and 594 in the township. Only the white population was broken down by age and sex, and it was nearly evenly divided in gender, with 446 males and 451 females.

22. "An Act to Incorporate the Village of Worthington," 9 Mar. 1835, *Laws of Ohio,* OHS, FLM 249, vol. 33.

23. *General Ordinances of the Village of Worthington, Ohio* (Columbus: Gazette Printing House, 1885). Officers of the village from 1836–84 are printed in this publication.

24. Abner Putnam Pinney had lived most of his married life on a farm in Delaware County, but he "retired" to the village in the 1830s—a pattern that would become common for the rest of the century.

25. "An Ordinance for preventing or removing nuisances and obstructions in the town of Worthington," 20 Feb. 1836, *General Ordinances,* 13–14.

26. *Delaware Patron,* 8 Apr. 1824. Persons were fined from $1.00 to $5.00 for leaving dead animals within the town.

27. "An Ordinance for preventing or removing nuisances and obstructions in the town of Worthington," 20 Feb. 1836, *General Ordinances,* 13–14.

28. "An Ordinance for restraining sheep and swine," 9 Aug. 1836, *General Ordinances,* 23–27. This was the first in a series of eight laws on this subject before 1884, which eventually covered sheep, swine, geese, cattle, horses, goats, and mules and created an impoundment facility and fines to support it.

29. "A By-Law Providing for making side-walks," 6 Sept. 1841, *General Ordinances,* 4.

30. "An ordinance to regulate public shows," 31 Mar. 1836, *General Ordinances,* 12–13.

31. U.S. Bureau of Census, 1830, Sharon Township, Franklin County, OHS, GR 17. Of the white inhabitants whose age is known, 242 of 315 in the village were 30 or younger, in the township 437 of 582.

32. Bartlett, *New Country,* 423.

Epilogue

1. M. H. Dunlop, *Sixty Miles from Contentment: Traveling the Nineteenth-Century American Interior* (New York: Basic Books, 1995), 3–50.

2. Worthington city ordinance, chapter 1177, 11 May 1987, a revision of the 1967 ordinance, Codified Ordinances of the City of Worthington, Ohio.

3. National Register of Historic Places, Worthington Historic District, 17 Apr. 1980.

4. James Kilbourne died at Worthington on Apr. 24, 1850. The only Scioto Company member to live longer was William Vining, who farmed northwest of the village.

5. McCormick and McCormick, "African Americans in Worthington before the Civil War," *Probing Worthington's Heritage,* 99–101; McCormick and McCormick, "Turk-Gilkey House," *Worthington Landmarks,* 58–59.

6. U.S. Census population figures are available from 1830 to the present. Ohio schedules for 1810 and Franklin County schedules for 1820 were destroyed.

7. McCormick, *Scioto Company Descendants*, 27–31, 207–9, 274–77.

8. The only institution of higher education in the Worthington area today is the Pontifical College Josephinum, an internationally known seminary for Catholic priests, which moved to the north side of Worthington in 1929.

Selected Bibliography

— ❖ —

Aldrich, Lewis C., ed. *History of Erie County.* Syracuse: D. Mason, 1889.

Ammon, Harry. *James Monroe: The Quest for National Identity.* 1971. Reprint, Charlottesville: University Press of Virginia, 1990.

Anderson, Virginia D. *New England's Generation.* Cambridge: Cambridge University Press, 1991.

Atherton, Lewis E. *Main Street on the Middle Border.* Bloomington: Indiana University Press, 1954.

Baker, John M. *American House Styles: A Concise Guide.* New York: W. W. Norton, 1994.

Baldwin, Leland D. *The Keelboat Age on Western Waters.* Pittsburgh: University of Pittsburgh Press, 1941.

Bartlett, Richard A. *The New Country: A Social History of the American Frontier.* New York: Oxford University Press, 1974.

Bass, Bernard M. *Handbook of Leadership.* New York: The Free Press, 1990.

Berquist, Goodwin, and Paul C. Bowers, Jr. *The New Eden: James Kilbourne and the Development of Ohio.* Lanham, Md.: University Press of America, 1983.

Bickford, Christopher P. *Farmington in Connecticut.* Farmington: Farmington Historical Society, 1982.

Bieder, Robert E. "Kinship as a Factor in Migration." *Journal of Marriage and the Family* 35 (Aug. 1973).

Billington, Ray A. *Frederick Jackson Turner: Historian, Scholar, Teacher.* New York: Oxford University Press, 1973.

Billington, Ray A., and Martin Ridge. *Western Expansion: A History of the American Frontier.* New York: Macmillan, 1982.

Biographical Directory of the American Congress. Washington, D.C.: Government Printing Office, 1971.

Blue, Frederick J. *Salmon P. Chase: A Life in Politics.* Kent: Kent State University Press, 1987.

Boatright, Mody C. "The Myth of Frontier Individualism," in *Turner and the Sociology of the Frontier.* Ed. Richard Hofstadter and Seymour M. Lipset. New York: Basic Books, 1968.

Bogue, Allan G., and Margaret Beattie Bogue. "Profits and the Frontier Land Speculator." *Journal of Economic History* 17 (Mar. 1957).

Boorstin, Daniel J. *The Americans, The National Experience.* New York: Random House, 1965.

———. *Cleopatra's Nose: Essays on the Unexpected.* New York: Random House, 1994.

Brown, Samuel R. *The Western Gazetteer: or Emigrants' Directory.* Auburn, N.Y.: H.C. Southwick, Printers, 1817.

Buley, R. Carlyle. *The Old Northwest: Pioneer Period, 1815–1840.* Reprint, Bloomington: Indiana University Press, 1978.

Burns, James MacGregor. *The Vineyard of Liberty.* New York: Alfred A. Knopf, 1982.

Bushman, Richard L. *The Refinement of America: Persons, Houses, Cities.* New York: Alfred A. Knopf, 1992.

Calhoun, Arthur W. *A Social History of the American Family.* New York: Barnes and Noble, 1945.

Campen, Richard N. *Ohio: An Architectural Portrait.* Chagrin Falls, Ohio: West Summit Press, 1973.

Carley, Rachel. *The Visual Dictionary of American Domestic Architecture.* New York: Henry Holt, 1994.

Cayton, Andrew R. L. *The Frontier Republic: Ideology and Politics in the Ohio Country, 1780–1825.* Kent: Kent State University Press, 1986.

Cayton, Andrew R. L., and Peter S. Onuf. *The Midwest and the Nation: Rethinking the History of an American Region.* Bloomington: Indiana University Press, 1990.

Chase, Philander. *Bishop Chase's Reminiscences: An Autobiography.* Boston: James B. Dow, 1848.

Clark, Christopher. "The Household Economy, Market Exchange, and the Rise of Capitalism in the Connecticut Valley, 1800–1860," *Journal of Social History* 13 (Winter 1979).

———. *The Roots of Rural Capitalism: Western Massachusetts, 1780–1800.* Ithaca: Cornell University Press, 1990.

Cole, Charles C., Jr. *Lion of the Forest: James B. Finley, Frontier Reformer.* Lexington: University of Kentucky Press, 1994.

"Common Pleas Court Records from the Organization of Franklin County." *Old Northwest Genealogical Quarterly* 15 (July 1912).

Compton, H. W. "The Seige of Ft. Meigs." *Ohio Archaeological and Historical Society Publications* 10 (1902).

Conrad, Ethel. "Touring Ohio in 1811: The Journal of Charity Rotch." *Ohio History* 99 (Summer-Autumn 1990).

Creasy, David. *Coming Over: Migration and Communication between England and New England.* Cambridge: Cambridge University Press, 1987.

Cummins, C.J. *Methodism in Worthington.* Worthington: Methodist Church, 1953.

Cummins, Mary Anne. "The Stanbery/Stanborough Genealogy." Typescript. Delaware County Historical Society.

Curti, Merle. *The Making of an American Community: A Case Study of Democracy in a Frontier County.* Stanford: Stanford University Press, 1959.

Dana, Edmund. *Geographical Sketches on the Western Country: designed for emigrants and settlers.* Cincinnati: n.p., 1819.

Dannenbaum, Jed. *Drink and Disorder: Temperance Reform in Cincinnati from the Washington Revival to the WCTU.* Urbana: University of Illinois Press, 1984.

Debates and Proceedings of the Congress of the United States. Washington, D.C.: Gales and Seaton, 1854.

D'Emilio, John, and Estelle B. Freedman. *Intimate Matters: A History of Sexuality in America.* New York: Harper and Row, 1988.

Demos, John. *A Little Commonwealth: Family Life in Plymouth Colony.* New York: Oxford University Press, 1971.

Doyle, Don Harrison. *The Social Order of a Frontier Community: Jacksonville, Illinois, 1825–1870.* Urbana: University of Illinois Press, 1978.

Dunlop, M. H. *Sixty Miles from Contentment: Traveling the Nineteenth-Century American Interior.* New York: Basic Books, 1995.

"Early Records of St. John's Church." *St. John's Banner* 1 (Jan. 1901).

Faragher, John Mack. *Sugar Creek: Life on the Illinois Prairie.* New Haven: Yale University Press, 1986.

Felter, Harvey Wickes. *History of the Eclectic Medical Institute, Cincinnati, Ohio, 1845–1902.* Cincinnati: n.p., 1902.

Filler, Louis. *The Crusade against Slavery.* New York: Harper and Brothers, 1960.

The First Ten Years of the Protestant Episcopal Church in the Diocese of Ohio, 1818–1827. Columbus: Scott and Bascom, 1853.

Ford, Lacy K., Jr. "Frontier Democracy: The Turner Thesis Revisited." *Journal of the Early Republic* 13 (Summer 1993).

Frohman, Charles E. *Sandusky's Yesteryears.* Columbus: Ohio Historical Society, 1968.

Fruehling, Byron D., and Robert H. Smith. "Subterranean Highways of the Underground Railroad in Ohio." *Ohio History* 102 (Summer-Autumn 1993).

General Ordinances of the Village of Worthington, Ohio. Columbus: Gazette Printing House, 1885.

Goldman, Perry M., and James S. Young, eds. *The United States Congressional Directories, 1789–1840.* New York: Columbia University Press, 1973.

Goodrich, Carter, ed. *Canals and American Economic Development.* New York: Columbia University Press, 1961.

Graumann, Carl F., and Serge Moscovici, eds. *Changing Conceptions of Leadership.* New York: Springer-Verlag, 1986.

Gray, Susan E. "Family, Land, and Credit: Yankee Communities on the Michigan Frontier, 1830–1860." Ph.D. diss., University of Chicago, 1985.

Green, Constance McLaughlin. *Washington: Village and Capital, 1800–1878.* Princeton: Princeton University Press, 1962.

Greven, Philip J., Jr. *Four Generations: Population, Land and Family in Colonial Andover, Massachusetts.* Ithaca: Cornell University Press, 1970.

Gutgesell, Stephen. *Guide to Ohio Newspapers, 1793–1973.* Columbus: Ohio Historical Society, 1974.

Hatch, Nathan C. "The Democratization of Christianity and the Character of American Politics." *Religion and American Politics.* Ed. Mark A. Nell. New York: Oxford University Press, 1990.

Hatcher, Harlan. *The Western Reserve: The Story of New Connecticut in Ohio.* New York: Bobbs-Merrill, 1949.

Hawke, David Freeman. *Everyday Life in Early America.* New York: Harper and Row, 1988.

Henretta, James A. "The Morphology of New England Society in the Colonial Period." *The Family in History: Interdisciplinary Essays.* Ed. Theodore K. Rabb and Robert I. Rothberg. New York: Harper and Row, 1973.

Hibbard, Benjamin H. *A History of the Public Land Policies.* New York: Peter Smith, 1939.

Hine, Robert V. *Community on the American Frontier.* Norman: University of Oklahoma Press, 1980.

"The Historic Setting of Granville." *Old Northwest Genealogical Quarterly* 8 (1905).

History of Crawford County and Ohio. Chicago: Baskin and Battey, 1881.

History of Delaware County and Ohio. Chicago: O. L. Baskin, 1880.

History of Franklin and Pickaway Counties, Ohio. Cleveland: Williams Brothers, 1880.

History of the Ohio Canals. Columbus: Ohio State Archaelogical and Historical Society, 1905.

Holbrook, Stewart H. *The Yankee Exodus: An Account of Migration from New England.* New York: Macmillan, 1950.

Hulbert, Archer Butler. *Historic Highways of America.* Cleveland: Arthur H. Clark, 1903.

———. "The Old National Road—The Historic Highway of America." *Ohio Archaeological and Historical Society Publications* 9 (1901).

Humphrey, Seth K. *Following the Prairie Frontier.* Minneapolis: University of Minnesota Press, 1931.

Huntington, C. C. "A History of Banking and Currency in Ohio before the Civil War." *Ohio Archaeological and Historical Society Publications* 24 (1915).

Hurt, R. Douglas. *American Farm Tools: From Hand-Power to Steam-Power.* Manhattan, Kans.: Sunflower University Press, 1982.

Jackson, Ronald V., Gary R. Teeples, and David Schaefermeyer. *Index to Ohio Tax Lists, 1800–1810.* Bountiful, Utah: Accelerated Indexing Systems, 1977.

Jenkins, Warren. *The Ohio Gazetteer and Traveler's Guide.* Columbus: Isaac N. Whiting, Printers, 1841.

Johnson, Allen, and Dumas Malone, eds. *Dictionary of American Biography.* New York: Charles Scribner's Sons, 1930.

Jones, Emma, ed., *A State in the Making: Correspondence of the late James Kilbourne.* Columbus: Tibbetts Printing, 1913.

Jones, Robert F. *"King of the Alley," William Duer: Politician, Entrepreneur, and Speculator, 1768–1799.* Philadelphia: American Philosophical Society, 1992.

Jones, Robert L. *The History of Agriculture in Ohio to 1880.* Kent: Kent State University Press, 1983.

"Journal of Nathaniel Little." *Old Northwest Genealogical Quarterly* 10 (1907).

Kilbourn, John. *The Ohio Gazetteer.* Chillicothe: Builbache and Scott, Printers, 1819.

Kilbourn, Payne Kenyon. *The Family Memorial: A History and Genealogy of the Kilbourn Family.* Hartford: Brown and Parsons, 1850.

[Kilbourne, James]. "Autobiography of Col. James Kilbourne." *Old Northwest Genealogical Quarterly* 6 (Oct. 1903).

Knepper, George. *Ohio and Its People.* Kent: Kent State University Press, 1989.

Krout, John Allen. *The Origins of Prohibition.* New York: Alfred A. Knopf, 1925.

Larkin, Jack. *The Reshaping of Everyday Life, 1790–1840.* New York: Harper and Row, 1988.

Laws of Ohio. Ohio Historical Society. Microfilm 249.

Lee, Alfred. *History of the City of Columbus.* Chicago: Munsell, 1892.

Lee, Everett S. "A Theory of Migration." *Demography* 3 (1966).

Lewis, Samuel. "Third Report of the Ohio Commissioner of Common Schools." *Ohio Executive Documents* 17 (1839).

Leyland, Herbert. *Thomas Smith Webb: Freemason, Musician, Entrepreneur.* Dayton: Otterbein Press, 1965.

"Licensed Tavern Keepers in Sharon Township." *Ohio Genealogical Quarterly* 2 (April 1938).

Litwak, Eugene. "Geographic Mobility and Extended Family Cohesion." *American Sociological Review* 25 (June 1960).

Lockridge, Kenneth L. "Land, Population and the Evolution of New England Society." *Colonial America: Essays in Politics and Social Development.* Ed. Stanley N. Katz. Boston: Little, Brown, 1971.

Lonetto, Richard, and Donald I. Templer. *Death Anxiety.* Washington, D.C.: Hemisphere Publishing, 1986.

Mahoney, Timothy R. *River Towns in the Great West: The Structure of Provincial Urbanization in the American Midwest, 1820–1870.* Cambridge: Cambridge University Press, 1990.

Main, Jackson Turner. *Society and Economy in Colonial Connecticut.* Princeton: Princeton University Press, 1985.

Matthews, Jean V. *Toward a New Society: American Thought and Culture, 1800–1830.* Boston: Twayne Publishers, 1991.

Maynard, Elnathan. "A Few Personal Recollections of Bishop Chase." *St. John's Banner* 1 (July 1900).

McAlester, Virginia, and Lee McAlester. *A Field Guide to American Houses.* New York: Alfred A. Knopf, 1990.

McCormick, Robert, and Jennie McCormick. *Probing Worthington's Heritage.* Worthington: Cottonwood Publications, 1990.

————. *Worthington Landmarks: Photo-Essays of Historic Worthington Properties.* Worthington: Cottonwood Publications, 1992.

McCormick, Virginia E. *Scioto Company Descendants: Genealogies of the Original Proprietors of Worthington, Ohio.* Worthington: Cottonwood Publications, 1995.

McPherson, James M. *Battle Cry of Freedom: The Civil War Era.* New York: Oxford University Press, 1988.

Miller, Edward A. "History of the Educational Legislation in Ohio from 1803 to 1850." *Ohio Archaeological and Historical Society Publications* 27 (1919).

Millett, Allan R. and Peter Maslowski. *For the Common Defense.* New York: The Free Press, 1984.

Miyakawa, T. Scott. *Protestants and Pioneers: Individualism and Conformity on the American Frontier.* Chicago: University of Chicago Press, 1964.

Morgan, Ted. *Wilderness at Dawn: The Settling of the North American Continent.* New York: Simon and Schuster, 1993.

"Mr. Fitch's 'Mysterious Machine.'" *Ohio Historical Society Echoes* 10 (Apr. 1971).

"Mr. Kilbourn's Congressional Career." *Old Northwest Genealogical Quarterly* 6 (Oct. 1903).

Nelson, Julia L. "The Presbyterian Church of Worthington, Ohio." *Old Northwest Genealogical Quarterly* 7 (Jan. 1904).

Nelson, L. D., and C. H. Cantrill. "Religiosity and Death Anxiety: A Multi-Dimensional Analysis." *Review of Religious Research* 21 (Spring 1980).

New England in the Wilderness. Worthington: Worthington Historical Society, 1976.

Nylander, Jane C. *Our Own Snug Fireside: Images of the New England Home, 1760–1860.* New York: Alfred A. Knopf, 1994.

Ohio Lands: A Short History. Columbus: State Auditor, 1989.

"Organization of Franklin County." *Old Northwest Genealogical Quarterly* 15 (July 1912).

Peeke, Hewson L. *A Standard History of Erie County, Ohio.* Chicago: Lewis Publishing, 1916.

————. "Charles Dickens in Ohio in 1842." *Ohio Archaeological and Historical Society Publications* 28 (1920).

Perry, William Stevens, ed. *Journals of the General Convention of the Protestant Episcopal Church, U.S.A.* Claremont, N.H.: 1874.

Phelps, H. Warren. "Some Historic Records from Franklin County Commissioner's Books." *Old Northwest Genealogical Quarterly* 7 (July 1904).

Quillan, Frank U. *The Color Line in Ohio.* 1913. Reprint, New York: Negro Universities Press, 1969.

Rawls, Thomas H. *Small Places: In Search of a Vanishing America*. Boston: Little, Brown, 1990.

Reformed Practice of Medicine, by the Professors of the Reformed Medical Colleges of New York and Worthington. Boston: n.p., 1831.

"Report of James Kilbourne, Agent of the Scioto Company for the Summer of 1803." *Old Northwest Genealogical Quarterly* 6 (1903).

Reps, John William. *Cities of the American West: A History of Frontier Urban Planning*. Princeton: Princeton University Press, 1979.

Richey, Russell E. *Early American Methodism*. Bloomington: Indiana University Press, 1991.

Rohrbough, Malcolm J. *The Land Office Business*. New York: Oxford University Press, 1968.

Rohrer, James Russell. "Battling the Master Vice: The Evangelical War against Intemperance in Ohio, 1800–1832." Master's thesis, Ohio State University, 1985.

Rorabaugh, W. J. *The Alcoholic Republic: An American Tradition*. New York: Oxford University Press, 1979.

Roseboom, Eugene H., and Francis P. Weisenburger. *A History of Ohio*. Columbus: Ohio Historical Society, 1986.

Russo, David J. *Families and Communities: A New View of American History*. Nashville: American Association for the Study of State and Local History, 1974.

Ryan, Daniel J. "From Charter to Constitution." *Ohio Archaeological and Historical Society Publications* 5 (1900).

Ryan, Mary P. *The Cradle of the Middle Class: The Family in Oneida County, New York, 1790–1865*. Cambridge: Cambridge University Press, 1981.

Salomon, Richard G. "St. John's Church Sesquicentennial Address." 3 Jan. 1954. St. John's Parish records.

———. "St. John's Parish, Worthington and the Beginnings of the Episcopal Church in Ohio." *Ohio Historical Quarterly* 64 (Jan. 1955).

Scheiber, Harry N. "Urban Rivalry and Internal Improvements in the Old Northwest, 1820–1860." *The Old Northwest: Studies in Regional History, 1787–1910*. Ed. Harry N. Scheiber. Lincoln: University of Nebraska Press, 1969.

"The Scioto Company and Its Purchase." *Ohio Archaeological and Historical Society Publications* 3 (1894).

Sears, Alfred Byron. *Thomas Worthington: Father of Ohio Statehood*. Columbus: Ohio State University Press, 1958.

"Sexton Records of George H. Griswold, St. John's Episcopal Cemetery." *Ohio Genealogical Society Report* 30 (1990).

Shammas, Carole. "Constructing a Wealth Distribution from Probate Records." *Journal of Interdisciplinary History* 9 (1978).

Shannon, Timothy J. "This Unpleasant Business: The Transformation of Land Speculation in the Ohio Country, 1787–1820." *The Pursuit of Public Power: Political Culture in Ohio, 1787–1861*. Ed. Jeffrey P. Brown and Andrew R. L. Cayton. Kent: Kent State University Press, 1994.

Shedding Light on Worthington. Worthington: Presbyterian Church Woodrow Guild, 1931.

Sherman, C. E. *Original Ohio Land Subdivisions.* Columbus: Ohio Cooperative Topographic Survey, 1925.

Siebert, Wilbur Henry. "Beginnings of the Underground Railroad in Ohio." *Ohio Archaeological and Historical Society Publications* 56 (1948).

————. *The Mysteries of Ohio's Underground Railroads.* Columbus: Long's Book, 1951.

Sklar, Kathryn Kish. *Catharine Beecher: A Study in American Domesticity.* New York: W. W. Norton, 1976.

Smith, Daniel Scott. "All in Some Degree Related to Each Other: A Demographic and Comparative Resolution of the Anomaly of New England Kinship." *American Historical Review* 94 (Feb. 1989).

Smith, Mrs. Samuel Harrison. *The First Forty Years of Washington Society.* Ed. Gaillard Hunt. New York: Charles Scribner's Sons, 1906.

Smith, Page. *As a City on a Hill: The Town in American History.* Cambridge: Massachusetts Institute of Technology Press, 1966.

Smythe, George Franklin. *Kenyon College.* New Haven: Yale University Press, 1924.

Soltow, Lee. "Inequality Amidst Abundance: Land Ownership in Early Ohio." *Ohio History* 88 (Spring 1979).

Squirer, E. G., and E. H. Davis. *Ancient Monuments of the Mississippi Valley.* 1848. Reprint, New York: AMS Press for the Peabody Museum of Archaeology and Ethnology, 1973.

"St. John's Church." *Old Northwest Genealogical Quarterly* 6 (Oct. 1903).

Stevens, Harry R. "Folk Music on the Midwestern Frontier, 1788–1825." *Ohio Archaeological and Historical Society Quarterly* 57 (1948).

Stone, John S. *Memoir of the Life of the Rt. Reverend Alexander Viets Griswold, D.D., Bishop of the Protestant Episcopal Church of the Eastern Diocese.* Philadelphia: Stavely and McCalla, 1844.

Storey, C. M., ed. *Massachusetts Society of the Cincinnati.* Boston: Society of the Cincinnati, 1964.

Sweet, William W. *Men of Zeal: The Romance of American Methodist Beginnings.* New York: The Abingdon Press, 1935.

————. *The Presbyterians.* Vol. 2. *Religion on the American Frontier, 1783–1840.* New York: Henry Holt, 1931.

Taylor, W. A. *Ohio Statesmen and Hundred Year Book.* Columbus: Westbote, 1892.

Teeples, Gary R. *Connecticut 1800 Census.* Provo, Utah: Accelerated Indexing Systems, 1974.

"To Establish a Permanent Seat of Government." *Old Northwest Genealogical Quarterly* 15 (July 1912).

Turner, Frederick Jackson. *The Frontier in American History.* New York: Henry Holt, 1953.

Tyrrell, Ian R. *Sobering Up: From Temperance to Prohibition in Antebellum America, 1800–1860.* Westport, Conn.: Greenwood Press, 1979.

U.S. Census Office. *Census for 1820.* Washington, D.C.: Gales and Seaton, 1821.

Utter, William T. *The Frontier State: 1803–1825.* Columbus: Ohio State Archaeological and Historical Society, 1942.

———. *Granville: The Story of an Ohio Village.* Granville: Granville Historical Society, 1956.

Van Dusen, Albert E., ed. *The Public Records of the State of Connecticut.* Hartford: State of Connecticut, 1953.

Vibert, William M. *Three Centuries of Simsbury, 1670–1970.* Simsbury: Simsbury Tercentenary Committee, 1970.

Wade, Richard C. *The Urban Frontier: The Rise of Western Cities, 1790–1830.* Cambridge: Harvard University Press, 1959.

Waite, Frederick C. "Second Medical School in Ohio, at Worthington 1830–1840." *Ohio State Medical Journal* 33 (1937).

Walsh, Margaret. *The American Frontier Revisited.* London: Economic History Society, 1981.

Weigley, Russell F. *History of the United States Army.* Bloomington: Indiana University Press, 1984.

Wells, Robert V. "Demographic Change and the Life Cycle of the American Family." *The Family in History: Interdisciplinary Essays.* Ed. Theodore K. Rabb and Robert I. Rotberg. New York: Harper and Row, 1973.

Wiebe, Robert H. *The Opening of American Society.* New York: Alfred A. Knopf, 1984.

Wigger, John H. "Taking Heaven by Storm: Enthusiasm and Early American Methodism, 1770–1820." *Journal of the Early Republic* 14 (Summer 1994).

Williams, W. W., ed. *History of the Firelands, Comprising Huron and Erie Counties, Ohio.* Cleveland: Leader Printing, 1879.

Woodbury, Robert S. *History of the Lathe.* Cleveland: Society for the History of Technology, 1961.

"Worthington Genealogies." *Old Northwest Genealogical Quarterly* 6 (1903).

Wright, Louise Heath. "The Methodist Episcopal Church of Worthington, Ohio." *Old Northwest Genealogical Quarterly* 7 (Jan. 1904).

Young, James S. *The Washington Community, 1800–1828.* New York: Columbia University Press, 1966.

Young, John, ed. *Exploring Our Roots: A Story of the Worthington United Methodist Church, 1808–1986.* Worthington: United Methodist Church, 1986.

Index

— ❖ —

Abbott, Samuel, 136, 246
Abolitionists, 217–18
Abstinence from alcohol, 245–47. *See also* Temperance reform movement
Adams, Demas, 189, 198
Adams, H. R., 198
Adams, James, 110–11
Adams, Susan Barnes, 189
Adam style of homes, 188, 189
Adena-Hopewell earthworks, 34f, 292n20
Advance work party, 28–38, 60, 80, 98
Advertising, 126; for boarding students, 253; by Worthington Academy, 147, 148f, 153, 252; by Worthington Manufacturing Company, 160f, 162, 164, 166–67, 170; for runaway slaves, 216; for traveling, 208
African-Americans, 122, 214–19, 269–70. *See also* Slavery
African Methodist Episcopal Church, 270
Agricultural production, 3, 32, 198, 220
Ague fevers, 30, 140
Alcoholic beverages, 52, 104, 157, 246, 317n9. *See also* Temperance reform movement

Allen, Augustus, 85, 105–6
Allen, Ethan, 12
Allen, James, 78, 85, 105, 184
Allen, Joel, 278, 279, 285; and death of son, 85, 105–6; on doctors, 127–28; maps by, 54, 55f
American Colonization Society. *See* Slavery
American Institute, New York City, 230
Amesville Library, 295n8
Anatomical studies, 255–57
Ancient mounds. *See* Prehistoric earthworks
Andrews, Asa, 294n31
Andrews, Betsey, 81
Andrews, Cynthia. *See* Barker, Cynthia Andrews
Andrews, George, 260
Andrews, Hiram, 244
Andrews, Jesse, 81
Andrews, Moses, 40, 81, 278, 279, 284, 306n17
Andrews, Noah, 40, 81; as church chorister, 61; pledge to school, 121; as school trustee, 100
Andrews, William, 271
Anglican church, 237, 239
Anthony, 216

— 335 —

NEW ENGLANDERS ON THE OHIO FRONTIER
was composed in 9.9/13 Trump Mediaeval
on a Power Macintosh using QuarkXPress;
at The Book Page;
printed by sheet-fed offset
on 50# Lions Falls Turin Book Natural stock,
notch case bound over binder's boards
in ICG cloth,
and wrapped with dust jackets printed in two colors
on 80# Rainbow stock
by Braun-Brumfield, Inc.;
designed by Diana Dickson;
and published by
THE KENT STATE UNIVERSITY PRESS
Kent Ohio 44242